Rick Jamison

Rifleman's Handbook

A Shooter's Guide To Rifles, Reloading & Results

Rick Jamison
  Rifleman's Handbook

0-9621148-2-0

Copyright 1989 by PJS Publications, Inc.

*This book is dedicated to fathers
who teach their sons to shoot .22s
and then take them hunting.*

Acknowledgments

Editors

James W. Bequette
John Crowley
Holly J. Ferris
Randall Josephson

Production

Terry R. Boyer
Randall Cook
Keith Griepentrog
Marilyn Howard

Cover Illustration

David Taylor

Illustrator

Ken Clubb

Publisher

Jerry Constantino

PJS Publications
Box 1790
News Plaza
Peoria, IL 61656

Contents

Foreword

RICK JAMISON AND I go back quite a few years, back to when he moved to Arizona and went to work as an editor for Dave Wolfe's shooting magazines, *Handloader* and *Rifle*. I had an office in Wolfe's building then which gave me an opportunity to visit with Rick nearly every day.

Rick was educated, smart, and hard working, so in short order he learned a lot about the gun-writing trade. More important than that, he *thought* about what he learned, and therein is the reason he has become one of the brightest stars in the gun-writing firmament. Then, as now, Prescott, Arizona, offered probably the country's richest environment of shooting, hunting, gun building, and gun lore. Deer and pronghorn could be seen on the outskirts of town, elk were in nearby mountains, and mountain lions plagued local ranchers. Small game was never hard to find, and varmints rounded out a busy year of hunting. Within a short walk was the famed A&M Rifle Co., where superior barrelmaking and gun crafting were a nonstop event, while around the corner, at another gunshop, the astonishing Wells rifles were built. Thrust into such a gunmaker-scented atmosphere as this, Rick Jamison saw more, learned more, and *experienced* more in a few years than most gun writers will absorb in a lifetime.

But even with these advantages, what sets Rick apart from the ordinary gun writer is that rather than just reporting on what he learned, he forged new frontiers and became a teacher. For example, when he took up the artful craft of coyote hunting, he became *the* expert, the final authority, by virtue of his unique observations. And that takes us back to what I said earlier: He *thinks* about what he observes.

Guns and shooting, and everything connected thereto, are a wilderness of contradiction where facts tend to be fleeting and truth is often obscure. Rick has learned, as few writers have, how to dig his way through the dark tunnels of the shooting world and mine those hard-to-find gems of solid, *usable* truth. This skill, combined with his natural talent for writing, makes Rick Jamison an authority well worth listening to. He has earned what I consider the highest praise to which any gun writer can aspire: the title of a professional.

Jim Carmichel
Johnson City, TN
April 1989

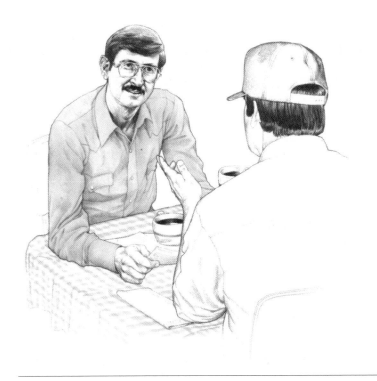

Rifles, Reloading & Rick

I'VE BEEN INTERESTED in guns and hunting for as long as I can remember. I was in the woods almost as soon as I could walk. Actually, I spent a lot more time in the woods than my father preferred. But I was fortunate that I grew up on a farm and in a family that viewed hunting as being as much a part of growing up as learning to drive a tractor.

During the Depression, my father market-hunted cottontail rabbits with a Winchester Model 1890 pump chambered only for .22 Shorts. He didn't want the Long chamber because all he could afford were Shorts. Twenty-two Shorts were 12 cents a box and Longs were 15 cents. He used that rifle to bag thousands of cottontails and squirrels. Few running rabbits escaped the second-nature sight-by-feel he had with the old .22 pump. He always shot running rabbits from the hip. Once they were in the bag and brought home, my mother helped skin them by lantern light. Twenty-two-shot rabbits were worth a quarter; those taken with a shotgun were worth only 15 cents.

My father first taught me to spot cottontails in hiding, then to stalk closely and take them with nothing more than a rock. It worked. He was teaching me to be a hunter first and a shooter second. The excitement was in the hunt, and I carry that excitement with me to this day.

When I moved up to a BB gun, it provided endless hours of entertainment—considering that we had thousands of unwanted sparrows around the barnyard.

When I was 13, Jim Steves, a brother-in-law, bought me a bolt-action Stevens Model 86C .22 rimfire as an eighth-grade graduation present. I was worried that my parents wouldn't let me keep it because it was a "household rule" that a boy could not own a real rifle until he was 15. But my father had smuggled his own .22 home in a load of shelled corn and kept it hidden in the barn because he was afraid his father would disapprove of the purchase. My parents realized I really needed the .22 and allowed me to keep it. I spent every spare moment in the woods, hunting rabbits, squirrels, coyotes, and foxes with that .22. It was with that rifle that I really learned to shoot. I remember visualizing Jack O'Connor's elk hunting stories and the .270 as I sighted-in squirrels. Factory iron sights were all I ever used on that rifle, and it wears the same sighting equipment today—and shoots as well as ever.

I got the .22 along with my diploma in May, and by fall, I had purchased a bolt-action 20-gauge shotgun. There was just too much good quail and duck hunting on our farm not to have some kind of bird gun.

One of the daily chores I had was to go to the pasture and bring up the milk cows. I used to leave a little early and walk the thick brushy areas where quail coveys hid out. Needless to say, my mother fixed many quail suppers.

I felt a little undergunned with the .22 rimfire when coyotes were the quarry. The Kansas prairie was open, and coyotes, being wary, were nearly always spotted at long range. One of the most exciting memories of hunting during my boyhood days was when I got the drop on a coyote by sneaking up within 10 feet of him.

I'd gone out to the cow lot to bring in the cattle one December evening. It was snowing and getting dark. Out of the corner of my eye, I saw a dark form drift out from behind a pile of hedge fenceposts and out into the hayfield about 200 yards away. I kept walking and slowly turned my head to see a big coyote eyeing me. There was a pneumonia-killed calf behind the pile of posts, which was why the hungry coyote was standing there watching me instead of running off. I figured he would be back at the calf as soon as I was out of sight in the barn.

Fighting the urge to run and get my gun, I herded the cows into the barn. As soon as the gate was closed on them, I was out of sight from the coyote and running at top speed for the house. I knew it was getting too dark for iron sights, so I grabbed the bolt-action 20 gauge and a handful of the most potent shells I had, the 2¾-inch magnums loaded with No. 2 shot I'd bought for geese.

In no time, I was back in the barn. I eased around the corner of the corral and looked into the darkness. There was no coyote to be seen. My only hope was that he was behind the post pile.

The snow was about three inches deep. Using a lot of restraint for a 13-year-old boy, I cautiously and quietly walked up to the backside of the post pile. It didn't seem possible the coyote could be there because I would be within 20 feet of him. I began walking around the post pile, watching for movement.

And then there he was, no more than 10 feet away and running. The first charge of No. 2s hit him at about 15 yards. It rolled him, but he got up and ran again, this time right at me! I worked the bolt and fired again. The coyote dropped again but just as quickly was back on his feet and still coming at me. The third and final round in the gun dropped him at about 12 feet, and I frantically opened the bolt and shoved a fourth round up the spout. Before the bolt was closed, the coyote was up and coming again. The fourth round hit him at no more than four feet, and I sidestepped to allow the coyote to roll and slide past me. He never moved again.

I decided that neither the .22 rimfire nor a 20-gauge shotgun was enough gun for coyotes, so I bought two rifles for the task. One was a Model 1917 Eddystone Enfield .30-06; the other, an Italian 6.5mm Carcano. I sent for both through the mail, and the guns were delivered to my door. If I remember correctly, the Carcano was $9.95, and the price included 100 rounds of ammo. The Enfield was $19.95, I believe, and the price included 200 rounds of military ball ammo.

During this time, I acquired a Lee tool for loading the 20-gauge shotshells. I loaded with that tool almost daily because I hunted daily during the fall seasons. Even if I only fired five or six shells when I went to bring in the cows, I filled those hulls after the milking was finished that night.

I bought a Lyman tong tool for the .30-06. Monk Bryant, an older fellow in the neighborhood, was the only one I knew locally who loaded rifle ammunition, and he used a tong tool. The gunshop owner who sold me the tool recommended 110-grain bullets and IMR-4320 powder for crows and coyotes. I bought Winchester 110-grain spirepoints, along with the powder and primers, and headed home.

I didn't have a powder measure or even a scale. I went to Monk for advice before I started to reload. He went through various items in his loading tool box and finally pulled out a brassy tube capped at one end. It was about an inch long and about ¾ inch in diameter. He filled it with IMR-4320 and weighed it on his scale. He repeated the process three or four times. Then he indicated that I should fill the tube level full of powder for the right charge. I later noticed that the tube had a Revlon logo on the cap. I think it was the cap from a tube of lipstick which had been cut off.

I used the tong tool, the Winchester 110-grain bullets, Winchester primers, and the measure of powder to load ammo for months, not knowing what the powder charge was. All I knew was that it worked, and I took a lot of crows and coyotes with it. As I recall, I could hold eight- or 10-inch groups at 200 yards with the battle sights.

In the summer during my high-school days, I got a part-time job working as a laborer on a construction job. I spent my entire first paycheck on a custom-built Mauser .244 Remington with a Weaver K-8X scope. I bought the rifle for crows and coyotes at long range. From what I had read, the rifle was capable of doing the job. It was. That rig proved to be extremely accurate.

About that time, I decided I wanted to try all the centerfire rifle calibers, to own rifles for them, and to reload them. I knew I couldn't own them all at once, so I traded rifles as I felt I had experienced what there was to experience with each one. In short order, I'd tried a .222 Remington, .222 Remington Magnum, .30-40 Krag, .30-30 Winchester, 6.5mm Swedish Krag, and .243 Winchester.

I left the farm and went to college, first to the University of Kansas on a track scholarship. I liked to run the mile, and Kansas was the top track school in the country. I went there for two years. Then I visited my brother Jip in Arizona, and had the opportunity to experience western hunting. I was hooked and knew I had to live in the West. When the track coach at Northern Arizona University heard I was interested in living in Flagstaff, he offered me a scholarship, and I moved.

I had classes three days a week and hunted 4½ days. The extra half-day in the week came about because I cut classes at least that much to hunt. I remember failing an important test because it was opening day of deer season, but I wouldn't have changed anything. Being exposed to big-game hunting for the first time was one of the happiest periods in my life. I have long forgotten the subject matter of the test I flunked, but I'll never forget my first bear or my first elk.

I was working on a construction crew in Flagstaff, Arizona, when I got a copy of the game regulations that summer. Bear season was the first general big-game hunt that opened that fall. I began inquiring about the possibility of hunting bears. Most of the people I worked with were hunters, but they had never seen a bear in the wild and didn't think there was much chance of getting one, at least not without dogs. One of my brother's friends finally revealed where he and his father used to run bears with dogs years ago. It was up on Mormon Mountain, about 30 miles south of Flagstaff. Opening morning of bear season found me there.

I was still too naive to consider the poor odds of bagging a bear, but it really didn't matter. I was in unknown and beautiful country, hunting bear, and that was what was important. It was an adventure.

The gun I carried was the old 1917 Eddystone Enfield .30-06. By this time, I had done a considerable amount of work on it. I had used my father's emery wheel to grind off the rear sight protector and to shape the receiver for a Redfield bridge-type scope mount drilled for a Model 70 Winchester. I used a file to do the final contour work. Then I tried to drill the receiver with an electric hand drill. The receiver was too hard, and the bit wouldn't bite in. I managed only to scratch the receiver, so I took the rifle to a gunsmith who completed the job the right way. The scope was an inexpensive 4X of a now-defunct make. I had fashioned a serviceable sporter stock out of a piece of seasoned walnut I'd acquired from a friend of my father's who owned a sawmill.

In the predawn light, I parked my '59 Chevy at the base of Mormon Mountain and loaded the rifle. As daylight came, I walked up the side of the mountain and went clear to the top, moving up through pine, spruce, and aspen. There was a clearing on top of the mountain, with a waterhole along the edge where I approached. Tall grass in the clearing was wet with dew, and there was a clearly defined trail where something had gone through the grass, knocking off the dew. I couldn't see tracks, and I thought a hoofed animal like an elk would have left tracks in the soft soil, so I assumed the critter was a soft-footed bear.

I followed the trail. After a quarter-mile or so, it ran along the top edge of a rockslide. I moved over to the edge of the slide to view the countryside. On the rocks about 75 yards below, was a black bear. He was looking back at me!

I shouldered the rifle, settled the crosshair on the right spot, and fired. The bear growled, bawled, stood on his hind legs, twirled around, and was off the rock and out of sight in a split second. I glanced down near my feet and saw two empties. I couldn't remember firing twice and chambering a third round, but I had.

I went down to the rocks and found blood and other signs of a hit, but no bear—and no blood trail. I spent the next three hours combing the dense spruce for the bear, fearful that the bear might be wounded and waiting for me. Just as I was about to give up and go for help, I saw a pinhead-size droplet of blood on the forest floor. I marked it and got down on my hands and knees and found another, then another. I finally found the bear, stone dead.

I had shot him with a 150-grain Sierra ahead of 50.0 grains of IMR-4064, and it had done an admirable job, penetrating his shoulder, smashing it, traversing lungs and liver, and exiting the flank on the opposite side. The bear somehow still traveled several hundred yards.

The next fall, I killed my first elk, a six-pointer. I had a bull permit and hunted five solid days from daylight until dark in northern Arizona without seeing so much as a calf elk. It was Thanksgiving day, and I was supposed to be home at 6:30 for a late turkey dinner. I was walking around the eastern rim of Anderson Mesa, looking for elk in the dense junipers below. Since it was about 5:30 and I was about an hour from town, I decided to head for home. Then I saw movement in the junipers below, raised the binoculars, and saw a calf elk standing in the clearing. I immediately jerked off my sweatshirt, wadded it up, and placed it on the rock ledge for a forend rest. I belly-flopped down on the rock and found the opening through my scope.

The calf walked out of the opening, followed came a cow elk. The cow stopped momentarily in the opening and then walked through. I was sizing up the distance. It was a far distance to be shooting, but I was hungry for an elk. I had hunted too long and hard, and elk were too scarce to pass up an opportunity. I had a rock-steady rest. There was no wind.

While I was sizing up the distance, a six-point bull elk stepped into the clearing. I knew I didn't have long to make a decision. This time, I was carrying a .300 Winchester Magnum in a rechambered Model 1903 Springfield. I steadied the Weaver 4X crosshair just over the shoulder of the bull and the rifle roared. The elk went down as if poleaxed!

I didn't get home until almost 10 p.m. My wife had several friends at our place. They had planned to call the search-and-rescue squad if I wasn't home by 10!

It was a struggle for me to get through my four years of college. My major was zoology, and I was thinking of getting into the field of wildlife management. My grades weren't great, but I won the conference championship in the mile my senior year. There weren't many job possibilities in the wildlife field back then, and the Vietnam conflict was in full swing. My brother Mick had just bought a dairy farm in Kansas and offered me the opportunity to come back and farm it. I decided to take him up on his offer.

After a year and a half milking cows twice a day, 365 days a year, I figured the Army couldn't possibly be worse. I was right. I volunteered for the draft and found basic training was a breeze. It was nothing compared to the discipline I had received from my father growing up and nothing compared to the physical activity on the farm. It was almost like I had retired.

I'll never forget the look on the drill instructor's face when I ran the mile as fast as I did with combat boots, lapping everyone on the track. About the end of the second lap, he was yelling at me to slow down, and I realized that he really was afraid that I was going to hurt myself at that speed.

I maxed every P.T. test and topped the company on the rifle range. As a result of all this, I never pulled K.P. during basic training.

I was stationed at Aberdeen Proving Ground for awhile and later had a tour of duty in Vietnam.

It was during my stint in the Army that I decided I needed to do something worthwhile with my life. A lifetime spent milking cows was a prison sentence. Construction work rated just a notch higher. The thought of doing either for a lifetime seemed terrible.

I credit my mother with making me believe I could do anything I wanted. I wanted to hunt for a living; she said I couldn't make a living doing that.I was out to prove her wrong. As I read a copy of *Field & Stream,* it suddenly occurred to me that *this* was what I wanted to do. I wanted to hunt and fish and write about it for a living like those guys.

I got every book I could read on the subject of magazine article writing while I was in the service. I learned that "all" that was necessary was to be a good writer and photographer and to mail in an article. It would be accepted or rejected on its merits.

I learned the proper format and submitted two trapping articles to *Fur, Fish & Game.* Both sold, netting me $20 and $30, as I recall. Even in 1968 dollars, that wasn't much, but the encouragement was worth an untold amount.

I got a copy of *Writer's Market* and found that *Field & Stream* paid a lot better. I sold my third attempt at writing to that publication for $500. It was then that I knew this was the way to go. I didn't realize how lucky I was. The piece was called "Out-Of-State Budget Hunting" and appeared in the March 1972 issue.

While I had been successful with my first three pieces, I wanted to know that I would be able to make a living in the field. I decided to go back to Northern Arizona University and major in journalism. I would then get an in-house job on a magazine, and if the money looked like it was there, I would try my hand at freelance writing.

I found I needed three more semesters of work to complete a bachelor's degree in a new major. Incentive and purpose does wonders. I made the dean's list at NAU and graduated with a journalism degree in 1973.

Right out of school, I got an assistant editor's job at *Rifle* and *Handloader* magazines in Prescott, Arizona. When I went to apply, I was armed with the best scholastic credentials, ready to impress the person doing the hiring. Editor Neal Knox was the man, and he never looked at my grades. He was more interested in whether I could answer questions like:

"What is a rebated rim?"

"Name the cartridges that have a rebated rim."

"How did the .30-06 get its name?"

I passed the questioning and got the job.

Having the opportunity to work on those technical gun magazines was a real education for me. During the five years I spent there, I had the opportunity to travel to firearms seminars and to the NRA and SHOT shows. I learned more about the industry and met most of the editors of other magazines as well. Part of my job at *Rifle* and *Handloader* was editing *NBRSA News,* the publication of the National Bench Rest Shooters Association. During this time, I traveled to benchrest matches around the country to compete and to report on them.

At the end of five years, I quit my job to pursue my goal of becoming a full-time writer. That was in the fall of 1978, and coyote pelt prices were at their peak. Working in an office all day every day is tough for an outdoors person. Even though I camped out many weekends and hunted before and after work, I wanted more of the outdoors. My plan was to hunt coyotes all winter and then write gun and hunting articles at the end of the winter.

The coyote hunting went well. I went at it seriously. I had a wife and two kids to support at the time and felt compelled to "make it." I figured everyone thought I was nuts for quitting a good job to hunt coyotes. The pressure was on. I hunted hard, from daylight until dark, calling early till late, and skinning after dark. I slept in a pickup camper and hunted out of a Bronco. While I had been very successful calling coyotes for sport, doing it for a living took on a whole new meaning. Missing a shot at a coyote was serious. I really bore down and used a Remington Model 788 in .22-250 with a custom Canjar trigger. I really learned how to use that rifle. I also learned how to connect on coyotes, whether at long range or running flat out. Living with a rifle at your side and shooting it every day brings out shooting skills that one would not have thought possible. One also loses these skills in just a few months if they aren't practiced. I averaged 3.3 coyotes per day during the first 19 days I hunted. During the last month, I averaged more than four coyotes per day.

Within two weeks after I quit my job at Wolfe Publishing, I received a call from *Field & Stream.* Dave Petzal wanted to know if I would be interested in the position of associate shooting editor of that publication. I was, went to New York for an interview, got the job, and began writing a column every other month. Within six months after the coyote season, I was also field editor at *Petersen's Hunting* and wrote a handloading column for *American Hunter.* During this period, I began writing for *Shooting Times.* ST treated me well, and I've been with the magazine since 1981.

A lot of people have asked me how to get into the gun or outdoor writing business. The best way I know is to first have a love for what you're doing and learn all you can about the subject. A knowledge of guns or the outdoors is a lifetime experience and is acquired through a natural interest.

I know. I've been there . . . and I'm still learning and enjoying every minute of it.

Rick Jamison
Springfield, OR
April 1989

Rifles

Rating .22 Rifle Actions

THE .22 RIMFIRE is everyone's cartridge. Whether you're selecting a rifle strictly for small-game hunting or choosing one to complement a big-game gun, there is a .22 rimfire rifle style to fit any purpose or whim. In no other chambering, rifle or shotgun, are all five basic action types so uniformly accepted and used.

Generally, sportsmen in certain regions of the country prefer one type of action over the other. In the Southwest, for example, the bolt action is most prevalent among big-caliber hunters, while in the heavily timbered sections of the Northeast, the slide or lever action gets the nod. Shooters usually prefer the bolt action for long ranges, and the slide, semi-auto, or lever for close range hunting in thick timber or undergrowth.

If you like the feel of a lever or pump better than a bolt, there's certainly no reason not to choose one. Just pick one that feels good and enjoy it. Though I grew up shooting a tubular magazine bolt-action rifle, it's a treat to change actions from time to time just to spice up the hunting or plinking sport.

I recently experimented with all five basic action types—lever, bolt, semiauto, single shot, and slide—and compared them for handling characteristics. The guns used were a Browning BL-22 tubular magazine lever-action rifle, a Marlin Model 781 tubular magazine bolt action, a Ruger Model 10/22 semiauto with box magazine, a Stevens Model 72 Crackshot single shot, and a tubular magazine Remington Model 572 slide action.

The rifles were fired from benchrest for group size at 50 yards (two five-shot groups). Ten shots were then fired for time at a distance of 25 yards. Though this was partially an attempt at measuring action-cycling time, accuracy was also a factor, for all shots were placed within the theoretical small-game vital area (2½ inches) at the 25-yard distance. The two timed five-shot groups were fired from the kneeling position. In the timed segment, five shots were fired on one target and five were fired on another. This was the most enjoyable portion of the testing.

The rifles were fired with factory-standard iron sights. Four of the rifles had provisions for mounting a scope—either with tip-off mount grooves or, as in the case of the Ruger, the receiver drilled and tapped for centerfire rifle scope mount bases. The Stevens Crackshot was the exception; it has no provision for mounting a scope.

As most experienced shooters know, iron sights don't have the aiming precision necessary to determine accuracy potential. It's possible the group sizes obtained during the slow-fire sequence are more indicative of the sighting potential than the accuracy potential of the rifle. All groups went between two and 2.5 inches, with the exception of the Remington pump, which averaged 1.4 inches. Two five-shot groups are limited indicators, and this "average" could very likely be an exception rather than the norm for that rifle and sight combination.

I experienced difficulty maintaining a uniform sight picture during trigger squeeze. None of the triggers had outstanding target accuracy. Most had considerable creep, and some felt rough or had a heavy weight of pull.

When I was done shooting, I scaled the trigger pulls and made an attempt to measure creep. To determine creep, I used an inside caliper to first measure the distance between the inside front of the trigger guard and the trigger. Then I applied pressure with the caliper until the rifle fired, at which point I read the indicated measurement. The difference between the measurements is creep. (See the accompanying chart.)

The Ruger and Browning triggers could almost be considered two-stage triggers. They pulled quite a distance before meeting any resistance. The initial takeup is not included in the creep measurement. In other words, the first measurement was taken at the beginning of the second stage.

With an overall length of 36¾ inches, the Browning BL-22 runs neck and neck with the Ruger 10/22 for compactness in a repeater. The Browning's tubular magazine makes for plenty of firepower, accepting 15 Long Rifle cartridges, 17 Longs, or 22 Shorts. The ammunition can be fed into the action in any combination without a hitch.

The Browning has a noticeably short lever throw at 33 degrees. The entire trigger guard and trigger finger lever swings down along with the action-operating lever. This is convenient in that it precludes any finger pinching against the trigger when the lever is swung upward. The lever throw is so short that a thumb grip around the stock can be maintained while the lever is operated. Thinking that speed of fire

.22 RIFLE COMPARISON

	Ruger (Semiauto)	Marlin (Bolt)	Remington (Slide)	Stevens (Single Shot)	Browning (Lever)
Time for 10 Aimed Shots (Seconds)	15	31	23	80	23
Average Group Size Timed Fire (Inches)	2.3	1.4	1.7	1.6	1.6
Average Group Size Slow Fire (Inches)	2.0	2.5	1.4	2.0	2.1
Trigger Creep (1/32 Inch)	1 (two-stage pull)	1.5	2	1.5	.75 (two-stage pull)
Trigger Pull Weight (Ounces)	100+ (off scale)	55	72	75	80
Barrel Length (Inches)	18½	22	23	22	20
Published Overall Length (Inches)	37	41	42	37	36¾
Published Average Weight (Pounds)	5	6	5½	4½	5
Sight Radius (Inches)	15	19	20	18	15¼

could increase using this technique, I attempted the grip while working the lever. However, at the first shot during the rapid-fire stage when I swung the lever down, the hammer merely came back and contacted my thumb. The action could not be opened completely until I moved my thumb out of the way. I lost a second or two during the rapid-fire stage on this initial shot.

Still, the Browning lever tied with the Remington pump for the No.

2 spot in speed of action cycling.

The Browning had a very positive feeding mechanism; the lifter carried the cartridge high – almost in alignment with the bore before the breech-bolt shoved it forward into the chamber. Most actions present the car-tridge to the chamber at an angle.

The breechbolt and parts of the feeding mechanism on the Browning are quite hefty. They appear to be machined steel rather than the stamped thin-sheet steel parts seen in some of the other .22 rifles. There is a delicate-looking ejector and a tiny coil spring that actuates it. How-ever, no problems were experienced in this area during the tests.

When the action is closed, there are almost no openings for foreign material to enter – a decided plus. The receiver, which is grooved for tip-off scope mounts, is very thin, making for a flat, compact action. The two-piece stock is finished in a gloss, while the black plastic buttplate is installed without white-line spacers.

The sight radius on the Browning is about 15¼ inches, and the rear sight leaf has an integral vertical adjustment activated by loosening two screws and sliding the interior notch blade vertically. A small amount of windage adjustment can be accomplished in the same way. If more is needed, drive the sight laterally in its dovetailed slot.

The Browning BL-22 is a very compact, quick-pointing, easy-carrying .22 rifle that is a joy to operate.

At six pounds, the Marlin Model 781 bolt action is the heaviest of all the rifles tested. It has a 22-inch barrel and a 19-inch sight radius. It features a tubular magazine that accepts 25 Short, 19 Long, or 17 Long Rifle cartridges. There is a thumb safety on the right side of the receiver that pivots from within the stock. A red cocking indicator at the rear of the cocking piece shows whether the rifle is cocked or not.

The ramp front sight is hooded and resembles those found on quality big-game guns. The flat spring rear sight contains vertical adjustment via a sliding step-notched wedge. Horizontal adjustment for windage is accomplished by driving the rear sight laterally in its dovetailed notch on the barrel.

The receiver is grooved for tip-off scope mounts, and the feeding mech-anism is constructed of pressure-formed thin sheet steel. The feeding sys-tem lacks some of the tiny, delicate working parts seen in other types of bolt-action .22 rimfires.

During the timed rapid-fire shooting, stovepipe jams occurred on a number of occasions, but the rifle functioned perfectly as long as the ammo was chambered normally. The stock has impressed checkering panels on its pistol grip and forend. It also has a Monte Carlo hump but no cheekpiece. The black plastic buttplate is installed with a white-line spacer, and the trigger is plated in a gold-color material. At 31 seconds for 10 aimed shots, the Marlin bolt was the second slowest action type – as could be expected.

The Ruger 10/22 semiautomatic is short and relatively lightweight. In that respect, the 10/22 is similar to the BL-22, but the Ruger's receiver and stock are much thicker laterally than the Browning's. The Ruger has a 10-shot rotary magazine for Long Rifle cartridges only, and it produces a very positive feeding into the action. The entire feeding mech-anism, with the exception of the breechbolt, is contained within this magazine. The magazine was much slower and more difficult to load than the tubular types. It contains a very stiff spring so considerable pressure is required to force the cartridges into the box.

The Ruger's action is very simple and lacks the delicate wires or other parts often seen in .22 rimfire rifles. The 10/22 functioned flawlessly during the load tests.

Ruger's crossbolt safety is located in the forward portion of the trigger guard. Unlike most .22 rimfire rifles, the Ruger contains a wide flat-top receiver that is drilled and tapped for big-game rifle scope mounts.

Similar to the Browning, Ruger's rear sight is vertical and has a small amount of lateral adjustment, which is accomplished by loosening two screws and sliding the notch. Greater horizontal adjustment can be attained by driving the dovetailed sight base laterally. The Ruger's sight radius of 15 inches is the shortest of any gun tested. A barrel band behind the forend tip secures the stock and barrel. The stock is of a fancy grain, but it is finished dull.

The buttplate is military style and wraps around the top portion of the stock. This style has drawn complaints from shooters because it is often poorly fitted, with the stock wood projecting beyond the plate at the sides and the toe of the butt. The test rifle was no exception.

One advantage to the Ruger's rotary magazine is that, though it holds 10 rounds, it is designed to fit flush with the lines of the stock. Other straight-line box magazines that hold the same number of rounds protrude beyond the stock at the balance point and make the rifle uncomfortable to carry.

The Stevens Model 72 Crackshot could be called the most unusual of the test guns. Most of today's single-shot rifles are of the bolt-action design; the Crackshot is a tipping block or falling block action. At 4½ pounds, this rifle is a half-pound lighter than the other two compact versions tested. Unlike the other compact rifles, however, the Stevens Crackshot sports a lengthy 22-inch octagon-shaped barrel while maintaining a short 37-inch overall length.

The sight radius on the Crackshot is 18 inches, and the flat spring rear sight is adjustable for elevation by sliding a step wedge. Lateral adjustment is accomplished by driving the sights, front and rear, laterally in their dovetailed barrel notches. There is no provision for mounting a scope on the Crackshot.

This old design features a simple exposed hammer, and the action-operating finger lever is of the classic "S" style. The traditional single-shot extractor on my test specimen did not eject the empty case free of the barrel. It merely extracted the brass from the breech so that the case could be plucked out of the barrel with the fingers. As would be expected, this action is by far the slowest to cycle, requiring 80 seconds to complete 10 aimed shots.

The Crackshot's receiver has a pleasing color-casehardened appearance. Like the Browning BL-22, the Crackshot has a two-piece stock, a plastic buttplate, and no pistol grip.

The Remington Model 572 slide action has the longest overall length at 42 inches and the longest barrel at 23 inches of any rifle used during the test. Its tubular magazine holds 20 Short, 17 Long, or 14 Long Rifle cartridges, which can be loaded interchangeably. The action is activated by a single push-rod from the handfilling forend. Being quick and easy to operate, it fed cartridges smoothly during the test series without a hitch. The crossbolt safety is located in the rear of the trigger guard. The breechbolt is nothing more than a ¼-inch rod with extractors projecting from either side. The ejection port in the side of the receiver is quite small, but there are openings around the breechbolt that are susceptible to weed seeds, dust, small sticks, and any other debris. Since this gun was not used in the field, whether this would actually pose a problem is unknown.

The gun has a long 20-inch sight radius. A step-notch wedge is used for vertical adjustment in the rear sight, while lateral adjustment is accomplished by driving the front sight laterally in its dovetailed slot. The rear sight is attached to the barrel via two screws and has no lateral adjustment. The receiver is grooved for tip-off scope mounts. The forend slide contains deep vertical grooves for a positive nonslip gripping surface, while the buttstock contains no checkering or other embellishments. The plastic buttplate is attached without a white-line spacer.

Although this Remington is the longest overall of any gun tested and contains the longest barrel, it does not feel awkward in the slightest. To the contrary, its pointing and swinging qualities are pleasing. This, in conjunction with the rapid-operating slide, makes the rifle pleasant to function and shoot. And the Remington pump produced the smallest groups, firing a 1.4-inch average at 50 yards.

After trying all the action types, I'm right back where I started. When it comes to .22s, I like to shoot them all. Selecting an action type primarily involves personal preference and hunting style. Just pick an action that you like and enjoy it. After all, that's what the .22s are for.

Ruger 77, Remington 700, Winchester 70

TODAY'S AMERICAN sporting rifles are among the best the world has ever known. They're strong, reliable, aesthetically pleasing, and made to last several lifetimes. There are, in fact, so many good models that making a choice can be difficult. It normally isn't too difficult to select an action type because a shooter usually has a decided preference for a lever, pump, auto, bolt, or single shot. When the choosing goes beyond the five basic types of rifle actions, however, shooters get sweaty palms, wrinkle their brows, and go into a state of nervous indecision.

American shooters, for the most part, are bolt rifle oriented. The bolt-action rifle is the one most frequently written about, is chambered in the widest range of cartridges, and has the reputation for being the most accurate and reliable.

Many of the questions I receive ask, "I've decided to buy a .30-06 and have narrowed the choice down to the Remington Model 700, Winchester

Model 70, or Ruger Model 77. Which one is the best choice?"

Well, what if . . .

• you've just returned from an Alaskan brown bear hunt, one on which you bagged a monster with your .338 Magnum in a Ruger Model 77.

• you've bought a Remington Model 700 in .22-250, mounted a scope on it, taken it to the range, and put five shots into one hole at 100 yards.

• you've grown up using the Model 70 with its three-position safety, and any departure from this safety system leaves you fumbling for the button while the trophy whitetail makes off through the undergrowth.

Three different examples. Three different answers.

For those of you who haven't yet made the decision and feel there are so many unique characteristics about this popular trio that you need to learn more about each of the rifles' designs, read on. Be forewarned, however, that you could become one of those shooters left uneasy when faced with choosing only one.

First, all three makes and models—the Remington Model 700, Winchester Model 70, and Ruger Model 77—are two-lug, front-locking bolt-action rifles. This basic Mauser design has been around longer than most of us; its reliability for those in military uniform and in the hunting field is legendary. Beyond the basic two-lug design, however, the similarities in the three popular models end. I'll examine the differences among the three. Perhaps you can utilize the information to help in your decisionmaking.

The boltfaces of all three rifles are recessed. The Remington is the only rifle with a boltface rim formed by the recess encircling the brass case head practically to the forward edge of the extractor groove; the Winchester boltface rim is relieved for the extractor; about half the Ruger's rim is cut away to make room for the claw extractor when the bolt is turned down or opened.

All three bolts have spring-loaded plunger-type ejectors, and all the ejectors are located at approximately the same position in relation to the bolt lugs.

The rifles have distinctively different extractors. The Remington Model 700 extractor is a ring-like affair riveted into the inside of the bolt-face recess. The ring is spring steel and has a hook along one edge which serves to engage the case rim so the cartridge can be withdrawn from the barrel.

The Model 70 Winchester has a laterally sliding extractor recessed into the forward face of the bottom locking lug (when the action is locked). When the bolt is being closed on a chambered cartridge, the spring-loaded extractor slides laterally in this recess to allow the head of the cartridge to contact the boltface. When the case rim clears the extractor, the extractor reverses direction and snaps into the extractor groove, where it is ready to withdraw the case from the barrel when necessary.

The Ruger Model 77 retains the original Model 98 Mauser extractor. This extractor is much larger than the other two designs and is a long spring system positioned parallel to the bolt body, extending along most of its length. It is attached to the bolt by means of a ring encircling a recess in the bolt body behind the locking lugs. Regardless of its size, this type of extractor has long been favored by Mauser-action fans due to its strength and positive action.

The Model 700 bolt has a slot in the bottom or right locking lug which mates with a guide rib along the right side of the rifle's receiver. The Model 70 has the same characteristic. Proponents say this serves as an antibind device for smoother action operation. When comparing smoothness of action cycling and bolt "wobble" among the three rifles, however, I'm unable to detect a difference. Perhaps this is because the Model 77's long extractor serves as a type of guide rib in the lug raceway.

The Remington and Winchester both differ from the Ruger in two other respects: the jeweling on the bolt and the checkering on the bolt handle. Remington and Winchester have both features; the Ruger has neither. The Remington bolt knob has two oval-shaped panels which are checkered. The Winchester has a single band of checkering running around the circumference of its pear-shaped bolt knob.

All three bolts have different sizes and locations of gas escape ports. The Model 700 has a port between the two locking lugs in the left side of the bolt body (when the rifle action is locked). This circular port is approximately ⅛ inch in diameter. There is a circular gas escape port in the left side of the Model 70's bolt. Larger in diameter than Remington's (approximately ³/₁₆ inch), it is located about 1½ inches behind the forward face of the bolt. The Model 77 has three gas escape ports located behind the bottom locking lug as the rifle action is locked. The ports are covered by the ejector when the bolt is unlocked. The first port is a little more than an inch behind the boltface and is approximately ¼ inch in diameter. In addition, there are two oval-shaped ports located behind the extractor collar; each is approximately ¾ inch long, and ³/₁₆ inch wide.

The safeties on the three rifles are also different. The Model 700 safety is located to the right of the receiver tang and protrudes from a stock cutout made for the mechanism. This safety pivots fore and aft and is positioned so it can be operated by the thumb of the firing hand.

With the Model 70, the safety is located on the cocking piece shroud at the rear of the bolt body. This is a three-position safety which pivots fore and aft. When the safety is in the forward position, the rifle can be fired and the bolt can be manipulated. When the safety lever is in the center position, the bolt can be manipulated but the rifle will not fire. When the safety is in the rearward position, the rifle cannot be fired, nor can the bolt be worked.

The Model 77 has a sliding safety position on the top center of the receiver's long tang. Both the Model 70 and Model 77 safeties are designed to be manipulated with the thumb of the firing hand.

Like the safeties, the bolt releases are different on the three rifles. The bolt release on the Model 77 is located at the left side of the rear receiver bridge and pivots outward similar to the old Model 98 Mauser design. The Model 70's bolt release is located just behind the left side of the rear receiver bridge. Depressing the tab-like extension releases the bolt so it can be withdrawn from the rifle. The Model 700's bolt release is located inside the trigger guard just in front of the base of the trigger. Depressing this toward the top of the rifle releases the bolt.

Turn each of the three rifles over, and you'll notice the floorplate hinges and releases are all different. The hinge/action screw in the Model 77's floorplate is positioned so it is covered by the forward extension of the floorplate when the latter is closed. In order to expose the forward action screw, the floorplate must be unlatched and swung open. To release the Model 77's floorplate, a serrated knob at the lower forward edge of the inside of the trigger guard is pushed down and forward.

The Model 700 has a serrated button located in the top forward surface of the inside of the trigger guard bow. It is pushed up and forward to release the floorplate. The release on the Model 70 is located at the top outside forward surface of the trigger guard bow. The latch pin is pressed away from the floorplate in order to release the plate so it can be swung down and forward.

The Winchester and Ruger are "three-screw actions," while the Remington is a "two-screw action." The forward screw of the Model 70 enters the action at a right angle approximately $9/16$ inch behind the large recoil lug at the front of the receiver. The forward action screw of the Model 77 enters the center of a very small recoil lug; unlike the other two action designs, it enters the recoil lug at a 45-degree angle. Increasing tension on this screw pulls the recoil lug down into the bottom of the stock and pulls it back into its recess as well. The forward action screw on the two-screw, round-bottom Model 700 enters the action approximately $13/16$ inch behind the recoil lug.

Once the screws have been removed, the barreled actions can be pulled from the riflestocks, and you can take a closer look at bedding surfaces and triggers. While both the Model 77 and the Model 70 have recoil lugs integral with the receiver, the lug of the Model 700 is actually an extension of a washer fitting between the shoulder of the barrel and the rifle's receiver.

While the aesthetics of the Model 700's recoil lug might be a strike against the rifle, its trigger is considered to be excellent. A competent gunsmith can readily adjust a Remington trigger to a very light, crisp pull weight. The trigger on the Model 70 can also be adjusted, but it's an entirely different system. Trigger adjustments should be left to a competent gunsmith. The Model 77 trigger has a hex screw in the base of the finger lever which provides some degree of adjustment, but this is frequently insufficient to provide the type of trigger pull a shooter wants. While this trigger is not as easily adjustable as the other two designs, a competent gunsmith can make a Model 77's trigger lighter.

The Model 77 has a decided plus, according to many shooters, in its unique scope mount system, which has bases that are integral with the rifle's receiver bridges drilled and tapped for conventional scope mounts.

Concerning bedding surfaces, the Remington Model 700 has a *round-*bottom receiver; the other two have *flat* bedding surfaces. The pros and cons of these bedding surfaces can be argued ad infinitum, and since most rifles are shot just as they come out of the factory carton, with no bedding alterations, it's a moot point.

The rifles come in a selection of calibers to encompass hunting game anywhere in the world. All three are available in so many options, options which are constantly changing or going out of style, that it's hard to keep up with them. There are short and standard-length actions in all three models. There are variations in buttplates, recoil pads, stock finishes, forend tips, floorplates, and stock designs.

The time has come to make the decision. Which will it be?

The Lever Action

T HE LEVER ACTION is usually overlooked as a deer hunter's first choice for a repeating rifle, but it has a lot more to offer than most shooters think. The lever action was the first repeating rifle design to gain any real measure of popularity, and it has been a proven performer under hard use in the field for over 100 years. It is not a rifle design time has passed by. Actually, today's most popular lever-action rifles, rather than being modern variations on a basic early design, are the *same* designs that were in widespread use around the turn of the century.

The popular Savage Model 99, for example, has been in continuous production since 1895. The ubiquitous Winchester Model 94 has been around since 1894. And neither has undergone any appreciable change since its introduction. The Marlin Model 336 series has changed slightly but remains fundamentally the same as it was during the 19th century.

These lever guns had taken every species of big game on the North American continent long before most of us were born. They've performed in the face of outlaws and in the big-game fields. Who are we to say they aren't as good as anything going today for deer hunting?

I once knew a fellow who used a Winchester Model 94 in .30-30 to hunt deer, antelope, bear, coyote, and elk. It seemed like every time he went hunting, he bagged game. He always came home with a bragging-size deer, and it was always shot through the heart. He was a hunter in the true sense of the word, and he selected his shots carefully. He always claimed that if he wasn't "hunter enough" to get the shot he wanted with his old .30-30, he had no business shooting. And the only rifle he ever used was that old .30-30.

.358 WINCHESTER LOAD DATA

Bullet	Powder (Type)	(Grs.)	Primer	Case	Velocity (fps)
	Browning BLR 20-inch barrel				
Hornady 200-gr. spirepoint	IMR-3031	47.0	Win. LR	W-W	2477
Hornady 200-gr. spirepoint	RL-7	42.0	Fed. 210	W-W	2471
Speer 250-gr. spitzer	IMR-4064	44.0	Fed. 210	W-W	2171
Hornady 250-gr. spirepoint	IMR-4320	46.0	Fed. 210	W-W	2263
Speer 250-gr. spitzer	IMR-4320	46.0	Fed. 210	W-W	2311

NOTES: Velocity was taken with an Oehler Model 33 Chronotach and is an average of 10 shots 10 feet from the muzzle.

One reason the .30-30 cartridge is so popular is the rifles that chamber it. They're light, short, easy carrying, quick pointing, rugged—in other words, they get the job done. For years, saddle scabbards were designed around a slab-sided .30-30. Today, slip one under the seat of the pickup and forget it's there—until you need it. It may have months of fine road dust and dried-out boot mud in its mechanism when you pull it out. Miles of rough roads may have worn it shiny in spots, and vibrations may have loosened the buttstock, but it'll get the job done. It doesn't matter if it's a Marlin, Savage, or Winchester; they all come through, just as they have since they were nothing more than newfangled, not-to-be-trusted repeatin' guns. Those three makes and the Browning BLR (which is still a "new" gun by comparison) make up the most popular lever guns used for deer hunting.

.308 WINCHESTER LOAD DATA

Savage Model 99-E
22-inch barrel

Bullet	Powder (Type)	(Grs.)	Primer	Case	Velocity (fps)
Nosler 150-gr. Solid Base	RL-7	38.0	Fed. 210	Fed.	2786
Nosler 150-gr. Solid Base	H4895	46.0	Fed. 210	Fed.	2909
Nosler 150-gr. Solid Base	W748	49.0	Fed. 210	Fed.	2909
Hornady 180-gr. spirepoint	BL-C(2)	44.0	Fed. 210	Fed.	2519
Hornady 180-gr. spirepoint	IMR-4895	41.0	Fed. 210	Fed.	2503
Hornady 180-gr. spirepoint	H335	41.0	Fed. 210	Fed.	2429

NOTES: These loads were *maximum* in the test rifle. Be sure to reduce charges by at least 10 percent to begin your load development. Velocity was taken with a Model 500 Custom Chronograph with Model 600 Ambient Light screens and is an average of five shots 7½ feet from the muzzle.

There are a few other lever guns that should not be passed over without mention. Browning reintroduced two venerable old lever guns, the Model 1895 and the Model 1886, but they are limited-production items and aren't likely to be serious contenders for "popular" status.

The best-designed lever gun ever, in my opinion, has been discontinued. The Winchester Model 88 was a good-looking, smooth-operating rifle, with the advantages of a front-locking bolt, one-piece stock, and detachable box magazine that has not been equaled. The Model 88s I've had would shoot on par with most bolt rifles. The trigger was difficult to adjust, and the bedding system was a trifle eccentric, but other features made this an excellent rifle overall. With the advent of high-performance, short-action cartridges like the .308, .243, .358, and .284, Model 88s had a lot to offer.

* * *

The current popular lever guns have two-piece stocks and are variations on a rear-locking design—with the exception of the new Browning BLR. This little beauty is a gear-activated, front-locking, multiple-lug lever-action rifle strong enough for pressures on par with bolt actions. For this reason, the Browning BLR can handle any high-pressure cartridge that fits this action size. As a result, it is available in a class of chamberings that the traditional tube-magazine lever guns are not.

The Browning BLR is an efficient design that retains compactness and light carrying qualities. The flat-sided receiver, two-piece stock, and exposed hammer have the look of a traditional lever gun. However, the unique gear-driven action makes the lever throw considerably shorter and faster to operate than on traditional lever guns. In addition, the trigger swings down with the lever so a shooter won't jab his finger with the tip of the trigger when he hurriedly swings the lever up.

The BLR also has the advantage of a detachable box magazine. Even though it retains the basic "western" look, the nontubular magazine means spitzer bullets can be loaded in the BLR. A look at ballistic tables shows how much advantage a pointed bullet has over a flatnose at reasonable hunting distances. The Browning BLR also has side ejection and a solid-top receiver that is a natural for low scope mounting.

* * *

The Savage Model 99 also carries a very strong action. Though this basic action design is virtually unchanged from its original version, the postwar Model 99s seem to have a lot more strength than early guns of this model. While early guns I've owned in this model are prone to case stretching, later guns handle loads on a par with bolt-action rifles. Consequently, the Model 99s are now chambered for the high-pressure (52,000 psi) .243 and .308 Winchester cartridges. This increase in strength is a result of improved metallurgy and fit of the locking parts.

Unlike the other three popular lever guns, the Model 99 does not have an exposed hammer, but it does have a box magazine that will handle spitzer bullets. It is easy to mount a scope low over the Model 99's receiver. The old receiver design had to be drilled and tapped for scope mounts; current models are ready for scope mounting.

The Savage lever action also has a slightly longer barrel than the other three popular lever guns. At 22 inches, it is noticeably longer than Marlin's, Browning's, or Winchester's 20-inch standard barrels.

* * *

The Marlin rifle, truly a traditional saddle gun, has features that make it highly desirable for today's deer hunter. First, the Marlin has a very smooth lever throw. It has side ejection and a solid-top receiver that

.300 SAVAGE LOAD DATA

Savage Model 99-E
22-inch barrel

Bullet	Powder (Type)	(Grs.)	Primer	Case	Velocity (fps)
Nosler 150-gr. Solid Base	RL-7	37.0	Fed. 210	Fed.	2756
Nosler 150-gr. Solid Base	IMR-4895	43.0	Fed. 210	Fed.	2776
Nosler 150-gr. Solid Base	W748	46.0	Fed. 210	Fed.	2828
Hornady 180-gr. spirepoint	BL-C(2)	42.0	Fed. 210	Fed.	2474
Hornady 180-gr. spirepoint	IMR-4895	40.0	Fed. 210	Fed.	2494
Hornady 180-gr. spirepoint	H335	39.0	Fed. 210	Fed.	2389

NOTES: These loads were *maximum* in the test rifle. Be sure to reduce charges by at least 10 percent to begin your load development. Velocity was taken with a Model 500 Custom Chronograph with Model 600 Ambient Light screens and is an average of five shots 7½ feet from the muzzle.

allows low scope mounting. Standard models come with a pistol grip buttstock, unlike the Winchester or Browning rifles. Another plus for the Marlin lever action is that it's easy to remove the breechbolt, allowing you to look through the bore or clean the barrel from the breech. The most recent Marlin lever rifles have a unique crossbolt safety in addition to the conventional hammer. This safety, a round button that slides laterally in the receiver just forward of the buttstock, is an added safety feature.

Like the Winchester, the old Marlin design has a tube magazine. Roundnose or flatnose bullets are required for multiple loading.

.375 WINCHESTER LOAD DATA					
Savage Model 99 22-inch barrel					
Bullet	Powder (Type)	(Grs.)	Primer	Case	Velocity (fps)
Hornady 220-gr. FN	RL-7	39.0	Fed. 210	W-W	2273
Speer 235-gr. semispitzer	RL-7	37.0	Fed. 210	W-W	2141
Winchester 250-gr. Power-Point	Factory load				1915

NOTES: These loads were *maximum* in the test rifle. Be sure to reduce charges by at least 10 percent to begin your load development. Velocity was taken with an Oehler Model 33 Chronotach and is an average of five shots 10 feet from the muzzle.

Another decided difference is the chamberings available. Lever guns really come into their own in the deer woods—the thick undergrowth where big bucks lay up during the day. The Marlins are chambered in cartridges made for the brush. For example, the other three popular lever guns aren't chambered for the .45-70 or excellent .444 Marlin cartridges. If a cartridge and bullet ever make a difference when it comes to bucking brush, these will. The big, heavy, slow-moving bullets can plow through a lot and still have the power to put a deer down with authority.

* * *

The Winchester Model 94 has probably ridden in more pickups and been carried in more scabbards than any other. This rifle is so popular and has been around so long that almost every deer hunter knows it on sight. The rifle epitomizes the term "saddle gun." The rifle that's always pulled out of the saddle scabbard in western movies, it's the gun that's done the most to give the .30-30 cartridge its reputation for reliability.

The Model 94 Winchester is characterized by the traditional tube magazine, straight-grip stock, exposed hammer, and top ejection. This top ejection prevented the mounting of scopes over the receiver until the introduction of the "Angle Eject" version. A slight alteration in the positioning of the ejector and a lowering of the ejection port at the right side of the receiver are the basics of the modified rifle. When used in conjunction with a unique scope mount that straddles the breech top, scopes can be mounted low over the bore of the Model 94AEs.

The Model 94 has a locking system designed by John Browning that is different from the other current lever guns. It is recognizable at a glance by the vertically sliding locking device that interlocks the breechbolt with the receiver sidewalls at the rear of the action. Swinging the lever down and forward lowers this block just before the breechbolt slides to the rear, exposing the breech and allowing the bolt to pick up another cartridge from the lifter.

In recent years, the Model 94 rifle has undergone changes besides the Angle Eject feature. Some rifles have been beefed up in the receiver sidewalls so they can handle higher pressure cartridges like the .375 Winchester and the .307 and .356 Winchester cartridges. The barrels of these latter two rifles have also been increased in diameter, resulting in improved accuracy over the old lightweight mild-caliber rifles.

Tube magazines can affect the point of impact and accuracy of the lever guns. The rifles often shoot better with a full magazine than with an empty one. The magazine, being attached to the barrel, apparently affects the barrel's vibration qualities. A heavier barrel seems to counteract this.

Like thousands of others, I shot my first deer with a Winchester Model 94 in .30-30. The young buck was standing broadside and never heard the "click" of the rifle's hammer engaging the fullcock notch. The Winchester 170-grain factory load hit the deer behind the front leg, two-thirds of the way down on its body—right where I had aimed. In all my years of deer hunting, with everything from .243s to .300 Magnums, I have never killed a deer "quicker." When the bullet met its mark, the deer dropped, and I've since learned this sort of performance is typical of the .30-30. This cartridge was *made* for deer.

.30-30 LOAD DATA

Marlin Model 336CS
20-inch barrel

Bullet	Powder (Type)	(Grs.)	Primer	Case	Velocity (fps)
Speer 150-gr. FN	H335	35.0	Win. LR	W-W	2412
Sierra 150-gr. FN	RL-7	28.0	Win. LR	W-W	2307
Sierra 150-gr. FN	MR-223	33.0	Win. LR	W-W	2268
Hornady 170-gr. FN	H335	33.0	Win. LR	W-W	2194
Hornady 170-gr. FN	H335	34.5	Win. LR	W-W	2305
Sierra 170-gr. FN	IMR-3031	28.0	Win. LR	W-W	2007
Remington 170-gr. softpcint Core-Lokt	Factory load				2230
Winchester 170-gr. Power-Point	Factory load				2227

NOTES: Velocity was taken with an Oehler Model 33 Chronotach and is an average of 10 shots 10 feet from the muzzle.

.444 MARLIN LOAD DATA

Marlin Model 444
22-inch barrel

Bullet	Powder (Type)	(Grs.)	Primer	Case	Velocity (fps)
Hornady 240-gr. HP	IMR-4198	46.0	Rem. 9½	Rem.	2304
Speer 240-gr. Magnum SP	IMR-3031	54.0	Rem. 9½	Rem.	2219
Hornady 265-gr. FP	IMR-3031	51.0	Rem. 9½	Rem.	2124
Remington 240-gr. softpoint	Factory load				2231

NOTES: Velocity was taken with an Oehler Model 33 Chronotach and is an average of 10 shots 10 feet from the muzzle.

Bullets loaded in the cartridge are made for optimum performance, specifically in the .30-30 and specifically for lever-action carbines with 20-inch barrels. Other .30-caliber bullets are loaded to perform well in everything from the .300 Savage to .300 Magnums and with many different barrel lengths. You never know whether you're getting "compromise" performance with one of these. With the .30-30, there is no question. The gun, load, and bullet are designed for deer at ranges inside 150 yards. This sort of singleness of purpose is something you seldom receive from other cartridges.

.30-30 LOAD DATA

Winchester Model 94
20-inch barrel

Bullet	Powder (Type)	(Grs.)	Primer	Case	Velocity (fps)
Sierra 150-gr. FN	W748	38.5	Win. LR	W-W	2465
Speer 150-gr. FN	RL-7	28.0	Win. LR	W-W	2235
Speer 170-gr. FN	BL-C(2)	30.0	Win. LR	W-W	1920
Hornady 170-gr. FN	W748	35.0	Win. LR	W-W	2144
Hornady 170-gr. FN	RL-7	25.5	Win. LR	W-W	2026
Remington 170-gr. softpoint Core-Lokt	Factory load				2108

NOTES: Velocity was taken with an Oehler Model 33 Chronotach and is an average of 10 shots 10 feet from the muzzle.

.356 LOAD DATA

Marlin Model 336ER
20-inch barrel

Bullet	Powder (Type)	(Grs.)	Primer	Case	Velocity (fps)
Winchester 200-gr. Power-Point	Factory load				2351
Winchester 250-gr. Power-Point	Factory load				2065

Winchester Model 94 Angle Eject
20-inch barrel

Bullet	Powder (Type)	(Grs.)	Primer	Case	Velocity (fps)
Speer 180-gr. FP	IMR-4320	48.0	Win. LR	Win.	2442
Sierra 200-gr. RN	W748	48.0	Win. LR	Win.	2213
Hornady 200-gr. RN	BL-C(2)	47.0	Win. LR	Win.	2234
Hornady 200-gr. RN	IMR-4895	45.0	Win. LR	Win.	2366
Winchester 200-gr. Power-Point	Factory load				2310
Winchester 250-gr. Power-Point	Factory load				2838

NOTES: Velocity was taken with an Oehler Model 33 Chronotach and is an average of 10 shots 10 feet from the muzzle.

Get a Marlin Model 336 or Winchester Model 94 in .30-30, load it with 150- or 170-grain factory loads, and you're ready to hunt deer. In this age of flat-shooting magnum cartridges, you might think the .30-30 is a bit light for deer. I saw my first elk taken with a .30-30 in 1966. I was standing close by when my brother shot a bull at about 40 yards with his Model 94. The elk was dead in surprisingly short order.

Winchester 170-grain factory loads have been chronographed at 2110 fps from my Model 94. The .30-06, which no one would dispute is large enough for elk, is frequently loaded with 180-grain bullets. The Winchester .30-06 Power-Points chronograph 2544 fps from my Model 700 Remington. When considering this, along with ballistic coefficient (.248 for the .30-06 bullet and .254 for the .30-30), the .30-30 load hits with the same energy at 50 yards that the .30-06 does at 190 yards. No one considers 190 yards to be too far for taking an elk with the .30-06.

The .30-30 is considered to be a short-range cartridge. It might be more accurate to consider it a *hunter's* cartridge. You should be closer to the game when you fire. This means either stalking more closely or hunting in thick cover where shots inside 150 yards are the rule. The last antelope I shot was taken with a Marlin Model 336 in .30-30, and antelope hunting is considered anything but a short-range proposition. But I reasoned that there was a time when no one thought twice about hunting antelope with a .30-30. The country I hunted was devoid of vegetation large enough to hide a man, but there were low-rolling hills. I exercised a little stalking skill and shot the pronghorn at about 30 yards. I have never had as much excitement when shooting one at 300 yards with a high-power bolt-action rifle.

I've digressed from hunting deer to hunting elk and antelope in order to point out that the .30-30 is powerful enough for almost any deer and has ample range for deer hunting purposes. Both points are relative. There was a time when the .30-30 was considered to be fast and flat shooting. Today, in the presence of mighty magnums, even the .30-06 is not particularly powerful or flat shooting.

.307 LOAD DATA

Winchester Model 94 Angle Eject
20-inch barrel

Bullet	Powder (Type)	(Grs.)	Primer	Case	Velocity (fps)
Sierra 150-gr. FN	IMR-3031	40.0	Win. LR	Win.	2542
Speer 150-gr. FN	IMR-4895	41.0	Win. LR	Win.	2562
Hornady 170-gr. FP	H414	44.0	Win. LR	Win.	2346
Sierra 170-gr. FN	W760	45.0	Win. LR	Win.	2379
Winchester 150-gr. Power-Point	Factory load				2608
Winchester 180-gr. Power-Point	Factory load				2399

NOTES: Velocity was taken with an Oehler Model 33 Chronotach and is an average of 10 shots 10 feet from the muzzle.

I've used up a lot of space for the .30-30, but its popularity, performance, and longevity deserve more than casual mention. There are a lot of other excellent cartridge choices in the lever guns for deer. You should consider the .35 Remington to be at least the equal of the .30-30 in deer hunting performance. Deer I've shot with the 200-grain factory loads left profuse blood trails and went down with proper bullet placement. At the risk of offending many .30-30 fans, I would select this round over the .30-30; I just like fat bullets at short ranges. The .35 Remington is available in the Marlin Model 336, as is the .375 Winchester, another excellent deer round.

In the Marlin levers, you have the trio mentioned and the .356, .45-70, and .444 (Marlin's only proprietary cartridge currently in production). I haven't used the .444 on deer, but there's no doubt about its effectiveness. The Marlin rifles are also available in .357 Magnum and .44 Magnum, which are legal for deer in most states, but I consider all the previously mentioned cartridges far better choices.

In the Winchester rifles, there are the .30-30, .307, .356, and .375, all Winchester proprietary cartridges and all good deer-getters. Some consider the .356 and .375 to be excessively large for short-range deer hunting, but there's nothing wrong with putting a deer down with authority, even if you have to shoot through a bit of brush. Another advantage to a heavier, deep-penetrating bullet is that an exit hole produces a more profuse blood trail, a definite advantage if followup tracking becomes necessary.

In the Savage Model 99, there is the .308. While the 99 is also chambered for the .243, an adequate deer cartridge, I would go with the .308. There are also lots of used rifles in the .300 Savage chambering, which I consider an excellent choice for deer. It was a sad day a few years back when I learned Savage had dropped its proprietary .300 cartridge in favor of the more popular .308. The .308 is factory loaded to ballistics exceeding those of the .300 Savage and has undisputed deer hunting credentials. The .300 Savage has been around since 1920; the .308, 1952.

In the Browning BLR, good choices would include the 7mm-08 Remington, .308 Winchester, and .358 Winchester. Again, the .358 may be considered to be overdoing it for deer, but this round is one of my all-around hunting favorites in a lever gun. I have taken deer, bear, and elk with it, and it has always performed well. It's nice to have a cartridge that offers plenty of punch in case you want to hunt elk, bear, or moose with your favorite deer rifle. In the West, it's not unusual to hunt deer and elk at the same time, and for this type of hunting, the .358 is a good choice. Like the .284 Winchester, the .358 is another of those cartridges that is a lot better than its sales suggest. It isn't fully appreciated for what it has to offer.

When hunting deer in thick cover, particularly in foul weather, I like a lever gun that's fitted with a receiver peep sight. This type of sight is extremely quick to get on target, and it isn't affected by snow or rain the way a scope can be. For hunting in good weather, a low-magnification scope in the 1.5-2X range is extremely fast to get on target and offers advantages over the peep sight during low-light conditions early or late in the day. Pick one of these with an illuminated reticle like an Aimpoint (with zero magnification), and you have the best in a quick sight that doesn't fail in poor light.

In hunting country, where a longer shot is a possibility, I would select a cartridge like the .307 or .356 in the Marlin or Winchester rifles or the .308 in the Browning or Savage rifles. I would fit the gun with a 2X or 4X scope and be ready for deer out to 300 yards—at least with the latter two rifles.

What about accuracy with the lever guns? They don't shoot as well as bolt-action rifles, but *deer hunting accuracy* is the goal here. In nearly all instances, three-inch, 100-yard accuracy is all you need in most deer hunting situations anyway. Most lever guns are capable of this with the right loads. I've broken the two-inch, five-shot group average with a good many lever guns; a 1.5-inch average is possible.

I have found that the load used makes an important difference in many lever guns, so try as many deer loads, whether factory ammo or handloads, as you can before season. Select the one that shoots best, and you're ready to go.

Lever guns are good choices in deer rifles. They've put meat on tables for generations and will be doing so for years to come. Lever guns have a history and personality all their own, and taking a deer with one provides a sense of satisfaction that's quite special. Why not enjoy this experience next deer season?

My Dream Gun

THE RANCH was big, and it had lots of coyotes—calf- and sheep-eating coyotes. I was hoping to get a few pelts and help the rancher in the process as I eased the four-wheel-drive vehicle toward my first calling stand of the day. Coyotes are where you find them, and I didn't have to call to get a look at my first.

The canine spotted my pickup and began loping away at an angle, looking back over his shoulder as he ran. I braked the vehicle to a stop, and I quickly covered the loping animal with the Leupold scope's field of view. He was about 200 yards out . . . then 250 . . . 300 . . . I held my fire. He stopped, I held dead-on, squeezed, and in the next split second, the wildcat cartridge sped a 54-grain bullet out the muzzle at better than 4000 fps. The coyote didn't take another step. The bullet never exited his chest cavity.

Twenty minutes later, I was sitting under a juniper tree and using my predator call. In came a coyote that stopped 20 yards out to take a look. It was his *last* look. The 4000 fps cartridge performed just as well at 20 yards as 300 yards. The bullet fragmented inside the coyote and didn't exit, leaving only a .22-caliber entrance hole in the pelt.

Coyote hunting has taught me that a bullet capable of shooting fast and flat is a decided advantage; so is a crisp, consistent, light-pulling trigger; a stock that fits; and an accurate rifle, one that won't change point of impact as a result of wet weather, dry weather, or getting knocked around in a vehicle. There's also no sense wasting time with a scope and mounts that are less than the best.

With these elements in mind, I recently put together what I think is the best coyote hunting rifle I've seen . . . my dream gun. Actually, the combination is not unique, just serviceable. The same principles can be applied to your custom rifle, whether it's for whitetails in Pennsylvania, elk in Colorado, or prairie dogs in the Great Plains.

One of the first steps is to decide on a cartridge and select a rifle action to handle it. In the case of my coyote rifle, there was no question about the cartridge. I'm generally a fan of readily available factory ammo, but there's just no factory cartridge that will do what I want when it comes to hunting coyotes. That's why I use the .22-6mm CJ, a wildcat cartridge based on the 6mm Remington case necked down for .224-diameter bullets.

With a custom rifle, there's no reason not to use whatever cartridge you want. That's the whole point—to create a rifle that fits you and your requirements instead of adjusting to what's available. And with the CJ, conversion is no problem. An existing .22-250 can be rechambered, and making cases can be as easy as running 6mm Remington brass into the .22-6mm CJ sizing die. Furthermore, such cases generally feed well without magazine or feed rail alterations to the rifle, something that can't be said of a great many sharp-shouldered wildcat cartridge conversions.

In order to keep things simple—and costs down—I started with an Interarms Whitworth .22-250 barreled action. This action is basically a commercial version of the old military Model 98, an action with a reputation for reliability second to none. Its extraction and ejection features are legendary, and its gas-handling characteristics, in the event of a pierced primer or separated case, are excellent. This rifle has really withstood the test of time and field use; it remains virtually unchanged since it was introduced in 1898. The .22-250 action carries a 24-inch barrel and is available from Interarms in a wide variety of calibers. It's a simple matter to have the .22-250 chamber reamed for the wildcat cartridge.

Huntington's, the family that started RCBS, had chambered another .22-6mm CJ for me, and I recently learned the company is offering custom stocking with Brown Precision stocks. A synthetic stock is the logical choice over walnut. The people at Huntington's are some of the best in the business, and I decided to have them do both the metal and stock work for the new rifle.

One of the requirements was that the new rifle was to have subdued or nonglare metal and stock; camouflage is necessary for the most effective coyote calling combination. I elected to have a nonglare camouflage paint job on the stock and all the metal surfaced with a nonglare, bead-blast finish. The Leupold Custom Matte scope, with a similar finish, topped the rig. I decided on the Vari-X III 2.5-8X with the power selector detents and the range-estimating feature. I also chose Leupold rings and one-piece base. Huntington's bead blasted the base and rings along with the barreled action so that these metal parts have the same finish. This finish perfectly matched the matte surface on the Leupold scope.

Another advantage to a custom rifle is that you can get a stock that fits perfectly. Nearly all the factory rifle stocks are too short in length of pull for my long arms. They generally run 13¼ or 13½ inches, so I specified a 13⅞-inch length of pull on the new rifle.

Huntington's Tom Miller applied a camo finish and a wrinkle paint. It was subdued, nonglare, and nonslip over the entire stock, not just in the gripping portions. It was fitted with QD-type sling swivel studs and a Pachmayr black Old English recoil pad. While the entire rifle—stock, barreled action, scope, and mounts—is built for serviceability first and foremost, it looks exquisite.

Rather than stamping Xs over the original .22-250 caliber designation on the barrel, Miller milled a tiny oval flat and engraved the new caliber designation ".22-6mm CJ." This is a nice touch and a testament to the conscientiousness and craftsmanship of the gunmaker.

When I removed the barreled action from the stock, I could see the glass bedding looked good. The bedding material had been removed from the bottom, sides, and front of the recoil lug recess. Overall, the barreled action fit the stock nicely.

Even though the Interarms trigger is adjustable, it couldn't be adjusted quite as crisp and light as I like. I'm finicky when it comes to triggers and usually only a custom trigger measures up. In my opinion, trigger pull is one of the most critical factors when it comes to achieving a high level of accuracy and the ability to hit running predators. I sent the rifle to Timney Triggers and had a Featherweight Deluxe model installed and adjusted to 30 ounces, exactly as I requested. After the rifle and trigger work were complete, the gun and scope tipped the scale at 8¼ pounds.

The next step was to make cases and work out an efficient load for the rifle. I had the chamber cut with a tight neck; after the 6mm cases were necked to .22, I thinned the necks to the proper dimension with a Marquart turning tool. Then I loaded the brass with a variety of powders and seven different bullets ranging from 40 to 60 grains. I had some experience with the cartridge in other rifles, and this gave me an idea about which propellants to use. "Load From A Disk," a computer program distributed by Wayne Blackwell, was also used to determine the powders most likely to turn up top performance. The program suggested using medium-slow powders like IMR-4350 for bullets from 50 to 60 grains and slower burning propellants for bullets heavier than 60 grains.

In order to derive the maximum long-range performance with the cartridge, the bullets were chosen for their streamlined shape or high ballistic coefficients. One exception was the Speer 40-grain spirepoint. It was chosen for its light weight to get higher velocity and to see if the velocity obtained with it would compensate for the poorer ballistic coefficient.

All the bullets were seated with an RCBS Competition die. No more time and effort are required to use this quality seating die, and because of its micrometer-type click stops, it's truly a pleasure to use when adjusting seating depth.

A number of propellants were used in addition to those listed in the accompanying table; some were found to be unsuitable. Slower burning propellants like H870 and MR-8700 were too slow to produce adequate velocity before the capacity of the case was consumed. (Not enough powder could be put in a case to produce normal top operating pressures and velocities.)

A maximum load was developed for the Speer 40-grain bullet with one lot of IMR-3031. Forty-four grains of the initial lot produced 4251 fps at 10 feet from the muzzle. However, final chronographing was done with a different lot of propellant which produced only 4102 fps. This latter velocity is the one recorded in the accompanying table.

Another interesting development that cropped up during the testing involves the load with the Sierra 50-grain spitzer and 46.0 grains of IMR-4064. Among all the loads, this is the only one in which all the powder charges were weighed; all others were dispensed with a measure. I've always felt that as long as a powder measure is used which meters consistently, there's no need to take the extra time necessary to weigh each charge. In the accompanying table, however, I'm dealing with coarse, extruded propellants. Furthermore, I'm working close to maximum pressures with a case that has a large capacity and a small bore. My experience has been that when loading such a case, slight variations in any of the components can have a greater effect than if a small case with a relatively large bore is used. This might explain why the extreme

.22-6mm CJ LOAD DATA

Rechambered Interarms Whitworth (originally .22-250),
24-inch barrel, Huntington fiberglass stock;
Leupold Vari-X III 2.5-8X Custom Matte scope, Leupold mounts

Bullet	Powder (Type)	(Grs.)	Primer	Velocity (fps)	Extreme Spread	Standard Deviation	Energy (ft-lbs)	Recoil (ft-lbs)	Average Group Size (Inches)
Speer 40-gr. spirepoint	IMR-3031	44.0	Rem. 9½	4102*	135*	58*	1494	8.86	1.4
Sierra 50-gr. spitzer	IMR-4064	46.0**	Rem. 9½	4038	46	16	1810	10.68	.7
Sierra 52-gr. HPBT	IMR-4064	44.0	Rem. 9½	3850	119	33	1711	9.49	1.2
Hornady 53-gr. Match HP	IMR-4350	48.5	Win. LR	3963	93	25	1848	11.48	1.4
Nosler 55-gr. Solid Base	IMR-4320	43.0	Rem. 9½	3796	121	41	1756	9.38	1.5
Nosler 60-gr. Solid Base	MR-3100	49.0	Win. LR	3753	90	26	1877	11.51	1.3
Hornady 60-gr. spirepoint	IMR-4350	46.0	Rem. 9½	3673	97	29	1797	10.24	1.7

Bullet	400-Yard Velocity (fps)	400-Yard Energy (ft-lbs)	****400-Yard Wind Drift (Inches)	Time of Flight (Seconds)	Optimum Sighting-in Distance (Yards)	****Maximum Point-blank Range (Yards)	400-Yard Trajectory (Inches)	100-Yard Trajectory (Inches)
Speer 40-gr. spirepoint	1631	236	41.5	.475	240	275	-16.7	+1.53
Sierra 50-gr. spitzer	2403	641	18.5	.385	265	305	-9.4	+1.44
Sierra 52-gr. HPBT	2232	575	20.8	.410	250	290	-11.8	+1.47
Hornady 53-gr. Match HP	2304	624	20.0	.398	260	300	-10.4	+1.49
Nosler 55-gr. Solid Base	2366	683	17.4	.401	255	295	-10.8	+1.52
Nosler 60-gr. Solid Base	2370	748	17.0	.402	255	295	-10.9	+1.56
Hornady 60-gr. spirepoint	2187	637	20.4	.424	245	280	-13.0	+1.59

NOTES: Velocity is an average of 10 shots at 10 feet from the muzzle and was clocked with an Oehler Model 33 Chronotech. Group size is an average of three five-shot strings at 100 yards.
*This figure is based on only five shots.
**These charges were weighed; all others were measured.
***10 mph crosswind
****Based on trajectory within plus or minus two inches of line of sight

spread and standard deviation with the only weighed charges were half that of the other loads. The Sierra 50-grainer with 46.0 grains of IMR-4064 and the weighed charges produced an extreme velocity spread in 10 shots of only 46 fps. The standard deviation was 16. The load also produced the best accuracy at .7 inch for three five-shot strings and the highest velocity, with the exception of the 40-grain bullet, of 4038 fps.

Once the velocities were determined with the various loads, the figures, along with ballistic coefficient, were fed into my computer to derive downrange information and to compare the loads. This is an excellent way to determine which loads will perform best (based on your criteria).

Accuracy could probably be improved in all the loads, as it was with the Sierra 50-grain load, simply be dispensing more consistent charges. Velocity was now fixed with the loads listed; for the most part, they could be considered maximum. I was already using the most efficient bullets, so it was now a matter of selecting the load with the best downrange performance. For coyote hunting, it doesn't matter whether a 40-grain bullet or a 60-grain bullet is used. What matters is the drop, wind drift, and downrange energy performance of the loads. A computer can analyze this like no amount of actual shooting can.

First, I outlined the parameters of how the load would be used. For coyote hunting, I consider maximum point-blank range to be the maximum range at which a bullet can be fired without it rising or falling more than two inches from line of sight. The computer program told me what maximum point-blank range was and the optimum sighting-in distance to achieve it. Basically, what I was doing was using the computer as an aid to derive the maximum performance from each load and then compare the loads.

High velocity can offset a poorer bullet shape to some extent. A heavy bullet can offset wind drift somewhat, but it can't be fired as fast, which tends to negate some of the advantage. Only a computer can rapidly and efficiently determine the bottom line of all these tradeoffs.

The ballistic coefficient values of the bullets listed were obtained from the manufacturers. The Speer 40-grainer has a ballistic coefficient listed at .144, the Sierra 50-grain spitzer is .251, the Sierra 52-grain HPBT is .245, the Hornady 53-grain Match HP is .243, the Nosler 55-grain Solid Base is .282, the Nosler 60-grain Solid Base is .290, and the Hornady 60-grain spirepoint is .262.

Among the downrange comparisons, trajectory and maximum point-blank range were given primary consideration, followed by wind drift and then by energy. For interest, a recoil comparison was also made, and then the results were evaluated.

As mentioned, the Sierra 50-grain load came out on top in maximum point-blank range (with the flattest trajectory out to 500 yards, the maximum distance computed). Though it's not on top in wind drift out to 400 yards, it drifts only 1.5 inches more in a 10 mile-per-hour crosswind than the best heavy-bullet load using the Nosler 60-grain Solid Base. This difference in drift is of no consequence at 400 yards. The 50-grain load also has the shortest time of flight to 400 yards. Time of flight can be important, particularly among different cartridges. Game frequently moves after the shot is fired, and a short time of flight is a decided advantage for this reason. In addition, less lead is required on running game with a cartridge that has a shorter time of flight; this makes it easier to hit such moving targets. All the time of flight figures are very short with the .22-6mm CJ cartridge, and there's no significant difference among them.

The Sierra 50-grainer produced 641 ft-lbs of energy clear out to 400 yards, the maximum range at which coyotes are likely to be taken. This is generally considered to be more than ample energy for coyotes. The highest energy load was the Nosler 60-grainer at 748 ft-lbs, but the energy difference between the two loads was not considered to be as significant as the difference in trajectory. Actually, either the Sierra 50-grainer or the Nosler 60-grainer load would be top choices. The real clincher is the proven accuracy performance of the Sierra 50-grainer with a .7-inch average. Another reason for leaning toward the lighter bullet is that it tends to penetrate less. For coyote pelt hunting, I don't want the bullet to exit.

I decided the Sierra 50-grainer ahead of 46.0 grains of IMR-4064 was the load to use. With consistent .7-inch accuracy for five shots at 100 yards and a maximum point-blank range of 305 yards, it's going to be really effective. Out to 400 yards, the bullet is only 9.4 inches below the line of sight. That's flat shooting.

Combine this load with the reliability of a glass-bedded Interarms action resting in a fiberglass stock and topped with excellent optics, and I think it's an unbeatable outfit for coyotes – whether the range is 400 yards or 40 feet!

How To Buy A Used Rifle

B UYING A NEW rifle is one of the truly pleasurable experiences a hunter can have. The decision to buy is usually based on the recommendations of the salesman *and* finding a rifle chambered in a caliber that will do the job. And if anything goes wrong with the rifle, a very unlikely occurrence, there is usually a warranty.

However, buying a used rifle can carry the same excitement. A used rifle can be as serviceable as a new rifle. And there are many advantages to buying a used rifle. The most obvious is the cost savings. Used guns are generally cheaper than new ones. In addition to the direct cost savings for the firearm, one frequently has the opportunity to get a case, ammunition, scope, etc., thrown in with the deal for very little – if any – more money.

Other than the cost benefits in buying a used rifle, the older gun simply may be more desirable. Chances are, the older rifle is more broken-in so the action, safety, etc., function more smoothly. And for rifles that are no longer manufactured, the *only* way to get one is to buy it used.

And there are more advantages to buying used. For example, a rifle previously owned by a serious shooter may have supplementary accuracy data or load data. Shooters often experiment with various handloads, factory ammunition, etc., in a given rifle and keep records regarding the accuracy of each load. The previous owner often has a good idea about which loads the rifle prefers – saving you considerable time and ammunition in finding a top performing load.

However, even though there are many advantages to buying a used rifle, if you don't know what to look for, all the "advantages" can drift away and what started as a sweet deal can turn very sour.

As a practical matter, firearms made in this country by the major manufacturers have always been built to last a lifetime, given reasonable care. And there's no reason why even a well-used firearm can't continue to give many years of fine service.

There are a number of places where a special value or bargain can turn up. Friends, newspaper classifieds, and gun stores are usually the best sources. I'm constantly looking for good buys in the used gun market— even when I don't have anything specific in mind.

However, if you do have a specific reason for buying a used firearm, you should first decide what type of rifles fit that need. For example, the horseback hunter after deer in dense cover may be best served by the old, slab-sided Model 94 Winchester or Marlin Model 336 lever action. The avid bird hunter who spends the better part of the bird season with a pump-action shotgun might find that the slide-action rifle is much easier to become accustomed to than any of the other action types.

In addition to action type or rifle style, the cartridge is another area where the shooter would be wise to have some idea about what he wants *before* going rifle hunting.

More important than selecting an individual cartridge is to determine the purpose of the cartridge. Will it be used for hunting deer, elk, or bear? Will you be hunting in open country, where the ranges are likely to be long, or in heavily timbered country? Rather than limiting the selection to a single caliber, you might be wise to look for a cartridge that falls within a *range* of suitable calibers.

If you're looking for a deer rifle chambered in a caliber suitable for long-range shooting, you would be wise to consider all rifles in the .25-06, .270, .280, .30-06, and 7mm Magnum class. This increases the number of rifles you'll have to consider.

Buying a rifle is no different than buying anything else. "Let the buyer beware" is something you should keep in mind. It may help to mentally break down a centerfire rifle into parts and consider each one separately when evaluating a used model.

The parts consist basically of the action, barrel, exterior metal finish, stock finish, and sights or scope. The action can be further broken down into its functions. First, the action has a breechbolt or breechblock with the function of locking the cartridge securely in the barrel in order to contain the pressure when the rifle is fired. Next, it has some sort of an extractor to withdraw the fired case from the rifle's chamber. It also has an ejector to throw the empty case free of the action. If it's a repeating mechanism, the rifle will also have some sort of a magazine for introducing cartridges to the breechblock for subsequent chambering and firing. In addition, a trigger and safety or hammer are located somewhere on the action.

Before examining any gun, first make sure it's unloaded by looking into the breech *and* magazine for a cartridge. A second check, accomplished by opening the action and feeling in the breech for a cartridge is recommended, particularly if it's a semiauto. Once you're certain the rifle is unloaded it can be examined, but as always, keep it pointed in a safe direction.

Hold the rifle as you would carry it in a hunting situation, then shoulder it to see how it comes up. This quickly gives you some idea regarding its handling characteristics. There is a chance that the rifle may feel awkward; if this is the case, it may not be the rifle for you. However, if the rifle comes up nicely and points naturally, it may warrant further examination.

The next step is to cycle the action. If it's a lever, work the lever forward and back, as in chambering a cartridge. If it's a single shot, manipulate the lever to drop the breechblock, or cycle the bolt if it's a bolt action. The action should cycle smoothly without catching or grabbing. Like shouldering, the action should cycle comfortably and feel good. If any portion of action cycling is awkward, this could mean trouble. But if the rifle points well and the action cycles smoothly, you're ready to proceed.

Manipulate the safety to be sure it's in a convenient location and engages and disengages smoothly. Cock the action, engage the safety, and with the rifle pointed in a safe direction, pull the trigger to see if the firing pin falls. It shouldn't.

Disengage the safety and squeeze the trigger while paying particular attention to the way it pulls. Is it gritty or does it pull smoothly? Does it take an extreme amount of pressure on the trigger in order to get the rifle to fire, or does it fire with almost no pressure at all? While some triggers can easily be adjusted by a competent gunsmith to make them lighter or heavier or pull more smoothly, some triggers cannot be adjusted. Unless you know which is which, it's best to avoid any trigger which does not feel right.

Cock the rifle again and, with the safety disengaged, bounce the butt on the floor from a height of three or four inches (if it has a rubber recoil pad). This should not cause the rifle to fire. If the rifle has a hard steel or plastic buttplate, I bounce the butt on a carpeted floor. This doesn't harm the rifle; it's simply a test to see if the trigger mechanism can be jarred enough to allow the rifle to fire when it shouldn't. Also, the striker or hammer should not fall when the action is cycled harshly or the bolt slammed home hard.

If this all checks out, examine the action to verify that an extractor and ejector are present and appear to function properly. The extractor is generally hooked, which grasps a cartridge case by the rim to withdraw it from the chamber. The ejector is a device, generally located in the rifle's boltface, that throws the empty case from the rifle when the action is opened. It is usually some sort of a spring-loaded plunger affair which pushes on the base of the case opposite the ejector. When the empty case clears the chamber, it is automatically flipped out of the action by this plunger pressure.

If "dummy" rounds are handy, manually cycle them through the magazine and action to see that the gun feeds and ejects them smoothly. If dummy rounds aren't available, it's *not* wise to cycle live rounds through the action while in a sporting goods store—nor will it likely be permitted by the owner. If you're dealing with an individual, it may be possible to travel to the range or to some safe shooting area to see how it functions. But even this may be impractical. In that case, I generally rely on the appearance of the action itself and I ask the owner if I can return the gun if it doesn't function well. I've never been denied this request, and I've never had to return a used rifle because it didn't function.

The barrel is the most important part to consider when examining any used rifle. It warrants very close scrutiny. Though rifles are made to last a lifetime under normal use, there is a limit to the number of rounds which can be fired through a barrel before it becomes worn.

The number of rounds a barrel can handle depends to a large extent on the rifle's caliber. High-intensity cartridges will wear a barrel out in short order. Though I scrutinize any used rifle barrel for wear, I am particularly cautious about examining rifles chambered for cartridges having a very large case with a relatively small bore. If the cartridge is of a caliber commonly used for varmints, I am even more cautious because generally many more rounds are fired at varmints than are fired at big game. For example, if the rifle is chambered for a cartridge such as the .220 Swift or .22-250 Remington, examine the rifle very closely for barrel wear resulting from a lot of shots.

This type of wear is usually noticed first at the origin of the rifling near the breech. A barrel generally wears out quicker in this region than it does farther down the bore. One reason is that the burning powder and gas are hotter toward the breech. This hot gas and unburned propellant particles are blasted from the cartridge case into the small bore of the rifle.

It does little good to examine a bore until you've cleaned it because dust flecks can look like rust pits, and an oily bore can appear very worn when it isn't. In short, to see all you need to see, the barrel must be clean. Besides, there's no better way to detect roughness resulting from erosion, rust, bore damage, etc., than by passing a tight-patched cleaning rod through the barrel. With this, you can feel the roughness as the patch passes over it, revealing where in the barrel it's located. This section of barrel can then be examined visually after the bore is clean.

To clean the barrel for visual examination, it's best to scrub it with a bore brush that's been dipped in a gun cleaning solvent. The bore is wiped clean and dry with several patches; this is when you feel for roughness. Make certain the solvent has been dried out of the bore; again, a wet bore can falsely appear to be worn.

If possible, remove the rifle's bolt or lower the breechblock so that the bore can be viewed from either end of the barrel. Introduce light into the bore from the opposite end you're viewing through. It helps to have a device commonly called a Bore-Lite to illuminate the interior of the rifle's barrel for examination. If you don't have a Bore-Lite, light reflected from white paper works fine.

If the rifle's action is a pump, lever, or semiauto, you'll probably have to view the bore from the muzzle only because the breechblock can't be easily removed. But even if it were removed, the action contour might prevent straight-through viewing. In this instance, and if a Bore-Lite isn't available, a slender piece of paper can be folded and inserted in front of the breechblock of an open action to reflect light through the bore. In either case, carefully scrutinize the shoulders of the rifling lands. If they appear indistinct or rounded, this is probably due to bore wear. If the rifling appears almost smooth except for very thin black lines near the breech, as mentioned earlier, consider the barrel to be worn out, no matter how distinct the rifling appears to be farther down the barrel.

I have seen rifles with the first two or three inches of the barrel worn smooth. I have also seen cases where the lands weren't worn smooth, but they were very rough for the first couple of inches of bore. This is another reason to believe the barrel is completely worn out. Sometimes this roughness cannot be seen clearly; if it is seen, it may appear only as a dark area.

Besides those used for varmint shooting, other cartridges can be highly erosive to barrels. The .264 Winchester Magnum, .25-06 Remington, and .270 Winchester are just three examples. Again, any cartridge with a large case capacity in relation to bore should be cause for close examination of the barrel for wear.

In addition to examining the bore for wear, examine it for neglect and consequent rust pitting. This pitting is generally seen as a "peppered" bore surface. Sometimes it can be clearly seen by looking in the muzzle of the rifle without any auxiliary light. Examine carefully for this if the gun is very old and may have once fired blackpowder cartridges. Even later guns chambered for military cartridges like the .30-06 or .30-40 Krag may have had corrosive primer ammo fired in them.

After examining the rifling, be sure to scrutinize the chamber of the rifle. A previous shooter may have experienced a separated case or had a case stuck in the chamber. It's common practice to use a hardened-steel icepick or other makeshift "tool" to remove such an obstruction. Unfortunately, this can permanently damage a rifle's chamber. If you notice any scratches in the chamber region, avoid purchasing the rifle.

Take a close look at the crown or muzzle of the barrel. It's important that the barrel's crown be near perfect. A slight burr can cause accuracy to sour as this region has the last effect on a bullet as it exits a barrel. However, a burr on a crown is not that uncommon. If the crown is in bad condition, recrowning can usually be accomplished by a competent gunsmith for a small fee. This should not necessarily be the reason for rejection of the rifle.

The exterior finish, both metal and wood, can give some insight about the care the rifle has had. While some rifles show "honest" wear around the muzzle or perhaps bolt handle or lever, there are other types of finish blemishes that result from neglect. The most common blemish is rust, but severe scratches can come from crossing a barbed wire fence, dropping the rifle on rocks, etc.

While the finish has no direct bearing on the serviceability of the rifle, it has an effect on the salability of the rifle should you decide to peddle it sometime in the future. For this reason alone, the stock and metal finish are important considerations.

You can tell a lot about a rifle by simply looking it over. Examine the sights to see if they're intact. If there is a scope on the rifle, examine it for serious dents, dings, and scratches. Examine the scope mounts to make sure all the holes line up and that the mount bases match the contour of the receiver. Sometimes makeshift or ill-fitting mounts are substituted for the sale.

It was once my goal to own and handload for rifles in every commercial chambering. Though I have not yet reached that goal, I have come a long way and a good portion of the rifles I have owned have been purchased used. And they have all been highly serviceable. Though it sounds like there's a lot to check out in order to determine whether a used rifle is in good condition, it really doesn't take very long to get an accurate reading. As long as you examine the gun closely and avoid purchasing those that are questionable, you'll no doubt find one with a lifetime of service left—and one you'll be proud to own.

Shortening Rifle Barrels

I'VE CHRONOGRAPHED many loads in different firearms over the years, and I've learned there are some "rules of thumb" which do not always hold true in practice. One contrary to common belief is the velocity loss resulting from shortening rifle barrel length. It is commonly held that 25 fps of velocity is lost for every inch the barrel is shortened. For example, if you cut a rifle barrel from 26 to 24 inches, you can generally expect 50 fps of velocity loss. Of course, this rule of thumb only holds up within the range of popular barrel lengths, say from 18 to 26 inches. There is a point at which, when you increase barrel length, there is no gain in velocity. In fact, exactly the opposite can result in some instances.

I've learned I can normally expect some velocity loss as a rifle barrel is shortened. Even this is not always the case, however. My chronograph data reveals some cartridges are more prone to velocity loss when a barrel is shortened. My test shooting seems to indicate a cartridge which has a large case capacity and a relatively small bore loses more velocity as the barrel is shortened than does a rifle firing a cartridge with a relatively large bore and small case. Put another way, I've experienced more velocity loss with the .243 Winchester when a barrel is shortened than I have with a .308 Winchester. Both cases are about the same size; the difference is the larger bullet a .308 fires.

My data also tends to indicate there is generally less velocity loss with heavy bullets than with light bullets when a barrel is shortened. With the .308 Winchester, there was not nearly as much velocity loss in the shorter barrel with 200-grain bullets as there was with 130-grain bullets.

Contrary to what I once believed, propellant burning rate has a relatively minor bearing on velocity loss when a shorter barrel is used. Most of my test shooting has involved comparing 22-inch barrels to 18-inch barrels. My thinking is that if any appreciable velocity loss is to be experienced, it will certainly show up in a barrel length difference of four inches. To my surprise, virtually no velocity loss was experienced *with some loads* in the .308 Winchester when cutting a barrel from 22 to 18 inches. A chronograph is required to determine which loads are affected.

A few months ago, I planned to hunt Cape buffalo in Africa. It was strongly recommended that whatever rifle was selected, it shouldn't have a barrel longer than 22 inches. The reasoning was a short barrel would swing easier in the dense undergrowth where we would be hunting. Most rifles used for dispatching game of this size commonly have 24- or 26-inch barrels.

My choice was a .375 H&H Magnum. I'd planned to take a fiberglass-stocked rifle built by H-S Precision in Prescott, Arizona. The rifle was based on a Winchester Model 70 action with an Atkinson stainless-steel barrel. Tom Houghton, owner of H-S Precision, dropped the barrel to 22 inches.

Unfortunately, the Cape buffalo hunt was canceled, so there I was with a rifle specially built for a specific purpose, one I was eager to test on game in the field. But what do you use a .375 H&H Magnum for in the Lower 48 states? The answer was a Colorado elk hunt.

A 270- or 300-grain softpoint would no doubt dispatch a big bull decisively as long as I did my part and the range wasn't too long. I thought a .375 with a 22-inch barrel would not be the greatest performer at the long ranges frequently encountered above timberline, but a close look at the ballistic tables indicated otherwise. The .375 H&H Magnum with a 270-grain bullet appeared to be on par—trajectory wise—with a .30-06 Springfield using 180-grain bullets.

The .375 has a decided advantage over the .30-06 in the energy and momentum categories when it comes to killing power at long range. I wanted to see whether velocities from the 22-inch barrel would measure up to long-range shooting.

In my experience, elk are frequently found above timberline at the crack of dawn on opening day of the season. At this time, shots can be on the long side. After a day or two of hunting pressure, however, elk are more frequently encountered in the thick patches of dark timber where a 50-yard shot can be a long one.

If the velocity of the .375 H&H Magnum could hold up, the cartridge could perform well on long-range shots, and it would also perform well for an angling shot on rapidly departing game, a situation where a lot of penetration is a decided plus. For these reasons, the .375 H&H Magnum seemed a reasonable choice for elk hunting, provided high velocity could be maintained with the short barrel.

I assembled a variety of handloads for the .375 H&H Magnum with three different bullets—the Hornady 270-grain spirepoint, the Speer 285-grain Grand Slam, and the Sierra 300-grain spitzer boattail. I'd loaded for several .375 H&H Magnum rifles in the past and knew from experience that the slow-burning IMR-4350 and -4831 numbers are a bit too slow burning to reach top pressures in the .375 H&H Magnum. Not enough of it can be put in the case, and my rifle was based on a standard-length Model 70 action. Bullets had to be seated deep in the case in order for cartridges to feed properly. As a result, case capacity was reduced even further.

I decided to begin the test series with DuPont's IMR-4064 and Winchester's W760. All loads were assembled in Remington cases and sparked by Winchester No. 120 primers. To make a long story short, I received surprisingly good velocities from the 22-inch Atkinson barrel with both propellants.

Working up gradually with Winchester's W760 and the Sierra 300-grain spitzer, I found 78.5 grains of this propellant turned up a 2572 fps average for a five-shot string. The extreme velocity spread was a miniscule 30 fps. Seventy-seven grains of the same propellant with the same bullet produced a 2504 fps average. With the Speer 285-grain Grand Slam, 78.5 grains of W760 clocked 2556 fps, while 68.0 grains of 4064 went 2480 with the same bullet. Using the Hornady 270-grain spirepoint, 80.0 grains of Winchester's W760 turned up 2567 fps; 69.0 grains of 4064 produced 2549 fps.

The top velocity load with the Sierra 300-grain spitzer boattail would be the choice for elk. This streamlined bullet would probably be a good performer for long shots. It shot very well at the 100-yard range, turning in 1½-inch, three-shot groups (as did most of the other loads).

The H-S Precision rifle was a consistent performer regardless of the loads fired. In all honesty, I doubt if the 1½-inch group reporting does the rifle justice. It probably has the potential to shoot even better. The fiberglass-stocked rifle with the short, lightweight barrel, complete with a Zeiss 4X scope in Weaver mounts, weighed only 8½ pounds. To say the least, it belts you good when it's fired from the benchrest. Shooting tiny groups with such a rifle is tough. Still, the groups were plenty small for elk hunting.

While at the range, I also chronographed the Remington 270-grain soft-point factory ammo at 2540 fps. Past records indicate this same factory ammo was once chronographed from a standard Winchester Model 70 with a 24-inch barrel. In that particular rifle, it produced 2536 fps—a four fps *higher* velocity with a barrel two inches shorter.

Indeed, 2572 fps with the handloaded 300-grain bullet from a .375 H&H Magnum is decent velocity from any barrel length, whether it be 24 or 26 inches, and I was able to safely obtain it with a 22-inch barrel.

The .375 H&H Magnum chronographing tends to coincide with previous testing. I would classify this cartridge as having a relatively large bore diameter in relation to case capacity, which is the type of cartridge that doesn't produce as much velocity loss as more severely bottlenecked numbers. Furthermore, I was using the 300-grain bullet, which also tends to reduce velocity loss in short barrels.

This is something to keep in mind if you're thinking about chopping a barrel or obtaining a custom rifle with a short tube. You may not experience as much velocity loss as the 25 fps-per-inch rule of thumb leads you to believe. On the other hand, you could be experiencing an even greater velocity loss.

Only a chronograph will reveal what you're getting.

Barrel Erosion

I NCREASED PERFORMANCE is one of the primary reasons people handload. But handloaders, particularly varmint shooters who fire a lot of rounds, are sometimes concerned about what this performance costs them in terms of barrel erosion. It's no secret that loads fired at maximum pressure and velocity are more erosive on barrels than milder loads.

Barrel erosion can be reduced, however, by manipulating components. It's been mentioned many times that spherical or ball powders burn with a lower flame temperature and are less erosive than extruded propellants. There has also been some discussion about the difference in erosion qualities between boattail and flatbase bullets, though I don't believe any tests are conclusive.

Besides the components used, case capacity in relation to bore has some bearing on barrel or throat wear. In other words, a large case that funnels a lot of powder and gases through a relatively small bore is more conducive to throat erosion than a case holding a relatively large bullet.

Heat is another major contributor to barrel erosion. Though heat is a constant insofar as that developed by the powder/primer combination, it is variable in terms of rapidity of fire. One of the quickest ways to wear out a barrel is to continue firing maximum loads after it heats up from shooting.

Improper cleaning techniques can also cause a barrel to wear prematurely. It's been said that more barrels are worn out by improper cleaning techniques—or no cleaning at all—than by shooting too many rounds.

Benchrest shooters are particularly aware of the fact that cleaning rod wear can be one of the major contributors to throat erosion and sometimes uneven throat erosion. That's why these handloading accuracy buffs use cleaning rod guides. This tool somewhat resembles a rifle's bolt with a length-wise hole to admit a cleaning rod. This aligns the rod tip with the bore when it's inserted into the breech and makes the cleaning rod enter the leade on-center. But even if you use a cleaning rod guide, wearing a barrel unevenly by putting a bow in the cleaning rod is possible.

I used to shoot and share rifles with Neal Knox, who was at one time NBRSA National Heavy Varmint Rifle Champion. One particular .222 rifle that we had been sharing began to shoot erratically. A cursory visual examination indicated the throat was not worn to the extent that the poor groups might indicate, even though the rifle had a lot of rounds through it.

A closer examination with the bore scope revealed that the rifling was worn considerably more from the 11 o'clock position than in any other area around the lands. After talking with more experienced benchrest shooters, and after a bit of experimentation in examining our cleaning techniques, we found this wear was resulting from the cleaning rod we were using—not the bullets.

The cleaning rod is another potential source of barrel wear. A one-piece steel rod is probably best. Steel resists grit or other abrasive particles from becoming imbedded in its surface and can easily be wiped clean.

There has been talk about certain cartridges being particularly hard on barrels. "Overbore" rounds like the .220 Swift, .264 Winchester Magnum, and other large-capacity cases generally receive the brunt of the criticism. In my experience, however, as far as the average shooter is concerned, shooting out a barrel in a big-game rifle is more theoretical than actual. Even with some of the high-intensity varmint calibers in rifles that have been shot a considerable amount, most barrels withstand a lot of hunting use before going sour from wear. For example, several years ago, when a .222 benchrest rifle began shooting at a level somewhat less than benchrest accuracy (benchrest accuracy at that time was considered to be ¼-inch or smaller five-shot groups at 100 yards), Knox decided to figure out how many rounds had been fired through it. By figuring the number of shots generally fired in a match and the number of matches fired, he could account for about 6000 rounds which had been put through that barrel. These loads, contrary to what some would believe, were hot.

Admittedly, by today's standards, the .222 Remington cartridge is a mild one when compared to the .22-250 or .220 Swift. In most cases, hunters have no idea how many rounds they've put through a barrel when it begins shooting poorly. When it comes to hunting rifle accuracy, even varmint hunting rifle accuracy, a sour-shooting rifle generally begins to give indications that it's had it by throwing occasional shots wild and generally low.

I was firing a shot-out .22-250 Winchester Model 70 when I noticed it was throwing occasional shots way off point of aim. I continued shooting and later began noticing that some bullets were kicking up dust only 50 yards or so in front of me when the intended target was a prairie dog several hundred yards downrange! A closer examination of the barrel's interior with the bore scope indicated that the first couple of inches of bore were eroded severely.

Most people handload a variety of different combinations for varmints and don't keep track of the numbers of rounds fired. A barrel will last many years in most cases, and it's just too troublesome to keep track of rounds. But there are a few shooters who do keep meticulous records, and C.W. Wade is such a shooter. During the course of a prairie dog shoot near Goodland, Kansas, Wade mentioned that he recorded not only the numbers of rounds he had fired to wear out a couple of barrels, but the loads he used as well. I seized the opportunity to expand my knowledge on the subject, and he dug out his records when we returned home. They revealed the numbers of .22-250 rounds it took to wear out two Remington factory chrome-moly steel barrels on 40-XB rifles. In these two instances, the same load was used for the life of both barrels – 33.0 grains of IMR-3031 powder behind a Sierra 53-grain hollowpoint bullet and a Remington No. 7½ primer. The records indicated 6159 rounds had been fired through one barrel before it began throwing "flyers." The other barrel had 6196 rounds through it – surprisingly close to the number of rounds that we had fired through the .222 benchrest rifle before it went sour.

Even though the .22-250 is a more severe cartridge in terms of bullet acceleration and velocity and an increased amount of powder and gases go through the bore, the accuracy level required for the .22-250 on varmints is not as critical as the accuracy required from the .222 Remington for benchrest shooting.

Even for a varmint rifle, 6000 rounds is a lot of shooting. Think about it. How long would it take you to fire that many rounds, and what would it cost? Remember, we're talking about an extreme in terms of wearing out a barrel quickly, for few other types of shooting afford opportunities to fire as many rounds in a short period of time. Considering the price of ammo, the cost of rebarreling would be minimal.

In my experience, when it comes to big-game shooting, wearing out a barrel (even with one of the big belted magnum cartridges) is more myth than reality since there are few hunters who shoot so much big game that they can wear out a barrel even in their lifetime. For this reason, I believe the bore wear resulting from the big belted magnums in a hunting rifle is insignificant.

Jim Hull at Sierra Bullets also keeps meticulous records on the number of rounds fired through his rifles. Hull, a competition shooter, related one instance when he fired a perfect score at 600 yards with a .30-06 rifle that had over 10,000 rounds through the barrel. He related another instance when a .308 rifle had over 5500 rounds through it, and at that point he shot a string of 10 five-shot groups averaging .185 inch. Shortly thereafter, Hull removed six inches from the chamber end of the barrel and rechambered it, removing the eroded throat portion. After 10,000 rounds, that barrel still shot under ¼-inch groups. The .308 load used in this instance was 39.0 to 40.0 grains of H4895 behind the 168-grain Sierra Match bullet. Hull, who has considerable competition-shooting experience, indicated that as long as the bullet could be seated out to touch the lands, a high level of accuracy could generally be maintained.

All is not rosy, however. Steve Hornady of Hornady Bullets says that in some cases as few as 800 or 900 rounds can wash the throat out of a rifle firing a cartridge like the .264 Winchester Magnum.

In my experience, the average handloader need not be concerned about wearing out a barrel under today's hunting conditions. I'll simply do my hunting, and if the barrel does wear out, it'll just be replaced for another decade of shooting.

Cartridges

Rifle Cartridges:
What's In... What's Out... What's Up?

AMERICAN SHOOTERS can be a fickle lot. Take rifle cartridges, for example. A great many new rounds have enjoyed a grand introduction and then simply faded away. Others have stuck around for a few years, possibly being chambered in thousands of rifles before they stepped off. Still others—seemingly obsolete—have gotten a second chance through renewed interest. Included in this third group are numbers like the .22 Hornet, .250-3000 Savage, .257 Roberts, 7x57mm, .220 Swift, and .45-70.

I'll begin with a look at the ones lucky enough to be granted reprieves....

The .45-70, a cartridge which fires very heavy bullets at low velocity, was thought to have been six feet under. Adopted by the U.S. military in 1873, it remained the official cartridge until 1892. Although the production of .45-70 rifles ended with the 1886 Winchester in 1935, ammunition has been available ever since.

Just a few years ago, Ruger chambered the .45-70 in both the No. 1 and No. 3 single-shot rifles, and Marlin brought it out in the Model 1895 lever action. Browning introduced a .45-70 single shot in the form of the falling block Browning B-78. Modern reproductions of the old Trapdoor

---

Springfield are also in current production.

According to the *Speer Reloading Manual Number Ten*, original ballistics of the .45-70 included a chamber pressure of about 25,000 to 28,000 cup. With the introduction of new rifles, however, handloaders had the ability to load the .45-70 to much higher 50,000 cup pressures in stronger rifles like the Ruger and Browning.

* * *

Introduced by Winchester in 1930, the .22 Hornet was chambered in several bolt-action rifles, including the Savage Model 23 and the Winchester Model 54. With the advent of higher intensity varmint cartridges like the .222 Remington after World War II, the popularity of the .22 Hornet waned. Today, the .22 Hornet has regained ground by being chambered in the Ruger No. 3 carbine, the Thompson/Center Contender, and the Kimber and Anschutz rifles.

Though ballistics of the Hornet are tame when compared to other centerfire .22 calibers, it obviously fills a need.

* * *

Introduced in 1935, the .220 Swift was the first factory cartridge that delivered a muzzle velocity over 4000 fps. Over the years, however, the Swift has received a lot of bad press. It quickly gained a reputation for producing erratic pressures, stretching cases, and eroding barrel throats. When the Swift was introduced, barrel steels were not up to the standards they are today, and the high-pressure cartridge probably did produce exceedingly rapid throat erosion in early barrels.

Winchester discontinued the production of .220 Swift rifles. In 1964, the company introduced what it thought would be a replacement, the .225 Winchester. With its chambering in the Ruger Model 77 rifles, however, the .220 Swift appears to be outlasting its "replacement."

* * *

The .257 Roberts, which consists of the 7x57 case necked down to hold .257 bullets, was designed by N.H. "Ned" Roberts, a respected gun writer and experimenter, around the turn of the century. The first rifles in this caliber (called the ".25 Roberts") were made by Niedner's rifle company about 1928. In 1934, Remington introduced the .25 Roberts as the .257 Roberts, chambering its Model 30S bolt-action rifle for the round. Later, Winchester brought out the Model 70 in this chambering.

When the .243 and .244 Remington cartridges were introduced in 1955, the popularity of the .250 Savage and the .257 Roberts declined; as time passed, both seemed headed for obsolescence. Now, however, the .257 Roberts is chambered in a limited run of Remington Model 700 Classic rifles and has been chambered in a short run of Ruger Model 77s.

* * *

The .250 Savage, introduced in 1915 by the Savage Arms Co. in its Model 99 rifle, is an excellent combination varmint/deer cartridge. It can be chambered in short-action rifles, and unlike the Roberts, bullets can be seated well out of the case in these short actions. The .250 Savage (or .250-3000 Savage) is loaded to a relatively mild 45,000 psi and is a pleasant cartridge to shoot.

The original .250 Savage ammo was furnished with a lightweight 87-grain bullet at 3000 fps, hence the name .250-3000. No other commercial cartridge had been loaded to such a high velocity at that time. In 1921, Western Cartridge Co. introduced the first 100-grain .250 Savage bullet loading, and this round proved to be an excellent deer cartridge. Winchester also chambered its Models 54 and 70 for the cartridge.

After the success of the .243 and 6mm cartridges, the .250 appeared to be headed for the happy hunting ground until Savage reintroduced it in its Model 99 lever action in 1971. Ruger has also offered the chambering in the Model 77 bolt action, and Remington offered the Model 700 Classic in .250-3000 in 1982.

* * *

The 7x57 cartridge has been around since 1892, when it was designed by Paul Mauser as a Spanish military number. After the turn of the century, the 7x57 was chambered by custom gunmakers like Niedner, Griffin and Howe, and Sedgley. Winchester offered the cartridge in its Models 54 and 70 rifles, and Remington chambered it in the Model 30. The cartridge was thought to be obsolete. Then Ruger, Remington, and others began chambering the old number again.

Perhaps one reason for the reintroduction of these excellent old calibers is nostalgia. Another possible reason: they were excellent mild cartridges overshadowed for a time. Practically since the introduction of self-contained cartridges, there has been a movement toward cartridges producing higher performance—those with a larger case capacity in relation to bore to push bullets faster, flatter, and make them hit harder. Now there seems to be some interest in the opposite direction, and the mild cartridges are being touted for their own merits.

* * *

One of the latest reintroductions is the .300 H&H Magnum. In 1920, the .300 H&H Magnum appeared as a proprietary cartridge of the famous British firm of Holland & Holland. Originally called "Holland's Super .30," this round didn't appear as a factory cartridge in this country until 1925, when the Western Cartridge Co. introduced it. In 1937, Winchester chambered the Model 70 for the round.

The .300 H&H Magnum was put out of the running by higher performance, larger case capacity cartridges like the .300 Winchester Magnum, and other belted magnums like the 7mm Remington and .338 Winchester. Late in 1982, Remington announced the addition of this chambering in its Classic line of the Model 700.

* * *

Adopted by the military in 1892, the .30-40 Krag is another one that's pretty much gone by the wayside. Ruger offered this chambering in its No. 3 carbine rifle (though it has since been dropped in favor of more popular cartridges). The .30-40 Krag can't seem to buck the competition from .30 calibers like the .308, .30-06, and the .300 Winchester Magnum.

So much for cartridges that have been reintroduced. What about those excellent rounds which appear to be going or are almost gone as commercial rifle chamberings?

One such round is the .222 Remington Magnum. Though I don't have any rifles in this chambering, I once owned a very fine .222 Remington Magnum chambered in the Remington Model 722 rifle. The .222 Magnum was introduced in this rifle in 1958.

The cartridge case has about 20 percent greater capacity than the standard, highly successful .222 Remington and about five percent more than the .223. Many handloaders prefer the longer neck of the .222 Remington Magnum to the .223 Remington. When the .223 was standardized as a military cartridge called the 5.56mm, its success was practically ensured at the sacrifice of the very fine .222 Remington Magnum. It's amazing the .222 Remington (which had an excellent reputation for being highly accurate before the .223 was introduced) has held out as well as it has against the military .223.

* * *

Intended to be a replacement for the .220 Swift, the .225 Winchester was introduced in 1964. Its performance level is actually well below the Swift's. This round barely got off the ground when Remington introduced the .22-250 in 1965. The .22-250 had been a famous wildcat cartridge since the 1930s and already had an excellent reputation. Since it did produce performance slightly in excess of the .225 Winchester, it stole the show, and the Winchester round succumbed to the Remington competition. There are no .225 Winchester rifles chambered in this country.

During its short existence, the .225 gained an excellent reputation, and firearms writers across the country praised the excellent accuracy received from most .225 Winchester rifles. Many writers credit the ammunition produced by Winchester for such a high level of accuracy. Winchester apparently took great pains when assembling .225 ammunition.

The round was chambered in the Winchester Model 70 and in the Savage Model 340. Quite simply, the .225 Winchester and the .222 Remington Magnum are excellent cartridges that never caught on.

* * *

Another excellent cartridge falling into this category is the .284 Winchester. The .284 Winchester is unique among American cartridges due to its rebated rim (the case body is of a larger diameter than the rim). The .284 rim is of a standard .308/.30-06 diameter, but the case body is larger; this increases capacity while retaining the standard rim diameter. The .284 Winchester was designed to function through short actions while still allowing capacity on the order of the .270, .280, and .30-06 family of cartridges, which requires a longer action. The .284 case design did achieve this goal.

Many shooters complained about the bullets, particularly in heavier weights, saying they had to be seated so deeply into the case that they intruded on powder capacity. The .284's short neck was generally blamed for the deep bulletseating. These shooters apparently overlooked something. The reason the neck was so short was a result of case capacity being increased to the rear of the neck. Since action length does not permit a longer case, a longer case body and shorter neck are the way to increase capacity.

To take full advantage of the round's potential, you should chamber the .284 in a long action so bullets can be seated out. Still, this offers little advantage over a standard .280 Remington cartridge. A long action actually defeats the .284's advantage.

The .284 Winchester was introduced in Winchester's lever-action Model 88 and autoloading Model 100 rifles in 1963. Both Ruger and Browning made .284 rifles, and Savage chambered it in the Model 99 lever action.

* * *

The .256 Winchester Magnum began life as a handgun cartridge chambered in the single-shot Ruger Hawkeye, but it was also chambered in the Marlin Model 62 Levermatic rifle. This detachable box magazine, lever-action rifle was light and handy.

The .256 Winchester Magnum cartridge is based on a necked-down .357 Magnum case. Actually, the .256 Winchester Magnum is nothing more than a souped-up version of the old and once-popular .25-20 Winchester.

You'd think shooters would have a yen for a fun-to-shoot, reloadable cartridge with this bullet diameter and case capacity for plinking and varmint shooting. I have owned two Marlin Model 62 Levermatic rifles, and one was extremely accurate. In any event, the cartridge seems to have flopped as a rifle round and as a handgun round.

These four cartridges—the .225 Winchester, .222 Remington Magnum, .284 Winchester, and .256 Winchester Magnum—are excellent rounds. Adverse press and other cartridges superseding their popularity, not any shortcomings on their own, resulted in their demise.

* * *

The 6.5mm Remington Magnum and .350 Remington Magnum were introduced in Remington's now-out-of-production Model 600, a light rifle with the 18½-inch barrel. The .350 was introduced in 1965; the 6.5mm, in 1966. Both promptly flopped, although these stubby belted rounds do turn up high performance for such small actions and short barrels. The .350 Remington Magnum is considered excellent for even the largest North American game, and the short, easy-carrying rifles in this chambering are still eagerly sought by Alaskan and Canadian hunters.

Like the .284 Winchester, these cartridges were a good way to obtain a lot of power from a short action. And like the .284, they received a lot of bad press regarding the depth to which bullets had to be seated within the case. This, of course, was the result of the limitations on action and magazine length though it is generally blamed on the short case neck. The necks could have been longer, but the overall length and bullet-seating depth would not change if magazine and action length were not increased. Again, the short neck is a result of *increased* case capacity to the rear of the neck.

The .264 Winchester Magnum is not the most popular cartridge on the American list. The large-case .264 Winchester Magnum is an exceedingly high-performance cartridge, however, and for the shooter who wants a very flat-shooting round for wide-open spaces and long ranges, the .264 Winchester Magnum is tough to beat.

Like the .220 Swift, the .264 Winchester Magnum has received a lot of bad press regarding its barrel throat erosion characteristics. Unlike the .220 Swift, however, the .264 Winchester Magnum is not a varmint cartridge. Consequently, there are not as many rounds fired through .264 Winchester Magnum barrels. Even though the .264 Winchester Magnum does erode barrels severely, rifles in this chambering can last a big-game hunter many years.

* * *

Though there are a few real "gaps" in the lineup of American rifle cartridges, I think we're going to see more cartridge introductions, and a few of the vanishing cartridges will perhaps again be chambered in new rifles. For example, I think the .284 Winchester is ideally suited to the new short-action Model 70 and would provide higher performance than is currently available from the rifle.

I think we're going to see a high-velocity .22 centerfire—something to top the Swift. Perhaps the case would take the form of the European 5.6x57mm that is loaded with a 74-grain bullet by RWS. The American version would probably be loaded with a lighter bullet at a much higher velocity. I've been shooting a wildcat 6mm necked down to .22 with potential that's too good to pass up.

I think introductions in ammunition are going to advance far beyond the reshaping of the traditional brass case. We're going to have improvements in bullet design, with departures from the usual lead core encased in a jacket. The accuracy and expansion characteristics of a liquid core bullet are an obvious field for exploration.

We're also going to experience changes in case metallurgy and design. Omark has already entered this area with the aluminum-cased Blazer handgun cartridges. A steel case for rifle cartridges isn't out of the question. The steel heads strengthen the weakest link in the modern bolt rifle/ammo combination, allowing higher operating pressures for improved performance.

In the distant future, I think the conventional bullet and the rifled bore will become the low-performance combination. Smoothbores, sabots, and flechettes offer greatly accelerated velocity and improved accuracy possiblities.

Sporting rifle/cartridge development is rather unique in our highly technological world. Shooters want tradition, nostalgia, and the hunting challenge of their forebears. Consider the resurgence of muzzleloaders and the revival of other old rifles and calibers—the Model 92 and 95 rifles, the single-action handgun, and the .45-70 cartridge. For these reasons, I think sporting firearms and ammunition, though improved in performance, won't depart radically from tradition.

The Size And Shape Of .22 Centerfires

T HE .22-CALIBER centerfires are to varminting what the .30s are to big-bame hunting. And as is the case with their large-caliber cousins, the .22 bullets are boosted into action by powder from cases varying in capacity.

In fact, powder capacity and overall cartridge length are the basic differences among the .22 centerfires. It sounds simple, but these differences have important effects on the performance and application of each cartridge—for various hunting situations and for the type of rifle used.

Cartridge rims are another significant difference when it comes to rifle suitability. Glancing at a list of the currently manufactured .22 centerfires, Remington dominates the field in terms of the number of proprietary cartridges. And it's interesting to note that all the Remington versions—the .222, .223, the .22-250, and the almost obsolete .222 Magnum—have the rimless design, while the other .22 centerfires are either rimmed, semirimmed, or belted. For example, the diminutive .22 Hornet is a rimmed case, the .220 Swift and the defunct .225 Winchester are semirimmed, and the .224 Weatherby is belted.

When looking at a cartridge lineup, the most obvious difference between all of the .22 centerfires is the size of the case. As most shooters realize, case capacity translates directly into potential bullet velocity, assuming all else is equal. How important is maximum velocity? It depends on the game hunted, and the shooter's hunting style and preference.

There are shooters who argue that "efficiency" is important. It's no secret some of the smaller cases produce more fps per grain of powder used. To other shooters, the difference between using 12 grains of powder or 46 grains is virtually of no consequence when it comes to hunting, while velocity *is* important.

Actually, the .22 rimfire is the most "efficient" .22 we have, obtaining the most velocity per grain of powder. But how many shooters would pit a .22 rimfire against a .220 Swift when the targets are prairie dogs at 300 yards? *That's* how important "efficiency" is.

There are handloading hunters who feel it's senseless to purchase anything but the largest-capacity case since it's simple to reduce powder charges if a lower velocity is required. In other words, a .220 Swift can always be loaded to .222 Remington or .22 Hornet velocities, but the reverse—loading the .22 Hornet up to Swift velocities—is not possible.

Their argument: Why even consider cartridges of lesser capacity?

And there are other factors determining which case size is best for you. One important factor to consider is that cases of greater capacity have a greater overall cartridge length, and cartridge length dictates rifle action length. For example, the .220 Swift is generally chambered in rifles having a standard or .30-06-length action, while the shorter, slightly smaller capacity .22-250 can be chambered in the shorter .308-length action. The smaller .222, .223, etc., can be chambered in even shorter actions (like the Sako L-461), and there are decided advantages in having such a compact, lightweight rifle with a short bolt throw.

The .22 Hornet, on the other hand, carries a good thing too far. This particular case is so tiny that bolt actions and feeding systems must be specially designed. The Hornet is too large for rimfire designs and too small for conventional bolt actions.

The .220 Swift, at the other extreme of the case capacity spectrum, is not without its problems when it comes to rifle design. Because of this case's semirim, magazines must be specially constructed to prevent the top cartridge rim from hooking over the cartridge stacked below when the bolt shoves the top round forward.

The .220 Swift magazine box is designed with an angling surface at its rear so each cartridge rim stacks ahead of the one below. This prevents rim hooking as a cartridge is chambered. This semirim design has plagued the mixed success of the Swift and very possibly hurried the demise of the .225. There's no doubt: Rimmed or semirimmed cartridges are not ideally suited to most bolt-action rifle designs.

Because they are varmint cartridges, most of the .22s are chambered in bolt guns or high-quality single-shot rifles, both having reputations for superb accuracy.

There are, of course, a few exceptions—the .223 for one. This particular cartridge, with a military designation of 5.56mm, has been chambered in thousands of government-issue rifles.

"Imitation" service rifles, like Colt's semiauto AR-15 and the Ruger Mini-14, which are chambered for the .223, have also promoted the expenditure of millions of rounds of .223 ammo.

The .22s have long been known for accuracy. An overwhelming majority of the benchrest rifles chamber cartridges with a .22-diameter bullet, not to mention that varmint hunters are among the most demanding when it comes to accuracy.

There's no question that a precision bullet is one of the most important components of accuracy. Because of the demands from varmint and benchrest shooters, and because of the relatively high numbers of .22 bullets fired, manufacturers produce a vast array of them. And from all these designs and weights, the shooter can select a projectile that suits his purpose.

CASE CAPACITY COMPARISON
COMMERCIAL .22 CENTERFIRE CARTRIDGES

Cartridge	Case Capacity (Grains, H380)	Rim Design
.22 Hornet	11.5	Rimmed
.222 Remington	23.3	Rimless
.223 Remington	27.3	Rimless
.222 Rem. Magnum	29.0	Rimless
.224 Weatherby	34.7	Belted
.225 Winchester	39.0	Semirimmed
.22-250 Remington	41.5	Rimless
.220 Swift	44.7	Semirimmed

The most popular .22 cartridges use .224-diameter bullets, while the pre-war Hornet rifle barrels were cut for .223 bullets. The lesser known .22 Savage Hi-Power fired the odd-size .228 bullet, and these are still available, even though .22 Hi-Power rifles are almost obsolete.

The .22 centerfires, though varying widely in case capacity, are designed for varminting. They provide a high degree of accuracy with almost unnoticeable recoil. And the high-velocity .22-250 and .220 Swift cartridges have wind-bucking abilities on par with some of the high-velocity 6mm and .25-caliber cartridges.

Wind is known to affect lighter bullets more severely—if all is equal. However, all is not equal. Time of flight also makes a dramatic difference when you're speaking in terms of wind drift. The longer wind has to affect the bullet, the more it is going to drift at a given range. Therefore, if a bullet moves faster, it drifts less. That's a fact often overlooked by varminters.

The *Sierra Bullets Reloading Manual* cites more specific examples. The 85-grain spitzer can be safely fired from a 6mm Remington at 3300 fps muzzle velocity. At 300 yards, a constant 10 mile-per-hour wind will drift this bullet 6.51 inches off course. The big-case .25-06 can start a 90-grain boattail hollowpoint bullet over 3400 fps, but this bullet will be blown 9.29 inches off course by the same 10 mph wind at 300 yards. The little 55-grain .22 spitzer from a .220 Swift, starting out at a safe 3900 fps, will be blown 7.53 inches by the 10 mph wind at the same distance. This is more than 1¾ inches *less* than the .25-06 or only an inch more than the 6mm!

Few can consistently fire three-inch groups in gusty 10 mph wind conditions. In other words, when it comes to practical application, there is no noticeable difference in wind drift between the hot .22s and the larger 6mm and .25s.

The tiny .22 bullets have more than enough punch for a varmint, and they can be fired with less recoil and less expenditure of powder and lead. The latter two may not be significant in hunting situations, but recoil can be an important factor—even among varmint cartridges.

You don't think the 6mm and .25-06 have much recoil? Maybe not when you're talking about big-game cartridges. (I'm not particularly recoil sensitive. I prefer some of the belted magnums for big-game hunting when only a few rounds will be fired, most likely from a sitting, kneeling, or offhand position.) But try firing 200 rounds from the prone position. That's not unusual in prairie dog or ground squirrel hunting situations, and under these conditions, you'll be wincing from the kick of the "diminutive" 6mm Remington by the end of the day!

The .22-250 and .220 Swift are considered to be "long-range" varmint cartridges, while the .222 and .223 Remington cartridges are often looked at as "mid-range" cartridges, and the .22 Hornet a "short-range" round.

In the past, it has been popular to categorize each cartridge as being suitable for a given maximum range. The Hornet's range is generally 175 yards, the .222 or .223 are usually 225 or 250 yards, and the Swift and .22-250 are approximately 350-400 yards.

The faster a bullet travels, the flatter it flies, which is the reason for higher velocity producing a longer "point-blank" range (the maximum distance at which a target can be hit with a center hold without under shooting or producing midrange misses from over shooting). A three-inch mid-range trajectory is often used as maximum for varmint shooting (due to the size of the game) when figuring point-blank range.

If this is the case, the Sierra manual reveals that 175 yards is about right for the Hornet and 225 is about right for the .222. However, the Swift would be more correctly listed at 275 instead of 300 or 400. In other words, the "point-blank" range varies only 100 yards between the fastest and slowest .22 centerfires.

When actually shooting at long range, holdover and wind drift have to be doped, no matter which cartridge is selected. I have seen hunters in the prairie dog fields hold their own with .222s when others were shooting .22-250s or Swifts.

As a practical matter, it is a bit naive to classify cartridges with "maximum" range limits when it comes to varminting. A solid hit from any of the centerfire varmint cartridges on the near side of the quarter-mile line will drop the animal. And the hitting depends upon the skill and luck of the man squeezing the trigger.

I believe the .22 centerfires – from the .222 on up – are the best of the bunch when it comes to varminting. The size and shape of the case, whether it be .222, .223, or .22-250, can be discussed, debated, and disputed ad infinitum, and there will still be differences of opinion.

Just remember: When it comes to varminting, pick any of the .22 centerfires with the assurance that you will have made a wise choice.

The .222 Remington

THE MODEL 788, Remington's economy bolt-action rifle, has earned an enviable reputation during its relatively short lifespan. Serious shooters once considered rear lockup actions and multiple locking lugs a drawback to any bolt action. The Model 788, which features both, has produced the kind of accuracy and serviceability in the field to dispel any myths.

Introduced by Remington in 1950 and originally chambered in the Model 722 rifles, the .222 Remington marked a major step in cartridge development. The .222 was based upon a totally new head size, and unlike most cartridges, this one was not developed around any pre-existing case head size. The .222 Remington was also the first rimless commercial case in .22 caliber. The .222 Remington later gave rise to the popular .223 Remington and others like the .222 Remington Magnum, .17 Remington, and .221 Fire Ball.

According to the *Speer Reloading Manual Number Ten*, the .222 Remington has a SAAMI-recommended maximum operating pressure level of 46,000 psi, which puts it a little below the 50,000 to 52,000 psi of some of the other more high-intensity cartridges. This could be one reason why the .222 Remington has such a reputation for long barrel life.

At one time, more benchrest records had been established with the .222 Remington than any other cartridge. From the time it was introduced until perhaps the mid-1970s, the .222 Remington dominated the 100- to 200-yard benchrest classes where .22-caliber cartridges were allowed.

The .222 Remington has such a high level of accuracy potential that, according to the *Sierra Reloading Manual* (copyright 1971), all .22-caliber bullet accuracy testing at Sierra is done with the .222 Remington cartridge. In other words, this cartridge is the one used to test the accuracy potential of all .22-caliber bullets at the Sierra factory. This certainly says a lot for the cartridge.

Most literature suggests the .222 Remington is a 250-yard varmint cartridge. It is generally suggested lightweight .22-caliber bullets at .222 Remington velocities are drifted a considerable amount in the wind –

enough so other cartridges are frequently viewed as better choices for long-range varmint shooting. On paper, of course, this is certainly true, but other factors enter into the picture which can't be clearly illustrated with ballistics figures.

For example, one reason the .222 Remington is such an "accurate" cartridge, in my opinion, is due to the decreased recoil and muzzle blast of the diminutive cartridge when compared to larger numbers like the .22-250 Remington and .220 Swift. Many shooters don't even believe these larger .22 calibers have recoil of any consequence. In many varminting situations, however, particularly when shooting prairie dogs or ground squirrels, the shooter might have an opportunity to fire several hundred rounds in a day's outing. When firing ammo in such quantities from the prone position, the recoil of the large-case .22-caliber cartridges becomes noticeable.

The effect of recoil is not that simple. Other factors enter into the picture. For example, most varmint shooters select scopes of at least 8X, 10X, or 12X magnification when going after prairie dogs or ground squirrels. Those who do a lot of varmint shooting with a variety of calibers soon realize the recoil of a .220 Swift or .22-250 Remington seems to be just enough to cause the targets to disappear from the high-magnification scope's field of view when the shot is fired.

There is a definite advantage to detecting where a bullet impacts in varmint-shooting situations. With the smaller .222, you can frequently see where the bullet impacts by watching for the puff of dust through the scopes' field of view. This is a major advantage to hitting at long range, particularly when you don't have someone else spotting the shots. Simply hold dead-on, squeeze a shot off, see where it hits, and then allow accordingly for the second shot. Consequently, even when the target is beyond the "250-yard range" of the .222, your success becomes a matter of holding over the target if the bullet hits low or into the wind if the bullet hits right or left.

For these reasons, the varmint shooter familiar with a .222 can frequently be as effective in the field as another shooter firing a heavier bullet at higher velocity, even though the higher velocity and heavier bullet look better on paper. When I'm shooting at a very small target at extreme range, any sort of wind means holdover and wind drift still have to be doped and allowed for – no matter whether I'm firing a .25-06 or a .222. The shooter who can spot his bullet impact point and allow for it accordingly with the smaller caliber might do better than the shooter with the cartridge turning up higher "peformance."

Years ago, I was a real .222 fan. I had a Remington Model 722 rifle in this chambering topped with a Weaver K8 scope. This was one of my favorite varmint rigs. Then I began shooting the higher velocity .22s, and the .22-250 chambering became my varmint-shooting choice. Though the .22-250 looks better on paper, I couldn't swear I was taking any more varmints with the high-velocity cartridge than with the mild .222.

To check the effectiveness of the .222, I worked up some loads for my Remington Model 788. I wanted to see how the 788 performed with a variety of bullet weights from the Speer 40-grain spirepoint through the Speer 70-grain semispitzer. I used a half-dozen propellants, a couple of different primers, and three case makes to assemble handloads for the

.222. In addition, I fired three factory loads consisting of the Remington 50-grain Power-Lokt hollowpoint and the Frontier 50- and 55-grain SX spirepoints.

For the testing from the benchrest, I selected a Leupold 3-9X Compact scope, which is one of the latest additions to the Leupold line. The scope was attached to the rifle via Weaver rings and bases.

I assembled 10 different handloads in batches of 15 rounds each for firing three five-shot groups with each load. The first step was to collimate the rifle and then sight it in with the Remington factory ammo to get the shots printing fairly close to the aiming point. During the sighting-in process, I found the new Leupold scope moved the point of impact precisely as the adjustments on the turret knob indicated.

.222 REMINGTON LOAD DATA

Remington Model 788, 24-inch barrel
Leupold 3-9X Compact, Weaver mounts

Bullet	Powder (Type)	(Grs.)	Case	Primer	Velocity (fps)	Extreme Spread	Standard Deviation	Group Size (Inches)
Speer 40-gr. spirepoint	H335	26.0	W-W	CCI 450	3601	165	50	1.9
Sierra 45-gr. spitzer	IMR-4198	20.5	R-P	Fed. 200	3288	84	30	1.4
Nosler 50-gr. Expander	BL-C(2)	24.5	W-W	CCI 450	2914	57	15	.9
Sierra 50-gr. Blitz	IMR-4198	19.5	R-P	Fed. 200	3013	111	32	.9
Hornady 50-gr. spirepoint	RL-7	20.0	Frontier	Fed. 200	3147	26	7	1.1
Sierra 52-gr. HPBT	H335	24.0	W-W	CCI 450	3204	55	17	.9
Hornady 53-gr. spirepoint HP	H322	22.0	W-W	CCI 450	3198	78	29	1.2
Hornady 55-gr. SX	W748	24.5	W-W	CCI 450	3067	53	16	1.5
Hornady 60-gr. spirepoint	IMR-3031	21.0	Frontier	Fed. 200	2771	75	24	1.3
Speer 70-gr. semispitzer	IMR-4895	21.0	Frontier	Fed. 200	2657	59	22	1.4
Remington 50-gr. Power-Lokt hollowpoint			Factory load		3138	126	35	1.2
Frontier 50-gr. SX spirepoint			Factory load		2933	45	13	.9
Frontier 55-gr. SX spirepoint			Factory load		2925	44	16	1.4

NOTES: Velocity is an average of 10 shots and is instrumental at 10 feet from the muzzle. Group size is an average of three five-shot groups at 100 yards.

After all the shooting was completed and the results tabulated, I found the loads turned up velocities ranging from 2657 fps with the heavy Speer 70-grainer to 3601 fps with the Speer 40-grain lightweight. The point-of-impact shift with all these different bullets didn't vary more than an inch with any of the bullets tested. The difference in point of impact between the fast 40-grainer and the heavy 70-grainer consisted of the heavyweight bullet impacting approximately one to 1½ inches lower at 100 yards.

In terms of accuracy, four of the loads shot a .9-inch average for three five-shot groups, one load grouped 1.1 inches, and two loads went 1.2 inches. *All* the 50-, 52-, and 53-grain loads, both handload and factory load alike, fell into this category. The loads which didn't break the 1.2-inch mark were the 40-, 45-, 55-, 60-, and 70-grain numbers.

On the surface, bullet weight might appear to have something to do with accuracy, but I'm not certain this is the case. There is a caution in the *Hornady Handbook of Cartridge Reloading, Third Edition*, stating its heaviest 60-grain bullet might be too long and heavy to stabilize in the standard 1:14 twist of most .222 Remington rifles at velocities turned up by this cartridge. During the test shooting, however, there was no sign of bullets impacting the targets at anything other than a point-on position. Furthermore, both the Hornady 60-grainer and the Speer 70-grainer shot quite well in the .222 Remington rifle, the 60-grainers turning up a 1.3-inch average and the 70-grainers producing a 1.4-inch average. In one five-shot group fired with the Hornady 60-grain spirepoints, four shots clustered into .4 inch.

The group-size average for three five-shot groups does not always tell the whole story. Sometimes you must look at the targets to determine a potentially accurate load. The groups fired with the Nosler 50-grain Expander ahead of 24.5 grains of BL-C(2) powder are an example. The load turned up an excellent .9-inch average, which is still no better than three of the other loads. However, a look at the targets fired with the Nosler bullets tends to indicate this particular load has perhaps the greatest potential of any of the loads fired. In two of the three instances, four shots clustered into .4 inch with "flyers" enlarging these two groups to 1.1 and .9 inches, respectively.

When firing the lightweight Speer 40-grain spirepoint ahead of 26.0 grains of H335, I found this particular load turned up a 1.9-inch average, the worst of all loads fired. When looking at the targets, however, you can see that in two of the three instances, four shots clustered into .4 and .3 inch, respectively. In the largest group of the three at 2.8 inches, four shots clustered into 1.3 inches. If an average was taken for these clustered four-shot groups, it would have been .7 inch. This would have made it the best shooting load of all 13 fired. I'm not certain whether the flyers were the result of the gun, the bullet, the propellant charge, the primer, the case, the barrel heating, the conditions, or the shooter. If the flyers could somehow be eliminated (by changing a powder charge, for instance), the group relationship would be changed around altogether.

In all, the .222 Remington cartridge in the Model 788 turned up excellent shooting performance from the factory rifle. In fact, with a proper selection of loads, this rifle, which does not have a heavyweight barrel, could turn in shooting performance on varmints which would be second to none, whether handloads or factory loads were used.

It is interesting to note in the chart that the 20.0-grain charge of Reloder 7 turned up an extreme spread among 10 shots of only 26 fps for a standard deviation of only seven. During my benchrest-shooting days, Reloder 7 was my selected powder for a high level of accuracy. I used this propellant on the suggestion of Neal Knox, onetime Heavy Varmint Nationals champion. One of Neal's major criteria for working up a good shooting load for a benchrest rifle was to consider extreme velocity spread in a string of shots. He thought a well-made benchrest rifle would shoot all loads very well, and if a load were developed to produce a very low extreme velocity spread, it would more likely produce a higher level of accuracy downrange. Reloder 7 propellant in the .222 Remington cartridge has always turned up a very low extreme spread and standard deviation in any rifle I've used.

My benchrest shooting load was somewhat hotter than the 20.0-grain charge, although the 20.0-grain charge produces adequate velocity and is apparently consistent.

The bottom line is that a shooter with a bolt-action rifle in .222 sacrifices nothing in performance.

The .223 Remington

T HE .223 REMINGTON is one popular rifle cartridge. Sales of ammunition and bullets indicate that more .223 ammo is fired than any other centerfire rifle fodder. The last time I checked the RCBS chart of loading die sales, the .223 was almost at the top of the heap, rivaling the respected .30-06.

But the .223's history is not very glamorous. It was developed for the military specifically to decrease the weight of a rifle, lessen recoil, and enable a soldier to carry more ammunition. It was developed at the request of the Continental Army Command between 1957 and 1959 and was standardized by the Army in 1964. Remington also offered it as a commercial cartridge that same year.

The .223 doesn't have the claim to accuracy fame that the .222 Remington enjoys, and it doesn't have the velocity advantages of the .22-250. The .223 replaced a cartridge that is identical in application, the .222 Remington Magnum. Some even like the longer neck and six percent greater case capacity of the .222 Remington Magnum. Unfortunately, the .222 Remington Magnum did not become a military case. According to the *Sierra Bullets Reloading Manual,* "While not quite as good a cartridge as the .222 Remington Magnum, it will probably survive that cartridge because of the availability of surplus brass and ammunition."

I said the .223's history wasn't glamorous. Still, a cartridge used as much as the .223 must have something going for it. And it does.

For a .22 centerfire cartridge comparison, I filled several different .22 centerfire cases with H380 powder and weighed the amount that each held. The case capacities went like this: .222 Remington, 23.3 grains; .223 Remington, 27.3 grains; .22-250 Remington, 41.5 grains; .220 Swift, 44.7 grains. Since the .223's capacity falls between the .222's and .22-250's, those calibers will carry the most relevant comparisons.

While the .223 doesn't have the benchrest accuracy record of the .222, it has more accuracy than anyone can use in the field. You won't be able to tell any difference between the accuracy of a .222 and a .223 with off-the-shelf hunting rifles.

And though the .223 doesn't offer the high velocity of the .22-250, it does have advantages. Both cartridges are varmint loads, and that's where the comparisons should center. (Though larger species of game are killed with both cartridges, no .22 centerfire should really be considered for big-game hunting.)

The .223 offers longer barrel life because it burns less powder and produces less heat and erosion. This is a decided advantage to a shooter who may use hundreds of rounds in a day's prairie dog outing. And since the .223 burns less powder, a can of propellant goes farther. For example, a pound of 4895 will load 269 rounds of .223 ammo and only 205 rounds of .22-250. Factory ammunition is also less expensive for the .223.

.223 REMINGTON: 10 FAVORITE LOADS

HANDLOADS

Bullet	Powder (Type)	(Grs.)	Case	Primer	Velocity (fps) (10 Feet)	Five-Shot Group (Inches)	Gun	Remarks
Sierra 52-Gr. HPBT Benchrest	BL-C(2)	25.5	R-P	Fed. 205M	2913	.5	23-inch TCR '83	Most accurate in TCR
Hornady 53-Gr. Match HP	W748	26.0	R-P	Fed. 205M	3013	1.1	23-inch TCR '83	All-around varmint load
Speer 45-Gr. spitzer	H4198	22.5	R-P	Win. SR	3409	.9	22½-inch Kimber M84	Fastest load listed; accurate
Sierra 50-Gr. spitzer	RL-7	22.3	R-P	Win. SR	3149	1.0	22½-inch Kimber M84	Coyote load
Hornady 55-Gr. FMJ	IMR-4895	25.0	R-P	Win. SR	3102	1.1	22½-inch Kimber M84	Fox load

FACTORY LOADS

Bullet	Powder (Type)	(Grs.)	Case	Primer	Velocity (fps) (10 Feet)	Five-Shot Group (Inches)	Gun	Remarks
Hornady 55-Gr. spirepoint	Factory load				3192	1.1	22½-inch Kimber M84	Good velocity
Remington 55-Gr. FMC	Factory load				3060	1.2	23-inch TCR '83	Fox-calling load
Winchester 55-Gr. PSP	Factory load				3058	1.3	23-inch TCR '83	All-around varmint load
Black Hills 52-Gr. Nosler HP	Factory load				3030	1.2	22½-inch Kimber M84	All-around varmint load
Black Hills 60-Gr. SP	Factory load				3040	1.1	24-inch Mossberg M1500	Shoots well in quick-twist barrels

The .223 also kicks less, which becomes a factor two ways in a varminting situation. Shooting several hundred rounds with a .22-250 from the prone position can give you a sore shoulder. A .223 is less likely to do that if an equal-weight rifle is used. The .22-250's kick often knocks the varmint from the field of view of the high-magnification scopes used on varmint rifles. The .223's lighter kick allows the shooter to see more easily the bullet's impact. This is important if the shot is missed because the shooter then knows where to hold for the next round.

Another nice feature of the .223 is its shorter length. Check out a rifle with an action made specifically for this short little cartridge and you'll see the best reason of all for using the .223. (I have a Kimber Model 84 made specifically for this length cartridge; it's one of those rifles that I just want to carry and look at.)

The .223 is also a "handgun" cartridge. Among fanciers of the single-shot Thompson/Center Contender, the .223 is undoubtedly the most popular varmint round. Remington has even forsaken the .221 Fire Ball in favor of the more popular .223 for its bolt-action XP-100. If you've never shot one of these scoped, single-shot firearms, you'll find it amazing what one can do at long range with such an abbreviated firearm with no buttstock.

I don't usually have a lot of comment regarding loading idiosyncrasies with most cartridges, but a few things bear comment about handloading for the .223 Remington. First is case size. Handloaders accustomed to working with cartridges having a standard head size like a .22-250 or .30-06 know there are decided signs of excessive pressure regarding the primer and brass. But signs of a given pressure level are not as readily apparent with the .223's smaller case and primer. This factor is often overlooked by handloaders. Your criteria for pressure judging visually must be modified when loading for the .223. You must also rethink if you judge pressure by miking case head expansion. If all else is equal, it takes much less total expansion to equal a given pressure level with a smaller case.

Another caveat often mentioned in conjunction with semiauto and full-auto rifles is port pressure. Gas-operated actions rely upon some of the pressure developed by the load to operate the action. Tiny holes in the barrel allow a small amount of the expanding gases to bleed off to function a piston and hence open the action. These holes are located down the barrel, away from the chamber. If the load is too mild and the port pressure too low, the action will not function reliably. If port pressure is too high, the action will be operated too violently and jamming will occur. This could lead to the eventual breakage of rifle parts.

Excessive port pressure is a greater problem with the M-16/AR-15 action than with the Mini-14 because of the differences in their operating systems. Port pressure doesn't really have much to do with chamber pressure. A 52,000 cup chamber pressure is the maximum allowable for the .223, but it's the time/pressure curve that bears importance in this matter. As a bullet moves down the barrel under the pressure of expanding gases, the pressure begins to diminish. The rate at which it diminishes depends in part on the burning rate of the propellant. Too-high port pressure results when slower-burning powders are used and pressure is still high by the time the bullet passes the gas port(s) which allow gases to enter the action-operating system. If you load for an AR-15 or M-16, stay with the quicker-burning powders that are recommended in the loading manuals. Your action will function better and last longer.

If you load for one of the semiautos, it's best to be on the safe side and crimp case mouths into bullets. This will prevent the bullets from being set back inside case mouths under the force of feeding. Bullets with cannelures should be used. Fortunately, a good many .22 bullets are available with cannelures, specifically for .223s.

When crimping, cases must all be the same length or problems will develop. A case that is too short won't be crimped at all, and a case that is too long will buckle or bulge in the neck area and may not even chamber. If you crimp–and you need to with autoloaders–trim your cases regularly.

One final warning on loading the .223. When using a .223 with a 1:10 twist barrel, such as a Ruger Mini-14, avoid using fragile bullets like the Hornady SX. According to the *Hornady Handbook of Cartridge Reloading*, "The rapid twist can cause these fragile bullets to come apart in flight, especially at maximum velocities."

TOP FIVE RIFLES					
Make/Model	Barrel (Inches)	Sights	Weight (Pounds)	Finish	Rifling (Twist)
Kimber M84	22½	Leupold 2-7X Compact	6 pounds, 8 ounces	Satin	1:12
Thompson/Center TCR '83	23	Weaver 10X	7 pounds, 5 ounces	Satin	1:12
Mossberg M1500	24	Redfield 4-12X	9 pounds, 5 ounces	Gloss	1:12
Remington Model Seven	18½	Burris 4-12X	6 pounds, 4 ounces	Satin	1:12
Browning M1885	28	B&L 3-9X	8 pounds, 13 ounces	Satin	1:12

Since the .223 is a military cartridge, you may acquire some military cases. As with most military cases, you'll find the spent primers are sometimes difficult to eject because of crimped pockets. But after they are ejected, you'll need some way to remove this crimped-in brass before you insert fresh primers. This is usually accomplished by reaming or swaging the crimped-in brass to allow easy insertion of a fresh primer. Fortunately, it's an operation that needs to be done only once.

Aside from this, loading the .223 is not much different from loading other rifle cartridges. If you use a lot of ammo, you may want to try one of the newer progressive tools. With the proper attachments, it will swage primer pockets as well as trim case necks. If you do use one of the progressive tools, fill the propellant hopper with a ball or spherical powder and not an extruded powder. This makes for more positive or uniform powder dispensing.

The .223 is a varmint cartridge, and it doesn't matter whether the critter is a crow, woodchuck, jackrabbit, prairie dog, or coyote. The .223 performs admirably on each. I use a TCR '83 and a Kimber Model 84 quite a lot. Some writers have placed some sort of range limitation upon the various varmint cartridges. As a practical matter, you probably couldn't tell much difference in the field. In a varminting situation, more depends upon the shooter than on the cartridge. His ability to judge range, his familiarity with the rifle, trigger, and load, and his ability to dope wind are far more important than the differences between the .222 and .223 – and perhaps even a .22-250.

I once shot prairie dogs with a couple of guys who were carrying heavy-barreled .243 Winchester rifles. As we unloaded our rifles and ammunition early one morning, the prairie wind was already picking up. One of the shooters was surprised that I pulled a .223 out of the case. He remarked that it would be tough to shoot well in the wind with such a light cartridge. (I thought so too.)

They used the "buddy" system: one hunter spots while the other shoots. The spotter tells the shooter where his shot landed so that he'll have a better chance of hitting on the second shot. I usually do my varmint hunting alone. As it turned out, I could see each shot after a miss. A "foot at 300 yards" had different meanings to each shooter. Neither could effectively relate to the other just how far to the right or left or high or low the other missed because they each had different ideas about how far the shot actually missed. I didn't have to worry about someone else relating my misses because I could see them myself. I was popping about three times as many dogs as those two.

Some might question the effectiveness of the .223 on coyotes when compared with more powerful cartridges like the .22-250 and .220 Swift. But the coyotes I've killed with the .223 went down as quickly as they had with the larger .22 centerfires—as long as the shot was placed in the right spot.

More accurate bullets exist for the .22 calibers than for any other diameter. And a lot of good bullets are available for the .223—both softpoint and full metal jacketed. Try as many bullets as possible until you find the combination that performs best in your rifle. In my experience, the bullet is a major factor regarding how well a rifle shoots. Find the right bullet for your rifle, and you may be surprised at how accurate it is.

If you don't handload, a wide selection of factory ammo is available. All the major American ammomakers include it—as do some of the not-so-major ones. Figure in the foreign makers, and it adds up to a lot of ammo choices in the .223.

Though there are more accurate cartridges, the .223 has more accuracy than you can use in the field. Though there are more powerful cartridges, the .223 gets the job done in its own mild-mannered way. Maybe all that research and development poured into cartridge development by the military has some merit after all.

The .22-250

IF I WERE limited to one rifle cartridge for everything from crows to coyotes, the .22-250 would be it. If I were to pick the best all-around cartridge for prairie dog shooting, the .22-250 would be it. If I were to pick the best commercial cartridge for coyote pelt hunting, the .22-250 would be it.

The .22-250 is the varminter's answer, a gunmaker's delight, and a handloader's dream.

According to several sources, the .22-250 originated as a wildcat during the 1930s. It's based on a .250 Savage case that's necked down for a .22-caliber bullet and with the shoulder angle changed to 28 degrees. In *Pocket Manual for Shooters and Reloaders,* P.O. Ackley wrote, "The .22-250 is also known as the .22 Varminter and the .220 Wotkyns Original Swift. The .22-250 is one of the most flexible and accurate varmint cartridges ever designed . . . . It is better adapted to reduced loads than the standard Winchester .220 Swift and is one of the overall most satisfactory cartridges in the .22 caliber for all types of varmint shooting . . . . The name 'varminter' is a registered trademark, owned by J.B. Gebby, and can be used only with his consent . . . . This cartridge will probably be commercially available sometime during 1964."

As it turned out, Ackley was partially right about the .22-250's introduction. The 1963 Browning literature lists the High Power rifle as being available in a new chambering – the ".22-250 Wildcat." Browning listed both light and heavy barrels for the new chambering in its bolt-action rifle. Factory ammunition was not made available by Remington until 1965, when it introduced the chambering in a bolt rifle.

It's unusual for a rifle manufacturer to introduce a chambering when there is no ammunition commercially available. But the .22-250 was a success as a wildcat long before it was "legitimized." (It's probably the most popular hunting-oriented wildcat cartridge ever devised, and when it went "legit," it became even more popular. At last count, there were nearly two dozen rifle manufacturers offering this chambering.)

There are good reasons for the popularity of the .22-250. With the exception of the Swift, it has more case capacity than the other commercial .22 centerfires. This gives it the obvious advantage of higher velocity, which results in a flatter trajectory, decreased wind drift, and higher impact energy. The flatter trajectory and decreased wind drift mean it's easier to hit with the .22-250; a slight error in wind doping or range estimation isn't as significant with the .22-250 as it is with the .22 Hornet, .222, or .223, and higher impact energy means more violent bullet expansion and less chance of a ricochet – nearly always a plus in varmint bullet performance.

So what about the Swift, which tops the .22-250 in these categories? The Swift does have about five percent greater case capacity with the potential for slightly higher velocities, though many handloaders habitually "throttle back" on Swift loads. The case capacity advantage of the Swift is outweighed by the disadvantage of its basic semirim case design. Though the rim size is the same as the .22-250, the Swift has a slimmer body and a rim design that gives feeding problems in conventional box magazines. The .22-250 can be made to easily feed through most conventional box magazines, but the Swift requires a special magazine with an angled rear wall. This is no doubt much of the reason why there have never been a lot of different Swift rifles available – and why almost every rifle manufacturer chooses to chamber the .22-250 instead.

Even though the .22-250 has the advantage in velocity over the lesser .22s, this alone wouldn't be enough to maintain the .22-250's popularity. The .22-250 has other attributes. It is pleasant to shoot, generally shoots very well, and is extremely easy to load.

Just pick any production .22-250 bolt-action rifle and a box of factory ammo, and you're likely to get good groups. I've shot many half-inch groups with off-the-shelf .22-250 rifles and factory ammo. These are five-shot groups, mind you; for three-shot groups, I could say that one-holers are common. (I could make the same statement about the .17 Remington at 100 yards or the .222 Remington, but in my experience, the average .223 has not yet produced .22-250 accuracy.) For example, in some rifles, the new Federal Blitz with the fast 40-grain bullet shoots like it was trained to go to a hole. I can't figure why the stubby little slug shoots so well. It just does. I've shot the light-bullet ammo for a five-shot, three-group average at 100 yards in seven different rifles. The worst average it turned in was 1.5 inches. Though individual groups are often one-holers, the best average I've shot with this factory ammo was .6 inch. Despite Federal's claims of 4000 fps for the Blitz ammo, the average of all the velocity averages from these rifles was 3887 fps at 10 feet from the muzzle.

.22-250: 10 FAVORITE LOADS

HANDLOADS							
Bullet	**Powder (Type)**	**(Grs.) Case**	**Primer**	**Velocity (fps) (10 feet)**	**Five-Shot Group (Inches)**	**Gun**	**Remarks**
Speer 52-Gr. HP	H4895	35.0 R-P	Rem. 9½	3688	.8	24-inch Remington M700	Coyote-calling load
Sierra 52-gr. HPBT	H380	39.0 R-P	Rem. 9½	3572	.6	24-inch Remington M700	Accurate
Hornady 55-Gr. spirepoint	W760	41.5 R-P	Rem. 9½	3802	1.1	24-inch Ruger M77	All-around varmint/predator load
Nosler 55-Gr. Solid Base	H414	41.5 R-P	Rem. 9½	3861	1.0	24-inch Ruger M77	High velocity
Speer 55-Gr. spitzer	IMR-4064	36.5 R-P	Rem. 9½	3810	.8	24-inch Ruger M77	All-around varmint/predator load
FACTORY LOADS							
Federal 40-Gr. Blitz	Factory load			3916	.6	28-inch Browning 1885	Fast and very accurate
Federal 55-Gr. Premium HPBT	Factory load			3702	.9	28-inch Browning 1885	Accurate
Hornady 53-Gr. HP	Factory load			3686	1.0	28-inch Browning 1885	All-around varmint load
Hornady 55-Gr. spirepoint	Factory load			3643	1.2	28-inch Browning 1885	Coyote load
Remington 55-Gr. P-LHP	Factory load			3586	1.0	24-inch Remington M788	Coyote load

Federal Premium 55-grain HPBT ammo has also shot exceptionally well in my rifles. Five-shot group averages of less than one inch are common. I fired the ammo in five rifles for a five-shot, three-group average in each. The averages ran .6, .7, .9, .9, and 1.4 inches. The velocity average of four rifles was 3578 fps at 10 feet from the muzzle. Barrel lengths ran from 24 to 26 inches.

I have experienced a noticeable lot difference with this ammo. One lot had an unplated primer and a different weight of powder than another lot with plated primers. The second lot's accuracy didn't compare to that of the first. Actually, a powder weight, or even powder type, change is fairly common in factory ammo.

Remington's 55-grain P-LHP ammo shoots well in the rifles in which I've used it. I've probably shot as many coyotes with the .22-250 as any other cartridge, and I would as soon use this Remington factory round as any handload with a conventional bullet. (I qualify this statement with "conventional" bullet because I make my own nonconventional, fluid-core bullets for coyote pelt hunting, and they outperform commercial offerings.)

The Hornady 53-grain hollowpoint is another off-the-shelf loading that shoots very accurately. Individual groups I've received with this ammo can be tough to match with handloads.

If you handload, it's not difficult to find good loads. I've had very good luck with 4895 powder (with either the DuPont or Hodgdon label) and many different bullets. In my old 788, this powder and the Speer 52-grain hollowpoint bullet shoot very well and perform nicely on coyotes. I loaded 35.0 grains of H4895 in a Remington case, topped it off with the Speer 52-grain hollowpoint, and sparked it with a Remington No. 9½ primer. My Remington Model 700V averages .5 inch with this load and produced 3780 fps at 10 feet from the muzzle. If I team H4895 and Sierra's 52-grain HPBT, it not only shoots great, but with the boattail and tight nose hole, it has the shape for a downrange ballistics advantage over the Speer hollowpoint with the gaping hole in its nose.

But if you really want a high ballistic coefficient in a .22 bullet, try the Hornady 60-grain hollowpoint, the Nosler 60-grain Solid Base, or the Sierra 63-grain semipointed. The sleek Nosler 55-grain Solid Base is tops, along with the Sierra 55-grain spitzer. Push these bullets with an ample charge of the right powder, and you're starting to realize the potential of the cartridge. Besides 4895, H380, IMR-4064, IMR-4320, IMR-3031, Accurate Arms' 2520, BL-C(2), and W760 are good choices with the 55-grain bullet in the .22-250. This is one of the nice things about working with a tractable cartridge—it works well with many different bullets, cases, and primers.

Primers do make a difference with this cartridge. I've used Remington, Winchester, Federal, CCI, and others with the .22-250, and they all perform well with a preferred component combination. An experiment in developing loads with different primers can prove revealing.

At one time, cases for the cartridge were made from .250 Savage brass, but they can also be made from 7x57, 8x57, 6mm, and .257 Roberts cases. The .22-250 has become so popular that there's no need to make cases—just purchase new brass with the .22-250 headstamp. The primer used is the Large Rifle size.

Another nice feature of the .22-250 is that it takes to reduced-velocity loading. As always, never use a medium-burning or slow-burning powder to achieve reduced velocities. After conducting extensive reduced-velocity load testing with the old 788, I found it liked 9.0 grains of DuPont's 700-X behind the Sierra 45-grain high-velocity bullet. With this load, the rifle consistently averages around one inch for five shots. Weigh each 700-X charge. A rifle powder measure will cause the charges to vary too much, and accuracy goes out the window. A couple of tenths variation is a lot in a 9.0 charge, particularly with this load.

This load is very pleasant to shoot, both for noise and recoil, and it works very well for the thin-skinned foxes if you're concerned about pelts. Velocity is in the neighborhood of 2390 fps, however, so it isn't a long-range recipe. It does have the power to put a coyote down cleanly if he's hit vitally. I've shot lots of coyotes with this load and have recovered bullets that mushroomed perfectly. I've also taken countless jackrabbits with it; if you like to eat young jackrabbits, the load is not excessively destructive to meat.

TOP FIVE RIFLES

Make/Model	Barrel (Inches)	Sights	Weight (Pounds)	Finish	Rifling (Twist)
Remington M700 Varmint	24	Leupold 6.5-20X	9 pounds	Gloss	1:14
Savage M110 Varmint	26	Zeiss 10X	9 pounds, 4 ounces	Satin	1:14
Ruger M77	22	Redfield 2-7X	7 pounds	Satin	1:14
Browning M1885	28	B&L 6-24X	8 pounds, 13 ounces	Gloss	1:14
Winchester M70	24	B&L 3-9X	7 pounds, 12 ounces	Satin	1:14

Since the 788, I've found that this load shoots well in every .22-250 in which I've fired it. You'll notice that the case isn't even close to being filled with the quick-burning flake propellant, but it doesn't seem to matter. The powder is easily ignited and produces consistent velocities.

The .22-250 cartridge shoots so well in so many rifles that I would have a tough time recommending a single rifle that I've found to shoot best. In heavy-barreled rifles, I've fired exceedingly tight groups with a Savage Model 110V, a Remington Model 700 Varmint, and a Ruger Model 77V. A lot of people sell the Savage short as being a "cheap" gun, but in my experience, it more than holds its own with any other production rifle for accuracy.

In lighter rifles, I have a Winchester Model 70 Sporter Varmint in .22-250 that shoots so consistently well with so many different types of ammo that I place it at the top of the heap. Winchester came up with the designation "Sporter Varmint" when it dropped the heavy-barrel configuration. The Sporter Varmint has a standard-weight barrel, but mine shoots well and is virtually unaffected by barrel heating. It will shoot alongside nearly any heavy-barreled rifle.

As always, the Remington Model 700s shoot great, and I've had Ruger 77s that do, too. I have a Browning Model 1885 single-shot rifle that averaged .6 inch for three five-shot groups at 100 yards—with the Federal 40-grain Blitz ammo. Few heavy-barreled bolt rifles shoot that well with factory ammo.

Most of the .22-250 rifles are single shots or bolt actions. I know of no slide actions or semiautos chambered for this cartridge, but surprisingly, levers are chambered for it. Browning offers it in the BLR, and Savage chambered it in the Model 99 during the late 1970s, though the Model 99 is no longer available in this chambering.

If you're looking for a versatile varmint cartridge, one that's been thoroughly proven, produces mild recoil, is easy to load for, and shoots as well as any cartridge going, the .22-250 is the cartridge for you.

The 6mm And The .243

THE 6MM cartridges have a history that dates back to the last century, when 6mm (.236) rounds were adopted by the U.S. Navy. The Navy authorized a contract to Winchester for 15,000 rifles to be manufactured under patents granted to James Paris Lee. The rifles were issued in 1895. In 1897, after the Navy order was completed, Winchester offered the public a sporting version of the military rifle. The sporting firearm was known as the Lee Straight Pull Rifle. The rifle got its name from the fact that the action was opened and closed by pulling the operating handle straight back, without the up and down motion of a conventional bolt action. Ammunition for it was loaded with smokeless powder, and the bullets had a hardened lead core with a copper jacket plated with tin. Velocity was reported to be 2550 fps.

The Lee Straight Pull never became popular. It was listed at $32 and was the most expensive rifle in the Winchester line. And there was also continued resistance to bolt-action rifles. As a result, the production of the sporting version of the rifle was less than 2000 units, and the Lee Model was dropped in 1900.

Phil Sharpe, the well-known shooter and writer, wrote, "This rifle died an early death simply because it was 40 years ahead of its day. Today, we are just commencing to appreciate the possibilities of the high-velocity, small-caliber arms, and if the 6mm were revived, it undoubtedly could be developed to a high accuracy and velocity far ahead of the 1895 era."

Sharpe was right about the potential popularity of the 6mm cartridge in the U.S, but it wasn't until 1955 (or 60 years later) that the 6mm bullet had its chance in two cartridges: the .243 Winchester and the 6mm Remington.

As with many commercial cartridge introductions, several wildcat versions existed before the cartridges from the major manufacturers. Two of the better known wildcats were the .243 Rockchucker, developed by Fred Huntington, and the .240 Page, created by Al Marciante and Warren Page.

The final form bestowed on the 6mm Remington is basically a 7x57 case necked down for 6mm bullets—but with a sharper shoulder angle (20 degrees, 45 minutes for 7x57; 26 degrees for the 6mm Remington).

The .243 is basically a .308 Winchester necked down and with the same 20-degree shoulder angle.

I had the opportunity to talk with the late Warren Page on several occasions. It is a well-known fact that Page pushed for the introduction of some form of 6mm cartridge. According to him, rather than its impressive terminal ballistics, the .243's initial success was due in large part to the accuracy of the free-floating, short-barreled Model 70 Featherweight in which it was introduced.

The competition between Remington and Winchester for the dominant 6mm cartridge is documented. Both considered the primary market to be varmint shooters. Remington introduced its .244 round in the plain Model 722 bolt-action rifle and Winchester introduced its .243 offering in the Model 70 bolt action and the Model 88 lever action. The Remington Model 722 had a 1:12 twist; each Winchester rifle had a 1:10 twist.

The top bullet weight in the Remington ammunition lineup was a 90-grainer, while Winchester offered a 100-grain loading. As it turned

					Velocity (fps)	Five-Shot Group		
	Powder							
Bullet	(Type)	(Grs.)	Case	Primer	(15 feet)	(Inches)	Gun	Remarks
6mm REMINGTON: FAVORITE LOADS								
HANDLOADS								
Sierra 60-Gr. HP	BL-C(2)	45.0	R-P	Fed. 215	3625	1.3	22-inch Rem. M700	Fast load
Speer 75-Gr. HP	H380	45.0	R-P	Fed. 215	3334	.9	22-inch Rem. M700	Varmint load
Sierra 90-Gr. FMJBT	H4831	48.5	R-P	Fed. 210	3157	.7	22-inch Rem. M700	Fur load
Hornady 100-Gr. spirepoint	IMR-4350	42.0	R-P	Fed. 210	3064	1.0	24-inch Custom M98	Deer/antelope load
FACTORY LOADS								
Remington 80-Gr. P-LHP	Factory load				3326	.7	24-inch Rem. M722 (Hart barrel)	Accurate load
Remington 80-Gr. PSP	Factory load				3282	.9	24-inch Rem. M722 (Hart barrel)	Varmint load
Federal 80-Gr. SP	Factory load				3422	1.2	24-inch Custom M98	Varmint load
Winchester 80-Gr. PSP	Factory load				3394	1.3	24-inch Custom M98	Varmint load
Remington 100-Gr. PSPC-L	Factory load				3082	1.2	24-inch Rem. M722 (Hart barrel)	Deer/antelope load

out, there was a big demand for the 6mm rifles to shoot the heavier bullet weights for use on deer. Word got out that the slower twist of the Remington rifles did not stabilize the heaviest bullets well.

The .243 Winchester flourished, but the .244 Remington languished. Remington finally dropped the .244 Remington chambering then reintroduced it in 1963 as the 6mm Remington. Though the .244 and 6mm cartridges are the same, 6mm rifles have a 1:9 twist to ensure the proper stabilization of the longest 6mm bullets. Remington puts a 1:9 twist in all barrels for this bullet diameter, whether they're chambered for the 6mm Remington or .243 Winchester.

It's interesting to note that Winchester's prototype cartridge was called the "6mm Winchester" for a time. Another little-known fact is that the 6mm Remington came close to being named the "6mm Remington Magnum." In fact, some rifles were stamped with this designation. Rifles I've seen with the stamping have the "Mag" rollmark x-ed over, but it is still readable.

.243 WINCHESTER: 10 FAVORITE LOADS

Bullet	Powder (Type)	(Grs.)	Case	Primer	Velocity (fps) (15 feet)	Five-Shot Group (Inches)	Gun	Remarks
HANDLOADS								
Sierra 60-Gr. HP	W760	47.5	Win.	Rem. 9½	3548	.7	26-inch Custom M98	Accurate
Hornady 70-Gr. spirepoint	IMR-4064	41.5	Win.	Win. 8½-120	3376	1.3	22-inch Win. M88	Varmint load
Speer 80-Gr. spitzer	H4831	46.0	Win.	Win. 8½-120	3282	1.4	22-inch Win. M88	Varmint load
Sierra 90-Gr. FMJBT	IMR-4350	43.0	Win.	Win. LR	3095	1.3	22-inch Win. M70	Fur load
Hornady 100-Gr. spirepoint	H4831	44.0	Win.	Win. LR	2996	1.5	22-inch Win. M88	Deer/antelope load
FACTORY LOADS								
Hornady 75-Gr. HP	Factory load				3362	1.4	23-inch TCR '83	Varmint load
Winchester 80-gr. SP	Factory load				3320	1.7	22-inch Win. M88	Varmint load
Remington 80-Gr. PSP	Factory load				3126	1.9	22-inch Win. M70	Varmint load
Hornady 100-Gr. SPBT	Factory load				2927	2.3	23-inch TCR '83	Deer/antelope load
Norma 100-Gr. FMJ	Factory load				3078	1.8	23-inch TCR-83	Fur load

I've owned, handloaded for, and hunted with all the rifles that the cartridges were introduced in—and several other factory rifles made since the introduction of the cartridges. I've also owned custom-made rifles in .243, .244, and 6mm configurations. I've used them to take hundreds of varmints and numerous deer. One of my favorites was an early Winchester Model 88 chambered for the .243. I glass bedded the rifle, topped it with a Weaver 4X scope, and used it to take lots of coyotes, bobcats, and deer. The rifle would shoot 1½-inch groups all day with the Hornady 100-grain spirepoint and 44.0 grains of H4831. One-inch groups were commonplace. I used the load for both deer and predators. It's excessively destructive to coyote and bobcat pelts, but those were the days when pelts weren't worth much and predators were called as a favorite pastime.

I remember one custom-built .243 with a 26-inch heavy barrel and topped with a Lyman 10X scope. I used Sierra's 85-grain HPBT ahead of 46.0 grains of H4831 to snipe numerous coyotes at long range with that rifle. The Hornady 87-grain spirepoint atop the same powder charge was the choice for prairie dogs. Either load shot as accurately as any varmint shooter could hold.

I've used the ultralight Sierra 60-grain HP in both the .243 and 6mm with excellent accuracy results. The stubby little slugs don't look like they would shoot well, but they are exceptional performers in some rifles. I've used the bullets for called-in coyotes with mixed success insofar as pelt damage. Sometimes the bullet stays inside; other times, the bullet exits, producing a large hole in the pelt.

For those of you who have heard the .244 (with the 1:12 twist) won't shoot heavy bullets, I once had a custom-stocked 722 Remington that would shoot one-hole clusters with the Speer 90-grain FMJ and 40.0 grains of IMR-4064. I also owned a Hart-barreled .244 which favored the Remington 80-grain P-LHP factory ammunition. I never got a handload to equal the accuracy of the lot of factory ammo I used.

I think the primary reason the .243 and 6mm are so popular is that they're small enough to be pleasant to shoot, yet they're deemed large enough for deer. Varmints and deer are the reasons that most center-fire rifles are bought, and it's nice to have one rifle that will do both jobs. Furthermore, a rifle that's used for varmints generally gets used a lot. It's carried whenever one goes into the field, and it's used on the occasional crow, woodchuck, coyote, or fox. When deer season rolls around, it makes sense to take a rifle that you know. As a result, the shot will be better placed. The .243 and 6mm class of cartridges has a reputation for being excellent for use on deer. But I think this reputation has been earned because shots have been well placed for the reasons mentioned and not because there is any inherent advantage in the cartridge.

I think the .243 and 6mm are excellent varmint cartridges for occasional use on deer. If you need a light-recoiling cartridge in order to avoid flinching and to shoot well, then these may be the ticket for your use on antelope/deer-size game. However, I think there are many cartridges better suited for big game. The 6mm rounds should not be considered for use on elk-size game. For deer-size game, .243 and 6mm cartridges should be used only with the heavier bullets and shots should be carefully placed.

I used the Speer 105-grain spitzer to take three deer last fall. It was loaded to produce just over 3000 fps, and it worked well, but the shots were placed well and the deer were not large.

I also lost the biggest whitetail I've ever shot, and it was with a .243 Winchester. I was hunting in central Pennsylvania when a big buck came crashing through the underbrush. I shouldered the Model 88 Winchester loaded with Hornady 100-grain spirepoints, fired, and the deer went down. The hit looked good, but the deer regained its feet. I shot again as it wobbled down the mountain. There was no doubt the deer would have expired in a short distance. Unfortunately, the big buck ran headlong into a group of hunters from Ohio. They shot it several more times. These hunters weren't to be argued with regarding ownership of such a large-racked deer. (I really lost the buck to other hunters, but I couldn't help feeling a cartridge with more punch would have anchored the buck sooner. The Hornady 100-grainer has performed well on other deer I've taken, and so has the Nosler 100-grain Solid Base.)

There's nothing strange or difficult about loading either of the current 6mm cartridges. Most say there isn't enough difference between them to worry about. If given a choice, I would pick the 6mm over the .243. The 6mm has greater capacity, and slightly higher bullet speed is possible with it. When all else is equal, I think the 6mm will produce 100 to 150 fps more speed than the .243 with a 100-grain bullet. True, the advantage in that margin of velocity is slight in a hunting situation, but it's still an edge.

Some handloaders prefer the longer neck of the 6mm, though I see no advantage in a longer neck except that it means more case capacity. Others like the sharper shoulder of the 6mm, saying this results in less forward flow of the brass on firing with maximum-pressure loads. However, when loading heavy loads in standard chambers, I've always discarded cases due to enlarged primer pockets—not too-thick necks.

The best powder I've found for heavy bullets with either cartridge is Hodgdon H450. It produces the highest velocities with heavy bullets. I lean toward IMR-4350, IMR-4831, MR-3100, and IMR-4320 when it comes to the heaviest bullets. For the lighter bullets, I've had good success with IMR-4064 regarding both accuracy and velocity. Other numbers such as H335, BL-C(2), IMR-4895, W760, H414, and IMR-3031 should not be overlooked in your search for good accuracy at high velocity with a given bullet.

As for bullets, I like those weighing 70 to 85 grains for varmints and slugs 90 grains and heavier for deer and antelope. I know hunters who swear by the 85-grain weights for deer and antelope. When considering whether something is adequate, think about shooting when the game is at a poor angle or standing behind brush. And consider the possibility of a poorly placed shot—no matter how good a hunter you are.

	Barrel		Weight		Rifling
TOP FIVE RIFLES					
Make/Model	Barrel (Inches)	Sights	Weight (Pounds)	Finish	Rifling (Twist)
Remington M700	22	2-7X	7 pounds, 4 ounces	Gloss	1:9
Winchester M70	24	3-9X	7 pounds, 12 ounces	Satin	1:10
Ruger M77	22	Depends	7 pounds	Satin	1:10
Sako	21¾	on intended	7 pounds	Satin	1:10
Mossberg M1500	22	use	7 pounds, 10 ounces	Gloss	1:10

Cartridges and bullets which are marginally adequate or those which do well under ideal conditions can become inadequate under less favorable conditions.

The .243 Winchester and 6mm Remington are excellent long-range varmint cartridges with the proper bullets. For example, the streamlined Speer 85-grain softpoint boattail has a ballistic coefficient of .404. If you load this bullet to a muzzle speed of 3375 fps and sight-in 1¼ inches high at 100 yards, it will be dead-on at 215 yards. It will be no more than 1.5 inches above or below the line of sight out to 250 yards for a varmint-shooting point-blank range. At 300 yards, it's only 4.5 inches low. And at 350 yards, it's about 10 inches low.

With the proper bullets and under the right conditions, the 6mm and .243 are also adequate for deer and antelope. With a streamlined bullet like the Hornady 100-grain spirepoint loaded to 2950 fps at the muzzle, it reaches the 300-yard mark with a little more than 1000 ft-lbs of energy, a level sometimes deemed minimally adequate. Place your shots with care and avoid shots at distances greater than 300 yards, and the .243 and 6mm Remington will fare well in the deer woods.

The .25-06

NECKING THE .30-06 up and down since its introduction has resulted in an excellent line of sporting cartridges. Some of the better ones—the .270 Winchester and .280 Remington (7mm Express Remington)—are commercial chamberings; a number of others—the .22-06, 6mm-06, and .35 Whelen—have remained wildcat chamberings; the .25-06, one of the best of the bunch, was a wildcat for many years before being chambered in a production gun.

The .25-06 originated about 1920 and was developed by the famous gunsmith A.O. Niedner. Originally known as the .25 Niedner, it was nothing more than a .30-06 case necked down to hold a .25-caliber bullet. Over the years, there have been a number of variations to the .25-06 cartridge, primarily in shoulder angle, although none offer any advantage over the standard 17½-degree shoulder common to the .30-06.

When developed by Niedner, the .25-06 cartridge was really ahead of its time. None of the powders available then were able to utilize the large capacity of the .25-06 case. In fact, the .25-06's potential wasn't fully realized until the development of modern slow-burning propellants like IMR-4350 and IMR-4831.

In 1969, 49 years after Niedner's introduction, Remington announced the .25-06 would be commercially available in its Model 700 bolt-action rifle. Today, the .25-06 is chambered by several manufacturers. With the advent of the popular 6mm Remington and .243 Winchester, the .25-caliber cartridges (namely the .250-3000 and .257 Roberts) rapidly lost ground. Remington's commercialization of the .25-06 rekindled interest in the .25 calibers, and now even the .250-3000 Savage and .257 Roberts are enjoying some degree of renewed interest.

The popular 6mms (or .24 calibers) overshadowed the .25s for a time, primarily as varmint/deer cartridges, but the .25-06 has the edge in terms of bullet weight and energy, making this larger bullet diameter a better choice for game like deer and antelope. Besides having the edge for big game, the .25-06 will do everything the flat-shooting 6mm Remington will do at the extreme ranges of varmint shooting. About the only disadvantage to the .25-06 is recoil. Heavier bullets, higher velocities, and more powder mean more kick.

There is a wide range of bullet weights available in .25 caliber; they run from 75 through 120 grains. The .25-06 case offers enough capacity to produce very high velocities with any of these bullet weights. The 75-grain bullet can be pushed to 3700 fps with proper .25-06 loads, while the 120-grain numbers can exceed 3000 fps. These muzzle velocities, combined with bullets of a high ballistic coefficient, mean a flat trajectory with excellent retained energy. This makes the cartridge excellent for both long-range varminting and big-game hunting.

The 120-grain Hornady hollowpoint bullet, for example, has a ballistic coefficient of .388; if started at 3000 fps muzzle velocity and with a 200-yard zero, the bullet will be only 21.1 inches low at 400 yards according to the Hornady manual. Though the hollowpoint bullet is not generally thought of as a big-game bullet, my hunting partner Dan Martin used this Hornady 120-grainer last fall to take a four-point mule deer at 90 yards. The bullet dropped the broadside-standing buck in its tracks.

With the Hornady 75-grain hollowpoint and an initial velocity of 3700 fps (again with a 200-yard zero), this bullet will be only 14.4 inches low at 400 yards. The 75-grain hollowpoint has a ballistic coefficient of .302. These big-game and varmint bullet figures compare favorably with almost any long-range cartridge. In fact, the .25-06 Remington cartridge is actually a "magnum" without the name or the belt.

For years, shooters formed their own .25-06 cases, usually by necking down .30-06 brass (though it can also be formed by necking down .270 Winchester or .280 Remington cases). Any of these three operations is simple. If you form .25-06 Remington cases from brass of other calibers, particularly the .270, it's a good idea to check overall length after forming to make certain the reformed cases do not exceed the specified length. A too-long case can crimp the neck into the bullet when the round is chambered—with no room for bullet release.

In some instances, it's also important to thin the necks (such as when forming .243 cases from .308 Government brass). Neck turning generally isn't necessary when forming .25-06 cases from .30-06 cases, but case neck thickness is something any handloader should be aware of.

As experienced handloaders know, excessive brass thickness in the case neck area, particularly in conjunction with a tight-necked rifle chamber, causes the case neck to be forced tight against the bullet when the round is chambered, much like a too-long neck does. The worst part comes when the rifle is fired, for this situation does not allow the case neck to expand or open enough to release the bullet without high pressures. This can raise chamber pressure to a dangerous level.

One way to see whether case necks are a bit on the thick side is by trying to insert a bullet into a fired case neck. A bullet of the proper caliber for the case should easily drop into a fired case. If it doesn't, the brass in the case neck is too thick. This problem can easily be corrected by outside case neck turning or inside neck reaming, depending on the equipment available.

Remember, case necks are thickened by forming cases *down* to a smaller bullet diameter. Again, however, this is not as much of a problem with the .25-06 as it is when forming some other wildcat cartridges. Today's .25-06 cases are readily available, and there's no need to form them.

Regardless of what some experts would have you believe, the .25-06 is not an elk cartridge. Of course, many elk have been taken with the .25-06, but this does not make the .25-06 adequate for the average elk hunter under most conditions.

The first introduction I had to the .25-06 was when Bill Mills, a friend of mine, and I were shooting prairie dogs. He had just received a new custom-built .25-06 based on an Enfield action; this rifle had a heavy barrel and thumbhole stock. I was impressed by what Mills was doing with the .25-06 at extreme range.

I was intrigued by the performance of the .25-caliber cartridge, but I didn't get the opportunity to use one until Remington commercialized it. I've handloaded for the Remington Model 700 .25-06, using 12 different bullets, eight propellants, and three separate primers. I have also fired two factory loads; the Remington 87-grain Power-Lokt hollowpoint and the Remington 120-grain Core-Lokt pointed softpoint.

.25-06 LOAD DATA

Remington Model 700, 24-inch barrel; Bushnell 3-9X Banner scope

Bullet	Powder (Type)	(Grs.)	Case	Primer	Velocity
Sierra 75-gr. HP	W785	60.0	W-W	Win. 120	3667
Hornady 75-gr. HP	W760	55.0	W-W	Win. 120	3687
Hornady 87-gr. spirepoint	IMR-4064	48.0	W-W	Win. 120	3516
Sierra 90-gr. HPBT	IMR-4831	55.0	W-W	Rem. 9½	3343
Speer 100-gr. HP	H205	51.0	R-P	Rem. 9½	3170
Nosler 100-gr. Solid Base	IMR-4350	52.0	R-P	Rem. 9½	3278
Sierra 117-gr. spitzer BT	W785	53.0	W-W	Win. 120	3074
Hornady 117-gr. RN	H370	63.0	W-W	Fed. 215	2940
Sierra 117-gr. spitzer flatbase	IMR-4350	49.0	W-W	Rem. 9½	2984
Sierra 120-gr. HPBT	IMR-4350	48.0	W-W	Rem. 9½	2914
Nosler 120-gr. Partition	H450	50.0	W-W	Win. 120	2961
Hornady 120-gr. HP	IMR-4831	50.0	W-W	Rem. 9½	2966
Remington 87-gr. HP P-L	Factory load				3415
Remington 120-gr. PSP C-L	Factory load				3045

NOTES: All loads were clocked at 10 feet with a Custom Chronograph and are an average of five shots.

The .25-06 is easy to load for, as much so as the .270, .280, or any other bottleneck case. The case is also suitable for a wide range of burning rate propellants. With the 75-grain bullets, for example, I achieved high velocity with both Winchester's W760 (3687 fps) and the much slower burning Winchester W785 (3667 fps). I used standard Remington No. 9½ and Winchester No. 120 primers throughout the load testing except when loading 63 grains of the slow-burning H870 propellant, which was sparked with a Federal No. 215 Magnum primer. The H870 was used to push the 117-grain Hornady roundnose to an impressive 2940 fps.

All velocities were clocked in a Remington Model 700 (24-inch barrel) that sported a Bushnell 3-9X Banner scope with a rangefinding reticle.

With the scope set at 9X, I proceeded to fire three five-shot groups with the Remington 87-grain factory load. These turned up a 1.4-inch average. Then I selected one of the light bullet handloads, the Sierra 75-grain hollowpoint with 55 grains of Winchester's W760, and again proceeded to fire three five-shot groups. This load turned up a 1.2-inch average.

These groups were fired with the Model 700 as it came out of the box. The trigger was typically stiff and pulled hard, no doubt due to the fact that some extra margin of safety is built into the rifle. With a little trigger pull lightening and load development, I have no doubt this .25-06 could have been made to shoot one-inch groups, the general accuracy requirement for a varmint-class rifle. And in a big-game rifle, one-inch accuracy is more than anyone will use under field conditions.

According to the new *Speer Reloading Manual Number Ten*, the SAAMI maximum average pressure for the .25-06 Remington has been established at 53,000 cup, which is 3000 cup greater than the .30-06 or the .280; however, this is 1000 cup less than the .270 Winchester. Whenever 50,000 cup is exceeded with a bottleneck cartridge like the .25-06, the shooter or loader is able to get very high velocity from the round.

If I were using the .25-06 for the smaller species of varmints – prairie dogs, ground squirrels, or woodchucks – I would use bullets ranging from 75 to 100 grains. It's usually best to lean toward the 75-grain hollowpoints in more settled areas. If I were to hunt antelope or other deer-size game, I would apply the 117- or 120-grain numbers for their more controlled expansion capabilities and greater mass for deeper penetration.

In my experience, the Nosler Partition bullet is an excellent choice for those hunters who want minimal destruction from a high-velocity cartridge like the .25-06. This bullet generally expands with a small frontal area. As most hunters know, high-velocity cartridges on the order of the .25-06 are capable of severe destruction if improper bullets are used. Using a lightweight bullet designed for varmints in a .25-06, for example, can result in inadequate penetration on a deer-size animal.

The .25-06 is one of the best cartridges going when it comes to decisively putting down a coyote-size predator, but it isn't the best for preserving pelts. For saving fur at top velocities, I would opt for a heavier bullet with more controlled expansion capabilities. There are times when the explosiveness of the lightweight varmint bullets can be excessively damaging to a coyote or bobcat pelt.

Overall, the .25-06 is an excellent combination varmint/deer cartridge that is flat shooting and easy to load. It accepts a wide variety of propellants and bullet weights, making it suitable for game from ground squirrels to deer. If you've bypassed the .25s but have been thinking about giving one a try, the .25-06 Remington is definitely one of the best.

The .270 Winchester

WINCHESTER'S FIRST entry into the heavy-caliber bolt-action rifle field was the Model 54, which was introduced in 1925. The rifle was initially chambered for a well-known and respected cartridge, the .30-06. It was also offered in a new chambering called the .270 Winchester, a round basically the same as the .30-06, but with a bullet measuring .277 inch instead of the .30-06's .308.

Jack O'Connor, one of the best-known gun writers of all time, is sometimes credited with the popularity of the .270. He's said to have written more articles on the .270 Winchester than anyone else, and he certainly contributed to its success. According to his writings, O'Connor killed more game with the .270 Winchester than any other caliber. In *The Rifle Book,* O'Connor wrote:

"In the first years of its experience, the .270 ran into tough competition. All the gun editors of that day were singing the praises of the .30-06. Some of them went so far as to say that the .270 was less accurate than the .30-06 and there was nothing it could do that the .30-06 could not do better. Furthermore the government was selling ammunition for as little as one cent a shot for 1918 wartime ammunition in .30-06 . . . . "

In another of his books, *The Hunting Rifle,* O'Connor said:

"It would appear that in those far distant days, shooting writers were a much less breathless lot than they are today. The gun editor of one leading hunting and fishing magazine didn't even mention the fact that there was such a cartridge for several years . . . . Another editor decided, apparently without trying the .270, that it wasn't as good as the .30-06 and let it go at that. It took even the august *American Rifleman* three years to get around to running an article on the new cartridge. If anyone wanted to find out about the .270, he was driven to reading the Winchester ads."

O'Connor goes on to say that shooters finally began realizing the attributes of the .270—that it shot a little flatter than the .30-06 with popular bullets and loadings at that time and kicked a bit less. Once the .270 caught hold, there was no stopping it. Besides the .30-06 and .270, the Model 54 Winchester was subsequently chambered in several other calibers, but the .30-06 and .270 were by far the most popular. If you come across a Model 54 rifle, chances are it'll be chambered for either the .270 or .30-06. The .270 Winchester is now one of the most popular big-game cartridges going.

Even gun writers have changed their attitude about the .270. Whenever anyone writes about the .270, "flat shooting" and "accurate" nearly always turn up in the copy. Those more enamored with the old cartridge would almost have us believe it has magical powers beyond the current level of ballistics knowledge.

Aside from all the good press, there's been a lot of controversy surrounding the .270 Winchester. There's usually no argument about the .270's efficiency on deer-size game; it's when the critters reach elk size that some dispute the .270's suitability.

To gain a little perspective on this well-liked cartridge, we currently have a couple of closely related rounds for comparison—rounds that weren't available back when the .270 had only the .30-06 for competition. The .270 is more closely related to the .25-06 Remington and .280 Remington than it is to the .30-06 Springfield. All four cartridges have basically the same case size. The only difference of any significance is the diameter of the bullet and consequently the bullets and loadings available. The .25-06 shoots a .257-inch-diameter bullet; the .270, a .277; and the .280, a .284. As you can see, the .270 falls right between the .25-06 and .280 Remington. As with all cartridges, within reason, the size of the .270's case and bullet are indicative of its practical applications.

The .270 is controversial for elk hunting because it's one of those borderline cartridges. Even those who consider it to be adequate for elk don't often consider any smaller cartridge to be adequate. It's interesting that such a borderline cartridge can often be touted as the "best possible selection."

Judging a cartridge's suitability for this or that species of game can be difficult because any species can be taken with any centerfire cartridge under the right circumstances. Suitability depends greatly upon the individual hunter, where and how he hunts, and the type of shots he takes. Trying to judge suitability on the basis of whether a cartridge performs well for some people is not necessarily a good measure of its effectiveness for general use. In any comparison of cartridges, it's best to stick to the ballistic facts, and the .270 is no slouch in this area.

For example, 130-grain bullets can be loaded to 3000 fps in the .270 with a 24-inch barrel; 150-grain numbers reach close to 2900 with a few loads. This compares with about 3100 for the .30-06, using the latter bullet weight. However, a .270 bullet of equal weight and similar shape has a higher sectional density (SD) and ballistic coefficient (BC) owing to its smaller diameter. A Hornady 150-grain .30-caliber spirepoint has a .358 BC and .226 SD; a Hornady 150-grain .270 spirepoint rates a .443 BC and .279 SD. Let's translate these into downrange figures.

Although the 150-grain bullet is not considered to be the best long-range choice in the .270, neither is it the best choice in the .30-06. But the 150-grain weight does allow a fair comparison because it's available in both diameters.

The 150-grain .270 bullet starting at 2900 has 2802 ft-lbs of energy and reaches the 300-yard mark with 2284 fps of velocity and 1737 ft-lbs of energy. Starting at 3100 fps, a bullet with the same weight from a .30-06 has 3202 ft-lbs of energy and reaches the 300-yard distance with 2317 fps of velocity remaining for 1789 ft-lbs of energy.

At close range, the .30-06 has advantages in velocity, energy and bullet diameter; at 300 yards, however, its decided advantages have decreased in number to primarily bullet diameter alone. With all else being equal, a larger bullet diameter produces a larger frontal area on impact. The better sectional density of the .270 may cause it to penetrate more at that distance even though there is less tissue destruction along the bullet's path.

Since the .270 is so popular, there is a wide variety of rifles and ammunition available for it. Practically any maker that chambers the .30-06 also chambers the .270. Like the .30-06, the .270 requires a standard-length action. The currently popular short actions, designed for such rounds as the 7mm-08 or .308, just won't do. During Jack O'Connor's era, such high-performance, short-action cartridges weren't popular in bolt-action rifles; some of them weren't even available. When a bolt-action rifle was considered for big game, one automatically thought of a standard-length .30-06 action. If the more compact short actions and cartridges were widely available back then, O'Connor's pick for a lightweight mountain rifle might have been something other than a .270.

The .270 is often considered to be a versatile cartridge, one suitable for any game on this continent. In a .30-06/.270 question of bullet selection versatility, however, there is no contest. The .30-06 wins hands down. In factory ammo, the .30-06 has bullets weighing 55 to 250 grains. The handloader has more than 69 different .30-caliber hunting bullets available just from Hornady, Speer, Sierra, and Nosler. There are 23 hunting bullets for the .25-06, 27 for the .270, and 34 for the .280. There are no plinkers available for the .270.

On the other hand, there are plenty of bullets for the .270 to do practically anything you want. As a practical matter, few hunters go after fur or small game with a .270 Winchester. With a good selection of 100- and 110-grain bullets available, one doesn't go wanting for good varmint bullets. If you're into really fast muzzle speed, load the Sierra 90-grain hollowpoint, teaming it with about 54.0 or 55.0 grains of H380. It's a sizzler.

With a wide variety of the popular 130-grain weights available for deer-size game, you'll fill the need for 90 percent of the .270's applications. This bullet weight is the uncontested king for the cartridge. The slower burning powders such as 4350, 4831, and 3100 produce the highest velocities with this middleweight.

TOP FIVE RIFLES

Make/Model	Barrel (Inches)	Sights	Weight (Pounds)	Finish	Rifling (Twist)
Winchester M70	22	Weaver 2.5-7X	6 pounds, 12 ounces	Satin	1:10
Ruger M77	22	Redfield 4X	7 pounds	Satin	1:10
Savage M110	22	Bushnell 3-9X	7 pounds	Satin	1:10
Remington M700	22	Leupold 2-7X	7 pounds, 4 ounces	Satin	1:10
Browning A-Bolt	22	B&L 4X	6 pounds, 11 ounces	Satin	1:10

If you really want to go after big game, the plentiful 150-grain weights or the superb Nosler 160-grain Partition is all you'll need for anything on the North American continent. If you want a real heavyweight, there's the Barnes 180-grain roundnose with a .032-inch copper jacket. Use it with H4831. The new IMR-7828 might be the ticket with this weight slug; I just haven't tried this combination yet.

One might add a qualifier to taking the really big, dangerous species of bears with a .270 . . . something to the effect that a hunter after such game should choose his shots with care. Then again, it's prudent to choose shots with care whenever such game is hunted.

As I mentioned earlier, the .270 is a controversial cartridge when applied to elk. In addition to the dispute about whether the cartridge is adequate, there is a question of the best bullet weight for this purpose. Some shooters consider the 150-grain weight to be the best for deep penetration on these large animals; others say a more rapidly expanding 130-grain bullet, placed in the ribs, will take elk more decisively.

My own experience has been that a considerable amount of tissue damage is desirable to put an elk down with authority. Greater expansion and a larger bullet frontal area are achieved at the sacrifice of penetration. While a larger bullet frontal area destroys more tissue, it also penetrates less. If you use a heavy, tough-jacketed bullet, you're better prepared to angle a shot through a lot of muscle and bone in order to reach the vitals. If you use a more rapidly expanding bullet, be sure to avoid meaty areas and choose your shooting angle with care. If you do, the game will often die more quickly when lung shot with a more rapidly expanding bullet than with a tough-jacketed one in the same place.

.270 WINCHESTER: 10 FAVORITE LOADS

HANDLOADS

Bullet	Powder (Type)	(Grs.)	Case	Primer	Velocity (fps) (10 Feet)	Five-Shot Group (Inches)	Gun	Remarks
Speer 100-Gr. spitzer	IMR-4064	52.0	Frontier	Fed. 210M	3274	1.6	22-inch Win. M70	For varmints only
Sierra 130-Gr. spitzer	IMR-4350	55.0	Frontier	Fed. 210M	2926	1.4	22-inch Win. M70	Deer/antelope load
Nosler 130-Gr. Partition	H450	58.5	Norma	Fed. 210M	2973	1.6	22-inch Win. M70	All-around load for smaller game
Hornady 150-Gr. spirepoint	W785	58.0	Norma	Fed. 210M	2897	1.0	22-inch Win. M70	Mid-size big-game load
Speer 130-Gr. BT	IMR-4350	54.0	R-P	Rem. 9½	3002	1.2*	22-inch H&R M340	High ballistic coefficient

FACTORY LOADS

Bullet	Powder (Type)	(Grs.)	Case	Primer	Velocity (fps) (10 Feet)	Five-Shot Group (Inches)	Gun	Remarks
Federal 130-Gr. spitzer	Factory load				3031	1.1*	22-inch H&R M340	Deer/antelope load
Winchester 130-Gr. Power-Point	Factory load				2994	1.3*	22-inch H&R M340	Deer/antelope load
Remington 130-Gr. Bronze Point	Factory load				2933	1.1*	22-inch H&R M340	Streamlined bullet
Hornady 130-Gr. spirepoint	Factory load				2798	1.5	22-inch Win. M70	Mild load
Remington 150-Gr. RN	Factory load				2648	1.3	22-inch Win. M70	Mid-size big-game load

*Three-shot groups

The .270 is an excellent all-around cartridge, but it is in the open country of the West, with mule deer as the game, that the .270 Winchester really shines. The 130-grain weight is the uncontested choice for this purpose. (Eastern deer hunters also recognize that a long-range, flat-shooting cartridge is really no handicap on a short-range shot, and they are flocking to the .270. In fact, the .270 is the most popular deer cartridge in some regions of the East.)

When I was hunting for Coues whitetail, I couldn't help thinking about O'Connor. I was after the same game and carrying the same caliber he wrote about so often. Instead of carrying a stock Model 70 Winchester, my rifle was custom built by H-S Precision Inc. and was based on a Model 70 action but fitted with an H-S Precision Fiberthane stock and an Atkinson stainless barrel.

I had been hunting for several days and was sitting on top of a small mountain, glassing a likely looking big mountainside opposite my position. The mountain I was watching was ideal Coues habitat, with brush-choked canyons running down from cliffs above and with openings here and there where the Coues grazed early in the morning.

I finally spotted two Coues bucks more than a half-mile away. I could tell they both had sizeable antlers, but I couldn't tell how good they were. I watched the pair for some time while they browsed and worked their way uphill through small openings. They disappeared into a patch of brush and didn't come out—just what I had been waiting for.

After a long, careful stalk, I knew I was close to where the deer must be. It was difficult keeping quiet in the dry desert brush, and I spooked the deer.

The buck moved quickly, and there wasn't much time to shoot. I could see the gracefully curving antlers as the scope's reticle met the deer. The rifle roared just as the deer reached the top and disappeared into thick brush on the opposite side.

It took about 30 minutes for me to work my way up the opposite slope toward the brush patch that I had carefully marked in my mind's eye. I climbed out of the canyon and located blood droplets on the rocky ground. A few yards away, I found the buck, a real trophy and the best Coues whitetail I had ever taken.

The .270 is fast and flat. I didn't have time to think about the bullet's trajectory before I shot, nor did I need to. There was only an instant for the bullet to get there before the deer disappeared, and the .270 did the job. Did the cartridge give me the edge I needed to get that deer? I think it did.

The .30-30

THE .30-30 has been around a long time. According to several sources, it appeared with the Winchester Model 94 lever-action rifle in 1895. According to the *Speer Reloading Manual Number Ten,* the original .30-30 loading was a 165-grain bullet ahead of 30.0 grains of powder for an advertised velocity of 1970 fps.

Since its introduction in the Model 94, the .30-30 has been chambered in the Winchester High Wall and other rifles built by Marlin, Remington, and Savage. I once owned a Winchester Model 54 and a prewar Savage Model 99 chambered for the rimmed .30-30. At one time, Remington offered a rimless version of basically the same cartridge which was called the .30 Remington, but it never achieved the popularity of the .30-30 or

.30 WCF. The .30-30 Winchester has been chambered in the excellent Remington Model 788 bolt action, the Savage Model 170 slide action, and the Savage Model 219 break-action single shot. These three rifles have been discontinued.

Lever guns much like those originals in which the cartridge was introduced still form the bulk of the .30-30 rifles, generally short, lightweight rifles like the Winchester Model 94 and Marlin Model 336 which have been given the credit for the sustained popularity of the .30-30. It's been said the .30-30 has put more venison on tables than all other cartridges put together. Effectiveness is what has kept shooters using the rimmed .30-30 cartridge in the little lever guns more than any other cartridge, even though many other rounds have been offered in the same guns.

For the most part, the venison taken with the .30-30 has been put on the table with factory loads, not handloads. This being the case, can one benefit by handloading for the .30-30? Well, handloads might not be needed for deer hunting with the .30-30, but in my opinion, handloading for any cartridge is beneficial. I find handloading to be an enjoyable means of reducing the cost of ammo and increasing the amount of shooting I can do. The .30-30 lever guns really are a lot of fun to shoot, and the mild loads mean the barrels last indefinitely, so there's little worry about shooting out a throat. Furthermore, handloading adds versatility not available in factory loads.

.30-30 REDUCED LOAD DATA
(not for use in tubular magazine rifles)
Savage Model 340, 22-inch barrel, Williams receiver sight

Bullet	Powder (Type)	(Grs.)	Primer	Case	Velocity (fps)
Speer 100-gr. Plinker	SR 4756	12.0	Fed. 210M	W-W	1688
Hornady 100-gr. Short Jacket	Red Dot	10.0	Fed. 210M	W-W	1848
Speer 110-gr. Varminter*	Unique	11.0	Fed. 210M	W-W	1861
Hornady 110-gr. spirepoint	RL-7	20.0	Fed. 210M	W-W	1950
Speer 130-gr. spirepoint	IMR-4227	20.0	Fed. 210M	W-W	2175
Speer 130-gr. HP	H4198	20.0	Fed. 210M	W-W	1700
Speer 130-gr. FN*	IMR-3031	25.0	Fed. 210M	W-W	1790

NOTES: Velocity was recorded with a Custom Chronograph Model 500 and is an average of five shots at 10 feet from the gun's muzzle. All loads are considered small game/plinking loads by author.
*These bullet loadings can be used in tubular magazine rifles.

When handloading for the .30-30 lever guns, however, the shooter is limited in load construction and development. The popular Winchester Model 94 and Marlin Model 336 rifles have tubular magazines. The tip of one bullet rests against the primer of another, meaning blunt bullets must be used when handloading for these .30-30 lever guns. Spitzers should not be loaded in these guns unless a single round is carried in the magazine. A sharp-pointed bullet tip resting against the primer of another round could be detonated in the magazine under the force of recoil. Due to the spring tension of the tubular magazine, the blunt bullets must also have a cannelure or groove running about their mid-section for crimping the case mouth. Without a cannelure, the case mouth can't be effectively crimped into the bullet, and the latter will set back inside the case under the force of magazine spring tension.

The amount of propellant placed inside a case is limited in those loads producing 38,000 cup or less, according to SAAMI specs. This is in contrast to the 50,000-plus psi pressures commonly used in ammunition

.30-30 FACTORY LOAD DATA		
Load	Advertised Muzzle Velocity (fps)	Application
Remington 55-gr. Accelerator SP	3400	Varmints
Federal 125-gr. HP	2570	Varmints
Federal 150-gr. Hi-Shok SP	2390	Deer-size game
Hornady/Frontier 150-gr. RN	2250	Deer-size game
PMC 150-gr. SP	2390	Deer-size game
Remington 150-gr. Core-Lokt SP	2390	Deer-size game
Winchester 150-gr. FMC	2390	Deer-size game
Winchester 150-gr. P-P(SP)	2390	Deer-size game
Winchester 150-gr. Silvertip	2390	Deer-size game
Federal 170-gr. Nosler Partition	2200	Deer-size game
Federal 170-gr. Hi-Shok SP	2200	Deer-size game
Hornady 170-gr. FP	2100	Deer-size game
PMC 170-gr. SP	2200	Deer-size game
Remington 170-gr. Core-Lokt SP	2200	Deer-size game
Remington 170-gr. Core-Lokt HP	2200	Deer-size game
Winchester 170-gr. P-P(SP)	2200	Deer-size game
Winchester 170-gr. Silvertip	2200	Deer-size game

loaded for use in strong bolt-action rifles. There are good reasons for this low pressure limitation, and they involve the design of both rifle and cartridge brass.

There are some very old .30-30 rifles around. Even the popular modern lever guns are old designs with rear-locking breechbolts and relatively thin receiver sidewalls. When a high-pressure round is fired in such a gun, the breechbolt compresses and the receiver walls stretch. There is a limit to the amount of backthrust safely produced in such a gun. And .30-30 brass is quite thin and generally isn't as strong as the brass of other high-intensity cartridges. This is the primary reason why the Speer manual and others recommend against loading the .30-30 cartridge up to high pressure levels.

These are the reasons why handloaders should not increase ballistics over factory rounds with this particular cartridge. If you want to hand-load the .30-30 in order to soup it up, forget it. On the other hand, you will have greater versatility in bullet weight and load selection. As far as accuracy is concerned, the .30-30, like any other rifle/cartridge combination, does respond well to load variations. In other words, you can experiment with different components until the optimum combination is derived to obtain all the accuracy possible out of a particular firearm.

I reviewed a series of .30-30 loads in the Marlin Model 336 and the Winchester Model 94. I decided to stick with the factory iron sights on the top-ejection Model 94 since that's the way most of these rifles are used.

With the Marlin, however, it's easy to mount a scope low over the bore, and I topped if off with a Tasco 1.75-5X scope. In addition, I chronographed some reduced loads in the Savage Model 340 bolt-action rifle. This gun was fitted with a Williams receiver aperture or peep sight.

.30-30 LOAD DATA
(for tubular magazine rifles)

Winchester Model 94, 20-inch barrel, factory open iron sights
Marlin Model 336CS, 20-inch barrel, Tasco 1.75-5X scope, Tasco mounts

Bullet	Powder (Type)	(Grs.)	Primer	Velocity (fps)	Average Group Size (Inches)	Rifle	Application
Speer 110-gr. HP	H335	42.0	Win. LR	2886	5.7	Model 336CS	Varmints
Speer 110-gr. HP	H335	43.0	Win. LR	2905	5.7	Model 336CS	Varmints
Speer 110-gr. HP	IMR-4198	29.0	Win. LR	2579	3.3	Model 336CS	Varmints
Speer 110-gr. HP	RL-7	33.5	Win. LR	2765	4.1	Model 94	Varmints
Sierra 125-gr. HP	H322	33.0	Win. LR	2382	4.5	Model 94	Varmints
Sierra 125-gr. HP	W748	38.0	Win. LR	2438	4.0	Model 336CS	Varmints
Sierra 125-gr. HP	RL-7	31.0	Win. LR	2516	5.0	Model 94	Varmints
Speer 130-gr. FN	IMR-4198	23.5	Fed. 210	2057	2.5	Model 336CS	Plinking
Sierra 150-gr. FN	W748	38.5	Win. LR	2485	3.8	Model 94	Deer-size game
Speer 150-gr. FN	H335	35.0	Win. LR	2412	3.7	Model 336CS	Deer-size game
Speer 150-gr. FN	RL-7	28.0	Win. LR	2235	6.1	Model 94	Deer-size game
Sierra 150-gr. FN	RL-7	28.0	Win. LR	2307	3.0	Model 336CS	Deer-size game
Sierra 150-gr. FN	MR-223	33.0	Win. LR	2268	3.8	Model 336CS	Deer-size game
Speer 170-gr. FN	BL-C(2)	30.0	Win. LR	1920	3.7	Model 94	Deer-size game
Hornady 170-gr. FN	W748	35.0	Win. LR	2144	5.0	Model 94	Deer-size game
Hornady 170-gr. FN	H335	33.0	Win. LR	2194	3.8	Model 336CS	Deer-size game
Hornady 170-gr. FN	H335	34.5	Win. LR	2305	3.1	Model 336CS	Deer-size game
Hornady 170-gr. FN	RL-7	25.5	Win. LR	2026	4.2	Model 94	Deer-size game
Sierra 170-gr. FN	IMR-3031	28.0	Win. LR	2007	3.5	Model 336CS	Deer-size game
Remington 170-gr. Core-Lokt SP	Factory load			2108	4.3	Model 94	Deer-size game
Remington 170-gr. Core-Lokt SP	Factory load			2230	3.0	Model 336CS	Deer-size game
Winchester Super X 170-gr. Power-Point SP	Factory load			2227	1.8	Model 336CS	Deer-size game

NOTES: Velocity was taken with an Oehler Chronotach and is an average of 10 shots at 10 feet from the gun's muzzle. Group size is an average of two five-shot groups at 100 yards. W-W cases were used in all handloads.

The bulk of the reduced load data for the bolt-action Savage Model 340 incorporates pointed or hollowpoint bullets. By using pointed bullets in a bolt action (or one at a time in the lever guns), you can increase down-range ballistics considerably over factory ammo without pushing pressures and muzzle velocities to the limit. Pointed or spitzer bullets heavier than 150 grains are designed for much higher velocities and should not be used in this cartridge for game. It's possible they won't expand reliably on game when fired at the slower .30-30 velocities.

Lever guns don't have the camming power bolt-action rifles do, and due to the cartridge-wedging effect from bolt compression during the first firing, a reloaded case could be hard to chamber. I recommend full-length sizing cases so there's no resistance in chambering. Also, crimp all case mouths into the bullet cannelure. The cases will not all be precisely the same length after a firing or two, which would not be a problem were it not for the necessity of crimping.

Crimping requires all cases be exactly the same length so they will crimp properly into the bullet groove; if they aren't, and if a case that's too long is pressed into the crimping die, the case neck wall will generally buckle, sometimes so severely that the round will not chamber. If a too-short case is pressed into the bulletseating/crimping die, the round will not be crimped at all. In some instances, the case mouth may not even reach the bullet's crimping groove. Consequently, loading for the tubular magazine rifles requires that cases be constantly trimmed and deburred. If you're loading for a bolt rifle like the Savage Model 340, this aspect of case trimming is no different than loading for any other bolt-action rifle. You just won't have to do it as often as with the lever guns.

After assembling and shooting 26 different handloads and two factory loads, I found the best five-shot group series was turned in by a factory round. The Winchester Super-X 170-grain Power-Point did it with a 1.8-inch average for five shots at 100 yards. Surprisingly, the shot-to-shot velocity consistency had nothing to do with this average because the velocity consistency was the poorest of all the loads tried, producing a variation of 163 fps in 10 shots.

The second most accurate load, a handload, was not far behind. This load was actually a reduced load consisting of the Speer 130-grain flat-nose backed by 23.5 grains of IMR-4198. The load produced a velocity average of 2057 fps and a 2.5-inch group average at 100 yards.

The handloads did win the honors for high velocity and velocity uniformity. The Speer 150-grain flatnose backed by 35.0 grains of H335 produced an extreme spread of 26 fps in a 10-shot string. The Remington 170-grain Core-Lokt factory load was not far behind, however, with a 31 fps spread. Both of these were received in the Marlin 336CS.

The highest velocity in the 150-grain bullet weight range was produced with the Sierra 150-grain flatnose and 38.5 grains of W748 for 2465 fps from the Winchester Model 94. At 2305 fps, the highest 170-grain bullet velocity was about 80 fps faster than the factory ammo in the Marlin 336CS and was produced by 34.5 grains of H335 behind the Hornady 170-grain flatnose. The fastest overall velocity was received with the Speer 110-grain hollowpoint and 43.0 grains of H335 producing 2905 fps. From looking at the 100-yard targets, it's obvious the bullets were not stabilizing properly because they did not produce round holes; some of them impacted the target sideways.

In the reduced load category, the Speer 100-grain Plinker and 12.0 grains of SR 4756 produced a 1¼-inch, five-shot group average at 50 yards and a mere 1688 fps. This load is also economical and very enjoyable to shoot due to the lack of recoil and muzzle blast. It was fired from the Savage Model 340.

Handloading for the .30-30 is an enjoyable proposition, although there are certain aspects to observe regarding the popular lever guns, aspects which cannot be avoided. By handloading, you can definitely save money, shoot more, find a load your particular rifle likes, ar.d make your gun more versatile than is possible with factory ammunition. If you have a yen to handload for your .30-30, go to it.

The .308 Winchester

IN 1952, the .308 Winchester cartridge was introduced to the sporting market after extensive government testing. Its development goes back to World War I, when the government was looking for a cartridge for light semiauto and fully automatic firearms. It was obvious a shorter cartridge would mean lighter and more efficient gun mechanisms. Much of the developmental interest centered around the .300 Savage and what was dubbed the "T-65" round. The primary difference between the two is that the T-65 has a neck about ³/₁₆ inch longer. The T-65 finally won out and was adopted in 1954, two years after Winchester introduced it as the .308 Winchester.

The .308 Winchester was not an instant winner in the sporting market, but like other military cartridges, it was destined for success. The stubby round obviously doesn't have the case capacity of the established .30-06, but it has other things going for it. One major feature is that it functions through short actions. When the .308 was introduced, the standard-length action was the .30-06, and popular cartridges utilized the action and magazine length of those actions. But the short action has become very popular and is an action length through which the .308 will function. The .30-06 will not.

What's the big deal about a short action?

A shorter action makes for a shorter bolt throw and a shorter, handier overall rifle or carbine length. Only during recent years have shooters utilized this advantage to full potential in big-game rifles. In fact, cartridges like the .308 Winchester are responsible for bringing about the popularity of short bolt-action rifles. The Winchester Model 70, for example, one of the longest-lived bolt-action sporting rifles, was not available in a short action until just 198 . Previously, the magazine box was simply blocked at the rear to decrease its interior capacity, and the boltstop was changed to accommodate short cartridges. Now there is a Model 70 built specifically for cartridges like the .308.

Besides its small size, the .308 is an efficient cartridge. The small powder chamber produces high velocities and a high level of accuracy with a wide range of powders.

The .308 Winchester is chambered in sporting rifles of all action types, from the Browning, Remington, and H&K semiautos to the Remington pumps, Thompson/Center TCR single shot, and an array of bolt actions. There are also the excellent Browning BLR and Savage Model 99 lever rifles. The makers of the ancient Browning Model 99 even dropped the .300 Savage for the .308 Winchester. Remember, to the handloader, the .308 is little more than a .300 Savage with a slightly longer neck.

Among factory loads, it's a different story. The .308, having come along much later than either the .300 Savage or the .30-06, makes use of higher pressures. According to the *Speer Reloading Manual Number 11,* SAAMI pressures for the .308 Winchester run 52,000, while .300 Savage factory loads are held to 46,000, a considerable difference.

I once performed an extensive review with two Savage Model 99 rifles with only one serial number separating them. One was chambered for the .300 Savage; the other was chambered for the .308 Winchester. When both were loaded to the same pressure levels with similar brass, the .308 averaged a velocity advantage of only 57 fps over the .300. During the review, nine different bullets and powders were loaded to maximum in each rifle.

Nevertheless, the .300 Savage is gone, and the .308 Winchester is doing better than ever. In a factory load comparison with the longer .30-06, the .308 still comes up looking good. The factories load .30-06s milder than .308s. For handloading, however, the .30-06 is head and shoulders above the .308 in performance. Don't let anyone tell you they're ballistic twins. And don't take my word for it. Look in the *Hornady Handbook of Cartridge Reloading.* Maximum velocity for the 150-grain bullet in the .308 is 2800 fps. Maximum velocity listed for the .30-06 is 3100 fps. Other bullet weights bear a similar velocity difference. Both rifles listed in the Hornady manual are Model 70 Winchesters, and both have 22-inch barrels. While the difference with your loads may not be as great, the point is that there is a significant difference in handload performance potential.

All this is not to detract from the .308's good points. It's a fine cartridge. Many have touted the .308's efficiency. I believe "efficiency," as it is applied to cartridges, is often misunderstood and overrated. A smaller case generally requires a smaller increase in powder charge to attain a given velocity increase when compared to a larger cartridge. However, a smaller case will not produce velocity equal to the larger case when both are loaded to equal pressure levels.

When I say efficiency is overrated, I mean in relation to a big-game cartridge. What does it matter if five more grains of propellant are required to achieve a noticeable increase in velocity? Sure, more powder and a higher velocity are going to erode a barrel faster, but who wears out a .308 or .30-06 barrel on a big-game rifle? And yes, more powder and velocity mean more recoil. But who can really tell the difference in recoil between a .308 and .30-06 without looking at the cartridge being chambered? In the Hornady manual, for example, a charge of 44.9 grains of IMR-4064 starts the 150-grain bullet at 2800 fps in the .308. In the .30-06, 56.1 grains of W748 are used to start the same bullet at 3100 fps. Recoil for an eight-pound .308 rifle with this load is 14.2 ft-lbs. Recoil for an eight-pound .30-06 is 18.8 ft-lbs. That's 4.6 ft-lbs of additional recoil and 11.2 grains more powder for a velocity gain of 300 fps. See what I mean by "efficiency" being overrated? People who talk about efficiency generally ignore performance, which is the truly important consideration in a big-game cartridge.

Besides being efficient in terms of getting a relatively high velocity from a small case, the .308 is one of those rounds that has an affinity for working well with shorter barrels. Since the .308 Winchester is a short-action cartridge, it's ideal for a short overall rifle, one with an abbreviated barrel. I once conducted a series comparing two .308 rifles, one with a 22-inch barrel and one with an 18-inch barrel. With bullets of 150 grains and lighter, velocity favored the longer barrel by 75 to 150 fps. This is somewhat less than the 50 foot-seconds of velocity per inch of barrel rule of thumb often quoted. When I loaded heavier bullets, however, the velocity difference was incredibly low, running from only 15 fps to 83 fps (maximum) with the loads used. In other words, there was virtually no velocity advantage to four more inches of barrel.

The .308 is a very easy cartridge to load for because it is not the least bit finicky about powder charges or powder types. Accurate bolt-action .308 rifles generally shoot well with an assortment of loads. However,

.308 WINCHESTER HANDLOAD PERFORMANCE

Bullet	Powder (Type)	(Grs.)	Primer	Case	Velocity (fps)
Savage Model 99E, 22-inch barrel					
Speer 130-gr. HP	IMR-3031	44.0	Fed. 210	Fed.	2900
Speer 130-gr. HP	IMR-3031	46.0	Fed. 210	Fed.	3019
Speer 130-gr. HP	IMR-4895	47.0	Fed. 210	Fed.	2985
Speer 130-gr. HP	IMR-4064	49.0	Fed. 210	Fed.	3003
Speer 130-gr. HP	IMR-4350	49.0	Fed. 210	Fed.	2490
Speer 130-gr. HP	H380	50.0	Fed. 210	Fed.	2604
Nosler 150-gr. Solid Base	RL-7	38.0	Fed. 210	Fed.	2786
Nosler 150-gr. Solid Base	H4895	46.0	Fed. 210	Fed.	2909
Nosler 150-gr. Solid Base	W748	49.0	Fed. 210	Fed.	2909
Hornady 180-gr. spirepoint	BL-C(2)	44.0	Fed. 210	Fed.	2519
Hornady 180-gr. spirepoint	IMR-4895	41.0	Fed. 210	Fed.	2503
Hornady 180-gr. spirepoint	H335	41.0	Fed. 210	Fed.	2429
Remington Model 7B, 22-inch barrel					
Speer 130-gr. HP	IMR-4895	45.0	Win. LR	Rem.	2874
Hornady 165-gr. SPBT	IMR-4320	43.0	Win. LR	Rem.	2520
Hornady 165-gr. SPBT	AA-2460	42.0	Fed. 210	Rem.	2540
Nosler 165-gr. Ballistic Tip	AA-2460	41.0	Fed. 210M	Fed.	2487
Sierra 165-gr. SP	AA-2460	44.0	Fed. 210	Rem.	2619
Winchester Model 70 Featherweight, 22-inch barrel					
Hornady 110-gr. spirepoint	RL-7	41.0	Win. LR	Fed.	2971
Sierra 125-gr. SP	W748	50.0	Win. LR	Fed.	2909
Speer 130-gr. HP	H380	52.0	Win. LR	Fed.	2748
Nosler 150-gr. Ballistic Tip	IMR-4895	45.0	CCI 200	LC-72	2920
Nosler 150-gr. Ballistic Tip	IMR-4350	48.0	CCI 200	LC-72	2672
Nosler 150-gr. Ballistic Tip	IMR-4064	42.0	CCI 200	LC-72	2620
Savage Model 110S, 22-inch barrel					
Speer 130-gr. HP	IMR-3031	46.0	Fed. 210	Fed.	3197
Speer 130-gr. HP	IMR-4895	47.0	Fed. 210	Fed.	3023
Speer 130-gr. HP	IMR-4064	49.0	Fed. 210	Fed.	3070

NOTES: Velocity is an average of 10 shots clocked at 10 feet from the guns' muzzles.

there are several things to keep in mind when you load it. Bullets heavier than 200 grains are really impractical for use in this short-action round. The projectile must be seated deeply into the powder space in order to function through short actions. Consequently, it's difficult to get ample velocity to make expanding bullets perform properly with the short case. There's really no need for 220-grain heavyweights in the .308 anyway. If you feel the need for heavier bullets and more case capacity, use a blunt-tipped projectile like a 180-grain roundnose and stay away from sharply pointed spitzers and boattails. For a given overall cartridge length, the base of a blunt bullet is seated farther out of the case.

Some .308 rifles are built on standard-length actions and magazines, and as long as the throat is also long, bullets can be seated farther out for an effective increase in case capacity. But overall loaded cartridge length generally must be held down to about 2.8 inches or about a half-inch shorter than the .30-06.

Regarding brass, it's always a good idea to separate cases by headstamp prior to loading, but this is especially true with the .308 Winchester. You might also weigh them to get some idea regarding capacity. A heavier case generally means thicker brass and reduced capacity. It won't take as much powder with such a case to obtain equal velocity. Looked at another way, a given load will produce higher pressure and velocity with a heavier case. Government brass, for example, will hold an average of about two grains less water than some commercial cases.

Size cases full length to restore the factory dimensions when loading for a semiauto, pump, or lever. This ensures they'll feed and chamber smoothly. Go for a zero headspace tolerance or "crush fit" by partial or neck sizing only with a bolt-action rifle. These guns have the camming power to allow it—if it isn't overdone.

The .308 Winchester has the advantage of all those .30-caliber bullets and is a versatile cartridge. In terms of accuracy, I've had excellent results with the Sierra 110- and 125-grain lightweights. The Speer 130-grain hollowpoint is also a good choice if you want to make a varmint rifle out of the .308.

For the lightweight 110-grain bullets, Hodgdon's H380 and H335 produce very high velocity, as do IMR-4064 and -3031. Velocities in excess of 3100 fps can be attained from most 22-inch barrels with these propellants. In fact, these powders, along with BL-C(2), W748, 4895, AA-2460 and AA-2520 remain top choices with all popular bullet weights in the .308 Winchester. Even slow-burning 4350 produces good velocity with the heavier 180- and 200-grain bullets.

The stubby .308 Winchester case doesn't look like a long-range round, but it doesn't fare badly. Use a streamlined bullet like a Nosler 150- or 165-grain Ballistic Tip or Solid Base and load it to top velocity, and the .308 Winchester shoots surprisingly flat. I've used a Winchester Model 70 Featherweight to hunt antelope, a quarry that's noted for producing long-range shots, and I never felt lacking for a flat-shooting cartridge when the crosshairs settled on the antelope.

The .308 Winchester doesn't have the case capacity of a belted magnum, but it's a versatile round with bullets weighing from 110 to 200 grains. It produces good accuracy with many different powders and a moderate velocity with small charges. The .308 can be had in short, lightweight actions and doesn't kick as much as larger cartridges. Fact is, the .308 Winchester will do about anything an astute handloader asks of it—from varmints to moose to benchrest competition.

* * *

If you're loading for a semiauto, keep in mind that the load you use affects the way the ammunition functions in your firearm. I'm speaking of port pressure. Gas-operated semiautos have tiny ports partway down the barrel which extend into the rifle's bore. When the base of the bullet passes this port, gas shoots through the tiny opening to operate the action and chamber another round. The internal pressure at the time the bullet passes this opening is quite important. If port pressure is too high, the action is operated violently, which is hard on both brass and gun; if the port pressure is too low, the empty case may not eject, and the action may not pick up another round from the magazine.

In order to avoid problems in this area, I've found it's best to use extruded powders in the medium burning rate range. This isn't a problem since so many of them are ideal for the .308. Powders like 4895 or 4064 work well.

If you're loading for a semiauto, give the empties a trip through a case tumbler or vibrator. Then, before you seat primers, check each flash hole to make sure it's not clogged with a bit of gravel or cleaning media before you seat the primer.

The .30-06

THE .30-06 has its roots in the military Springfield rifle, developed and manufactured at the Springfield Armory in 1902 to replace the Model 1898 Krag Jorgensen the Army was using at the time. The first of the new rifles was issued to the service during the winter of 1904-05 and was chambered for the Model 1903 cartridge.

This cartridge was similar to the current 1906 round, but the neck of the case was slightly longer and the bullet was heavier—a blunt-point 220-grain projectile similar to the bullet used in the old Krag cartridge. According to Major Townsend Whelen's book, *American Rifle,* "The (1903) shell was loaded with sufficient Laflin and Rand W.A. (nitroglycerine) powder to give a muzzle velocity of 2350 feet per second. It was soon found that with this powder charge, the erosion was so excessive that the barrels wore out in about 800 rounds. The powder charge was therefore reduced to produce a muzzle velocity of 2200 fps. The breech pressure was about 44,000 pounds per square inch, and the maximum range 4247 yards."

In 1905, however, the Germans developed a light, sharp-pointed bullet for their 8mm cartridge which produced an extremely high velocity of 2880 fps. As a result, trajectory was flattened, increasing the effective range.

Quoting Whelen, "Our own ordnance officers were not slow to recognize the improvement, and the Model 1903 rifle proved capable of certain small alterations to enable it to use the new ammunition. Experimental bullets were made and tried in the 1903 shell, and it was found that by slightly shortening the neck of the shell, a 150-grain bullet with a six diameter sharp point could be used. It was decided to adapt this cartridge to the new rifle. The new cartridge is called the .30-caliber, Model 1906 cartridge, so we have a Model 1903 rifle using Model 1906 ammunition. To adapt the rifle to the new ammunition it was necessary to rechamber all the rifles already manufactured, cutting the barrel off at the breech and shortening it slightly. The barrel of the original rifle was 24 inches long, and this shortening for the 1906 ammunition accounts for the present standard length of barrel being 23.79 inches long. At the beginning we had to use the old W.A. nitroglycerine powder, and the erosion was very serious. The DuPont Co., however, quickly developed a pyro-cellulose powder for the rifle. Pyro-cellulose powders burn with a much cooler gas than nitroglycerine powders and give very much less erosion. The powder has been steadily improved until today the present powder, DuPont Military Rifle Powder No. 20, is a most stable, cool-burning powder that gives an accuracy life for the barrel of from 8000 to 11,000 rounds, over 10 times the life of the bore with the old nitroglycerine powder."

According to Whelen, this latter loading with a 150-grain bullet produced about 2700 fps at the muzzle with 51,000 psi of pressure. The .30-06 has been chambered in a score of military rifles used around the world. In the U.S., besides the 1903 Springfield rifle, there were the 1917 Enfield, M-1 Garand, 1918 series Browning automatic rifle (BAR), 1917 and 1919 series and Model 37 machineguns, late Gatling guns, and the Johnson military rifle. The list is almost endless.

After its initial development as a military cartridge, the .30-06 saw service during two World Wars and Korea and was destined to become the most popular centerfire cartridge for sporting use ever in America. The lever-action Winchester Model 1895 rifle, patented by John Browning, was the first sporting rifle chambered for it in the form of the .30-03 version beginning in 1904. This rifle was subsequently chambered for the .30-06 cartridge in 1908. The Remington Model 30 (basically the 1917 Enfield action design) was chambered for the round in 1921, the Winchester Model 54 in 1925, and the Savage bolt-action rifles in 1928. Today, every major rifle manufacturer chambers it in every rifle that's suited to this cartridge size.

The .30-06 Springfield is as close to being all things to all shooters as any cartridge can be. It has held all the .30-caliber target records and has won the 1000-yard Wimbledon match many times. It has taken every species of big game in the world, even though it is not recommended for the largest game. Many hunters use only the .30-06, taking everything from varmints to the largest game on the North American continent.

With the wide range of bullet weights (from 55 to 250 grains) available in factory ammunition, the .30-06 cartridge can be matched to everything from groundhogs to brown bears. At the light-bullet end of the factory ammo spectrum, Remington's 55-grain Accelerator is the ultrahigh-velocity answer to the varmint shooter's needs. The ammo has a "plastic" sabot that encases a .22-caliber 55-grain bullet until it leaves the .30-06's bore. The result is a bullet that leaves the muzzle at more than 4000 fps.

At the heavy-bullet end of the range, Barnes Bullets loads a 250-grain roundnose softpoint in the .30-06 that many shooters consider to be the answer to large, heavy game like Alaskan moose or brown bear. Between these extremes are factory loadings for any North American big game or varmints you may hunt. Many varmint shooters prefer the 110- and 125-grain bullets, which are generally designed to expand rapidly upon impact. Bullets weighing from 150 to 180 grains are generally considered best for small- to medium-size big game, while those 200 grains and heavier are usually designed for reduced expansion and deeper penetration to reach the vitals of the largest game.

The .30-06 offers more versatility in factory ammunition than any other cartridge. I'm aware of more than 40 .30-06 loadings available to the American shooter. Besides that, every major commercial ammunition manufacturer in the world loads the .30-06, so if you run out of ammo in Germany, Sweden, Australia, or South Africa, you'll be able to purchase .30-06 ammo locally.

.30-06 SPRINGFIELD: 10 FAVORITE LOADS

HANDLOADS

Bullet	Powder (Type)	(Grs.)	Case	Primer	Velocity (fps) (10 feet)	Five-Shot Group (Inches)	Gun	Remarks
Speer 165-Gr. BT	H205	58.0	W-W	Rem. 9½	2692	1.5	23-inch TCR '83	High ballistic coefficient
Hornady 180-Gr. spirepoint	IMR-4350	54.0	R-P	CCI 200	2592	.9	22-inch Savage M111	All-around big-game load
Sierra 180-Gr. BT	IMR-4350	54.0	Frontier	CCI 200	2708	.9	26-inch Browning M78	Fast and streamlined
Speer 200-Gr. spitzer	H4831	56.0	R-P	Rem. 9½	2537	1.7	22-inch Remington M78	Elk load
Hornady 165-Gr. BT	H205	58.5	R-P	Rem. 9½	2756	1.3	22-inch Remington M78	Large-range load

FACTORY LOADS

Bullet	Powder (Type)	(Grs.)	Case	Primer	Velocity (fps) (10 feet)	Five-Shot Group (Inches)	Gun	Remarks
Remington 55-Gr. PSP Accelerator	Factory load				4176	.9	24-inch Colt Sauer	For varmints only
Federal 150-Gr. Premium SPBT	Factory load				2797	1.4	22-inch Remington M78	Fast and streamlined
Hornady 165-Gr. SPBT	Factory load				2765	1.3	22-inch Remington M78	Long-range load
Norma 180-Gr. Protected Power Cavity	Factory load				2617	1.3	23½-inch Mauser M77	Excellent expansion characteristics
Norma 200-Gr. Protected Power Cavity	Factory load				2544	1.5	23½-inch Mauser M77	Elk/moose load

NOTES: All groups were fired at 100 yards.

When a firearms manufacturer introduces a new centerfire bolt-action rifle to the market, it's usually a .30-06 – and with good reason. Nothing outsells it. The standard-size bolt action was designed around this cartridge. Rifles chambered for the shorter .308 cartridge are often built around .30-06 actions. Likewise, larger cartridges like the .300 Winchester Magnum were designed to function through the standard .30-06-length action. The boltface of the .30-06 action has influenced the rim size of many other cartridges under development. It was with surplus .30-06 actions that many wildcatters were able to experiment with cartridge design.

The .30-06 is not only available in practically every bolt-action rifle in production, it is offered in the pump action in the Remington rifles; the single-shot Thompson/Center, Ruger, and Browning rifles; and the semiauto Remington and Browning rifles. It was introduced in a lever action, the Model 95, but instead of carrying the Winchester label, it sold under the Browning name (Model 1895). However, the design is the same as the original patented by John M. Browning.

The .30-06 is a versatile cartridge. To take advantage of this versatility, the shooter must select the proper bullet for the task at hand. With the exception of the sabot-housed 55-grain Accelerator round, the handloader has an even wider selection of bullets available than does the shooter of factory ammunition, with 60 different bullet shapes, weights, and constructions for the .30-06.

Selecting the proper bullet for the task is partially related to bullet weight. The lightest bullets generally available to the handloader are the Hornady 100-grain Short Jackets and Speer Plinkers. These are ideal choices for reduced-velocity loadings that might be used for low-recoil practice or even small-game hunting. Loading 14.0 grains of DuPont's 700-X behind either of these bullets often produces good accuracy, low noise, and low recoil. Velocity is 1976 fps from one of my 22-inch barrels.

The varmint hunter/handloader has bullets weighing from 110 to 130 grains that generally offer extremely rapid expansion at top .30-06 velocities. I've taken many prairie dogs, crows, coyotes, and jackrabbits with bullets in this weight range and can attest to their rapid expansion qualities. With Sierra 110-grain spitzers, I've had good results with 54.0 grains of IMR-4320 or 53.0 grains H4895 for about 3100 fps. Behind the Sierra 125-grain bullets, I've used 52.0 grains of H4895 that produced nearly 3000 fps.

The hunter after the smaller species of big game (under 400 pounds) cannot go wrong with the 150- or 165-grain bullets. It has often been said that the 165-grainer is the ideal weight, ballistically, for this cartridge. A sleek 165-grain boattail bullet fired at top velocity with perhaps 50.0 grains of IMR-4064 does produce a flat trajectory for a hunting bullet, and bullets in the aforementioned weights have worked very well for me on antelope and deer-size game.

I've hunted quite a lot in Colorado, where both deer and elk are hunted simultaneously. In this instance, the 180-grain bullet is my first selection. I've taken deer and elk with the Hornady 180-grain spirepoint ahead of 54.0 grains of IMR-4350. Using the Remington case and a CCI BR-2 primer, the combination has produced superb accuracy in several rifles. If I were to select a 180-grain bullet specifically for elk where deep penetration was wanted, I would opt for the Nosler 180-grain Partition.

Bullets in the 200-, 220-, and 250-grain weight range get the nod for the largest game in North America. The Barnes 250-grainer or the Nosler 200-grain Partition are top choices for deep penetration on large, tough game. A slow-burning powder like H4831 produces top velocities with these heavy bullets.

One of my first centerfire rifles was a .30-06. I bought an Eddystone Enfield along with 200 rounds of military ammunition for about $25. I shot all the military ammo and then bought a Lyman tong tool with .30-06 dies. I found it necessary to use a special primer punch to eject the crimped-in primers. I then purchased a primer pocket reamer to eliminate the crimp. I was ready to reload. My first reloads included Winchester No. 120 primers, IMR-4320 powder, and Winchester 110-grain softpoint bullets, which are no longer available for handloading. With those components and the military sights, I could hold eight-inch groups at 200 yards. The Enfield barrel was 26 inches long and had two grooves. I later used this rifle to down my first black bear, using a Sierra 150-grain spitzer backed by 51.0 grains of IMR-4064. It only took one shot.

A few years ago, I purchased a Remington Model 700 .30-06 for my nephew. He planned a black bear hunt in Washington State with a friend who had no rifle. My nephew shot a bear with the rifle; then he loaned it to his friend, who shot a black bear and a mountain lion on the same trip. His friend then headed to Canada and Alaska with the rifle. He took a goat, sheep, moose, and caribou. All were one-shot kills, and the ammunition used ranged from 165-grain handloads to factory ammunition. That's a *versatile* performer.

TOP FIVE RIFLES

Make/Model	Barrel (Inches)	Sights	Weight (Pounds)	Finish	Rifling (Twist)
Remington M78	22	Bushnell 4X	7 pounds, 4 ounces	Satin	1:10
Ruger M77	22	Burris 4X	7 pounds	Satin	1:10
Winchester M70	24	Leupold 2-7X	7 pounds, 12 ounces	Satin	1:10
Mossberg M1500	22	Redfield 2-7X	7 pounds, 10 ounces	Satin	1:10
Browning A-Bolt	22	Zeiss 4X	6 pounds, 11 ounces	Satin	1:10

In 1985, I shot three big-game animals with the .30-06. The first was a South African nyala taken with a Thompson/Center single shot with iron sights. The ammunition was the Federal 165-grain softpoint boat-tail. One shot put the animal down cleanly. I also took two moose in Sweden with the Norma 180-grain Plastic Point Dual Core ammunition. Norma's 180-grain PPC loading is tough to beat in a factory load, either for accuracy or expansion on game. Another of my top choices in factory ammunition is the Federal 180-grain Premium loaded with the Nosler 180-grain Partition bullet. You won't be disappointed with these factory selections for practically any big game, medium or large.

The .30-06. There is no better all-around choice for hunting big game in North America. The .30-06 is the most versatile cartridge ever. It has performed admirably under every conceivable hunting condition, and after more than 80 years of hard use, it's still the most popular center-fire. What more can you say?

The .300 Winchester Magnum

T HE .300 WINCHESTER Magnum is new as .30-caliber cartridges go, but since its introduction in 1963, it has become one of our more popular big-game numbers. The .300 marks the end of a line of four belted magnum numbers introduced by Winchester. The first was the .458 Winchester Magnum, introduced during 1956, followed by the .338 Winchester Magnum in 1958 and the .264 in 1959.

Though the .300 Winchester has the same belt and rim diameter as the other cartridges in the Winchester family, the similarity ends there. While the other three cases in the line are 2.5 inches long, the .300 is 2.620 inches long. The .264 and .338 have a base-to-shoulder length of 2.040 inches; the .300's is 2.180 inches. As a result, it has considerably more capacity than either the .264 or .338.

When the standard-action .338 case was introduced, wildcat shooters immediately took forming dies in hand. There is an obvious advantage in a cartridge that shoots the popular .308-diameter bullet in a standard-length action from a case with considerably more capacity than the old '06. By necking the .338 case down to accept .308 bullets, wildcatters had a fast, flat-shooting .30-caliber cartridge that could be used in standard .30-06-length actions. The .30-338 continues to enjoy mild success as a wildcat cartridge.

Before the .300 Winchester Magnum was announced, and due to the success of the .30-338, rumor had it that Winchester would introduce a .30-caliber magnum based on the .338 case. Then, in 1961, Norma beat Winchester to the punch by offering a necked-down version of a case which it formerly sold as a straight-walled basic case. The new cartridge was called the ".308 Norma Magnum." Winchester surprised everyone in 1963 with an entirely new case design with more capacity and performance potential than either the .30-338 or the .308 Norma Magnum. It still had the primary advantage of fitting a standard-length action.

The idea of a .30-caliber belted magnum goes all the way back to 1920, when the British firm of Holland & Holland introduced the .300 H&H Magnum. Even Weatherby had its .300 Magnum by 1948. The problem with these older belted magnums is that they require a rifle with a longer-than-standard action. The .30-338, .308 Norma, and large-capacity .300 Winchester changed all that. For example, the big .300 Winchester, with an overall maximum cartridge length of 3.34 inches, is exactly the same as the .30-06, yet the .300 Winchester betters the performance of the old .300 H&H and is hot on the heels of the .300 Weatherby. A good load with the 180-grain bullet in the .30-06 produces 2700 fps. In the .300 Winchester, it's 3000 fps, and in the .300 Weatherby it's about 75 fps more, given equal barrel length.

I acquired my first .300 Winchester Magnum rifle during the summer of 1966. It was nothing fancy, just a rechambered and restocked bolt-action Springfield. Fact is, it was downright ugly. With the rifle, I purchased a box of ammo, loading dies, and about 100 cases. I loaded some ammo with Sierra 180-grain bullets and H4831, which I purchased in bulk back then, and headed to the range with my "new" rifle.

The first three bullet holes punched by the factory ammo touched. I then fired several groups with handloads, increasing the powder charge a grain for each group. The heavier the charge, the tighter the groups became. When I reached my top load, the cluster measured less than an inch.

A few weeks later, I shot a large black bear, followed by a four-point mule deer, and then a six-point elk – all with the same Sierra 180-grain handloads. I was impressed by the performance of the new cartridge, and my confidence in the rifle/cartridge combination soared. Consequently, I used the ugly .300 a lot. I've taken more than 30 head of big game with the .300 Winchester Magnum, including more than 20 deer, 10 elk, three bears, one antelope, and one sheep. I've also taken countless jackrabbits and coyotes. It continues to have my respect as a first-rate cartridge for North American game. Given a choice of using only one cartridge for big game, I would unhesitatingly choose the .300 Winchester.

The .300 Winchester Magnum has it all. The .30-06 may be revered as the cartridge that's suitable for everything and can do no wrong, but the fact is that the .300 Winchester Magnum has everything the .30-06 has and a whole lot more. As mentioned earlier, the .300 Winchester is used in the same action size as the .30-06, yet the .300 has much greater powder capacity, which results in a higher velocity. While 2700 fps is normal velocity for a popular 180-grain bullet in a .30-06, the .300 Winchester Magnum easily pushes it over 3000 fps with standard-length barrels.

.300 WINCHESTER MAGNUM: 10 FAVORITE LOADS

HANDLOADS

Bullet	Powder (Type)	(Grs.)	Case	Primer	Velocity (fps) (10 Feet)	Five-Shot Group (Inches)	Gun	Remarks
Nosler 180-Gr. Ballistic Tip	H4831	75.0	Win.	Fed. 215	3138	.9	25½-inch KDF K-15	Explosive expansion
Hornady 180-Gr. spirepoint	MR-3100	73.0	Win.	Fed. 215	3009	.8	25½-inch KDF K-15	Accurate
Sierra 150-Gr. spitzer	IMR-4350	75.0	Win.	CCI 250	3216	1.2	24-inch S&W M1500	Antelope load
Speer 200-Gr. spitzer	H4831	72.0	Win.	CCI 250	2831	1.6	24-inch S&W M1500	Elk load
Nosler 200-Gr. Partition	IMR-4831	70.0	R-P	Fed. 215	2866	1.6	24-inch S&W M1500	Deep penetration

FACTORY LOADS

Bullet	Powder (Type)	(Grs.)	Case	Primer	Velocity (fps) (10 Feet)	Five-Shot Group (Inches)	Gun	Remarks
Remington 150-Gr. C-L PSP			Factory load		3258	1.2	25½-inch KDF K-15	High velocity
Remington 180-Gr. C-L PSP			Factory load		3042	1.3	25½-inch KDF K-15	All-around load for N. American big game
Federal 150-Gr. SP			Factory load		3215	1.9	24-inch Winchester M70	Fast
Winchester 180-Gr. Power Point			Factory load		2924	2.2	24-inch Winchester M70	All-around load for elk/deer
Federal 180-Gr. SP			Factory load		2940	1.9	24-inch S&W M1500	All-around load for deer/elk

The advantages in higher velocities are obvious. A flatter trajectory means that precise range estimation is not as critical. Higher velocity means that the wind drifts the projectile less. It also means more impact energy and more reliable bullet expansion—which means more killing power.

The .300 Winchester Magnum does it by burning more powder,

but the expense of the additional powder is of no consequence in a big-game cartridge.

The belted cartridge also turns up more recoil than the .30-06, about a third more with a heavy-loaded 180-grain bullet. But most shooters probably couldn't tell the difference between the recoil of a .300 Winchester Magnum and a .30-06 if they did not see the size of the cartridge. (A difference certainly wouldn't be noticeable if a trophy six-point elk were in the scope. And if the range were long, it would be comforting to have the added power and flatter trajectory of the .300 Winchester.) If the thought of 10 more ft-lbs of kick psyches you out, the .300 Winchester can be handloaded to produce .30-06 velocity and recoil. However, most shooters appreciate and use the improved performance of the larger case.

Another alternative for reducing recoil is the installation of a muzzle brake on your rifle. I have a KDF muzzle brake on one of my .300 Winchester Magnum rifles, and it makes the kick feel like a .243.

The .300 Winchester Magnum gains performance from the standard-length action, not only by virtue of a fatter case, but with a shoulder that is farther forward. This results in a shorter case neck, a feature that has been maligned by some, though I can't understand why. The neck is more than long enough to secure the bullet, and what else should a neck do?

Some shooters think that the short case neck means decreased powder capacity since the bullet must be seated deeply into the case neck. In fact, the length of the neck has nothing whatever to do with bulletseating depth. The length of the action, magazine, and the throating of the chamber dictate bulletseating depth, and these have nothing to do with the cartridge. Case neck length is reduced from the rear to increase the capacity of the case, not reduce it. Even after a Nosler 180-grain bullet is seated to the maximum overall length in both the .30-06 and .300 Winchester Magnum (taking into account water displacement by the bullet), my .30-06 cases have 62.8 grains of water capacity and the .300 Winchester Magnums have 82.4.

The .300 Winchester Magnum is also easy to handload, and it isn't the least bit finicky about its diet. I've found that a single load using the 180-grain bullet works fine for practically anything you may wish to hunt on this continent. This bullet weight is quite efficient and well-balanced for the case. I've taken game with 180-grain handloads using bullets from Nosler, Hornady, Sierra, and Speer. The Nosler Partition bullet offers unparalleled penetration and minimal tissue destruction; the more conventional bullet designs offer greater tissue destruction and sometimes quicker kills on lung-shot game. The best choice depends on the performance sought. If you want a really long-range load, the .300 Winchester Magnum will propel a sleek 165-grain boattail at better than 3100 fps or a 150-grain bullet at 3200.

A few years ago, I chose the .300 Winchester Magnum for a trophy antelope hunt. The rifle was custom-built by H-S Precision in Prescott, Arizona. It weighed only 7.5 pounds and had a 24-inch stainless Atkinson barrel and a Fiberthane stock. It shot very well. I fitted the forward sling swivel stud with a Harris bipod so I could better use its accuracy in antelope country, where there are few rocks or limbs to use for a rest.

Some might question the use of the .300 Winchester Magnum on game as small as antelope, but after taking many head of this size game, I don't hesitate to use the .300 Winchester. The load I use—74.0 grains of IMR-4350 behind the Hornady 165-grain boattail (a load that's maximum, so don't use it without starting low)—turns up 3186 fps in a 24-inch barrel. The Hornady bullet has a ballistic coefficient of .459, which means that with my rifle sighted-in 2¾ inches high at 100 yards, the bullet is right on the money at 280 yards and only 11 inches low clear out at 400 yards. That's not bad for a cartridge that's "too large."

Tissue destruction is a function of bullet performance, and bullet performance is affected by impact velocity. Those who say that magnums are too destructive of tissue forget that the impact velocity of a magnum is no greater than some lesser cartridge's at a shorter distance. For example, the impact velocity of my .300 Winchester Magnum load at 300 yards is the same as that from a comparatively loaded .30-06 at 150 yards with the same bullet. As long as a proper bullet is used for the task, the .300 Winchester Magnum is no more destructive to tissue than a favorite .30-06 load. (I have never understood how the .300 Winchester can be considered too large when many hunters use cartridges like the .308 or .30-06 on antelope.)

If you're after varmints, imagine the explosiveness of a 125-grain spitzer at nearly 3500 fps muzzle velocity or a 110-grainer at 3600. There's nothing that tunes up the big-game shooting eye and reflexes like running jackrabbit shooting. I've used the Sierra 125-grain spitzer to dispatch a lot of jackrabbits.

For really heavy big game, where deep penetration is a primary consideration, I can think of nothing better than the Nosler 200-grain Partition, which can speed from the muzzle at nearly 2900 fps. That calculates to 3735 ft-lbs of muzzle energy. This heavy bullet is also a sleek one that retains velocity well. Its ballistic coefficient is listed at .584, which means that the same load reaches the 300-yard mark with 2614 ft-lbs of energy. The round has plenty of punch for adequate bullet expansion and penetration for the largest game on the continent—clear out as far as you're likely to shoot. This can't be said of many cartridges.

I remember hunting elk in Colorado several years ago on a cold November day. I followed the tracks of a large elk for several miles and then came upon a small band of mule deer. The deer descended into a canyon, and I watched as they started to climb the opposite slope. They jumped a trophy elk that had been bedded on a rocky outcrop far across the canyon. It's difficult to judge distance across a canyon, and I thought the elk was more than 350 yards away—but I wasn't sure. He started to move out of the canyon. There was no time to get closer.

It was comforting to be shooting a .300 Winchester Magnum that I knew had the punch to bring down the bull even if the distance were 500 yards. I held just over the back of the bull, and the sound of the shot echoed across the snow-covered canyon. It was a solid hit, and the elk dropped. Had I been carrying a .308 or .30-06, I probably wouldn't have had the confidence to attempt such a shot.

The best powders for the .300 Winchester Magnum, particularly with big-game bullets, are the slower burning numbers. Since the obsolescence of W785 and H450, I had been using only three powders in the .300 Winchester: 4831, 4350, and MR-3100. Since the advent of IMR-7828, there has been another selection that should be ideal in the case, particularly with 200- or 220-grain bullets. Using DuPont-recommended charges, I received 2822 fps with 74.0 grains behind Hornady's 180-grain spirepoint bullet. Loading 71.0 grains behind Speer's 200-grain spitzer produced 2663 fps for an average. The cases were Winchester, and the primers were Remington No. 9½M. These velocities and loads in no way indicate the potential of IMR-7828; they just reveal the velocities I received at those load levels with my lot of propellant.

TOP FIVE RIFLES

Make/Model	Barrel (Inches)	Sights	Weight (Pounds)	Finish	Rifling (Twist)
Remington M700	24	Leupold 3-9X	7 pounds, 12 ounces	Satin	1:10
Winchester M70	24	Bausch & Lomb 3-9X	7 pounds, 12 ounces	Satin	1:10
KDF K-15	25½	Zeiss 3-9X	7 pounds, 10 ounces	Gloss	1:10
Ruger M77	24	Zeiss 4X	7 pounds	Satin	1:10
Browning A-Bolt	24	Bausch & Lomb 4X	7 pounds, 3 ounces	Satin	1:10

Regarding 4831 and 4350, both numbers are offered by DuPont and Hodgdon. However, do not consider these to be identical. You cannot interchange data—particularly with 4831. In my experience, a maximum powder weight charge with H4831 could very probably be over maximum with IMR-4831. All of these powders—H4831, IMR-4831, H4350, IMR-4350, and MR-3100—are in the same slow-burning powder category and are ideally suited to the .300 Winchester, but handloaders should treat each one as an individual.

The .300 Winchester Magnum surpasses our most popular big-game cartridges. If you can judge the cartridge's performance in the field without bias, it could become one of your favorites.

The .444 Marlin

A FEW YEARS AGO, a friend and I went deer hunting in central Pennsylvania. Though I had never hunted in the area, he lived there and knew the region well. Our preseason scouting trips had indicated plenty of deer were around, but all the vehicles we passed along the road indicated there were going to be plenty of hunters as well.

I was carrying a .243, and my friend had a Marlin lever action with a half magazine. We were making our way up the side of a mountain and hadn't gone more than 200 yards when I heard a stick break above me and saw a whitetail buck running to my right. My friend's rifle roared, and the running buck tumbled end over end and slid down the mountainside for a few yards.

I whooped out loud at the sight of such an impressive shot, and we hurried toward the still buck. "Great shot! What did you hit him with?"

"A .444 Marlin."

"He sure wasn't going anywhere after that."

"That's why I use it," he explained. "I don't like following wounded game, and I don't want another hunter getting a shot at my deer."

The buck had been shot in the neck, explaining the instant effect of the hit, but a gaping exit wound ensured a blood trail that couldn't have been overlooked.

What my friend said was really hammered home when I later shot a running whitetail with my .243. Though the buck faltered, he continued on, and in just a few yards, he was perforated by multiple shots from several Ohio hunters. There was no telling where my first shot had hit, and there was no blood trail leading from where I'd hit the deer. (There often isn't with a small caliber like the .243.) I decided then that a large caliber, one shooting a bullet which exits, has a decided advantage in heavily hunted deer woods.

The .444 is Marlin's only proprietary cartridge. At one time, the firm had at least three other cartridges which carried its name: the .25-36 Marlin, the .40-60 Marlin, and the .45-85 Marlin. These cartridges were introduced before the turn of the century and have long since gone out of production.

When the .444 was introduced in 1964, the .45-70 Marlin and .356 Winchester lever-action rifles did not exist. Winchester had dropped its lever action chambered for the .348 in 1958, and Marlin saw a need for a big-bore round.

Early .444 Marlin rifles were fitted with 24-inch barrels (on the long side for a rifle to be used in close-cover situations). Current .444s carry nominal 22-inch barrels. A tape measure indicates 21⅞ inches on my rifle.

The .444 is designed to use the same bullet diameter as the .44 Magnum handgun cartridge. Its case is about an inch longer than a .44 Magnum and has a semirim. According to the *Speer Reloading Manual Number Ten*, both cartridges are loaded to similar pressures: a maximum 44,000 cup for the .444 Marlin and 43,500 for the .44 Magnum.

While Marlin is the only large manufacturer that currently chambers the round, Remington is the only producer of ammunition. The factory cartridges are offered with 240- and 265-grain softpoint bullets. The latter weight was specifically developed by Hornady for the .444 Marlin cartridge. I have heard rumors that the 240-grain weight is a handgun bullet and won't hold together on game. The reasoning is that handgun bullets simply won't withstand an additional 500 fps in velocity that the larger cartridge produces—when both are fired in rifle- or carbine-length barrels. It was for this reason (plus the fact that I would be hunting a larger species of game) that I ruled out bullets designed for handguns when I set out to find a .444 Marlin load for elk hunting. The Speer manual makes the following statement: "Heavier bullets (than 240 grains) would make the .444 a more useful big-game caliber."

Two firms make heavier hunting bullets designed specifically for the .444 Marlin cartridge: Hornady and Barnes. Hornady makes a single 265-grain bullet, while Barnes has 250-, 275-, and 300-grainers. I used these bullets, six powders, and four primers in my search for a good elk hunting load for the .444 Marlin.

My plan was to hunt in western Colorado. I would hunt for a trophy mule deer with a .30-06 and then go after elk with the .444 Marlin later in the season. After several days of heavy hunting pressure, elk in this region generally leave the more open mountain meadows and aspen groves to hole up in clusters of thick spruce or other dense cover. Nearly all shots are at close range, 20 or 30 yards being typical, and the .444 Marlin is ideal.

With a supply of bullets on hand, I turned to loading manuals for data on the .444 Marlin. With one exception, there is a scarcity of data on this cartridge with bullets heavier than 240 grains. The third edition of the *Hornady Handbook of Cartridge Reloading* lists a half-dozen loads, with as many different powders, for its 265-grain flatpoint.

It's typical of most loading manuals to ignore the heavier bullets offered by Barnes, but one exception is the excellent *Hodgdon Data Manual No. 25.* This manual has load data for .444 Marlin bullets ranging from 225 to 300 grains.

Another good feature of the Hodgdon manual is that data is included for all popular powders, not just Hodgdon's. It wasn't difficult, with data for 265- and 300-grain bullets and a bit of interpolation and extrapolation, to determine approximate 275-grain bullet loads.

With a load program charted, I opened a new box of Hornady dies. Since the .444 is an almost-straight case, three dies come in a set. The .444 uses the same shellholder as the .44 Special, .44 Magnum, and .45 Colt; all have a nominal .512- or .514-inch rim diameter.

Before assembling loads, I sized, chamfered, and belled case mouths on unprimed Remington brass. When I began seating bullets, I found the cannelures on all bullets are positioned to allow maximum overall cartridge length for the Marlin action. With some of the loads I used, a maximum charge was determined by the amount the case would hold. For example, 53.0 grains of H322 (behind the Hornady 265-grainer) was all I could get into the case and still seat the bullet to the cannelure. Hodgdon lists 54.0 grains as maximum, probably for the same reason. At any rate, a cannelure is a good thing to use on a cartridge of this type. Unless each case mouth is locked into this bullet groove, magazine spring tension and recoil can loosen bullets from cases. I loaded two different powders with each bullet and included the two Remington factory loads in the series.

My chronograph was soon indicating the most potent elk hunting recipes, and the 100-yard target revealed the sizes of the five-shot groups. I chronographed all loads at 10 feet with an Oehler Model 33 Chronotach and then computed muzzle velocity using the "Load From A Disk" computer program. It wasn't accuracy that pointed to the best load – it was performance.

Fifty-six grains of H335 behind the Barnes 300-grainer produced 2164 fps. The only loads I tried that shot faster had 240- and 250-grain bullets, and they were only slightly faster. That 300-grain bullet's muzzle energy is a whopping 3120 ft-lbs. As long as the bullet performed properly when it hit, I figured it should have plenty of potency.

The next step was to see how all the bullets expanded. I decided to fire the loads that produced the highest velocity for each bullet weight into a wet newsprint expansion medium at 20 yards. The reason I chose this distance was that I was expecting shots at close range. Also, if a bullet is going to break up, it's more likely to break up at a short distance when impact velocity is highest.

I have learned from experience that ideal bullet performance can generally be determined by firing at short range. The bullet should not come apart, yet a conventional jacketed bullet should mushroom until almost no shank remains. The bullet should turn almost inside out. With this sort of expansion, the shooter can generally be certain some bullet expansion will result at the longer ranges. A conventional bullet fired at a velocity which leaves a lot of its shank unmushroomed at close range may not expand at all when the range is long and the velocity is down.

.444 MARLIN DATA
Marlin Model 444SS, 21¼-inch barrel
Leupold 3-9X Compact scope, Weaver mounts

Bullet	Powder (Type)	(Grs.)	Primer	Case	Muzzle Velocity (fps)	Average Group Size (Inches)	Recoil Energy* (ft-lbs)	Muzzle Energy (ft-lbs)
Barnes 250-gr. FNSP (.214 BC)	IMR-4227	40.5	Rem. 9½	R-P	2255	1.9	18.94	2823
Barnes 250-gr. FNSP (.214 BC)	H4198	46.0	Win. LR	R-P	2063	3.2	16.80	2363
Hornady 265-gr. FP (.191 BC)	IMR-3031	52.0	CCI 200	R-P	2019	2.1	18.65	2399
Hornady 265-gr. FP (.191 BC)	H322	53.0	Fed. 210	R-P	2145	2.5	21.26	2708
Barnes 275-gr. FNSP (.239 BC)	H4198	44.0	CCI 200	R-P	1907	3.2	16.30	2221
Barnes 275-gr. FNSP (.239 BC)	RL-7	44.0	Rem. 9½	R-P	2009	2.9	18.11	2465
Barnes 300-gr. FNSP (.258 BC)	H4198	39.0	Fed. 210	R-P	1850	3.7	16.80	2280
Barnes 300-gr. FNSP (.258 BC)	H335	56.0	Win. LR	R-P	2164	2.3	26.86	3120
Remington 240-gr. SP (.146 BC)	Factory load				2227	3.2	18.26	2643
Remington 265-gr. SP (.193 BC)	Factory load				1960	4.3	15.86	2261

NOTES: *Recoil energy is based on the Marlin's eight-pound, 10-ounce rifle/scope combination. Velocity is an average of 10 shots clocked at 10 feet from the muzzle with an Oehler Model 33 Chronotach, then corrected to muzzle velocity. Computed downrange figures are based on manufacturers' published ballistic coefficients. Group size is an average of three five-shot strings fired from a benchrest at 100 yards.

I've also learned that bullet expansion is essential to dropping an animal quickly if it's shot in soft body parts. An animal shot at long range with a bullet that does not expand may give no sign of being hit.

All the bullets I tried expanded very well, including the lightweight 240-grain factory load. As far as I'm concerned, its performance destroys the myth that the 240-grain bullet comes apart—at least in the factory ammunition. In fact, this bullet had the highest percentage of weight retention—98 percent—of any bullet fired. When recovered, it also had the largest frontal diameter, at .77 inch, while penetrating 9.6 inches of the expansion medium. None of these lightweight factory bullets showed any tendency to come apart at the 20-yard firing range. It could be that Remington loads a special bullet, unlike most pistol bullets, in this weight. I didn't try handloading conventional revolver bullets. Doing so would reveal whether those bullets are up to the .444's higher velocity.

When I returned from the range, I pulled bullets from both factory loads. I wasn't surprised at the 265-grain bullet's appearance. Rumor has it that Remington loads Hornady bullets for this one, and they do look the same. This heavyweight factory load held 41.9 grains of an extruded propellant.

The stopper in the mouth of the lightweight loading is an unusual-looking bullet because it has two cannelures. A factory may sometimes apply two cannelures if a bullet is used in different cartridges with different seating depths required. However, I can think of no such application for this bullet. Another possible reason for two cannelures is for bullet identification. Could it be that this 240-grain bullet is specially designed for the .444 instead of being just another pistol bullet? In any event, it performs like it was made for the cartridge. Unlike the powder in the heavy load, the 240-grain loading was stuffed with 45.7 grains of a ball or spherical propellant.

As I mentioned earlier, accuracy was not the limiting factor for load selection regarding its intended purpose. The chosen 300-grain recipe averaged 2.3-inch groups from the Marlin rifle. The bullet that fired the best group average was the Barnes 250-grainer ahead of 40.5 grains of IMR-4227. This load averaged 1.9 inches. At 2255 fps muzzle velocity, it was also the fastest.

.444 MARLIN BULLET PERFORMANCE COMPARISON CHART

Bullet	Powder (Type)	(Grs.)	Primer	Impact Velocity (fps)	Depth of Penetration (Inches)	Retained Weight (Grs.)	Percentage of Retained Weight	Expanded Diameter (Inches)
Remington 240-gr. SP	Factory load			2112	9.6	234.8	98	.77
Barnes 250-gr. FNSP	IMR-4227	40.5	Rem. 9½	2174	9.6	197.0	79	.67
Remington 265-gr. SP	Factory load			1878	11.2	253.5	96	.74
Hornady 265-gr. FP	H322	53.0	Fed. 210	2058	10.8	256.7	97	.75
Barnes 275-gr. FNSP	RL-7	44.0	Rem. 9½	1941	12.2	261.9	95	.73
Barnes 300-gr. FNSP	H335	56.0	Win. LR	2097	11.5	269.5	90	.65

NOTES: Bullet performance is based on an average of three shots fired into a wet newsprint expansion medium at 20 yards. Impact velocity is computed with "Load From A Disk" computer program, based on chronographed velocity and manufacturers' published ballistic coefficients.

With a knowledge of the chosen 300-grain load's velocity, I was able to compute its downrange performance possibilities. Bluntnosed bullets, like those loaded for the .444's tubular magazine, have poor ballistic coefficients and don't retain their velocity and energy well. Along with decreased velocity and energy come increased drop and wind drift. I wanted to know what to expect of the chosen load just in case I had the opportunity for a shot longer than expected.

Drop from line of bore is 18.2 inches at 200 yards. If the rifle is zeroed at 200 yards, the bullet strikes 4.3 inches high at 100 yards, 3.6 inches high at 150, 3.0 inches low at 225, and 7.0 inches low at 250 yards. Its maximum height of trajectory is 4.3 inches above line of sight (from 100 to 125 yards). Even at 250 yards, the bullet is still packing 1495 fps of velocity and 1489 ft-lbs of energy. As such, the cartridge is a solid 200-yard elk cartridge and can be used up to 250. I decided I would try to get within 200 yards of an elk. If I misjudged the range and it turned out to be just a little farther, I would still be okay.

As luck would have it, I encountered a herd of elk when I was hunting deer, and I wasn't about to pass up a five-point bull just because I didn't have the right rifle. I shot it with a .30-06. I haven't yet taken an elk with the .444.

It was still a lot of fun to develop the load, and I have a lot of confidence in this cartridge for elk- and bear-size game at woods hunting ranges. If I wanted to put a deer down with decisiveness, I would opt for either the 240-grain factory load or the Barnes 250-grainer. These bullets in the .444 Marlin will get the job done.

...And Other Rifle Favorites

A LOT OF really good cartridges have been around at least as long as most of us. Many of them lost popularity for a time—due primarily to the influence of advertising literature touting newer "numbers." Some of the old cartridges were thought to be dead until a resurgence of interest in them and classic-lined rifles in recent years resurrected old followings and tastes. Here are a few of my favorites and my experiences with them.

* * *

The .22 Hornet originated in the 19th century in the form of the .22 Winchester Center Fire (WCF) cartridge, a blackpowder lead-bullet round. The .22 Hornet was a modification of this cartridge; Capt. G.L. Wotkyns, Col. Townsend Whelen, and others at the Springfield Armory are generally credited with the development of the .22 Hornet in the late 1920s.

The .22 Hornet gave rise to Hercules 2400 propellant when Col. Whelen and his cohorts turned to Hercules for a better smokeless powder. (The powder got its name from the velocity it produced with 45-grain bullets in the Hornet.)

Winchester got in the act and in 1930 began producing ammunition for the .22 Hornet. In 1932, Savage introduced the bolt-action Model 23 rifle for the Hornet, and Winchester followed in 1933 with the Model 54 bolt action.

The .22 Hornet was the first standard U.S. factory cartridge intended expressly for varmint hunting. It also marked the beginning of a long line of high-velocity small-bore centerfire cartridges. Early .22 Hornet rifles had barrels made for .223-inch bullets, but after World War II, Hornet rifles were made for the now-standard .224-inch bullets.

The Hornet was a popular cartridge until after World War II, when other high-velocity centerfire rounds began overshadowing the tiny rimmed case. For a time, the .22 Hornet cartridge appeared to be on the way out. Several years ago, however, the Ruger No. 3 rifle was offered in .22 Hornet, and Thompson/Center began chambering its single-shot Contender for the cartridge. (Most .22 Hornet rifles, American and European, carry a 1:16 twist; the Contender barrel has a 1:14 twist.)

Popular in Europe, the .22 Hornet carries a metric designation of 5.6x35R. For shooters who aren't familiar with this almost-forgotten round, it's a limited-capacity rimmed case with a very long, tapering shoulder. While its velocities aren't high by today's standards, the Hornet has always had an excellent reputation for being mild in terms of bore wear, noise, and recoil. The .22 Hornet offers the rifleman a cartridge turning up velocities somewhat better than the .22 Winchester Magnum and carries the bonus of versatility with the economy of being reloadable.

Whether your rifle barrel is cut for .223- or .224-inch diameter bullets, both are readily available. I've found that it's best to stay with the lighter bullets for the Hornet (in the 40- to 45-grain range). Heavier bullets sometimes give disappointing accuracy with the too-slow twist of most Hornet rifles. In addition, expansion might be a sometimes thing for hunting purposes at Hornet velocities.

The powders to try in your Hornet are H110, 2400, IMR-4227, W680, W296, and IMR-4198. I've had good luck with 11.5 grains of IMR-4227 behind the Speer 40-grain spirepoint. Velocity runs 2850 fps in my Anschutz Model 1432, and accuracy is better than any other load I've used in that rifle. The same powder charge behind the Nosler 45-grainer also produces excellent accuracy and 2695 fps. A 9.5-grain charge of H110 behind the Speer 40-grainer is another recipe that has done well for me accuracy-wise. It turns up 2634 fps in my Anschutz.

Since the Hornet produces relatively little noise, and since its range is more limited than other .22 centerfires, it's a good choice for varminting in more populated areas.

Possibly one of the things that has limited the popularity of the Hornet is the fact that it requires a very specialized action to handle it because it is such a small, rimmed cartridge.

* * *

The .220 Swift was introduced by Winchester in 1935. It is based on the 6mm Lee Navy case necked down to .22 caliber with a sharper shoulder and less body taper. This was the *first* factory cartridge to exceed 4000 fps in muzzle velocity. While the Swift has the reputation for being a 4000 fps round, in my experience it should only be considered in this category with bullets of 45 grains and lighter. And with a 45-grain bullet, 4000 fps is pushing it. With 55-grain bullets popular in the .22-250, the Swift's advantage is not great.

The Swift has gotten a lot of bad press for being hard on barrels. In my experience, it is no harder on barrels than its performance warrants. I suspect that some of the bad press originated when barrel steels were milder than they are today.

The Swift is also said to produce erratic pressures and be prone to stretch and thicken case necks, but the Swift is no worse in these characteristics than any other cartridge in this bullet diameter and performance level.

In recent years, the Swift has been overshadowed by the popular .22-250. The feature the .22-250 has going for it that the Swift doesn't is case design. The semirim of the Swift case necessitates a specially designed magazine box to assure smooth feeding while the .22-250 functions in a conventional action with a boltface of a conventional size. The Swift has been revived in recent years by the introduction of the Ruger chamberings for this excellent round.

The Swift is a fine cartridge for larger predators like coyotes. In this type of predator hunting, you don't generally fire as many rounds as is done with other types of varminting, and barrel wear is not particularly critical.

Favorite powders for the Swift today are IMR-3031 and IMR-4064. (Far and away the best propellant for the Swift was H450, but this propellant has been discontinued.) If you're looking for accuracy, try 34.0 grains of IMR-3031 behind a Speer 52-grain hollowpoint. Velocity runs only 3595 fps in my Ruger Model 77, but it shoots like a house afire.

For high velocity with a 50-grain bullet, try 40.0 grains of IMR-4064. That load is maximum in my rifle, and it turns up just a tad over 4000 fps. That's about the highest velocity you'll get with that bullet weight in that cartridge with a 26-inch barrel. But beware that 40-grain powder charge because it will be *over* the maximum in some rifles. Loading 38.0 grains of IMR-3031 with the same bullet weight will do almost as well in velocity. Again, those are hot loads in some guns, so don't use them without starting low and working up to maximum.

If you want barrel life, hold down your velocities. With 3031, the Swift seems to produce excellent accuracy, even at the milder charge levels.

* * *

In the mid-1920s, famed experimenter and gun writer N.H. (Ned) Roberts developed a new .25-caliber cartridge by necking down the 7x57 Mauser case. It was appropriately called the ".25 Roberts" at the time, and the first rifles in this caliber were made about 1928 by the Niedner Rifle Co. Later, Griffin & Howe in New York also made custom rifles for the new cartridge.

It wasn't until 1934, when Remington commercialized the cartridge by introducing a slightly altered version of the original ".25 Roberts" case, that it became a household name among riflemen. What Remington did was move the shoulder of the case slightly forward and change the shoulder angle from 15 to 20 degrees in order to facilitate factory production. The round was called the ".257 Roberts" to avoid confusion with other .25-caliber cartridges like the .25 Remington.

Remington chambered the new .257 Roberts in its Model 30S bolt-action rifle. One source indicates the first factory .257 Roberts cartridges were loaded with the then-new IMR-3031 powder. Winchester initially chambered the .257 Roberts in the Model 54; when the Model 70 was introduced in 1937, the .257 was chambered in it.

During the next 20 years, the Roberts became one of the most famous American sporting cartridges. Noted gun writers of the day praised it, and Remington later chambered its bolt-action Model 722 and slide-action Model 760 for the cartridge. The .243 Winchester and .244 Remington introduced in the mid-1950s went up against the .257 Roberts for the best combination varmint/deer cartridge. This resulted in a rapid decline of sales for the .257 Roberts and .250-3000 Savage.

There is no question that the heavier bullets and larger bore diameter of the .25-caliber cartridges give them the edge over the 6mms for big-game hunting. However, there are a couple of drawbacks to the Roberts that somewhat curtailed its popularity potential. One feature was the short throat and magazine length of early rifles chambered for the .257 Roberts. This was frequently written about and was seen as a black mark by the general shooting public.

Another albatross around the neck of the .257 Roberts was that the industry-standard working pressure for the cartridge was established at a relatively mild (for the strong-actioned rifles it is chambered in) 45,000 psi. The new 6mm cartridges, the .243 and .244/6mm, had a considerably higher 52,000 psi SAAMI maximum average chamber pressure. As a result, these new .24-caliber cartridges stole the show, and no new rifles were chambered for the Roberts or any other .25 for a while. The .25 calibers seemed destined to fade away.

In 1971, Savage reintroduced the Model 99 lever-action rifle in the .250-3000 chambering, and Ruger offered its Model 77 in the same caliber. Ruger followed with a Model 77 in .257 Roberts in 1972. (Ruger made only a short run of the Roberts-chambered rifles at the time.) There appeared to be some renewed interest in the Roberts-chambered rifles, but nothing more developed for this .25-caliber round until U.S. Repeating Arms chambered its Winchester Model 70 Featherweight for the .257 Roberts. Remington followed by offering its Model 700 Classic in the Roberts chambering.

The Roberts is still alive, but certainly not highly popular. It remains in the shadow of the more powerful, more popular .25-06 Remington, but it is no slouch on either varmints or deer, for which it was intended.

If you're after varmints, try the Hornady 75-grain hollowpoint ahead of 44.0 grains of IMR-4895. The load turns up 3584 fps in my Remington Model 700 with a 24-inch barrel and 3486 fps in my Winchester Model 70 with a 22-inch barrel. For deer, I would go with bullets of 100 grains or heavier. I loaded 48.0 grains of IMR-4831 behind a 100-grain Nosler Solid Base bullet for 3076 fps from the Remington and 3052 fps from the Winchester. Those loads should be considered maximum in the test rifles. They are *over* the maximum in other rifles.

* * *

Introduced in 1958 or 1959 (I don't recall the exact date), the .264 Remington Magnum was intended to be a long-range big-game cartridge. It is an excellent flat-shooting round for deer and antelope in the wide-open spaces. Many hunters have used it on elk with complete success—although cartridges with larger diameter bullets are better choices.

The round was initially introduced in the Winchester Model 70 with a stainless-steel barrel. Due to the relatively small bore in conjunction with the relatively large case, it is erosive to barrels. However, for a big-game cartridge, where relatively few rounds are fired, this may not be particularly important. I know several hunters who really like the round and use no other for big game.

Due to the aforementioned bore/case relationship, the slowest burning powders are the best choices for the .264 Winchester Magnum. A good all-around bullet for this cartridge is the Speer 120-grain spitzer. Putting it on top of 76.0 grains of H870 produced 3322 fps. The Speer bullet has a ballistic coefficient of .433, making it a flat-shooting load.

* * *

It seems that whenever popular cartridges are discussed, the Weatherbys are often omitted. It's a mistake because there are some excellent listings in the Weatherby lineup. The .300 Weatherby Magnum is one. It came along right after World War II, and ammunition has been commercially available since 1948. This round has had a lot to do with the making of the Weatherby name, and it's the most popular round in the Weatherby lineup.

I think the only reason Weatherby cartridges aren't more popular is because they're offered in relatively few rifles. There are only a few high-dollar rifles, besides the Weatherby, that offer Weatherby chamberings. If the Weatherby cartridges were chambered in the more common rifles and carried in a price comparable to other brands of ammo, several of the calibers would take off.

Most Weatherby cartridges offer the highest velocities for each respective bullet diameter of any commercial cartridge. The .300 Weatherby is no exception. The round offers more velocity and more downrange punch for the .308-diameter bullet than any other cartridge. It's an excellent round for elk, moose, and other large North American game. At the same time, it does fine on deer-size critters. This is one cartridge that offers plenty of punch for any North American game at any range you're likely to be shooting.

Loading 84.0 grains of IMR-4831 behind the Speer 150-grain magnum softpoint produced 3464 fps from my Mark V Weatherby. With a Hornady 180-grain softpoint, I teamed 77.0 grains of IMR-4350 for 3158 fps. Putting the Speer 200-grain spitzer on top of 75.0 grains of IMR-4350 produced 2982 fps.

* * *

The .358 Winchester is based on a necked-out .308 Winchester case. It was introduced by Winchester in 1955 and was chambered in the Model 70 bolt-action rifle. It was then chambered in the Model 88 in 1956. This latter rifle is an excellent vehicle for the .358 Winchester.

The .358 Winchester really fills a niche when it comes to short-action rifles and big game at ranges that aren't too great. It's my favorite lever-action cartridge for all-around woods hunting, and I've used it successfully on deer, bear, and elk. The .358 Winchester is one cartridge that is very easy to load for, with no tendencies whatsoever toward erratic pressures. It packs a lot of punch in a small package.

Besides the Winchester rifles, Savage chambered the Model 99 for the .358 for a while and Browning continues to offer it in the Model '81 BLR. I have taken game with both the Savage and Browning rifles in .358, and both of these guns shoot very well.

While the .358 Winchester is thought of as a cartridge for large game, I can think of no better choice for putting whitetails down with authority. It's my first choice for whitetails in heavily hunted thick woods regions.

I've used both the Hornady 250-grainer and Speer 250-grainer with complete success in the .358. Loading 46.0 grains of IMR-4320 behind the Hornady 250-grainer produces 2263 fps from my Browning BLR with a 20-inch barrel. I used that combination to take a whitetail last winter. I've used the same powder charge behind the Speer 250-grainer from a Model 99 Savage on bears and elk. It does the job.

* * *

The .375 H&H Magnum, introduced in 1912, was the first commercially successful belted cartridge. Holland & Holland introduced the new chambering as having the affinity for shooting all bullet weights to the same point of impact. At that time Kynoch loaded bullets of various types for the .375 in 235-, 270-, and 300-grain weights. All those same bullet weights are available to American handloaders.

I've owned and hunted with several .375 H&H rifles; a Winchester Model 70, an Interarms Alaskan, and a custom-built fiberglass-stocked Model 70 with an Atkinson barrel, to name only a few. I really like the cartridge. My only regret is that I can't think of more excuses to hunt with one. About the only thing I have justified hunting with it is elk. The round also is fine for moose and the large bears.

I have a friend who guides for elk and who really likes a .375 H&H loaded with the Speer 235-grainer. He says it does a good job if the animal is lung shot. This Speer 235-grainer is the single .375 H&H bullet available from the major American bullet manufacturers that's recommended specifically for deer- and elk-size game. However, I've found that other bullets in heavier weights also work well on elk. The Hornady 270-grain spirepoint, the Speer 285-grain Grand Slam, and the Sierra 300-grainer are all excellent choices for wapiti. In my experience, the Speer penetrates the deepest of the three and the Sierra expands with the largest frontal diameter. The Hornady has some of both these desirable characteristics and fits directly between the two.

The custom rifle mentioned earlier had only a 22-inch barrel, and I found that the .375 H&H is one of those cartridges where little velocity is lost when the barrel is shortened from 26 to 22 inches. Winchester's W760 is my first choice in propellants for the .375 H&H. Loading 77.0 grains of it behind the Sierra 300-grain spitzer produced 2504 fps in the 22-inch barrel, with an extreme spread of 11 and a standard deviation of five.

This round has survived since 1873, when it was adopted by the U.S. military. It remained the official cartridge until 1892, when it was replaced by the .30-40 Krag. The first round of production for .45-70 rifles ended with the 1886 Winchester in 1935. However, there were lots of military and civilian rifles around, and this kept the cartridge alive for a long time. Then in recent years, Ruger introduced its No. 1 and No. 3 single-shot rifles for the round, Browning chambered the B-78 single-shot rifle for it and Marlin built a lever action for it; and there have been modern reproductions of the Trapdoor Springfield offered by Harrington & Richardson, the reproductions of the Sharps Old Reliable by C.

Sharps Arms Co., and the replicas of the Remington rolling block by Navy Arms.

The industry-standard working pressure for the .45-70 is a very mild 28,000 cup, and with good reason, considering some of the old rifles still in use. Since the coming of the newer, stronger rifles, it has become fashionable to "soup up" the performance of the old cartridge. Loading manuals like those from Hornady and Speer list different classes of data, depending on the type of .45-70 rifle you own. Hornady, for example, lists three different classes of loads, depending on the rifle. There are loads for the 1873 Springfield/1886 Winchester/Remington rolling block class of firearms, loads for the Model 1895 Marlin in a second category, and loads for the very strong Ruger and Browning single shots in a third category. For this reason, check out those fine loading manuals for data on this 103-year-old number.

The .45-70 has found favor with many big-game hunters of the West and North who want the advantage of a big, heavy bullet, particularly at close range, where trajectory is of no consequence. The .45-70 will do the job on any game in North America—with the right load.

What Your .22-250 Loads Are Doing At All Ranges

THE NO. 1 reason why a varmint shooter buys a .22-250 rifle is the advantage the big case offers in shooting small targets at extreme ranges. It's at this greater distance that any advantage in the high-velocity .22-250 is realized over cartridges like the .222 or .223. If the handloader utilizes the potential the big case contains, he has a decided advantage over the smaller "numbers." If the handloader does not select his bullets and propellants wisely, the long-range potential of the big case is shortchanged and may be no better than the more "efficient" smaller rounds.

As an example, look at the criteria for a good long-range load as it applies to any hunting situation, regardless of caliber or game. First, the load must shoot "flat." Flatter trajectory makes long-distance range estimation less critical. If the shooter is firing a cartridge with a flatter trajectory and misjudges range slightly, he isn't as likely to miss the intended target as with a cartridge having a rainbow curve to its flight path.

Second, a long-range load must be accurate. Since the targets are farther away, the minute of angle requirements for precise shot placement are more stringent. A rifle that groups inside two inches at 100 yards is good for prairie dogs at 100 yards but not at 300 yards.

Third, loads that are less susceptible to wind drift produce a long-range advantage. The farther a target is from a shooter, the greater the problem of wind drift. As range increases, bullet velocity decreases and projectiles at lower velocity are more susceptible to wind drift over a given distance.

Fourth, a load must retain ample energy to dispatch the intended quarry at the impact distance. As the distance increases, velocity will decrease (as mentioned earlier) and impact energy will also decrease. Getting the bullet to the game won't mean much if it doesn't have enough energy left to get the job done.

Fifth, the bullet must expand properly, even at extended distances. At extreme range, the velocity drops off so much that bullets are not as likely to mushroom or expand properly. This is particularly important in a big-game hunting situation. A bullet that performs extremely well at relatively high 50- or 100-yard velocity might not perform well at the decreased velocity of a 500-yard shot.

Now that I've listed the criteria for any long-range load, I'll zero-in on the .22-250. First, the .22-250 is *not* a big game cartridge. In my opinion, it is strictly a varmint/predator number. Due to the high muzzle velocities attained with this cartridge, the small size of the intended targets, and the retained velocity, any normal .22-250 load has more than enough retained energy for even coyote-size predators out to 500 yards. Therefore, retained energy for long-range .22-250 loads is not a problem. If the load shoots fast and flat, it'll have what it needs to drop varmints at any reasonable range.

Long-range or low-velocity bullet performance generally isn't a problem with the .22-250. Nearly all the .22-caliber bullets are fragile; at midranges, these bullets expand violently—to the extent that the jackets come apart and become nothing more than tiny fragments. Even at extreme range (400 to 500 yards), these .22-caliber bullets expand very well. I have fired a number of the high-velocity .22-caliber bullets into coyotes and an expansion medium at reduced .22 Hornet velocities. I've found these bullets expand very well—even at 2000 to 2400 fps impact velocity. This stimulates a 400- or 500-yard impact velocity with a maximum .22-250 loading. Furthermore, due to the small size of the game, even minimal bullet expansion inflicts a lethal wound.

Another long-range load criterion—accuracy—is largely dependent on an individual rifle. When considering the stability of long-range loads, you must test-fire the load candidates in the rifle you intend to use to determine if they turn up suitable accuracy.

Accuracy is so interrelated with the rifle that it cannot be discussed in terms of the load only. An "accurate load" must be discussed in terms of both rifle and ammo. A load that groups inside one-half inch at 100 yards in one rifle may shoot 1½ inches in another. Generally, most .22-250 rifles currently manufactured shoot very well. And normally, there are several potential long-range loads that will produce suitable accuracy for shooting small targets at extreme range.

Differences in .22-250 loads are found in the remaining areas of flatter trajectory and less wind drift. They separate the long-range loads from the rest. These are the two areas where the larger cased .22-250 edges out the .222 or .223—if the handloader works up loads wisely.

Both of these desirable attributes in a long-range load—flatter trajectory and lessened wind drift—are achieved, in part, by the same means. A higher velocity will flatten a bullet's trajectory. Gravity is the primary component affecting bullet drop. Gravity, or the downward pull, on any two bullets of given weight is equal. No matter which bullet you use and no matter what the velocity, they will drop at the same rate. However, the faster bullet will travel a greater distance before it drops the same vertical amount as the slower bullet. Over a given distance, the faster bullet will drop less because it gets there quicker. If both bullet flight paths could be seen, there would be less arc in the faster bullet's path.

Higher velocity also means a shorter time of bullet flight from shooter to target. This is important because bullet drift, resulting from a crosswind, is directly dependent on time of flight or the time that a crosswind component has to act on a projectile. If the bullet gets to the target faster, there's less time for the wind to blow it off course.

A bullet's shape is another major variable in long-range loads. Some bullets are more streamlined and are able to overcome air resistance better than others. A bullet begins to slow down from the time it leaves the barrel, but if it is more streamlined, it retains velocity over a greater distance.

Ballistic coefficient is the number that describes a bullet's ability to overcome resistance in flight relative to the performance of a standard projectile used to compute ballistics tables. Mathematically, ballistic coefficient is the ratio of a bullet's weight to the product of the square of its diameter and its form factor.

Without getting into all the confusing calculations associated with ballistic coefficient, it's safe to say that the higher the ballistic coefficient for a bullet in a given caliber and weight, the more streamlined it is and the better it will retain velocity downrange. The ballistic coefficient for a bullet can be obtained from the bullet manufacturer loading manuals.

Sectional density is another component of velocity retention. Sectional density is the ratio of a bullet's weight in pounds to the square of its diameter in inches. The longer bullet in a given caliber has a higher sectional density if nose shapes are identical. When comparing two bullets of the same caliber, nose shape, and muzzle velocity, the longer, heavier bullet retains velocity and energy at a greater distance. But it's a bit more complex than this since the heavier bullet cannot generally be loaded to as fast a muzzle velocity as a lighter bullet can. As a practical matter, there is a point at which a bullet is too heavy and muzzle velocity is too low for it to be an optimum long-range load. That's what is called sectional density. Like ballistic coefficient, sectional density information can be obtained from the loading manuals.

The loading manuals are a valuable source of information regarding what it takes for a long-range load because they reveal not only ballistic coefficient and sectional density, but also have complete drop and wind drift tables. Sierra, Hornady, and Nosler publish excellent drop and wind drift tables for all practical hunting ranges. These loading manuals all specify the test rifle used for load chronographing. Most of the loads in these manuals are chronographed out of popular factory rifles currently available. Some data is from testing in long-barreled pressure guns. These guns may turn up velocities that aren't readily obtainable in your hunting rifle, so take note of the type of gun used when looking for your rifle's potential velocity.

Using all the manuals can be particularly beneficial when trying to determine the most ideally suited propellant to produce an ultrahigh-velocity load. Generally, all maximum load data in a given manual for a given caliber produces about the same pressure. Therefore, the propellant that produces the highest velocity is the most efficient for that particular cartridge.

Manuals differ in respect to the propellants used to produce the highest velocity with a given bullet weight. However, by using all the reliable load data sources available, you can get a more accurate picture about which powders are apt to produce the highest velocity. In many cases, three or more sources will list a single propellant as producing extremely high velocity. For that reason alone, you should try it.

By perusing all the manuals and taking notes, the handloader will soon determine that there are a handful of propellants producing the highest velocities with a given bullet weight in a given caliber. The handloader can then work with them when developing a maximum load.

After determining what a maximum velocity might be, you may then refer to the drop and wind drift tables to see how different bullets might stack up against other bullets in a given weight range.

The drop and wind drift tables in the loading manuals are figured mathematically, generally by computer. Ballistic coefficients and sectional density figures may be established by slightly different methods, depending on the bullet manufacturer. Due to the slight differences in computations, ballistic coefficients from different sources may not be directly comparable. In my own experience, however, the tables developed from these ballistic coefficient figures are the most accurate you can obtain.

Let's take a long-range load development step by step. First, look in the loading manuals and check the load data sections to see what velocity is likely to be maximum. For instance, the manuals suggest that in a .22-250, 3800 fps is the maximum velocity to be achieved safely with a 55-grain bullet. The manuals reveal that a velocity of 3900 fps is possible with a 50-grain bullet and 3600 fps is likely with a 60-grainer. Other bullet weights can be computed in the same way.

Next, turn to the drop and wind drift tables in the manuals to see which bullets shoot flattest and drift least at these potential velocity levels. A close look at the data indicates bullets in the 50-, 55-, 60-, and 63-grain weight range are likely the best choices in the .22-250 with existing shapes.

It's no surprise that the lightweight 45-grain bullets lose velocity too rapidly to be ideally suited for long-range shooting. Similarly, the heavy 70-grainers start out too slow and are generally too blunt to be ideally suited for long ranges. It *was* a surprise to me that the 52- and 53-grain bullets, often used in match shooting, do not generally turn in performances at long ranges as good (according to the tables) as some of the softpoint spitzers. The more blunt hollowpoint bullets, in general, do not look as good as the pointed spitzers in the long-range tables.

The next step is to select some of the suggested propellants that, according to the loading manuals, produce the top velocities, then work up to maximum with each of them in a specific rifle. I did this with a 24-inch heavy-barreled Ruger Model 77V. It's a good idea to use all the criteria for developing a maximum load—case expansion, case extraction, primer appearance, and, if possible, chronographed velocity—to safely determine when maximum is reached.

The next step is to chronograph five additional rounds at this maximum working level to determine an average velocity for the load. By using a chronograph, the handloader knows exactly what velocity his load is producing. The data in most loading manuals is rounded off in 100 fps increments. By knowing precisely what your particular load is turning up, you can figure out what a particular bullet will be doing in terms of drop and wind drift at 200, 300, 400, and even 500 yards.

.22-250 LONG-RANGE DATA

Bullet	Powder (Type)	(Grs.)	Velocity (fps)	Drop (200-yard zero) 300	400	500	Wind Drift (10 Mph Crosswind) 300	400	500
Sierra 50-gr. spitzer	H380	41.5	3668	4.6	14.2	30.2	8.4	15.9	26.3
Nosler 50-gr. Expander	IMR-4320	37.0	3806	4.9	15.1	32.6	9.3	17.8	30.0
Hornady 55-gr. spirepoint	W760	41.5	3802	5.0	15.8	34.3	9.4	18.2	30.7
Speer 55-gr. spitzer	IMR-4064	36.5	3810	4.9	15.0	32.2	Data not in Speer manual		
Nosler 55-gr. solidbase	H414	41.5	3861	4.6	14.2	30.0	7.6	14.4	24.0
Hornady 60-gr. spirepoint	W760	40.0	3612	5.4	16.7	35.8	8.9	16.9	28.3
Sierra 63-gr. semipointed	H414	39.5	3615	4.7	14.4	30.1	7.8	14.5	24.1

NOTES: Velocity is instrumental at 10 feet and is an average of five shots. All loads are maximum in the test rifle; start at a reduced level. Remington No. 9½ primers and R-P cases were used in all handloads.
Ruger Model 77V, .22-250, 24-inch barrel, and Bushnell 3-9X Banner BDC scope were used

After developing maximum loads with seven different bullets and chronographing them, I interpolated drop and wind drift. These figures are in the accompanying table. This table is not intended to be conclusive by any means. Rather, it illustrates how the potential long-range shooter can clearly determine which loads are likely to produce the best results.

In the accompanying table, it appears that the Nosler 55-grain solidbase bullet loaded with 41.5 grains of H414 is the best choice. It turns up a 3861 fps instrumental velocity, and with a 200-yard zero, it's only 4.6 inches low at 300 yards, 14.2 low at 400, and 30.0 at 500. The wind drift figures for a 10 mph crosswind are 7.6, 14.4, and 24.0 inches at the same distances quoted for drop.

The listed loads are excellent, to be sure, and there isn't a great difference among any of them. But rather than suggesting that the seven loads listed in the table are the ultimate in long-range recipes, or that they're all-inclusive, I offer them only as examples. They're only a guide that serves to indicate the array of potential possible.

Use these procedures and you'll not only be certain that you have one of the best long-range loads, but you'll be utilizing all the potential in your cartridge. Perhaps most important, you'll know precisely what your load is doing at all ranges.

My Favorite Varmint/Deer Cartridges

I T USED TO BE that there was no such thing as a "combination cartridge," nor was a cartridge meant to be used for anything specific. If your grandfather had a rifle chambered for the .44-40, he probably used it for everything from bears to rabbits. Then manufacturers started offering more choices in chamberings. Stronger guns, brass cartridge cases, and new powders meant higher pressures and velocities. This brought about a great proliferation of cartridges.

Now there seems to be a "need" for a specific cartridge for every hunting purpose. There are cartridges for plains game, calibers for elk, rounds for dangerous game, and chamberings for use in the mountains. If you're going after deer in the brush, you're probably taking a different cartridge and rifle than those you'd use hunting deer in open country. And when you think about it, this makes sense.

Elk have been killed with the .44 Henry Flat, but there are a lot of better, more efficient, more humane choices among the cartridges available today. The same approach applies to practically anything we hunt. A .25-06 is better for deer than a .22-250, a .30-06 is more suited for elk than a .243, and a .300 Winchester Magnum is more efficient for long-range shooting than a .30-30.

There's usually a limit to the number of different rifles we're likely to have standing in the corner of the closet, and there is usually a limited number of game species that we're likely to hunt every year. If you live in the West, deer and elk are the popularly hunted species; if you live in the East, the game could be deer and groundhogs. For such limited-use applications, single cartridges can serve multiple functions. Similarly sized animals—like deer, antelope, and sheep—are obvious applications for multiple-purpose cartridges. The varmint/deer combination is a little more extreme in size of quarry, but any one of several cartridges can serve this dual-purpose function quite nicely, particularly for the handloader.

The cartridges suited to, and generally used for, this dual-purpose function are those firing bullets of .24 and .25 caliber. The .243 Winchester, 6mm Remington, .240 Weatherby Magnum, .257 Roberts, and .25-06 Remington fall into this category. These cartridges are sometimes used for a single purpose only—either for deer or for varmints—and this function is about as likely to be for one as for the other. Rifles chambered for them are selected to hunt varmints for a couple of reasons. First, they shoot fast and flat. And while they aren't quite as fast at the muzzle as some of their smaller caliber counterparts, the strictly varmint cartridges, they provide in sheer momentum what they lack in muzzle velocity.

It's generally believed that .24- and .25-caliber cartridges have a big advantage over the .22s in terms of drop and wind drift at long range. This is another reason why rifles in these chamberings are bought strictly for varmints. This supposed advantage sometimes dissolves under actual shooting conditions with varmint-weight bullets. The ballistics tables and computer programs also illustrate this.

There isn't really a lot of difference between the .22 and .24 or .25 calibers when existing commercial cartridges are considered for varminting purposes out to 300 yards or so, where nearly all the shooting is done. Shoot Nosler's 55-grain Solid Base from the .220 Swift at a muzzle velocity at 3800 fps. The 300-yard drop from line of bore is 13.7 inches; the 300-yard wind drift in a 10-mile-per-hour crosswind is 8.8 inches and the 300-yard energy is 886 ft-lbs. Compare this with the .25-06, which starts a Hornady 75-grain hollowpoint at 3480 fps. At 300 yards, the drop is 16.2 inches, drift is 9.2 inches, and energy is 1035 ft-lbs. Pick another loading, and the advantages in drop and drift could just as easily go to the .25-caliber round.

Downrange energy isn't generally much of a factor for varmint cartridges because nearly all those I've listed, whether .22 caliber or .24 caliber, have more than ample energy for varmint-size critters at any distance a varmint hunter is likely to be shooting at them. Still, advantages in drop and wind drift are the usual reasons given for using the larger .24- and .25-caliber cartridges strictly for varmints. The disadvantages of using these combination varmint/deer cartridges are that they have too much recoil for some types of varminting and they're a bit more expensive for the handloader to shoot. Bullets of .24 or .25 caliber are a little more expensive than .22 bullets, and the cartridge cases with larger bullets usually require heavier doses of powder, making this component more expensive as well.

Deer hunters select the combination cartridges because they are generally accurate, have very mild recoil, and are slightly less expensive to shoot than larger calibers. The drawback in using the combination varmint/deer cartridges strictly for deer is that these cartridges are sometimes marginal for deer hunting, depending on the load, size of the deer, and shooting distance.

The combination varmint/deer cartridges are not long-range big-game cartridges. They're considered excellent long-range choices for varmints, but energy is not a factor for varmints; it becomes a factor when considering game the size of a large deer at long range.

When we're talking about varmint/deer cartridges, we're not talking about hunting both classes of animals at the same time. It's unlikely you'll take a shot at a woodchuck while you're hunting whitetails. We're talking about using the cartridge/rifle/scope for the different purposes at different times, possibly for woodchucks in late summer or early fall and deer later in the year. For this reason, selecting and using two different types of ammunition is not difficult.

Perhaps the most important factor is to match the bullet to the game being hunted. A bullet intended for deer should penetrate at least to the vitals to effect a clean kill. A bullet intended for varmints should expand violently to produce considerable tissue damage and also result in a clean kill. Varmints are sometimes shot at extreme ranges, and shots on these small critters frequently do not land in what is normally considered the vitals—the heart/lung/spine area. Due to the considerable amount of energy available in relation to the small size of the varmint, however, even a poor shot can produce a clean kill if the bullet expands violently enough.

When selecting .24- or .25-caliber bullets, the lightweight projectiles with quick-expanding characteristics are intended for varmints and the heavyweight bullets are intended for big game. There is a gray area in between where bullets could be classified as neither light nor heavy. As a general rule, bullets in .24 caliber weighing from 60 to 80 grains are generally intended for varmints; bullets from 90 to 105 grains are intended for deer. This is to be considered only as a guide. Lots of deer are taken, and taken cleanly, with 80-grain bullets. Still, to be on the safe side, stick to heavier bullets for this purpose.

I've shot hundreds of prairie dogs with the Hornady 87-grain spirepoint from a .243. I don't expect it would penetrate a great deal on game as large as a deer. I've also used the Sierra 85-grain hollowpoint boattail, another in-between 6mm bullet weight, for coyotes. It works great for this when fired from either a .243 or 6mm, assuming you don't want to save the pelts. But again, I wouldn't recommend this weight for deer. To be on the safe side, stick with the heavyweight slugs for deer: 95 to 105 grains in .24 caliber and 100 to 120 grains in .25 caliber.

I've taken several deer with the same .243 caliber mentioned earlier, all with 100-grain bullets. The cartridge will certainly do the job, as long as the shot is placed properly.

Getting back to the subject of predator pelt damage, you may be wondering what will work on these large "varmints." Well, if you're after minimal pelt damage, try one of the FMJ bullets. They're available in .24 caliber from Hornady, Speer, and Sierra. There isn't a wide selection of rifle-type FMJs for the .25s, but Barnes does list a 90-grain semi-spitzer in this diameter. (FMJs can be destructive to pelts if they're fired at high velocity and hit bone.)

In addition to bullet weight, bullet shape is important. Pointed bullets, those with a high ballistic coefficient, are the best choices for either purpose. A sleek profile can help to retain energy at long range, resist wind drift, and minimize bullet drop. Whether you're after deer or varmints, pick a pointed, streamlined bullet. Also try to increase the velocity—but keep your eye on the accuracy. I can quickly think of six advantages in higher velocity: less drop, less wind drift, higher impact energy, shorter time of flight, shorter barrel time, and more reliable bullet expansion.

Less drop and wind drift provide the obvious advantage of making hits easier at long range, no matter what the ambient conditions. Higher impact energy is especially important for hunting deer-size game; you'll need all the energy you can get from a light varmint/deer cartridge. A shorter time of flight means there's less time for a standing animal to take a step or move before the bullet gets there; it also means less lead is required on a moving target. Shorter barrel time means the bullet has less time to be acted on by a shooter's wobbles after the trigger is pulled.

I can think of only a couple of disadvantages in the "cost" of higher velocity, and they're questionable: increased barrel wear and slightly more powder consumed for a slightly greater cost. Barrel wear is immaterial in a deer rifle, a firearm that will be fired only a few times

LOADS FOR VARMINT/DEER CARTRIDGES

Bullet	Powder (Type)	Powder (Grs.)	Primer	Case	Velocity (fps)	Use	Optimum Sighting-In Distance (Yards)	Bullet Path at 100 Yards (Inches)	Maximum Point-Blank Range (Yards)	300-Yard Drop From Line Of Sight (Inches)	300-Yard Drift (Inches)	300-Yard Energy (ft-lbs)
.243 Winchester Winchester Model 70, 22-inch barrel												
Hornady 70-gr. spirepoint	IMR-4064	41.5	Fed. 210M	Win.	3384	Varmint	210	1.34	240	5.58	10.8	850
Nosler 75-gr. spitzer	IMR-4320	41.0	Fed. 210M	Win.	3326	Varmint	210	1.35	240	5.45	9.2	969
Nosler 100-gr. Solid Base	IMR-4064	36.0	CCI 200	Win.	2858	Deer	235	2.66	275	5.38	9.3	1032
Hornady 100-gr. spitzer BT	IMR-4350	42.0	CCI 200	Win.	2976	Deer	245	2.57	285	4.12	8.2	1160
6mm Remington Remington Model 700, 22-inch barrel												
Hornady 75-gr. HP	W760	48.5	Fed. 215	R-P	3495	Varmint	215	1.25	245	4.73	9.3	1038
Speer 85-gr. BT	H414	45.0	Fed. 215	R-P	3294	Varmint	210	1.29	240	5.08	6.9	1243
Sierra 100-gr. spitzer BT	H450	47.5	Fed. 215	R-P	3064	Deer	255	2.50	295	3.03	6.6	1331
Nosler 100-gr. Solid Base	MR-3100	47.0	Fed. 215	R-P	3129	Deer	255	2.48	295	3.09	8.1	1262
.240 Weatherby Magnum Weatherby Mark V, 26-inch barrel												
Hornady 70-gr. spirepoint	W785	59.0	Rem. 9½M	Why.	3755	Varmint	230	1.20	265	3.46	9.1	1085
Speer 80-gr. spitzer	H450	56.0	Rem. 9½M	Why.	3602	Varmint	230	1.25	265	3.39	6.8	1352
Nosler 100-gr. Partition	W785	52.0	Rem. 9½M	Why.	3206	Deer	260	2.42	305	2.61	7.8	1326
Speer 105-gr. spitzer	IMR-4831	49.0	Rem. 9½	Why.	3084	Deer	255	2.48	295	3.02	6.8	1391
.257 Roberts Remington Model 700, 24-inch barrel												
Hornady 75-gr. HP	IMR-4895	44.0	Rem. 9½	R-P	3584	Varmint	220	1.21	255	4.19	8.8	1108
Speer 87-gr. spitzer	IMR-4320	44.0	Rem. 9½	R-P	3364	Varmint	210	1.32	240	5.38	9.5	1127
Sierra 117-gr. spitzer BT	W785	47.0	Fed. 215	R-P	2830	Deer	235	2.63	275	5.24	7.9	1276
Nosler 120-gr. Solid Base	H205	46.0	Rem. 9½	R-P	2886	Deer	240	2.57	280	4.53	7.0	1417
25-06 Remington Remington Model 700, 24-inch barrel												
Sierra 75-gr. HP	W760	54.0	Win. 120	Win.	3563	Varmint	215	1.29	245	5.08	12.1	906
Hornady 75-gr. HP	H4831	58.0	Rem. 9½	R-P	3480	Varmint	215	1.26	245	4.76	9.2	1035
Speer 120-gr. BT	H4831	51.0	Rem. 9½	R-P	2930	Deer	245	2.63	285	4.14	7.5	1408
Nosler 120-gr. Partition	IMR-4350	48.0	Rem. 9½	R-P	2946	Deer	245	2.56	285	4.03	7.1	1455

NOTES: Loads were clocked at 10 feet from the muzzle with an Oehler Model 33 Chronotach or a Custom Chronograph Model 900 with Model 600 ambient light screens. Optimum sighting-in distance and maximum point-blank range are based on a trajectory that takes the bullet no more than 1.5 inches from the line of sight for varmint loads and 3.0 inches from the line of

106

each year; it may be a factor in a varmint rifle, say for a prairie dog hunter who fires 200 or 300 rounds a day several times a year, but it shouldn't be a consideration for the woodchuck hunter who may get 10 shots in a day's outing.

There are some shooters who say mild (reduced) loads are more accurate. Others claim hot loads are more accurate. I only know that there are a lot of high-performance loads that shoot very well. Finding one that will do well in most rifles (as long as the rifle is capable of decent accuracy) isn't difficult.

It's relatively simple to consult the loading manuals to determine which propellants will push a bullet of a given caliber and weight the fastest. It's also possible to determine the most streamlined bullets by referring to the ballistic coefficient, which is also listed in the loading manuals. Ballistic coefficient is a numerical value that describes a bullet's ability to overcome the resistance of air. The higher the number, the better its ability to retain velocity and downrange energy.

Considering these two factors, velocity and ballistic coefficient, I have selected several loads for each of five varmint/deer cartridges which should produce the desired performance. It will be up to you to fire the loads for group and see how accurate they are in your rifle. It'll likely be to your benefit to sight-in your rifle separately for the varmint loads and then again before you go deer hunting with the other deer loads. They not only might have different points of impact, but it's to your advantage to derive more out of each load's trajectory.

You can see in the accompanying table that I've included "optimum sighting-in distance" and "maximum point-blank range." The bullet's trajectory is utilized differently for a deer load than it is for a varmint load. The reason is the size of the animal. A path that takes a bullet three inches above and below the line of sight isn't excessive for a deer load, but it is for a varmint load. For this reason, I used a maximum of three inches above or below line of sight for deer and 1½ inches for varmints. Even this latter specification may be pushing it for a down-on-all-fours prairie dog or ground squirrel. If you're hunting the much larger woodchuck, you'll have a little more latitude in the varmint category. Perhaps you could even use two inches as maximum. In this case, you'll have a slightly longer optimum sighting-in distance and point-blank range. As a rule of thumb, consider 1½ inches a good guide for varmint hunting. Just look at the accompanying chart to see how high to sight-in at 100 yards with the various loads.

As far as selecting sighting equipment, the variety of excellent variable-magnification scopes makes it easy. A quality 2½-8X or 3-9X offers the field of view at the low end necessary for hunting deer in the thickest cover and provides enough magnification at the high end for the smallest varmint at long range. If you want a little more magnification, there is the 4-12X scope. If your deer hunting is primarily in open country, you might even want to consider something like a 6-18X. This gives you even greater magnification for those tiny varmint targets.

The varmint/deer cartridges shoot fast and flat as varmint cartridges go and, among the deer numbers, have very mild recoil. Select bullets wisely and place your shots with care, and the varmint/deer cartridges can handle both jobs quite admirably.

Top 10 Cartridges For Big Game

BRACING MYSELF against snow driven sideways by a biting wind and holding the binoculars steady, I could see the big buck's muscles ripple as he made his way up the opposite side of the canyon. Better than a 30-inch spread, his rack stretched out like the limbs on an old oak tree. There were too many points to count.

I wanted a crack at the buck, but my hunting partner Joe had spotted him first. Though we couldn't get closer before the deer topped out into doghair-thick junipers just over the canyon rim, there was plenty of time, and Joe had a good rest, a boulder padded with my coat. We figured the deer was about 300 yards away, within range of Joe's .308.

The buck finally stopped and turned broadside, nose to the wind. Joe's rifle roared, and a puff of dust shot up through the gossamer snowfall and left a dark streak on the otherwise white surface—*behind* and *below* the deer! The buck bounded behind a juniper. We never saw him again.

I was stunned. Joe is an experienced hunter who has bagged plenty of big deer.

"That buck was really a long way off . . . probably too far to be shooting at anyway," Joe said. Then he told me most of his deer had been bagged at spitting distance in thick junipers.

When Joe replaced the spent round, I noticed he was shooting round-nose bullets. I asked him why he'd used that bullet type, and he said he'd heard heavy, slow-moving bullets were best for bucking the brush. He was shooting 180-grain ammunition I later chronographed at 2502 fps. I also knew from past experience that he zeroed-in his rifle at 100 yards.

Although Joe is an experienced hunter, he simply wasn't prepared for a 300-yard shot into the wind. The bullet he was using had a reported ballistic coefficient of .250. At 300 yards, it was nearly two feet below his line of sight; furthermore, in a 25-mile-per-hour crosswind, the bullet was blown more than four feet off course! Compare this performance with the performance of the same rifle with the sighting and the load optimized for long-range shooting.

Suppose Joe had loaded his rifle with a lighter and more streamlined bullet, one like the Nosler Ballistic Tip with a ballistic coefficient of .441. Assume the load produced a realistic 2818 fps out of the muzzle of Joe's 24-inch barrel. Let's also use a sighting-in distance of 260 yards; more simply put, sight-in the rifle to hit 3.3 inches high at 100 yards. The rifle will now only be 3.3 inches low at 300 yards, and the bullet will drift only 19¾ inches in a 25-mile-per-hour crosswind. Compare these figures with Joe's two feet of drop and four feet of wind drift.

In addition, Joe's feeble load arrives at the 300-yard mark with only 1586 fps velocity and 1005 ft-lbs of energy. That's considered marginal energy for a clean deer kill. The new load arrives with 2210 fps of velocity and 1627 ft-lbs of energy—a dramatic difference. Had Joe used the more efficient load and sighting and held into the wind about a foot and a half, chances are he'd have been celebrating that night.

The point is that many sportsmen are walking in the woods with loads that are less than the best. If you're one of them, it could cost you a trophy. Assembling the best possible load isn't difficult, so why not be prepared?

I want to make it clear right off the bat that I'm not advocating hunters go out and intentionally try for game at extremely long range. I like to get as close as I can and consider anything over 250 yards to be a long shot. Many hunters should hold their attempts inside this distance. On the other hand, some are perfectly capable of taking game out to 300 yards or more as long as the conditions are right and there's no way to get closer. I've spent enough time with hunters to know that most will attempt such a shot, and it's not out of reason if they are prepared.

As we have seen, if you've got the best possible load, the deck is stacked in your favor. Ranges are also frequently misjudged. The deer thought to be 250 yards away turns out to be 325. A highly efficient, flat-shooting number can result in a clean kill instead of a wounded animal or a complete miss.

THE TOP 10 CARTRIDGES

1. .300 Weatherby Magnum
2. .300 Winchester Magnum
3. 7mm Weatherby Magnum
4. 7mm Remington Magnum
5. .270 Weatherby Magnum
6. .30-06 Springfield
7. .280 Remington
8. .270 Winchester
9. 7x57
10. .308 Winchester

As long as I'm looking at loads, I'll also look at cartridges— although evaluating cartridges isn't as simple as it sounds, even for a specific purpose. In this case, the specific purpose is hunting big game, primarily in the lower 48 states. This could be any game from antelope and deer to black bears, sheep, elk, and even moose. The various species of deer, black bear, and elk are undoubtedly the most frequently hunted.

Including game the size of elk helps to eliminate some of the smaller bore cartridges from the discussion (the .257s and the .264s), although they are extremely flat shooting and excellent choices for smaller big game like deer and antelope. Some of the numbers with bores (not cartridges) larger than .308 would be good choices, particularly for the largest game at long range. These include cartridge cases that shoot bullets of .338 and .375 diameter. However, these are generally considered to be excessive for deer-sized game, and they aren't as popular as the smaller numbers. Eliminating the .338 Winchester Magnum was a tough decision. It will outperform others on the list, but lines had to be drawn, and the cartridges encompassed ranged from the .277s through the .308s. Other excellent choices (like the .300 Holland & Holland Magnum and .284 Winchester) were eliminated due to their lack of popularity or availability. There was only room for 10, and popularity was part of the selection criteria.

So what criteria do you use to select and rate the best cartridges? With long ranges and large game among the factors, downrange impact energy

TOP LONG-RANGE BIG-GAME CARTRIDGE COMPARISON
(Factory-Published Figures)

Cartridge/Bullet	Mfg.	Velocity (fps)					Energy (ft./lbs.)				Drop From Line Of Bore (Inches)			
		Muzzle	100 Yds.	200 Yds.	300 Yds.	400 Yds.	100 Yds.	200 Yds.	300 Yds.	400 Yds.	100 Yds.	200 Yds.	300 Yds.	400 Yds.
.270 Winchester, 130-gr. Hi-Shok SP	Fed.	3060	2800	2560	2330	2110	2265	1890	1565	1285	2.0	8.4	20.1	38.3
.270 Winchester, 150-gr. Hi-Shok SP	Fed.	2850	2500	2180	1890	1620	2085	1585	1185	870	2.3	10.3	25.5	50.6
.270 Weatherby Magnum, 130-gr. Partition	Wby.	3375	3119	2878	2650	2432	2808	2391	2026	1707	1.6	6.8	16.2	30.5
.270 Weatherby Magnum, 150-gr. Partition	Wby.	3245	3036	2837	2647	2464	3070	2680	2333	2022	1.7	7.2	17.1	31.8
7x57, 140-gr. Hi-Shok SP	Fed.	2660	2450	2260	2070	1890	1865	1585	1330	1110	2.7	10.9	26.3	50.0
7x57, 175-gr. Hi-Shok SP	Fed.	2440	2140	1860	1600	1380	1775	1340	1000	740	3.1	13.7	34.1	62.8
.280 Remington, 165-gr. C-L SP	Rem.	2820	2510	2220	1950	1701	2308	1805	1393	1060	2.4	10.2	25.2	49.4
7mm Remington Magnum, 150-gr. Hi-Shok SP	Fed.	3110	2830	2570	2320	2090	2670	2200	1790	1450	1.9	8.2	19.7	37.8
7mm Remington Magnum, 175-gr. Hi-Shok SP	Fed.	2860	2650	2440	2240	2060	2720	2310	1960	1640	2.2	9.5	22.5	42.5
7mm Weatherby Magnum, 150-gr. Pt-Ex	Wby.	3260	3023	2799	2586	2382	3044	2609	2226	1889	1.7	7.2	17.2	32.3
7mm Weatherby Magnum, 175-gr. Pt-Ex	Wby.	3070	2879	2696	2520	2351	3220	2824	2468	2148	1.9	8.0	19.0	35.3
.308 Winchester, 150-gr. Hi-Shok SP	Fed.	2820	2530	2260	2010	1770	2140	1705	1345	1050	2.3	10.1	24.8	48.0
.308 Winchester, 180-gr. Hi-Shok SP	Fed.	2620	2390	2180	1970	1780	2290	1895	1555	1270	2.7	11.5	27.6	52.7
.30-06 Springfield, 150-gr. Hi-Shok SP	Fed.	2910	2620	2340	2080	1840	2280	1825	1445	1130	2.2	9.5	23.2	44.9
.30-06 Springfield, 165-gr. boattail SP	Fed.	2800	2610	2420	2240	2070	2490	2150	1840	1580	2.2	9.5	22.7	42.8
.30-06 Springfield, 180-gr. Hi-Shok SP	Fed.	2700	2470	2250	2040	1850	2435	2025	1665	1360	2.5	10.8	25.9	49.4
.30-06 Springfield, 220-gr. Hi-Shok SP	Fed.	2410	2130	1870	1630	1420	2215	1705	1300	985	3.3	14.2	35.2	69.2
.300 Winchester Magnum, 150-gr. P-P	Win.	3290	2951	2636	2342	2068	2900	2314	1827	1424	1.7	7.4	18.2	35.4
.300 Winchester Magnum, 180-gr. Hi-Shok SP	Fed.	2960	2750	2540	2340	2160	3010	2580	2195	1860	2.1	8.8	20.9	39.4
.300 Winchester Magnum, 220-gr. Silvertip	Win.	2680	2448	2228	2020	1823	2927	2424	1993	1623	2.6	10.9	26.3	50.3
.300 Weatherby Magnum, 150-gr. Partition	Wby.	3600	3307	3033	2776	2533	3641	3063	2566	2136	1.4	6.0	14.4	27.3
.300 Weatherby Magnum, 180-gr. Partition	Wby.	3300	3077	2865	2663	2470	3783	3280	2834	2437	1.7	7.0	16.6	31.1
.300 Weatherby Magnum, 220-gr. Semi Pt-Ex	Wby.	2905	2498	2126	1787	1491	3048	2208	1560	1086	2.3	10.2	25.8	52.6

TRAJECTORY
(Bullet path in relation to line of sight with optimum loads)

Cartridge/Load	Optimum Sighting-In Distance** (Yards)	Maximum Point-Blank Range* (Yards)	Distance (Yards) 100	200	300	350	400	450	Cartridge Rank
.270 Winchester, Speer 130-gr. boattail	290	340	2.94	3.44	− .63	− 4.63	−10.07	−17.09	5
.270 Winchester, Nosler 150-gr. Ballistic Tip	280	330	3.11	3.55	−1.38	− 5.83	−11.82	−19.46	
.270 Weatherby Magnum, Speer 130-gr. boattail	310	360	2.92	3.79	.57	− 2.78	− 7.43	−13.47	1
.270 Weatherby Magnum, Nosler 150-gr. Ballistic Tip	290	340	2.95	3.42	.63	− 4.55	− 9.85	−16.66	
7x57, Nosler 140-gr. Ballistic Tip	270	310	3.27	3.24	−2.28	− 7.36	−14.14	−22.75	9
7x57, Sierra 160-gr. spitzer boattail	250	290	3.20	2.55	−4.16	−10.06	−17.81	−27.54	
7x57, Sierra 175-gr. spitzer boattail	250	290	3.56	2.79	−4.52	−10.89	−19.22	−29.65	
.280 Remington, Nosler 140-gr. Ballistic Tip	270	320	3.15	3.13	−2.20	− 7.12	−13.68	−22.01	7
.280 Remington, Sierra 160-gr. spitzer boattail	260	300	3.33	2.98	−3.25	− 8.82	−16.18	−25.48	
.280 Remington, Sierra 175-gr. spitzer boattail	250	290	3.27	2.58	−4.20	−10.13	−17.89	−27.61	
7mm Remington Magnum, Nosler 140-gr. Ballistic Tip	300	350	3.07	3.75	0	− 3.73	− 8.83	−15.39	6
7mm Remington Magnum, Sierra 160-gr. spitzer boattail	280	330	3.07	3.30	−1.35	− 5.72	−11.56	−19.00	
7mm Remington Magnum, Sierra 175-gr. spitzer boattail	270	320	3.14	3.10	−2.16	− 6.96	−13.31	−21.33	
7mm Weatherby Magnum, Nosler 140-gr. Ballistic Tip	310	360	2.94	3.79	.57	− 2.75	− 7.32	−13.23	3
7mm Weatherby Magnum, Sierra 160-gr. spitzer boattail	290	340	2.98	3.44	− .63	− 4.55	− 9.84	−16.60	
7mm Weatherby Magnum, Sierra 175-gr. spitzer boattail	280	330	3.16	3.37	−1.37	− 5.79	−11.70	−19.17	
.308 Winchester, Nosler 150-gr. Ballistic Tip	260	300	3.31	3.00	−3.32	− 9.08	−16.80	−26.64	10
.308 Winchester, Sierra 165-gr. spitzer boattail	250	290	3.54	2.81	−4.61	−11.17	−19.84	−30.80	
.308 Winchester, Nosler 180-gr. Ballistic Tip	240	280	3.37	2.28	−5.59	−12.38	−21.27	−32.41	
.308 Winchester, Sierra 200-gr. boattail	230	270	3.40	1.84	−6.99	−14.44	−24.11	−36.14	
.30-06 Springfield, Nosler 150-gr. Ballistic Tip	280	320	3.23	3.50	−1.45	− 6.18	−12.60	−20.85	8
.30-06 Springfield, Sierra 165-gr. spitzer boattail	270	310	3.29	3.26	−2.30	− 7.44	−14.31	−23.07	
.30-06 Springfield, Nosler 180-gr. Ballistic Tip	260	300	3.35	3.00	−3.27	− 8.89	−16.32	−25.71	
.30-06 Springfield, Sierra 200-gr. boattail	240	280	3.28	2.22	−5.42	−11.98	−20.53	−31.22	
.300 Winchester Magnum, Nosler 150-gr. Ballistic Tip	300	350	3.01	3.71	0	− 3.76	− 8.93	−15.63	4
.300 Winchester Magnum, Sierra 165-gr. spitzer boattail	290	340	2.90	3.38	− .62	− 4.52	− 9.82	−16.62	
.300 Winchester Magnum, Nosler 180-gr. Ballistic Tip	290	340	3.16	3.62	− .66	− 4.78	−10.35	−17.46	
.300 Winchester Magnum, Sierra 200-gr. boattail	270	320	3.08	3.05	−2.14	− 6.87	−13.15	−21.09	
.300 Weatherby Magnum, Nosler 150-gr. Ballistic Tip	310	360	2.78	3.65	.55	− 2.69	− 7.20	−13.08	2
.300 Weatherby Magnum, Sierra 165-gr. spitzer boattail	300	350	3.08	3.77	0	− 3.77	− 8.93	−15.58	
.300 Weatherby Magnum, Nosler 180-gr. Ballistic Tip	300	350	3.05	3.71	0	− 3.68	− 8.70	−15.14	
.300 Weatherby Magnum, Sierra 200-gr. boattail	280	330	3.00	3.23	−1.32	− 5.58	−11.26	−18.48	

NOTES: *This is the maximum range in which the bullet is not more than four inches above or below the line of sight.
**This is the distance to sight-in to achieve the maximum point-blank range.

is a primary consideration. Having a bullet arrive on target doesn't do much good if it doesn't have enough velocity and energy to perform properly and produce a clean kill. This factor was given No. 1 consideration. Some sources recommend a minimum of 1000 ft-lbs of impact energy for deer-size game; others recommend 2000 ft-lbs for game as large as elk. This eliminates some of the top 10 cartridges for use on elk at the longer distances, and I think this is reasonable. Rounds like the .270 Winchester, 7x57, and .308 Winchester are marginal elk cartridges, and judgment should be exercised regarding the loadings used for this purpose (as well as at the range).

Downrange drop and trajectory are also important. These are the factors that determine the maximum range at which a cartridge can be used effectively to make long-range hits. Wind drift is important for the same reason. But even with these factors clearly outlined, a comparison still isn't easy. For example, whose figures do you use? There are factory figures, loading manuals, and even your chronograph figures. All are biased in one way or another.

Factory figures are the easiest to obtain and view, but these velocity figures are derived from pressure barrels that are frequently longer and not quite the same as an off-the-rack deer rifle.

Handloaders are fond of relying on loading manuals from the major bullet, propellant, and loading tool manufacturers. More often than not, however, the test rifle used to develop the data will not be the same as yours. The brand, model, or barrel length could be different. Those with chronographs soon realize there are a great many variations among individual rifles. There are also variations in bore or groove diameter, rifling width, rate of twist, throating, and chamber dimensions, etc. Even when developing your chronograph data for comparison, these variables can cloud comparisons with other rifles. Ultimately, the only valid data is what is obtained by actual chronograph testing with the specific guns and loads in question.

In my search for a cartridge performance comparison among the popular big-game numbers, I examined the factory-published figures from the ammunition manufacturers . . . and the data in loading manuals . . . and chronograph figures of factory ammunition as published in the *Speer Reloading Manual Number Nine* . . . and my chronograph figures. Overall, I could see various biases mentioned in all of them. I finally made a comparison based on mathematical formulas which eliminates as many variables as possible and provide a means to compare cartridges and loads without the distortions that always result from empirical data.

By "distortions," I'm referring to variations that always exist and keep comparisons from being valid. For example, I once had a 7x57 rifle capable of producing velocities far in excess of what one would expect for this cartridge. In terms of accuracy, it wouldn't shoot worth squat, but loads moved out fast. The velocities were attained with reasonable pressures from all indications. I later found the rifle had an exceptionally long throat and slightly oversized bore. Assuming that this rifle's performance was typical for all 7x57s would have been erroneous. In fact, nearly all of the powder charges I used to attain maximum loads in the rifle would have been excessive for other 7x57 rifles.

This is an extreme example, but it points out what I mean about em-

DOWNRANGE PERFORMANCE
(WITH OPTIMUM LOADS)

Cartridge/Load	Velocity (fps)				Energy (ft./lbs.)				Drop From Line Of Bore (Inches)			Cartridge Rank
	Muzzle	300 Yds.	400 Yds.	500 Yds.	Muzzle	300 Yds.	400 Yds.	500 Yds.	300 Yds.	400 Yds.	500 Yds.	
.270 Winchester, Speer 130-gr. boattail	3189	2553	2355	2169	2936	1881	1601	1358	17.9	33.5	55.5	8
.270 Winchester, Nosler 150-gr. Ballistic Tip	3009	2469	2300	2139	3016	2030	1762	1524	19.7	36.8	60.5	
.270 Weatherby Magnum, Speer 130-gr. boattail	3359	2703	2498	2304	3257	2109	1801	1532	16.0	30.1	49.7	5
.270 Weatherby Magnum, Nosler 150-gr. Ballistic Tip	3148	2593	2419	2252	3301	2240	1949	1689	18.0	33.5	55.0	
7x57, Nosler 140-gr. Ballistic Tip	2871	2346	2183	2028	2563	1711	1481	1278	21.7	40.6	66.8	
7x57, Sierra 160-gr. spitzer boattail	2713	2241	2095	1956	2615	1784	1559	1359	24.2	45.0	73.8	9
7x57, Sierra 175-gr. spitzer boattail	2588	2168	2038	1914	2603	1826	1614	1423	26.3	48.8	79.7	
.280 Remington, Nosler 140-gr. Ballistic Tip	2914	2384	2219	2062	2640	1767	1531	1322	21.1	39.4	64.7	
.280 Remington, Sierra 160-gr. spitzer boattail	2754	2277	2129	1988	2695	1842	1610	1404	23.5	43.6	71.5	7
.280 Remington, Sierra 175-gr. spitzer boattail	2674	2245	2111	1983	2779	1959	1732	1528	24.6	45.6	74.5	
7mm Remington Magnum, Nosler 140-gr. Ballistic Tip	3179	2620	2444	2275	3142	2134	1857	1609	17.6	32.8	53.9	
7mm Remington Magnum, Sierra 160-gr. spitzer boattail	3006	2502	2344	2192	3211	2224	1952	1707	19.6	36.4	59.5	4
7mm Remington Magnum, Sierra 175-gr. spitzer boattail	2881	2431	2289	2153	3226	2297	2036	1801	21.1	39.1	63.8	
7mm Weatherby Magnum, Nosler 140-gr. Ballistic Tip	3306	2735	2553	2380	3398	2325	2026	1761	16.3	30.3	49.6	
7mm Weatherby Magnum, Sierra 160-gr. spitzer boattail	3116	2602	2439	2282	3450	2406	2114	1850	18.2	33.8	55.2	3
7mm Weatherby Magnum, Sierra 175-gr. spitzer boattail	2954	2497	2353	2213	3391	2423	2152	1903	20.1	37.1	60.5	
.308 Winchester, Nosler 150-gr. Ballistic Tip	2818	2210	2027	1857	2645	1627	1368	1148	23.2	43.8	72.9	
.308 Winchester, Sierra 165-gr. spitzer boattail	2635	2113	1955	1807	2544	1636	1400	1196	26.2	49.1	81.1	10
.308 Winchester, Nosler 180-gr. Ballistic Tip	2578	2112	1969	1835	2657	1783	1550	1346	26.9	50.2	82.6	
.308 Winchester, Sierra 200-gr. boattail	2466	2048	1921	1800	2701	1863	1639	1439	29.2	54.2	88.7	
.30-06 Springfield, Nosler 150-gr. Ballistic Tip	3011	2377	2183	2002	3020	1882	1587	1335	20.2	38.1	63.4	
.30-06 Springfield, Sierra 165-gr. spitzer boattail	2880	2326	2156	1994	3039	1982	1703	1457	21.8	40.8	67.3	6
.30-06 Springfield, Nosler 180-gr. Ballistic Tip	2753	2266	2115	1971	3030	2052	1788	1553	23.5	43.9	72.0	
.30-06 Springfield, Sierra 200-gr. boattail	2589	2157	2024	1879	2977	2066	1819	1598	26.4	49.0	80.2	
.300 Winchester Magnum, Nosler 150-gr. Ballistic Tip	3255	2590	2384	2190	3529	2234	1893	1597	17.2	32.4	53.7	
.300 Winchester Magnum, Sierra 165-gr. spitzer boattail	3181	2593	2408	2233	3708	2464	2125	1827	17.7	33.1	54.6	2
.300 Winchester Magnum, Nosler 180-gr. Ballistic Tip	3058	2538	2374	2217	3738	2575	2253	1965	19.0	35.3	57.8	
.300 Winchester Magnum, Sierra 200-gr. boattail	2908	2442	2296	2155	3756	2649	2341	2062	20.8	38.6	62.9	
.300 Weatherby Magnum, Nosler 150-gr. Ballistic Tip	3425	2741	2526	2324	3908	2503	2125	1799	15.5	29.1	48.2	
.300 Weatherby Magnum, Sierra 165-gr. spitzer boattail	3191	2602	2416	2241	3731	2481	2139	1840	17.6	32.9	54.2	1
.300 Weatherby Magnum, Nosler 180-gr. Ballistic Tip	3175	2643	2475	2313	4030	2792	2448	2138	17.6	32.6	53.4	
.300 Weatherby Magnum, Sierra 200-gr. boattail	3016	2540	2389	2244	4040	2865	2535	2236	19.3	35.8	58.3	

pirical data being valid only for the specific rifle used. That's why I was interested in a mathematical comparison—theoretical in one sense, but closer to a true comparison in another. The formulas used to make such comparisons involving expansion ratio, powder burning rate, and chamber pressure, as well as the external ballistics, are not simple.

I used a computer program specifically written for such applications. Having such a program is a lot more convenient than using a calculator, but a considerable amount of information must be gathered in order to make the formulas work.

WIND DRIFT
10-MPH CROSSWIND
(With optimum loads)

Cartridge/Bullet	Distance (Yards)			Cartridge Rank
	300	400	500	
.270 Winchester, Speer 130-gr. boattail	6.2	12.0	20.2	7
.270 Winchester, Nosler 150-gr. Ballistic Tip	5.8	11.0	18.4	
.270 Weatherby Magnum, Speer 130-gr. boattail	5.8	11.1	18.6	4
.270 Weatherby Magnum, Nosler 150-gr. Ballistic Tip	5.4	10.3	17.2	
7x57, Nosler 140-gr. Ballistic Tip	6.2	11.9	19.8	8
7x57, Sierra 160-gr. spitzer boattail	6.2	11.7	19.5	
7x57, Sierra 175-gr. spitzer boattail	6.0	11.2	18.6	
.280 Remington, Nosler 140-gr. Ballistic Tip	6.1	11.6	19.4	6
.280 Remington, Sierra 160-gr. spitzer boattail	6.1	11.5	19.1	
.280 Remington, Sierra 175-gr. spitzer boattail	5.7	10.7	17.7	
7mm Remington Magnum, Nosler 140-gr. Ballistic Tip	5.3	10.2	17.0	2
7mm Remington Magnum, Sierra 160-gr. spitzer boattail	5.3	10.1	16.8	
7mm Remington Magnum, Sierra 175-gr. spitzer boattail	5.1	9.6	15.9	
7mm Weatherby Magnum, Nosler 140-gr. Ballistic Tip	5.0	9.6	16.0	1
7mm Weatherby Magnum, Sierra 160-gr. spitzer boattail	5.0	9.5	15.9	
7mm Weatherby Magnum, Sierra 175-gr. spitzer boattail	4.9	9.3	15.3	
.308 Winchester, Nosler 150-gr. Ballistic Tip	7.9	15.1	25.4	10
.308 Winchester, Sierra 165-gr. spitzer boattail	7.5	14.4	24.0	
.308 Winchester, Nosler 180-gr. Ballistic Tip	6.9	13.0	21.6	
.308 Winchester, Sierra 200-gr. boattail	6.6	12.5	20.6	
.30-06 Springfield, Nosler 150-gr. Ballistic Tip	7.1	13.7	23.0	9
.30-06 Springfield, Sierra 165-gr. spitzer boattail	6.6	12.6	21.1	
.30-06 Springfield, Nosler 180-gr. Ballistic Tip	6.2	11.8	19.7	
.30-06 Springfield, Sierra 200-gr. boattail	6.2	11.6	19.3	
.300 Winchester Magnum, Nosler 150-gr. Ballistic Tip	6.3	12.1	20.4	5
.300 Winchester Magnum, Sierra 165-gr. spitzer boattail	5.7	10.9	18.2	
.300 Winchester Magnum, Nosler 180-gr. Ballistic Tip	5.3	10.1	16.9	
.300 Winchester Magnum, Sierra 200-gr. boattail	5.2	9.8	16.3	
.300 Weatherby Magnum, Nosler 150-gr. Ballistic Tip	5.8	11.2	18.9	3
.300 Weatherby Magnum, Sierra 165-gr. spitzer boattail	5.7	10.8	18.1	
.300 Weatherby Magnum, Nosler 180-gr. Ballistic Tip	5.0	9.6	15.9	
.300 Weatherby Magnum, Sierra 200-gr. boattail	4.9	9.3	15.4	

First, the internal ballistics computations are based on the capacity of the case. It's necessary to fill fired cases with water to obtain volume. Next, overall cartridge length is obtained, along with bullet length. From this, a determination can be made regarding the capacity of the case after the bullet is seated. That's the important figure.

Cartridge Inequalities

Cartridge/Bullet	Ballistic Coefficient (Inch)	Highest Computed Muzzle Velocity** (fps)	Pressure Computed To Obtain Listed Velocity (ft./lbs.)	Maximum Pressure* (ft./lbs.)	Maximum Cartridge Length (Inches)	Effective Water Capacity In Fired Cases (Grs.)	Effective Bore Travel (Inches)
.270 Winchester, Speer 130-gr. boattail	.456	3189	53,500	54,000	3.340	65.0	21.785
.270 Winchester, Nosler 150-gr. Ballistic Tip	.522	3009	53,200	54,000	3.340	61.5	22.020
.270 Weatherby Magnum, Speer 130-gr. boattail	.456	3359	54,300	—	3.250	80.8	21.875
.270 Weatherby Magnum, Nosler 150-gr. Ballistic Tip	.522	3148	54,500	—	3.250	77.2	22.110
7x57, Nosler 140-gr. Ballistic Tip	.521	2871	49,200	50,000	3.065	53.2	22.195
7x57, Sierra 160-gr. spitzer boattail	.561	2713	49,300	50,000	3.065	53.1	22.205
7x57, Sierra 175-gr. spitzer boattail	.614	2588	49,900	50,000	3.065	50.5	22.365
.280 Remington, Nosler 140-gr. Ballistic Tip	.521	2914	47,300	50,000	3.330	62.3	21.930
.280 Remington, Sierra 160-gr. spitzer boattail	.561	2754	47,300	50,000	3.330	62.1	21.940
.280 Remington, Sierra 175-gr. spitzer boattail	.614	2674	49,300	50,000	3.330	59.6	22.100
7mm Remington Magnum, Nosler 140-gr. Ballistic Tip	.521	3179	51,100	52,000	3.290	78.5	21.970
7mm Remington Magnum, Sierra 160-gr. spitzer boattail	.561	3006	51,300	52,000	3.290	78.3	21.980
7mm Remington Magnum, Sierra 175-gr. spitzer boattail	.614	2881	51,400	52,000	3.290	75.8	22.140
7mm Weatherby Magnum, Nosler 140-gr. Ballistic Tip	.521	3306	54,900	55,100	3.250	80.1	22.010
7mm Weatherby Magnum, Sierra 160-gr. spitzer boattail	.561	3116	54,800	55,100	3.250	80.0	22.020
7mm Weatherby Magnum, Sierra 175-gr. spitzer boattail	.614	2954	53,500	55,100	3.250	77.4	22.180
.308 Winchester, Nosler 150-gr. Ballistic Tip	.441	2818	50,500	52,000	2.800	48.0	22.410
.308 Winchester, Sierra 165-gr. spitzer boattail	.494	2635	47,700	52,000	2.800	48.2	22.400
.308 Winchester, Nosler 180-gr. Ballistic Tip	.548	2578	50,100	52,000	2.800	47.1	22.460
.308 Winchester, Sierra 200-gr. boattail	.596	2466	51,700	52,000	2.800	45.2	22.560
.30-06 Springfield, Nosler 150-gr. Ballistic Tip	.441	3011	49,700	50,000	3.340	63.7	21.870
.30-06 Springfield, Sierra 165-gr. spitzer boattail	.494	2880	49,400	50,000	3.340	63.9	21.860
.30-06 Springfield, Nosler 180-gr. Ballistic Tip	.548	2753	49,100	50,000	3.340	62.8	21.920
.30-06 Springfield, Sierra 200-gr. boattail	.596	2589	48,400	50,000	3.340	60.9	22.020
.300 Winchester Magnum, Nosler 150-gr. Ballistic Tip	.441	3255	51,500	54,000	3.340	83.3	21.870
.300 Winchester Magnum, Sierra 165-gr. spitzer boattail	.494	3181	53,600	54,000	3.340	83.5	21.860
.300 Winchester Magnum, Nosler 180-gr. Ballistic Tip	.548	3058	53,500	54,000	3.340	82.4	21.920
.300 Winchester Magnum, Sierra 200-gr. boattail	.596	2908	53,000	54,000	3.340	80.5	22.020
.300 Weatherby Magnum, Nosler 150-gr. Ballistic Tip	.441	3425	54,900	55,100	3.562	94.6	21.648
.300 Weatherby Magnum, Sierra 165-gr. spitzer boattail	.494	3191	51,700	55,100	3.562	94.8	21.638
.300 Weatherby Magnum, Nosler 180-gr. Ballistic Tip	.548	3175	54,900	55,100	3.562	93.7	21.698
.300 Weatherby Magnum, Sierra 200-gr. boattail	.596	3016	54,500	55,100	3.562	91.8	21.798

NOTES: *These pressures were obtained from the *Speer Reloading Manual Number Ten.*
**These are the highest velocities listed by computer that are below maximum.

The next step is figuring out the bore travel of the bullet. Bore travel (not barrel length) is measured from the muzzle of the firearm to the base of the bullet as it's seated in the case and as it rests in the chamber.

The important points about all this are that overall loaded cartridge length is taken into consideration as well as how it affects bore travel. For example, a bullet from a short cartridge has a longer effective bore travel than a bullet from a long cartridge. This is frequently overlooked. Case capacity is measured from the base of the bullet after it's seated. In other words, cartridges which have bullets seated deeply inside the neck have less capacity. A given case with a longer, heavier bullet produces less case capacity but a longer bore travel. All of this information is taken into consideration.

FACTORY AMMUNITION CHRONOGRAPH DATA
(From *Speer Reloading Manual Number Nine*)

Cartridge	Gun	Barrel Length (Inches)	Factory Ammo	Bullet Weight (Grs.)	Muzzle Velocity (fps)
.270 Winchester	Rem. 700	22	Rem.	130	2849
.270 Winchester	Rem. 700	22	Win.	150	2710
.270 Weatherby Magnum	Custom	26½	Wby.	130	3425
7x57	Ruger	22	Fed.	139	2631
7x57	Ruger 77	22	Fed.	175	2348
.280 Remington	Rem. 740	22	Rem.	165	2628
7mm Remington Magnum	BAR	24	Fed.	150	3077
7mm Remington Magnum	BAR	24	Fed.	175	2817
7mm Weatherby Magnum	Not listed				
.308 Winchester	Win. 70	22	Rem.	150	2695
.308 Winchester	Win. 88	22	Fed.	180	2497
.30-06 Springfield	Win. 70	24	Fed.	150	2849
.30-06 Springfield	Win. 70	24	Fed.	180	2692
.30-06 Springfield	Rem. 700	22	Win.	220	2294
.300 Winchester Magnum	Win. 70	24	Win.	180	3000
.300 Winchester Magnum	BAR	24	Win.	150	3333
.300 Weatherby Magnum	Weatherby	26	Wby.	150	3130
.300 Weatherby Magnum	Weatherby	26	Wby.	180	3179

I spent the better part of a week taking such measurements and evaluating other data for a lot of big-game cartridges before feeding numbers into the computer. My goal was to come up with the best possible long-range loads for each cartridge before a comparison was made. To get the most out of a cartridge, the highest possible velocities within pressure limits are required. This takes the best-shaped bullets (highest ballistic coefficient) for the top downrange performance—higher retained velocity and energy and decreased time of flight, drop, and wind drift. In addition, the rifle must be sighted-in to make optimum use of its flat-shooting capability. The computer would help me do all this in a max-imally unbiased manner, but there are some built-in advantages that can't be avoided. For example, some calibers have bullets available with higher ballistic coefficients than others. The top ballistic coefficient for a 7mm bullet among the listings is .614 for the Sierra 175-grain spitzer boattail. The highest ballistic coefficient for the .30-caliber bullets is .596

for the Sierra 200-grain spitzer boattail. The light bullet spread for the two calibers is even more extreme—.521 for the .140-grain 7mm and .441 for the 150-grain .30 caliber.

Another area where there's a built-in prejudice among cartridges is in pressure level. The Sporting Arms and Manufacturers Institute (SAAMI) has established maximum allowable pressures for various cartridges based on such considerations as the design and strength of their components and the guns they're fired in. For these reasons, various cartridges have different maximum allowable pressure levels. The .30-06 has a maximum allowable pressure of 50,000; the .270 has a maximum of 54,000. When both cartridges are fired in guns of equal strength with equally strong cartridge brass and primer cups, the .270 Winchester seems to have an unfair advantage. It seemed prudent to stay with SAAMI recommendations for the computer. The ammo companies do. Throughout the computer data, this maximum pressure level was observed with one exception: the 7x57. SAAMI has established a maximum pressure for this cartridge at 46,000 psi cup. These maximum pressures are reported in the *Speer Reloading Manual Number Ten,* a respected book containing loads to 50,000 cup for use only in modern bolt-action rifles. For this reason, the computer data was compiled using this higher pressure figure.

The computer program lists pressures in increments, and the first increment below the SAAMI maximum was used for my computations. As a result, there is some variation, but these variations are far less than generally encountered with empirical data.

In my "Top 10" listing, the cartridges were rated in four categories: downrange energy, trajectory, wind drift, and recoil. All comparisons were made for rifles with 24-inch barrels. The results are the "theoretically" best obtainable velocities and the best downrange performances based on the most efficiently shaped projectiles.

For the overall rating, maximum emphasis was placed on downrange energy for reasons mentioned earlier. Slightly less emphasis was placed on trajectory and wind drift. There was not nearly as large a difference between cartridges in these categories. For example, the wind drift spread for all 10 cartridges was a mere 4.2 inches at 400 yards. It was much the same with the top five cartridges and the bottom five in the trajectory category—with the exception of the 7mm Remington Magnum in the top category (it wasn't as good as the others in the top five) and the .270 Weatherby in the bottom five (it was significantly better than the others).

Very little emphasis was placed on recoil due to the fact that it is so nebulous. Felt recoil cannot be measured and can be altered by the addition of a recoil pad, a muzzle brake, or a change in stock design. Recoil is only important insofar as it affects *your* shooting performance. If a given cartridge has more recoil than you want, you can either work on your tolerance or flinch or decide to use a less effective cartridge and accept its limitations along with its lack of recoil.

The downrange comparisons for the ratings were made at 400 yards because this is normally the maximum range at which anyone would be shooting at big game. The 500-yard figures are shown only for information. The .300 Weatherby Magnum took top honors in the overall category as well as in the energy listing. The .270 Weatherby Magnum is tops for trajectory, while the 7mm Weatherby is best for wind drift. The 7x57 wins in the category for the least recoil.

Included in my trajectory tables are columns supplying the maximum point-blank range and the optimum sighting-in distance. Maximum point-blank range is the maximum range over which the bullet's trajectory takes it no more than four inches above or below the line of sight. In other words, within this distance, you can aim dead center on a large game animal's vital area, and the bullet will impact within four inches of the aiming point. Optimum sighting-in distance is the distance at which the rifle must be sighted-in to achieve its maximum point-blank range (using the four-inch criteria). If you can't easily shoot over the longer distances mentioned at your range, you can use the sighting-in numbers listed at 100 yards. For example, if a .30-06 with the Nosler 180-grain Ballistic Tip bullet (at the listed muzzle velocity) is sighted-in to shoot to point of aim at 260 yards, it will have a maximum point-blank range of 300 yards. Your bullet will impact within four inches of your line of sight at any distance up to this point. But suppose you only have a 100-yard range for sighting-in. A look at the chart reveals where your bullet will impact at both 100 and 200 yards. Simply sight-in your rifle to hit 3.3 inches high at 100 yards, and you should achieve the same objective.

You may not be able to reach these published velocities in your rifle for any number of reasons. For example, your rifle may have a long throat and magazine. If so, you can seat bullets farther out of the case than the SAAMI-recommended overall maximum cartridge length. In this instance, your rifle will have an advantage not accounted for in my data.

This is the best comparison I've compiled in all my years of shooting, and I'll let the tables (figures) speak for themselves. If your favorite is well up in the listings, you can be assured it was compared against the stiffest competition going. If it isn't on top, take heart . . . neither is mine. But I've got the confidence and experience with my favorite to make it do what I want, and I know its limitations. That's something a computer can't measure.

Cartridges That Made Firearms History

C ARTRIDGES HAVE undergone a rather limited development throughout the last 100 years or so. The centerfire cartridge, brass case, rimmed, rimless, and belted case designs, along with smokeless propellant and jacketed bullets, have all been with us for at least 70 years. The developments during this period have generally revolved around changes in bullet diameter/case capacity ratio, shoulder angle, and neck length. These are all minor changes. In fact, whenever novel or unusual ideas like the Gyrojet or caseless ammunition crop up, they tend to flop. Hunters and shooters are basically a conservative lot, and the traditional cartridges and basic cartridge components have held us in good stead for many years.

Actually, there's no reason to change the basic design of sporting cartridges and firearms. Through the course of firearms history, however, there are certain cartridge designs that have attained special significance for one reason or another. At the top of the list would have to be the .22 rimfire, considered to be the real father of all metallic cartridges.

The development of the .22 rimfire can reportedly be traced back to a Frenchman named Louis Flobert in the mid to late 1840s. The first .22 rimfire consisted of nothing more than a lead ball pressed into the open end of a percussion musket cap. The musket cap was then shaped into a rimmed cartridge case, and Flobert began building breechloading rifles to fire it. Meeting with success, he founded a gunmaking firm and sold many thousands of these inexpensive rimfire plinking rifles. More importantly, this initial development fostered the later development of an entire line of .22-caliber rimfire cartridges which are still fired in greater number than all other ammunition. The .22-caliber rimfire cartridge, as most shooters know, is one of the best tools for learning to shoot and for hunting small game like rabbits and squirrels.

I began my hunting career with the .22 rimfire rifle, a bolt-action Stevens Model 86C to be exact. I received this rifle from a brother-in-law who was unaware (fortunately for me) of my father's position that no one should have a .22 rimfire before reaching the age of 15. I was only 13 at the time.

I lived on a farm where there were many acres of prime squirrel and cottontail habitat. After a few instructional sessions and hunting trips, I was able to take the rifle hunting all by myself. With it, I learned the value of shot placement on squirrels high in the treetops. Later, I experienced the problems associated with bullet drop and wind drift while shooting distant crows in a newly planted cornfield. Each puff of dust where the bullets hit was a clear indication about the effect of drop and wind drift.

Aside from hunting and teaching kids to shoot, the largest number of .22 rimfire rounds are probably expended in plinking everything from tin cans to dirt clods. Though not reloadable, the .22 rimfire round is inexpensive, and a Sunday afternoon spent firing .22 rimfire ammunition is not going to break anyone's wallet.

A strong case could be made that the rimfire cartridge design which originated with the .22 gave rise to all sorts of larger caliber rimfire cartridges. The larger rimfire cartridges blossomed for a time, but they were not destined to be the large calibers of the future. There are drawbacks with rimfire cases. As mentioned earlier, they're not reloadable; secondly, though relatively inexpensive to manufacture, the cases are not nearly as strong as cases of modern solid-head design, so stronger cases were also necessary when higher chamber pressures were standardized.

Numerous .22-caliber cartridges are associated with the development of this tiny rimfire round. They consist of the BB cap, which is a cartridge shorter than the .22 Short and very low powered. Then there's the CB cap, which is a little more powerful than the BB cap though cases are generally the same length. The .22 Short is next and remains popular today. The .22 Short was introduced in 1857 and has been in production longer than any other self-contained American cartridge. It was originally made for a Smith & Wesson revolver, and this firm is generally credited with its development. After the .22 Short is the .22 Long, which has a longer case than the Short but is generally loaded with a 29-grain bullet.

The .22 Long Rifle, which everyone is so fond of today, has a case the same length as the .22 Long but fires a heavier 40-grain bullet. There are the Long Rifle shot cartridges and the various hypervelocity .22s like the Stinger, Yellow Jacket, Viper, and Spitfire, which are generally loaded with lighter bullets, sometimes with longer cases for extremely high velocity.

The .22 Winchester Magnum rimfire (.22 WMR) is in a class by itself, producing greater muzzle velocity and energy and requiring a longer case than any of the others.

There were a couple of other .22 rimfire cartridges like the .22 Winchester Rimfire (.22 WRF), which was also referred to as the .22 Special, and there was a .22 Winchester Automatic. At any rate, the .22 rimfire is a top candidate among cartridges that changed firearms history.

The second cartridge on the list came along in 1888 and is known today as the 8mm Mauser. The 8mm Mauser cartridge was designed for the German Military Model 1888 Commission rifle. Used by Germany in World Wars I and II and adopted as a service cartridge by Poland, Czechoslavakia, and other countries, this was the first smokeless powder, military rifle cartridge with a rimless case to be adopted by a major power. Still a popular sporting rifle cartridge in Europe, it can be loaded to duplicate the performance of the .30-06.

The reason I've selected this cartridge? It fathered our most popular big-game cartridge head size. With a nominal rim diameter of .473 inch, it's the standard head size for such cartridges as the .22-250 Remington, .243 Winchester, .25-06 Remington, .270 Winchester, .308 Winchester, and .30-06 (just to name a few).

Thousands of 8mm Mauser military rifles turned up in this country after World War II. Many were used just as they came from the arsenal for hunting purposes; others were sporterized by shortening barrels, trimming down stocks, bending bolt handles, and installing scopes. Most importantly, these actions, designed for the 8mm cartridge, formed the basis for rifles built for numerous wildcat cartridges.

As many shooters know, experimenting conducted by the designers of wildcat cartridges has been a valuable asset to the evolution of American sporting cartridges. These cartridges explore unknowns in cartridge performance, and some of the better wildcat cartridge designs eventually turn up as commercial chamberings. Two such commercial cartridges are the .22-250 Remington and .25-06 Remington. Both utilize the 8mm/.30-06 head size.

Many custom rifles chambered for the wildcat versions were built on Model '98 actions originally chambered for the 8mm Mauser. Indeed, this 8mm cartridge head size has been one of the most popular for wildcat experimentation since strong bolt-action rifles became available.

The third cartridge on the list, the .375 H&H Magnum, is nominated for the same basic reason as the last: it gave rise to the belted magnum cartridges in common use today. Introduced in 1912 by the famous London gunmaking firm of Holland & Holland, the .375 H&H Magnum soon achieved a worldwide reputation for being a reliable hunting cartridge for some of the world's largest game.

Western Cartridge Co. finally introduced the .375 H&H to this country in 1925. Griffin & Howe began making custom rifles chambered for this cartridge in 1926, but a major production rifle, the Winchester Model 70, wasn't introduced for the chambering until 1937. There's a host of factory rifles still chambered in this caliber, and it still has an enviable reputation for being one of the top cartridges in the world for hunting large game.

The .375 H&H Magnum has a nominal .532-inch belt and rim diameter and, as such, is the father of the .458 Winchester Magnum, .338 Winchester Magnum, .338 Winchester Magnum, 8mm Remington Magnum, .300 Winchester Magnum, .300 H&H Magnum, 7mm Remington Magnum, and a number of others.

The .375 H&H Magnum has the case capacity and case strength needed to turn up top performance—for itself and for its long line of progeny. Considered to be adequate for hunting any game, the .375 H&H is frequently nominated the one-caliber choice for worldwide hunting. Though thought to be light for elephant, it will do the job with 300-grain solids. It is considered excellent for quickly stopping large, dangerous game like brown bear, and many Alaskan guides carry rifles chambered in this caliber. With its popular 270- and 300-grain softpoint bullets, the .375 H&H Magnum also performs well on smaller species of big game like whitetail and mule deer. The large bullets with controlled expansion characteristics aren't excessively destructive to the meat of these smaller species.

Though harsh, the recoil from a rifle chambered for the .375 H&H can be handled by most shooters, much more so than the recoil of the larger .378 Weatherby, .458 Winchester, or .460 Weatherby calibers.

The .375 H&H Magnum was the first really flat-shooting cartridge designed for very large game. The oft-quoted ballistics indicate it is as flat shooting as the popular 180-grain .30-06 loadings, making long-range shooting of game much easier than with earlier cartridges like the .450-400.

The fourth candidate is the .222 Remington, which was introduced by Remington for the Model 722 bolt-action rifle early in 1950. At the time of its introduction, the .222 Remington was an entirely new design for a rifle cartridge. An instant success, it quickly established an enviable reputation among benchrest shooters for producing a high degree of accuracy, and for a long while, most benchrest records were established with the .222. The .222 Remington remains a popular cartridge and produces the same performance it always did. No doubt its real popularity is rooted in low noise and low recoil advantages for varmint shooting.

The .222 Remington, with a nominal .378-inch rim diameter, is the father of the .223 Remington, .222 Remington Magnum, and .17 Remington—all considered to be excellent varmint cartridges.

If any cartridge can be said to be "inherently accurate," the .222 Remington qualifies. (In fact, this seems to be a characteristic of all five nominees. Not only did they give rise to other excellent cartridges, but these original cartridges produced excellent accuracy and performance in the game fields.) The .222 remains one of the top choices of varmint shooters, and most .222 rifles shoot very well. Furthermore, a lot of loads generally shoot well in any given .222 rifle.

Due to the position of this cartridge in competition shooting, more accuracy development has gone into .22-caliber bullets than any other caliber. In fact, accuracy standards for the manufacture of bullets in this caliber are sometimes more stringent than for bullets of other diameters. There are match bullet offerings in this caliber by all the major manufacturers, and there are hunting bullet weights available ranging from 40 to 70 grains.

This small, rimless cartridge usually produces very little point-of-impact shift with a wide range of bullets, making it an even more desirable cartridge. Even in the face of cartridges producing higher velocity (.223, .22-50, and .220 Swift), some of these characteristics preserve the .222's popularity.

The fifth and final candidate for making hunting rifle cartridge history is nominated for an entirely different reason than the others. The .30-06 Springfield, as today's version exists, was developed and introduced in 1906. The reason this round is nominated is obvious. Not only is the .30-06 one of the most popular centerfire cartridges remaining today, it is one of the best, the standard by which other cartridges are judged.

The .30-06 provides adequate power for any game in North America, and there's a wide range of bullet weights and propellant types suitable for the .30-06 — so wide it can be efficiently loaded to perform well for hunting any game on the continent. In fact, I can think of no better choice for taking big game shot by the largest portion of hunters in the U.S., including deer, elk, antelope, black bear, and all the other commonly hunted species. The recoil of the .30-06 is not ferocious, making it more ideally suited to the average hunter than the larger, more recent belted magnum cartridges.

The .22 rimfire, 8mm Mauser, .375 H&H Magnum, .222 Remington, and .30-06 Springfield are the five cartridges which have most changed firearms history. All five are still in production and quite popular. If a North American hunter were to select a firearms battery consisting of these nominees, he would have a gun battery and range of calibers ideally suited for hunting anything in the world. These cartridges, and their inventors, deserve all the special recognition they've received.

Reloading

How To Work Up
The Right Handload For A Rifle

WHEN A PERSON gets into handloading, one of the first things he does is select a specific firearm and then assemble bullet, powder, case, and primer into what he thinks will be the best combination for his gun and shooting requirements. The initial choice of components is often the result of the reloading store clerk's suggestion after a new shooter purchases handloading equipment. Or possibly a handloading friend suggests a particular powder and bullet. Eventually, however, in order to utilize the potential advantages handloading has to offer, the shooter will want to tailor his loads specifically to his individual gun, his hunting or target shooting habits, or the game he'll be hunting.

All it takes is a quick look in the loading manuals or a visit to any well-stocked handloading supply store to realize there is a seemingly unlimited number of load combinations for any given caliber. Obviously, a reloader needs guidelines when working up a load for a specific rifle, and one of the best places to start is to decide on the intended purpose for your rifle and cartridge. Will it be used for antelope hunting on the plains, elk

---

hunting in thick timber, varmint shooting in eastern Pennsylvania, or for some aspect of target shooting? Once you have decided on the intended purpose, the next step is to select a bullet suited to these shooting conditions in terms of expected range, type of game, vegetation, terrain, etc.

The varmint hunter going after groundhogs in eastern Pennsylvania may be concerned about ricochets and select an extremely fragile, lightweight projectile that would disintegrate on impact. For antelope hunting, where you could be taking long-range shots, you may want to select a very streamlined bullet, possibly a boattail design, which has a high ballistic coefficient for maximum velocity retention at extreme range. When hunting elk in heavy timber, the choice might be a long heavyweight slug with slower, more controlled expansion characteristics for deeper penetration. The bullet might even be a roundnose design since its long-range velocity retention would be insignificant.

The loading manuals can be an excellent guide when it comes to matching a *bullet* to a specific task. It has become popular in recent years for bullet manufacturers to provide information in loading manuals regarding the performance characteristics and intended uses for their bullets. By perusing such data, a handloader can get an excellent idea regarding which bullet is the best suited to a specific task. As a result, you can be certain you're not selecting a varmint bullet for big game or vice versa.

One reason I prefer to select the bullet before deciding on any other cartridge component is that the bullet, in any shooting situation, is the most important ingredient. The bullet has the sole responsibility of performing correctly once it leaves the rifle's muzzle. When you spot a bull elk and squeeze the trigger, you have no further control over the outcome. You've put all your chips on that tiny chunk of lead encased in a jacket, and it determines whether the animal is downed or not.

In a target shooting situation, the bullet's performance characteristics regarding how it is affected by wind, centrifugal force, air resistance, etc., determine how true it will fly and where it will impact on target. And even though the primer and powder are important and essential, they serve only to get things moving, to provide the impetus for speeding the bullet down the bore.

Since there is an almost infinite number of potential component combinations, the shooter would do well to simplify the process and avoid uncertainty by standardizing most of the components initially. I've found it's a good idea to stick with one bullet, primer, and case for the initial loading and shooting tests. By altering only the powder type and charge weight, the testing time is decreased considerably.

It doesn't really matter which primer brand you pick for the initial testing since you have no way of knowing which primer works best in your particular rifle. The testing of primers can come later. Remember: You're trying to simplify things. The choice between Magnum and Standard primer depends partially on the type of propellant that will be used.

As I mentioned, a loading manual is an excellent guide. In fact, it helps to have access to many different loading manuals so that they can be used as cross references. As an example, if four out of five manuals suggest using a Magnum primer with a particular type of propellant in a particular cartridge, you can figure you won't go wrong with the Magnum primer.

The case (or brass) to be used depends primarily on whatever the shooter has available. Brass is generally obtained from fired factory ammunition, and all cases currently manufactured in the U.S. are excellent. Cases do vary to some degree in terms of design, web thickness and weight, and this does mean a difference in effective chamber capacity, but all of these factors are within limited parameters. These slight variations in brass may produce a small increase or decrease in velocity, and this can usually be overcome by adjusting powder charge weight if desired. Case necks (the part that holds the bullet) can vary in uniformity and thickness, and this can make a small difference in accuracy and pressure. However, the shooter can spend a lot of valuable time checking everything precisely; for most applications, little—if anything—will be gained in the process.

One of the toughest decisions any handloader faces in developing a load for a specific gun and purpose is in the selection of a propellant. There are nearly 50 different ones available in the U.S., and how do we know which are ideally suited to a given cartridge and bullet weight? Surprisingly, the selection of a powder is one area where all the possible alternatives can be narrowed considerably without even going to the range.

Once again, the more loading manuals you have for reference, the better. First, the handloader should be aware that the Sporting Arms and Manufacturers Insitute (SAAMI) establishes maximum allowable pressure standards. The people who develop loading manual data observe these standards closely. With a few exceptions, all the data for a given cartridge in a given manual is accumulated by observing the same maximum pressure standards. In other words, all the maximum loads listed with a given bullet weight and a given cartridge produce the same maximum pressures. But as you can see in the manuals, velocities produced by these maximum loads with different propellants are not equal. Therefore, the powders that produce the highest velocities are the most efficient.

By using several manuals as a crosscheck reference, you'll frequently find three or four of them will list one particular powder as producing the highest velocities with a given bullet weight. This is the powder to pick. There are frequently two or more additional powders which produce velocities right behind the best propellant. Sometimes, one or two of the other loading manuals may list one of these secondary powders as producing the highest velocity, and you may want to try two or three of the top propellants. Follow this system, and you have a good idea about the most efficient propellant for your cartridge and bullet weight without even leaving your reading room.

There is a reason, besides efficiency, for basing the powder selection on velocity. In most situations, the shooter wants to get all the performance his cartridge is capable of. Higher velocity produces greater impact energy for the big-game hunter. For the target shooter, higher velocity means a shorter time of flight and consequently less wind drift. There are situations where the shooter does not want all the velocity his cartridge is safely capable of producing; he may want to load it to some reduced velocity for a specialized purpose. But this situation would be an exception.

Shooters often find loads which approach maximum velocities and pressures produce the best accuracy. If you're not utilizing all the velocity your cartridge is capable of, you may be better off going to a smaller capacity case. As an example, instead of using a .300 Winchester Magnum and shooting 180-grain bullets at 200 fps less than you can potentially obtain in this case, you may receive better accuracy with greater powder burning efficiency with a smaller case like the .30-06. I'll stick with developing a load that produces all the potential a cartridge is safely capable of.

Up to this point, a bullet has been selected that is best suited to the specific task; a case and primer have been chosen (based on what is available), and the loading manuals have been used to determine which powders are the most efficient. But we still haven't fired a shot—or even loaded a case. The next step is to determine which powder charge level is best to begin the initial shooting tests. The loading manual was used to select the best powder and bullet, but you still don't know for sure how much powder (in a case) your rifle is capable of digesting safely. The loading manuals list maximum charge levels and suggested starting levels.

At this point, you may want to decide how important every fps is. I'm not talking about "hotrodding," but rather about obtaining as much velocity as is safely possible. There is a chance that a powder charge weight a few grains below maximum will produce the highest level of accuracy in your rifle while sacrificing only a few fps in velocity. If you decide accuracy is going to be your foremost criteria—as it may very well be in a target shooting situation—you'll probably want to load ammo in five-round batches and shoot it for accuracy as you progress in powder charge weight. On the other hand, if you determine that velocity is going to be the No. 1 criteria in developing a load, you should work up to maximum with several powders before accuracy testing.

There are basically three ways that the average handloader can determine a maximum powder charge level for his particular rifle. By utilizing all three systems, the handloader can crosscheck his information and be more certain in his determination of a maximum load.

Probably the most-used method involves nothing more than observing the appearance of the primer and case and the feel of the case as it's extracted from the chamber. Once a shooter becomes familiar with the characteristics of a particular primer, he may be able to get a rough estimation regarding pressure levels by the amount of curvature or flattening at the edge of the primer in the primer pocket.

Some people use primer cratering as a criteria for judging pressure levels, but in my experience, this cratering effect can vary tremendously, depending on the size of the rifle's firing pin hole, the size and shape of the firing pin, strength of the striker spring, etc., up to the point where this information is of little value. One exception is when the shooter is thoroughly familiar with that particular rifle and how a particular primer has performed with many other loads. For instance, I once owned a rifle that would routinely pierce primers (considered by some to be a sign of excessive pressure) with almost any load. The real culprit was a too-large firing pin hole in the boltface. I had it bushed to a smaller diameter and the firing pin turned down, and that solved the problem.

Whenever a case extracts from the rifle's chamber with a sticky feel, be suspicious of high pressure, even though this is not always a sign of it. Go one step further and examine the case for a shiny or burnished-looking spot on its base (headstamp area). If the chamber pressure was great enough to force a bit of the brass case head into the boltface's ejector hole, this is a definite sign of excessive pressure. If the brass protrudes even a slight amount into this ejector hole, the turning motion when opening a bolt-action rifle's breech will burnish a shiny spot on the case head. If brass if forced into this hole more than just a little, the bolt handle can be difficult to lift.

Whenever pressures are great enough to deform brass appreciably, the load is too hot. Remember: With modern guns, the brass case is usually the weakest link in the gun/cartridge ability to contain pressure. Whenever the brass cartridge case begins to distort, the handloader should back off on his powder charge level. For example, enlarged primer pockets are a sign of high pressure. The increase in powder charge should stop before the brass is deformed appreciably. Primer appearance is one way to determine when the shooter is approaching maximum charge levels. This is a good reason for progressing in powder charge only a grain or one-half grain at a time with large rifle cartridges.

A second method of determining maximum pressures utilizes the fact that brass is deformed under pressure. The method has come into wide use only recently and is described in the instruction portions of at least two loading manuals: the *Nosler Reloading Manual* and the *Hornady Handbook of Cartridge Reloading*.

Basically, the case expansion system of pressure determination involves milking the web section of a fired cartridge case to determine how much (or if) it expands during the pressure of firing. Its expansion is compared to the amount of expansion produced with the same case fired with a factory load. A working description of this method of pressure determination is quite involved, so I'll refer you to the loading manuals mentioned to find out precisely how it's done.

The third method of determining maximum loads, or at least cross-checking maximum load data, is to use a chronograph. This method is frequently overlooked, though I have found it to be valuable in much of my reloading.

Velocities usually increase steadily as the powder charge is increased in small increments. However, when nearing a maximum charge level, there's generally a reduction in the amount of velocity gain per grain of powder added. In some cases, the velocity may even decrease. Only a chronograph reveals what's happening.

Secondly, whenever velocities received on your chronograph compare with velocities received at maximum pressure levels in the loading manuals, it's safe to assume that your pressures are approaching maximum, regardless of your powder charge. It generally takes a given pressure level to produce a given velocity with a specific propellant. Therefore, if your velocities are the same as the velocities received in the loading manuals (assuming the same type of rifle), your pressures are probably also the same, even though your powder charge may or may not be identical.

Whenever a rifle produces the velocities listed with maximum powder charge levels in the loading manuals, become extremely cautious—even though you may be using several grains less powder than the maximum listed load. If this happens, it's time to doublecheck for signs of high pressure. Mike case head expansion and closely observe the appearance of cases, primers, etc.

Utilizing all three methods of determining maximum, along with loading manual data, is the safest way to reload. There is very little need to push your loads to the limit when it comes to handloading. It's always better to utilize most of the cartridge's potential velocity while maintaining a safe margin below absolute maximum.

After reaching a charge level that you deem is a comfortable working load for your rifle, you will want to fire it for accuracy. Three five-shot groups fired from benchrest at 100 yards is the usual criteria. You may then want to compare the accuracy received from near-maximum charge levels of several powders because then it'll be easier to make a choice based upon which combinations produce the highest velocity, greatest accuracy, etc.

If there's nothing wrong with your rifle, its barrel, or bedding, one of the three or four powders selected should produce acceptable hunting accuracy. If not, try another bullet brand or two. Some rifles prefer one brand of bullet over another—even though the basic construction and performance characteristics of the bullets are the same.

The search for the "best" combinations can continue for as long as you choose, but by utilizing the techniques outlined, you also have a way to develop an efficient, useful load with the least expenditure of time and components. One of the greatest advantages in handloading is to suit your load to the particular task at hand. By developing a variety of different loads for a variety of different tasks, you have everything you need to go after any game with the perfect load.

Lightweight Bullets For Varmints

HUNTERS ARE looking to varmints to satisfy their hunting interests since most of the big game, upland game, and waterfowl seasons are over. Varmint shooters are some of the most demanding hunters in terms of shooting equipment and cartridge performance. These hunters generally want a fast-stepping, flat-shooting round for connecting with tiny targets at extreme ranges.

I find it amusing that the stereotype of the easterner is a fast-talking person with an air of haughtiness, while the westerner is supposed to be a slow-talking, easy-going type. When it comes to varmint shooting, however, westerners have traditionally reversed this role. With an air of haughtiness, the westerner is the one saying anybody ought to be able to hit one of those eastern groundhogs that's practically as big as a bear when compared to the West's prairie dog or tiny ground squirrel. It's the westerner who says you really don't encounter long-range shooting east of the Mississippi, while the West's wide-open spaces and high winds require the most in terms of cartridge performance.

Perhaps there is a bit of truth in those statements, but I can't resist curling the corners of my mouth when a shooter mentions lightweight bullets simply aren't up to the task of western varmint shooting or claims the smaller .22 calibers just don't have what it takes to battle the high winds of the West.

A longer, heavier bullet with the same nose shape as a shorter bullet does have a higher ballistic coefficient, and ballistic coefficient does have something to do with the bullet's ability to overcome air resistance, but many shooters overlook time of flight, which also has a great bearing on wind drift. In other words, the faster a bullet travels, the less time it has to be affected by a crosswind.

Using the Sierra, Speer, and Hornady loading manuals, I decided to compare the lightweight bullets with some of the heavier bullets to see just how much difference there is in wind drift. I used the loading manuals to determine ballistic coefficient and maximum listed velocity; I used light and heavy bullets of the same brand with all data from the same manual. In the case of the Speer manual, however, velocity had to be rounded off to the nearest 100 fps in order to utilize the wind drift tables available. To compare these bullets, I referred to Philip-Mannes' book, *Tables of Bullet Performance,* which was published by Wolfe Publishing Co. Using a 10-mile-per-hour crosswind as standard and maximum listed velocities for each bullet, I compared wind drift with light and heavy bullets at 300 and 400 yards.

The .22-250 was the first cartridge to be examined. In comparing the lightweight Sierra 45-grain semipointed bullet with a ballistic coefficient of .213 to the heavyweight Sierra 63-grain semipointed bullet with a ballistic coefficient of .300, I found there is a difference in wind drift between them. If the 45-grainer starts with an initial velocity of 4000 fps, it will be blown 10.4 inches off course at 300 yards by the 10-mile-per-hour crosswind and 20 inches off course at 400 yards. The heavyweight 63-grainer with an initial velocity of 3500 fps will be 8.2 inches downwind by the time it gets to 300 and 15.4 inches off by the time it reaches 400.

This difference is greater than most other bullets. But even the 4.6 inch discrepancy at 400 yards is practically negligible when considering the difficulty in maintaining this degree of accuracy at 400 yards under field conditions. There are few shooters who could keep most of their shots inside a 4.6-inch circle at that distance under most conditions.

For example, suppose the 10-mile-per-hour wind gusted to 15 miles per hour at the instant a shot was fired with the 63-grain bullet; the bullet would be drifted an additional 7.6 inches at 400 yards. Furthermore, if the wind velocity dropped to five miles per hour, the bullet would drift some 7.6 inches less.

In other words, a wind that fluctuates five miles per hour produces a variation of 15.2 inches in bullet drift and gusts in this range are not at all uncommon. Thus, actual field shooting conditions will produce a much greater bullet-drift variation than the variation between lightweight and heavyweight bullets.

The story is the same with some of the larger calibers. For instance, when firing the 6mm Remington, the Hornady 70-grain spirepoint with an initial velocity of 3600 fps drifts 8.5 inches in a 10-mile-per-hour crosswind at 300 yards and 16.1 inches at 400. The heavier 100-grain spirepoint with initial velocity of 3100 fps drifts 7.8 inches at 300 and 14.7 inches at 400. That's only a 1.4 inch discrepancy at the longer distance!

I used the .25-06 to compare the Speer 87-grain spitzer to the Speer 120-grain spitzer. The former, starting at 3700 fps, drifts 7.6 inches at 300 and 14.2 inches at 400. The heavier bullet, starting at 3000 fps, drifts 7.2 at 300 and 13.2 at 400.

Next, I used the .270 to compare the Speer 100-grain spitzer with the Speer 150-grain spitzer. The former, at an initial velocity of 3400, drifts 7.9 and 14.8 respectively; the heavyweight bullet drifts 6.6 and 12.1 inches—once again a negligible wind drift advantage for the heavier bullets.

Other serious varmint shooters contend it takes a cartridge with a larger bore to buck the wind better at extreme ranges. However, a cursory examination of wind drift tables again illustrates that this theory simply does not hold water.

The Sierra manual contains excellent wind drift tables, and I referred to these for a comparison of the .220 Swift, 6mm Remington, and .25-06 Remington cartridges. All of them are considered to be high-performance varmint cartridges in each respective caliber. I then selected ideal long-range varmint-shooting bullet weights in each caliber at maximum-listed velocities for a wind drift comparison at 300 and 400 yards under a 10-mile-per-hour crosswind.

When shooting the Sierra 55-grain spitzer in the .220 Swift with initial velocity of 3900 fps, the bullet will drift 7.53 inches off course at 300 yards and 14.08 inches at 400 yards.

In the 6mm Remington, with the Sierra 85-grain spitzer using an initial velocity of 3300 fps, the bullet will drift 6.51 inches at 300 and 12.05 at 400.

With the .25-06 cartridge (considered to be the ultimate in long-range varminting), the Sierra 100-grain spitzer, with an initial velocity of 3200 fps, will drift 6.59 inches at 300 yards and 12.20 inches at 400 yards.

Obviously, there is no significant difference between any of the high-performance varmint cartridges from the .220 Swift through the .25-06 Remington. In other words, there is no wind drift or bullet drop advantage to the .25-06 Remington over the .220 Swift.

The .25 caliber maintains greater energy downrange, but the .220 Swift is generally considered to be more than adequate for any varmint at all practical shooting distances. More importantly, the shooter of the larger calibers has to contend with greater recoil, and this is a factor to consider under varmint-shooting situations.

It's not uncommon to expend several hundred rounds from the prone position during a morning's outing. What's more, the .22s burn less powder, and the bullets are less costly than the larger calibers. That's something to consider when consuming ammo in varmint-shooting quantities.

Another advantage to lightweight small-caliber bullets is that they may be less prone to ricochet; if they do ricochet, the slugs will carry less energy. This factor obviously cannot be overlooked in a varmint rifle used in a populated area.

I'm sure my point of view will draw some heat from the large-caliber varminting afficionados, but it's the kind of disagreement that makes shooting fun.

Reduced Loads In Big-Game Rifles

THERE IS AN area of load development that serves a useful purpose, yet it has nothing to do with getting the most from a cartridge; in fact, its goal is the exact opposite. I'm talking about using reduced loads in a centerfire cartridge to get less recoil and less noise, all of which can be conducive to better shooting.

A lot of dry-firing is good medicine to remedy a flinch, but it precludes the actual shooting practice. Reduced loads actually allow the shooter to get shooting practice without the ear-abusing noise and shoulder-bruising recoil. Reduced-load shooting can be directly applied to plinking and to some hunting situations as well.

One type of hunting that frequently allows the expenditure of a large number of rounds is varmint shooting. When it comes to potting these small critters at extreme ranges, we need the higher velocity. Normally, I'll use a small-caliber centerfire that doesn't kick much but makes a lot of noise. The solution to ear-abusing noise in a prairie dog or ground-hog shooting situation is good hearing protection. For this type of varmint hunting, the shooter relies primarily on sight to locate the targets; he really doesn't need to hear them.

In much of the West, however, it's common to shoot jackrabbits as "varmints." There's no better way to sharpen the big-game shooting eye than to get a lot of preseason practice on running jackrabbits. But the problem is using the big-game rifle for shooting scores of rounds at these animals is noise and recoil. Recoil I can probably handle; most of the shots will be taken from the offhand or kneeling position. But there's no denying the fact that a milder recoiling cartridge would be more pleasurable toward the end of a day's red-hot shooting.

And noise is a problem in a jackrabbit hunting situation. The hunter must sometimes rely on his hearing to locate the game. Many times I've heard a jackrabbit rustle out of the brush beside me or behind me; I'd seldom detect them if hearing protection were being worn. Obviously, I am hesitant to shoot a large number of high-velocity rounds from a centerfire rifle without hearing protection because I know what it's like to have a headache and ears ringing for several days.

For this type of hunting, I've found reduced loads work ideally. Whether for plinking, target shooting, or preseason hunting practice, reduced loads actually have a wide range of applications. Additionally, they can serve as an ideal training tool for the beginner just getting into centerfire rifle shooting.

There are a couple of bullets specially designed for this type of plinking or target shooting. In fact, Speer has named it's lightweight .30-caliber bullet specifically for this hunting use, calling it the "Plinker." Hornady also has a bullet named the "Short Jacket." The "SJ" designation comes from the bullet's half-jacket design, which leaves a lot of lead exposed at the tip. Both bullets have a lot of soft lead exposed, which might be conducive to reducing ricochets. Ricochets are always a potential hazard when shooting any bullet at low velocity, and one way to avoid them is to shoot the more fragile projectiles.

There are few bullets in other calibers designed specifically for plinking, but the shooter wanting to utilize reduced loads still has a number of very good options. For instance, I have frequently used handgun bullets in rifle cartridges at reduced velocities with excellent results.

As an example, in the .25-caliber rifle, you could use the 60-grain bullets designed for .25-20 or .256 Winchester Magnum velocities. Besides the plinker bullets available in the .30 calibers, you may want to use one of the jacketed hollowpoint bullets designed for the .30 Carbine. They can perform quite well when fired from larger capacity cartridges at reduced velocity levels. The .357 Magnum handgun-type bullets can be fired in .35-caliber rifles like the .358 Winchester, while .44 Magnum and .45 ACP bullets can be used in rifle cartridges utilizing these diameter bullets.

Accuracy can be a problem with reduced loads, but with a little experimentation, you should be able to obtain accuracy on par with high-velocity loads in the same gun. For instance, I've used the Hornady 125-grain hollowpoint pistol bullet ahead of 60.0 grains of H335 in a .358 Winchester lever-action rifle and have printed one-inch groups at 60 yards.

In rifle calibers for which there are no handgun bullets available, just select one of the extremely lightweight projectiles that is very fragile. For instance, pick a 60-grain varmint-type bullet for the 6mm, the 90- or 100-grain bullet in the .270, the 115- or 120-grain bullet in the 7mm, etc.

Developing data for these reduced loads is easy. I've found most cast-bullet load data can be applied to jacketed bullets. By applying cast-bullet charge levels in a given bullet weight to jacketed bullets, I discovered the velocities are similar. I would expect pressures to be higher, since more engraving force is required with the harder jacketed bullets. In terms of pressure, however, the figures for most cast-bullet data are very mild.

One caveat in developing reduced-load data is to avoid the use of extremely slow-burning propellants. Using small quantities of slow-burning propellants in large-capacity cases is what has most frequently resulted in the secondary explosion effect (SEE). As you'll note, most cast-bullet data consists of small charges of fast-burning rifle or even handgun-type propellants.

If you haven't tried reduced-load shooting, give it a shot. You may be pleasantly surprised at how enjoyable your big-game gun can be to shoot more often.

Narrowing Down Component Combinations

W HAT'S THE BEST way to choose components when the different combinations of powder and bullets are seemingly unlimited? If you've handloaded for quite a few years, you may have accumulated a lot of different bullets and powders suitable for a cartridge and firearm you want a good load for. The problems in load development are the time required to do it and the expense for components. It seems there's no end to the possibilities, and one can never be sure he has chosen a good combination without trying them all.

I remember troubling over which bullet I was going to use. Then I tried various powder combinations with the bullet. It seemed this would be the least time-consuming route to a good load. The problem was that the firearm might not like the bullet I chose. I could waste a lot of time with a bullet or powder that just didn't have much potential in that particular firearm. Then I found that by exposing the firearm to a lot of different powders and bullets from the start I could quickly see what the rifle's tendencies in component preference were.

I now use this method to quickly narrow down the best possible choices, and the results have been great. I first select a powder the manuals say produces a high velocity for the caliber in question. Using this powder, I assemble loads in five-shot group batches, with all the different bullets I can, using the same powder charge weight for bullets of a given weight. I keep the case lot and primer type constant throughout. It's best if you can shoot three five-shot strings with each load.

Next, I select a bullet I think should shoot well, perhaps a match bullet, in the same weight class as the other bullets. Then I load all the different powders with it that I can, also in five-shot strings.

I shoot the combinations from a benchrest. Noting the most accurate bullets and the most accurate powders, I combine the best of both, selecting the best shooting powder and the best-shooting bullet; I try to develop a load around this combination. If there's time, I'll select the two best bullets and the two best powders and go from there. This method often produces excellent accuracy results in surprisingly short order. If you want, you can fine-tune the powder charge, try different primers, different bulletseating depths, etc., but you should be able to produce a good load without this.

Fine-Tuning Handloads

AFTER SHOOTING A wide variety of loads, the handloader will generally notice there are one or two powders that will produce high velocity and tight-shooting groups with a variety of bullets. Conversely, one or two bullets might produce tight groups with a wide variety of powders. These combinations are the ones the handloader is generally wise to work with, varying charges up or down a half-grain at a time in most varmint cartridges to see which load produces the optimum accuracy and velocity results. In the course of shooting and recording a wide variety of loading data, however, I began to rely on a couple of additional methods for fine-tuning a load which aren't usually discussed.

The use of a chronograph can help reveal exactly what a bullet and powder charge combination is producing—in terms of velocity and consistency. I've been recording information about loads that includes the consistency or extreme velocity variation between the fastest and slowest shots in a 10-shot string. Some powders are highly consistent, producing very little variation, while others are very inconsistent. Although the propellants producing the most consistent velocities may not produce the tightest groups all the time, consistency of velocity seems to be one measure of selecting an optimum powder for the cartridge and bullet weight.

Another major influence on velocity consistency is the primer. Once the handloader has determined a particular bullet shoots well with a variety of propellants and that one or two propellants shoot well with a variety of bullets, he can then narrow down his load testing to just a few combinations. And by changing primers to see what effect this has on velocity, velocity consistency, relative pressure, and accuracy, the handloader is really getting down to the fine points of tuning a load.

This final step will sometimes be found to have a major effect on both velocity and accuracy. You may be pleasantly surprised to find the load that was producing .9-inch groups at 100 yards will produce .6-inch groups simply by changing a primer. If you're working near maximum, however, it's important to back off on the powder charge a bit before switching primers and work from there.

You can't assume anything without checking. Still, the points mentioned here can serve as a guide and should make your fine-tuning go a little faster with less expenditure of components.

Handload To Maintain Load Consistency

THERE ARE MANY reasons to assemble your own ammunition. The ones repeated most often relate to the ability to specifically match the ammunition to the shooting purpose or hunting situation. There's also the added versatility over factory ammunition, with the ability to juggle propellant charges, bulletseating depths, etc., to obtain a higher level of accuracy. However, one of the handloading advantages seldom recognized is the ability to maintain the consistency of loadings.

Finding the proper load can frequently take substantial expenditures of time and money. Once a handloader finds a proper "recipe" for his particular rifle, he records it and uses the load repeatedly for a specific shooting purpose. The load generally performs well for a long period of time—until the rifle's throat becomes worn. Then a different bulletseating depth, propellant charge, or bullet might improve accuracy relative to the added barrel throat wear. It's no problem for the handloader to assemble fresh ammunition to his exact specifications time and again.

Such is not the case with factory ammunition. I checked out three very accurate .22-250 rifles, shooting three five-shot groups with each rifle from the benchrest at 100 yards with a single lot of factory ammunition. The .22-250 rifles turned up .7-, .9-, and .9-inch average group sizes, accuracy I consider excellent for factory ammunition and out-of-the-box rifles. Eight months later, I fired the same rifles at the same range with the same *nominal* ammunition. The only difference was I conducted the second test series with ammunition of a different lot. Those same rifles turned up average group sizes of 1.2, 1.5, and 1.5 inches. In other words, group sizes enlarged very consistently by .5, .6, and .6 inch.

At first, I thought the conditions had changed, causing the rifles to shoot poorly. A check of past shooting records indicated the first group series was fired during the middle of the day during a gusting wind when conditions were poor; the second groups were fired during near-ideal conditions.

My older chronograph records revealed the new lot of ammunition shot an average of 55 fps faster in all three rifles. When I returned home, I decided to pull out the few remaining rounds of the old lot of ammunition and compare it with the new lot. I noticed the old lot contained plated primers; the new lot was loaded with unplated primers. I pulled bullets to visually inspect and weigh all the components. The bullets and cases appeared the same and weighed the same. Both ammunition lots were loaded with an extruded propellant which resembled something on the order of IMR-4064, but the old lot of ammunition was loaded with 35.5 grains of the propellant; the new lot, 36.0 grains.

I've experienced this situation with factory ammunition in the past. It's common for a manufacturer to make minor modifications in bullet style, possibly the positioning of the cannelure, the propellant charge weight or type, etc. Sometimes the change is for the better; sometimes it is not. The handloader is in control and does not need to worry about such unknown changes in his ammunition.

I prefer being in control and keeping worries to a minimum.

Hot Tips On Burning Rates

HANDLOADERS ARE fortunate to have industry standards which ensure quality performance and a high degree of uniformity in components. Manufacturers knock themselves out maintaining specifications for bullet diameter, priming mixture, powder burning rate, etc. High standards are actually taken for granted by handloaders. As any manufacturer will attest, however, there is a whole range of circumstances beyond the maker's control.

We've all heard stories about the guy who uses too much powder or the wrong kind of powder, but not all handload variations result from such obvious circumstances. Components might not produce the expected results due to deterioration. Powder and primer performance can deteriorate with age or as a result of poor storage conditions. Powder stored in an attic, for instance, where the temperature can stay exceedingly high, might produce substandard performance.

Another area of propellant performance discrepancies involves burning rate. I'm not talking about burning rate variations among lots; I'm talking about burning rate shifts as a result of the loading conditions.

You should be familiar with the listings of powders by burning rate. Hodgdon, for example, in its *Data Manual No. 24,* lists all its powders

---

in order of approximate burning rate. The other manufacturers list propellants in order of increasing or decreasing burning rate. There are specific parameters established for the manufacturer's use. Much of this information is derived from "closed bomb" or "closed container" tests. Under carefully controlled laboratory conditions, a specified amount of propellant is placed inside a container of known volume, and the container is sealed. The propellant inside is ignited electronically, a transducer senses the pressure, and the time/pressure curve is recorded on an oscilloscope. This is one way a manufacturer has to monitor burning rate.

There is a chart in the *Sierra Bullet Loading Manual* which lists the relative burning rates of 71 different propellants from various manufacturers. A chart like this might seem like a pat answer to many of the handloader's load development questions, but since propellant burning rate can vary, depending upon the loading conditions, it should serve only as a guide.

Modern smokeless propellants are "progressive burning." They burn more violently when under pressure. When ignited in a gun's chamber, the powder begins to burn and release gas, which raises pressure inside the case and chamber. This causes the powder to progressively burn more violently. The manner in which it burns is controlled by the formulation, the size of the grains, the shape of the grains, perforations in the grains, and deterrent coatings on the grains.

Anything which serves to alter pressure also alters burning rate. Chamber size, for example, can alter burning rate; bullet weight and diameter can alter burning rate. Not only does burning rate change, but the powder relationships may change. Few handloaders realize this, but it points out why information from relative burning rate charts cannot be directly applied to load development. When considering two propellants which have burning rates very close to each other, one propellant might be faster than another under a given set of conditions, but change cartridges or bullet weights, and the other propellant could be faster.

Measuring Bullet-To-Lands Distance

THERE SEEMS to be confusion surrounding bulletseating depth for rifle cartridges and overall cartridge length.

Cartridge length is significant from several standpoints. First, it has a bearing on feeding. A too-long cartridge won't function through some actions, nor will it fit into some magazines. In fact, magazine size may dictate maximum overall cartridge length in some instances. Overall cartridge length also has a bearing on pressure and velocity. Jamming the bullet of a cartridge into the lands during chambering has a tendency to raise pressures when the round is fired. Conversely, a chambered bullet that has a gap to jump before it reaches the lands produces less resistance initially, particularly if this jump is a result of a longer chamber throat. Overall cartridge length has an indirect—though sometimes dramatic—bearing on accuracy. In fact, varying bulletseating depth, sometimes only slightly, can make or break a load in terms of accuracy.

Aside from the functioning aspect, overall cartridge length is insignificant unless the rifle's characteristics are also taken into consideration. Rather than overall cartridge length being significant, the bullet-to-lands distance is the important measurement. That presents the problem with listing overall cartridge length.

Suppose I fire a load that produces exceptional accuracy and great velocity. Further, I've seated the bullet so that it barely touches the lands when the round is chambered. If I then report the overall cartridge length measurement, shooters will look at the table and be delighted. But there's trouble with that . . . .

Suppose the load I used was maximum in my rifle. Let's also suppose that my rifle has a long throat. I've taken chamber casts from factory rifles which reveal that throat lengths vary a lot among different brands. Another shooter may reproduce the load exactly as published, complete with overall cartridge length, and then chamber it in a good bolt-action rifle with a lot of camming power. Due to all this camming power, he may not notice when the bullet is jammed hard into the lands because of a shorter throat. He may not know his rifle has a tighter chamber or that his lot of brass is thicker. He's now set up for a blown primer or a seized bolt. Due to the strength of today's actions, that's probably all that would happen, but he's probably not going to like that load, and it's all because of bulletseating depth.

Different rifles of the same make and model sometimes have different bullet-to-lands distance even though the bullet and seating depth are the same. The leade (origin of rifling) wears as a rifle is fired. Even the same rifle will have a leade which varies with wear. You may have to seat bullets a little farther out with your favorite load to maintain accuracy when the leade becomes worn. The point is that overall length is not necessarily significant. The bullet-to-lands distance is. All it takes is a caliper to measure overall cartridge length. It's not as easy to measure the bullet-to-lands distance.

Perhaps the simplest way to measure the bullet-to-lands distance for one's own use is to use a fired case. Squeeze the mouth together slightly. I sometimes bite it just enough to hold a bullet firmly when one is inserted. Insert a bullet, just like the one to be loaded, base first, as in a loaded round. Let the bullet stick out a long way, then carefully chamber the dummy cartridge and withdraw it. Next, handling the dummy with care to prevent the bullet from moving in the case mouth, measure the overall cartridge length and record the measurement for reference. If you want to seat a bullet .010 inch short of the lands, just reduce overall length by that amount, then load to that overall measurement.

While this method is easy, there is room for error with it due to the possibility of the bullet moving in the case mouth. I usually repeat the process several times to make certain I have the correct measurement. And remember that the reference measurement is valid only for that brand, weight, and style of bullet. If you change bullets, you'll need to derive a new reference measurement.

Another way to determine a bullet-to-lands distance is to hold a bullet firmly against the leade with a dowel rod inserted from the breech. Insert a cleaning rod into the muzzle until it contacts the bullet and mark the rod at the muzzle. This serves as a reference point. You can then chamber a dummy round loaded with the same bullet and use the same cleaning rod to check the depth it extends into the bore. The difference between the initial mark and the mark with the dummy round is the bullet-to-lands distance.

This method is imprecise simply due to the physical difficulty in marking the rod precisely at the right point. It's hard to keep pressure on the dowel and mark the rod precisely. Even if you have a friend to help, it's difficult to mark the rod at the exact origin of the bore. Remember, we're talking about a relatively short bullet-to-lands distance, so the marking needs to be precise to be of value.

There are a couple of commercial devices for measuring the bullet-to-lands distance which incorporate the same principles, but the bottom line is that it's not a quick and easy measurement to derive.

Overall loaded cartridge length is useful to the individual handloader since it is a reference for repeating a particular bullet-to-lands distance. If a test load shoots well, you can repeat the seating depth and hopefully the accuracy. Change rifles, however, and the reference is invalid.

Safely Working Up To Maximum Loads

"**P**RESSURE" developed by a cartridge is normally the key word when you talk about a maximum load for a rifle. Internal chamber pressure generated behind the bullet when a cartridge is fired is what provides the projectile with its velocity and energy.

Modern rifles operate at high pressures for greater bullet speeds and higher energy levels. For these reasons, pressure is not only beneficial to the shooter—it is a prerequisite for firing a bullet.

Excessive pressure is what can cause the shooter problems. Due to the industry standards regarding the manufacture of guns and ammunition, shooters have little reason to worry about excessive pressure with factory loads when they're fired in modern guns under normal conditions. It's the handloading shooter who must be concerned about this business of excessive pressure because he has the opportunity to put as much propellant into a rifle cartridge as he deems necessary. Only if he recognizes the signs of high pressure can he be certain he's staying on the safe side.

There was a time when the rifles were the limiting factor regarding the pressure a gun/cartridge combination could tolerate. Some of the old actions were only a fraction as strong as modern guns in design and metallurgy. Cartridge cases were also once weak (by today's standards) and had the affinity for causing all sorts of problems: blown primers, primers giving gas leaks, head separations, etc.

A lot has been learned about the manufacture of brass cartridge cases during the last 50 years. Today's brass is able to withstand much greater pressures with no problems whatsoever. The manufacture of rifles has also improved to the point that the *brass* is now the limiting factor (even with improved brass cartridge cases) with a strong bolt-action rifle like the Remington Model 700, Winchester Model 70, or any of the Mauser-type turnbolt actions. Today's rifles can normally withstand much greater pressures than cartridge brass.

Even though a rifle's action may not fail under excessive high-pressure loads, a cartridge case which fails and leaks high-pressure gas is nothing to sneeze at when considering today's operating pressures. Gas leaking back through a rifle's action, depending on the design of the action, can have a damaging effect. Unburned powder and brass particles, along with high-pressure gas, may come back around the rifle's action parts and cause injury. Gas leakage can also mean a damaged gun in the form of stock splitting or ruining the rifle's magazine box, extractor, or ejector.

Because today's rifles are so strong and operating pressures are so high, it's perhaps even more important that a handloader use care and judgment when assembling cartridges in order to not produce excessive pressures and still manage to get all the performance safely obtainable from his rifle. That's why it's necessary for a handloader to have guidelines he can observe which indicate how "hot" loads are before he goes overboard.

As mentioned, the brass case is the limiting factor with most modern bolt-action rifles. The rifle action will generally stand far more pressure than the brass. Fortunately, brass does not generally weaken without warning but begins to flow as pressure increases (in tiny increments for the careful handloader). The amount cartridge brass flows or deforms under high pressure is directly dependent on the amount of pressure applied. With this in mind, it's understandable that relative pressure levels can be determined by precisely measuring the amount of brass deformity in a cartridge case.

For years, the industry-standard cartridge pressure testing apparatus has been based on this same principle. A specialized pressure test barrel has a hole drilled into its chamber which is fitted with a piston. A lead or copper pellet (depending on the expected pressure level) of known dimensions and hardness is sandwiched between this piston and a fixed anvil held in place by an arbor.

When a cartridge is fired in this special gun, the internal chamber pressure on the piston is transferred to the copper or lead "crusher" and deforms it. Then, by carefully measuring the amount of deformity and applying the information to a tarage table, a pressure level in pounds per square inch can be determined.

The handloader can utilize this same principle; instead of using a copper or lead crusher, he can observe and measure the deformity of the cartridge brass to determine the relative pressure levels produced by his loads. This is generally what is done when a handloader utilizes the appearance of fired cases to determine if a load is excessive. A case deformed by excessive pressure may extract from the rifle's chamber with difficulty. The bolt handle may be difficult to lift or any action type difficult to unlock.

If brass flows enough to enlarge primer pockets so that primers fall out or extrudes into the boltface's ejector hole, this is definitely a sign of excessive pressure. Again, these are indications that any handloader should be aware of and immediately recognize as signs of excessive pressure. They're a warning indication to back off on the load.

Case and primer appearance is only one method of determining when an excessive load is produced. The best guide for keeping things safe is the use of many excellent handloading manuals available. By closely observing the data in all these manuals, the handloader is advised on how to keep himself out of trouble. In my experience, the maximums listed in the load manuals are *maximum*. The hotrodding handloader is asking for trouble when trying to exceed these suggested maximum powder charge levels. Loading manuals like Speer, Lyman, and Hodgdon give pressure data for some or all of the loads listed.

In some instances, there is little or no data available for possibly a new propellant, primer, case, or bullet make. In other instances, though data is available, pressure levels have been held low due to the fact that there are some very weak actions available for the listed cartridge.

The 7x57 Mauser cartridge data is a good example. Unless the data preamble specifically states the data is for strong, new guns capable of handling pressures generating 50,000 psi, it is likely held down to 46,000 psi due to the old military rifles still floating around. The *weakest* rifles available set the SAAMI standards for load data and factory cartridge pressure.

There is no reason why good brass in a strong new rifle like the Ruger Model 77, Remington Model 700, or Winchester Model 70 cannot withstand increased pressure levels of the 7x57 to improve performance.

For these reasons, it's beneficial for the handloader to have a good idea, without the aid of a manual, of the relative pressures his loads are producing. Eyeballing cases or feeling for sticky extraction–though a sure sign of high pressure–aren't good enough indicators. When these levels are reached, the shooter has already progressed *beyond* maximum.

Rather than just eyeballing for case deformity, measure the case with a micrometer. This way, relative pressure levels can be monitored as the handloader progresses, not after maximum operating pressure levels have already been exceeded.

One of the safest and simplest methods of determining your handload's pressure involves matching the pressure of your handloads to factory load pressure. The technique is outlined in the *Nosler Reloading Manual Number Two*.

First, fire a sampling of factory ammo of the chosen caliber in the test rifle and mike case expansion at the "pressure ring" or "expansion ring" just ahead of the case's belt on a belted case (or just ahead of the web on a rimmed or rimless case). Try to find the maximum amount of expansion by rotating the case and miking it at close intervals. Be sure to avoid miking over burrs or case scratches. You'll find the measurements will vary, so record the greatest one. It's a good idea to mike at least three cases to get an average.

This factory load case expansion measurement is used as a reference. Next, pull bullets from the other factory loads in the same box and empty the powder. Tap the case mouth on the bench and look inside to make sure none of the powder remains. Prepare the cases for loading by neck sizing, then starting at a low powder charge level, handload the cases in increasing charge level increments of one grain for large-capacity cases or .5 grain for smaller capacity cases. Load three cases at each charge level with the same bullet and seating depth.

Fire these handloads in increasing charge level increments and measure case expansion at each charge level as you proceed. When the factory load case expansion level is equalled with the handloads, the shooter can assume his handloads are producing pressures equalling factory loads. If he's working with a modern high-intensity cartridge having a SAAMI-recommended maximum pressure of 50,000 psi or so (the *Speer Reloading Manual Number Ten* reveals SAAMI-recommended maximum pressure), this is the time to stop.

I recently did this test with a new Remington Model 700 .25-06. When miking the factory load cases on the expansion ring, I came up with .4695-, .4691-, and .4691-inch-diameter readings. This averages out to .4692. Using a handload consisting of the Sierra 117-grain flatbase spitzer, a Remington No. 9½ primer, and DuPont IMR-4350 powder, I loaded cases beginning with 43 grains and increasing in one-grain increments all the way up to 56 grains.

A quick look at the loading manuals indicates that a maximum charge level, depending on the source, runs from 48.5 to 51.0 grains of this propellant. The accompanying chart illustrates the amount of case expansion received with each charge level increment. The 49-grain charge produced a .4692-inch-average case expansion which coincides with the factory case expansion attained. For all practical purposes, this should be considered a maximum load. Any handloader working up with a propellant for which there is no data available should stop at that point.

By coincidence, the 49-grain load velocity was similar to factory velocity – 2965 fps for factory-load velocity and 2991 fps for the 49-grain handload velocity. Chronographed data offers another cross-check to determine the relative pressure attained. If powder type and all else are equal, it takes a given pressure to produce a given velocity, in general. Therefore, if your load is producing maximum-class *velocity*, according to the manuals, you can figure your load is very likely producing maximum-class *pressure*.

As mentioned, there are handloaders who may want to go beyond factory-load levels when factory loads are very mild and when they're using heavily constructed new brass in a strong-actioned rifle. This is the *only* time a handloader can safely exceed factory-load pressure levels.

Any handloader who goes beyond factory-load pressure levels is on his own, although there are several guidelines which may serve to keep him out of trouble. The obvious and oft-quoted one is the primer appearance/-brass flow visual criteria mentioned. Again, however, these signs may not occur until *after* a dangerous pressure level has been reached. Once brass begins to deform noticeably, it may deform enough to cause an appreciable gas leak that could cause damage.

There's another method of measuring case expansion outlined in the new *Hornady Handbook of Cartridge Reloading, Third Edition*, which does not necessarily equate to factory case expansion. According to the Hornady manual, a fired case should be miked with a blade micrometer just ahead of the extractor groove on the solid web section. In other words, rather than measuring the bulging of the case body ahead of the web, the case web expansion is measured. Utilizing this system, the *same* cases are measured before and after firing to determine maximum loads.

The people at Hornady gauged many cases prior to and after firing in pressure barrels to determine a usable standard for the case head expansion system of measurement for pressure determination. According to information in the Hornady manual, it was found that case head expansion for low-pressure cartridges like the .30-30 should be .003 to .004 inch maximum, while mid-pressure range cases such as the .22-250 or .30-06 should be .005 to .006 inch maximum. Belted magnums should not expand more than .006 to .007 inch maximum. This data will vary slightly with different brands of brass due to variations in thickness, hardness, and composition, indicative of high pressure.

I decided to apply the Hornady-recommended system to the .25-06 cases that I fired to see what maximum was as indicated by the Hornady system. The first problem was I couldn't find a blade micrometer – and the contact anvil on my one-inch mike was too large to fit between the case rim and the expansion ring. My caliper has a very narrow blade edge, but measures only to three decimal places (or thousandths). To apply the Hornady system, I needed accuracy to four decimal places (or ten-thousandths).

I turned to barrelmaker Paul Marquart, who offered to chuck the fired cases in a lathe and take a .010-inch cut from the rims so that the webs could be easily measured with a conventional one-inch micrometer. It worked beautifully. The results can be seen in the accompanying table.

I did not mike the cases before firing, as outlined in the Hornady manual. Instead, I measured other unfired cases from the same lot. The average was .4646 inch. Applying the Hornady scale of .0005 to .0006 inch as being the maximum tolerable expansion for mid-pressure cases, this comes out to a .4651 to .4652 web expansion as being maximum. In my case, this equates with the 49-to-50 grain charge level – almost identical to the maximum level indicated by the expansion ring system of pressure determination.

The use of the visual brass flow (into the ejector hole) check, though expedient, is actually the poorest criteria since it requires the handloader to go beyond a "maximum" level before it becomes noticeable. Once brass deformity has been noted in the form of brass flowing into the ejector hole slightly or an expanded primer pocket, it is generally recommended that the handloader back off on his powder charge by five percent and that is said to be a maximum load. In other words, the handloader using this system fires cases at least five percent *beyond* maximum charge levels before high pressure signals are noted.

Just for the sake of pointing out what happens when the handloader proceeds to this point, I decided to use the strong Remington Model 700 and continue increasing charge levels until a noticeably sticky case extraction or brass flow was reached.

As can be seen in the accompanying chart, a very slight brass flow was not noticed until a 53-grain charge level was reached. Here, bolt lift became slightly more difficult than the previous 52-grain charge. It even required a close look to determine that brass had begun to flow slightly into the ejector hole and was burnished very slightly by the rotating bolt-face. When loading the 54-grain charge, the first two cases gave the same pressure indications that the 53-grain charge did, except when the third case was fired, the pressure deformed the case appreciably, causing both rim and primer pocket to enlarge noticeably. The action was difficult to open, and when it was opened, the primer fell out of the case. Noticeable gas leakage occurred through the action and could be smelled.

	CASE EXPANSION			
Charge Of IMR-4350 (Grains)	Average Maximum Expansion On "Expansion Ring" (Inch)	Average Maximum Expansion On "Web" (Inch)	Velocity (fps)	Velocity Increase (fps)
Unfired Factory Case Measurement		.4646		
Factory Load Remington (120-gr. PSP C-L)	.4692	.4648	2965	
43.0	.4678	.4644	2629	
44.0	.4679	.4644	2745	16
45.0	.4684	.4647	2791	46
46.0	.4688	.4648	2806	15
47.0	.4687	.4646	2871	65
48.0	.4690	.4647	2965	94
49.0	.4692	.4650	2991	26
50.0	.4694	.4652	3058	67
51.0	.4696	.4657	3118	60
52.0	.4700	.4666	3188	70
53.0	.4704	.4670	3240	52
54.0	.4717	.4703	3301	61

NOTES: Remington Model 700, .25-06, 24-inch barrel; R-P brass. Rem. No. 9½ primer, DuPont IMR-4350

Reducing this 54-grain charge level by five percent would again point to the 49-grain maximum which was also determined to be maximum by the other criteria. As can be seen, when the visual pressure level indications are reached, the handloader has gone considerably beyond what is deemed to be a maximum load. For this reason, it is not recommended. The case expansion system of pressure determination is much safer and is quite reliable according to several bullet manufacturers.

There are numerous cross-checks to make certain you don't exceed a safe charge level, or at least don't get into trouble. There is the manual data, chronograph data cross-check, case expansion ring measurement, case web measurement, case/primer appearance, and extraction characteristics. As a result, a handloader should be familiar with all methods of maximum load determination and take note of them any time he is developing load data. Safety should always be foremost in the minds of handloaders working on maximum loads.

Understanding High-Pressure Indicators

THOUGH SOME handloaders look at pressure as something undesirable, it's pressure that boots the bullet out the muzzle at high velocity. In fact, today's smokeless powders are designed to produce their maximum amount of energy under extreme pressure.

After the striker or hammer detonates the primer to ignite the propellant, the burning powder then releases expanding gases. This increasing pressure makes the powder burn even faster, i.e., the higher the chamber pressure, the more rapid smokeless powder burns. The tiny charge of powder in a rifle case develops some 25 tons of pressure in milliseconds to send the bullet speeding down the bore.

Generally, the greater the pressure, the higher the velocity. Of course, there are limits to how much pressure a rifle and cartridge can withstand without creating problems. No doubt, it's this area of excessive pressure that gives the term "pressure" an unsavory reputation among handloaders.

Insofar as the gun is concerned, manufacturers make barrels of ample steel strength and thickness to safely handle pressures that any normal load might generate. In general, it's the rear of the barrel—the breechbolt—that would fail first if the rifle were given an extreme overload. But here again, manufacturers have designed actions to be extremely strong with high-grade steel, ample lug-bearing surface, etc.

A fact often overlooked by handloaders is that backthrust on this breechbolt can vary considerably depending on case head size. Pressure is measured in pounds per square inch (psi). Therefore, to reduce backthrust on the breechbolt, we can either reduce the pounds or the inches.

For example, the .223 Remington, .308 Winchester, and 7mm Remington Magnum all operate at 52,000 pounds per square inch of chamber pressure as a SAAMI-recommended maximum. However, since case head sizes of all these cartridges are different, backthrust on the respective rifle's breechbolt will vary considerably.

The .223 Remington has a .378-inch-diameter case head, which computes to .1122 square inch of case head surface area. At 52,000 psi, there will be only 5835 pounds of backthrust at the case head. The .308, at a case head diameter of .473 inch, has .1757 square inch of case head area. At the same chamber pressure, the backthrust is considerably greater at 9136 pounds. The 7mm Remington Magnum, with a case head .532 inch in diameter, has .2222 square inch of case head area for a theoretical 11,557 pounds of backthrust. I use the word "theoretical" because this is assuming that all the internal chamber pressure is transferred to the breechbolt.

As a practical matter, when you develop a maximum load in a hunting rifle, the brass case is the limiting factor pressure-wise. Anyone who has developed maximum loads knows that when a charge gets too "hot," brass begins to create problems. Case extraction becomes more difficult, primer pockets can become enlarged or, in serious instances, cases can become completely stuck in the rifle's chamber.

Like pressure, the brass case should not be thought of as "weak" or "bad"; instead, it should be used as an indicator providing us with a warning for our own safety. Fortunately, brass begins to deform or flow under high pressure. The pressure at which it begins to flow is only slightly higher than maximum working pressures for most modern, high-intensity cartridges. Therefore, if the brass is deforming in some manner, you know that your loads are on the excessive side pressure-wise; the hotter the load, the more pronounced the brass deformity.

One such deformity often used as a high-pressure indicator by hand-loaders is the shiny spot on the case head. This results from brass flowing back into the ejector hole in the rifle's boltface. It is subsequently burnished to a shiny appearance when the bolt is lifted and rubbed across this high spot. Another more severe type of brass deformation is an enlarged primer pocket with gases sometimes leaking around the edge of the primer cup to produce a blackened ring.

A number of handloaders use a micrometer to take case head expansion measurements when working up to a maximum load. In large-capacity rifle cases, maximum loads are generally approached by loading cartridges in increasing charge level increments of a half grain or one grain at a time. By carefully miking the amount of case expansion just ahead of the case's web section after firing, a handloader can derive some idea about the relative pressure his load is producing.

In my experience, one of the best ways to approach load development using the case head expansion measurement system is to first obtain a good supply of factory ammunition. Most modern high-intensity rifle cartridges are loaded to near maximum pressure levels. It's a simple matter to fire three or four of these cases in your rifle and then carefully mike the expansion ring previously mentioned. Take several measurements around each case to get an average.

The next step is to pull bullets from the other cases and empty powder charges for loading your experimental cartridges. Resize the case necks and then load your experimental ammo, preferably in a minimum of three-round batches per charge level increment, starting well below maximum.

Fire these loads, starting with the lightest charge and progressing to heavier charge levels, miking cases as you go. When you reach a case head expansion measurement that duplicates the factory load expansion measurement, stop right there. Your handloads are equaling pressures of the factory loads.

It's best to neck size these cases only before reloading because any working of the brass tends to harden it. It's unlikely that even a full-length sizing die would work the brass in the base of a new case, but all you need to do is size the case neck to secure the bullets.

This system of case head expansion measurement is not as precise as some would have us believe, although it is true that the more experience you gain, the more reliable the system becomes and the more confident you'll be in its results.

Brass deformation is only one area of determining a maximum load. Primer appearance is another method frequently used by handloaders to gain a relative idea about the pressure a load generates. For example, the higher the chamber pressure, the more flattened and more cratered a primer generally appears. The important thing to remember when using primer appearance as a high-pressure indicator, however, is that it's necessary to be familiar with the individual primer and rifle being used. Handloaders often overlook the fact that differences in firing pin hole diameter, firing pin diameter, firing pin nose shape, and striker spring strength *all* make a difference in primer cratering.

For example, a primer that's been completely pierced in the area of the firing pin indent may indicate that the load was excessive. There are exceptions. I once owned a rifle that had a too large firing pin hole in the boltface; it would routinely pierce primers even with mild loads.

When I initially handloaded for the rifle, I immediately thought the loads were too hot and began backing off in powder charge levels. However, there was little change in the number of pierced primers. After scrutinizing the fired cases and noting that the edges of the primers were barely flattened at all, I took the rifle to a gunsmith who drilled and tapped the existing firing pin hole and turned a screw into it. Then he redrilled the hole in a smaller diameter. I never had a pierced primer in that rifle again.

As mentioned earlier, the edges of primers are rounded when they're pressed into the cases. The edges of the primers become increasingly flattened as chamber pressure goes up. Here again, however, this can be misleading. If a rifle has a bit of excessive headspace, or if an excessive headspace condition has been produced by the handloader setting the case shoulder back, a primer will sometimes come out looking like the load was excessive when actually it was not.

When the striker falls in a rifle with this excessive headspace condition, it will push the cartridge forward in the chamber before the primer detonates. At this instant, there is a gap between the rifle breechbolt and the base of the cartridge. When the primer detonates, pressure may force the primer back out of the case a little bit before powder ignition. Then, the high-pressure propellant gases drive the base of the case back hard against the boltface, sometimes riveting the primer around the primer pocket. The result is severely flattened edge of the primer.

Nevertheless, primer appearance is one of the easiest-to-use and most reliable indicators of high pressure. It's one that any handloader can utilize quickly on the spot and without special tools. Here again, however, the reliability of this method of pressure determination depends to a great degree on the shooter's experience.

A third method of doublechecking pressure level is one that few handloaders use—the chronograph. It cannot be depended on by itself, but it can still be quite useful. In general, it takes a specific pressure level to produce a given velocity in an individual rifle. Today's loading manuals almost always provide information regarding the rifle that was used to obtain the load data listed in the manual. If you happen to have the same rifle listed in the manual to develop data, your velocities should be somewhat comparable. By comparing the chronographed velocities you are receiving with those in the manuals, you can get some idea about the pressures your loads are generating.

Suppose 55 grains of W785 produces 3280 fps with the 100-grain Speer hollowpoint in your Remington Model 700 .25-06. The .25-06 data in the *Speer Reloading Manual Number Ten* was also shot with a Remington Model 700 with the same cases and primers you're using. Although the Speer manual says you can go up to 57.0 grains for its listed maximum, I wouldn't do it since it's this 57.0 grain charge that it lists as producing 3240 fps.

Though you've attained this velocity with two grains less powder, it's best to assume that your pressures are nearly the same as Speer's maximum load with two grains more powder. Again, it generally takes a given pressure level to produce a given velocity. Therefore, if your chronograph velocities are equal to those in the loading manual, you can assume that your pressures are pretty much the same as well.

Another thing I have noticed from using a chronograph is that velocity generally increases as charge level increases in pretty much of a linear progression. However, when maximum pressure levels are reached, unusual things occasionally happen. Sometimes velocity ceases to increase, jumps to an extremely high level, or even decreases! Any time something irregular like this occurs, I become extremely cautious and closely observe the other pressure signs.

You may not be interested in working up to absolute maximums in your particular rifle. But it is a good idea to be familiar with all these systems of pressure measurement since you never know what maximum is in your rifle. It could be several grains less than the maximum listed in the loading manuals. Handloaders who assume that the maximums listed in the loading manuals are maximums for their rifles are mistaken. In a number of instances, I have owned rifles that would not accept the maximum charges listed in several loading manuals.

It is best if you can utilize these three checks on relative pressure any time you are developing a new load. Even if you're starting well below maximum, it's possible to make an error in handloading—erroneously setting the powder scale, using the wrong powder, etc. It happens to the best of us. If you know the excessive pressure signs, you will be able to avoid any pressure problems and get even more out of this great hobby.

A Good Loading Manual

IF LOADING DATA is needed for nearly any bullet weight or payload available, a look at one of the loading manuals is all that's necessary. The manuals reveal approximately what maximum will be and what the velocity of the chosen load will be (at least in the ballpark). Most of us are so accustomed to using such data that we take it for granted.

I once attended a Winchester-sponsored ammunition components workshop. Dwain Kruse, senior engineer in research and development, described how loads were developed for the *Winchester Ball Powder Loading Data* booklet.

No matter whether rifle, handgun, or shotshell ammunition is to be loaded, the people at Winchester first use a reference lot of powder which has proven, via careful analysis, to be representative as average for that particular propellant type. Secondly, SAAMI reference ammo, which is standard throughout the shooting industry, is fired through the pressure and velocity barrels to check equipment functioning. This reference ammunition produces a known pressure and velocity, and it is the standard by which equipment is checked for later assessment of the handloads' pressure and velocity. This SAAMI reference ammo and the reference lot of powder form a known basis from which loads can be developed.

More specifically, shotshell loads are initially assembled using standard handloading-type tools to seat wads and crimp hulls. The loading tools chosen are representative of tools handloaders will be using. Powder and shot are charged by hand to obtain the maximum uniformity of loads. A shot size is used that coincides with the intended use of the load. Only loads which produce good-looking crimps are tested. If the components take too little or too much space in the hull, a poor-looking crimp results; any such load is discarded at the outset. Also, Winchester uses only primers with covered flash holes so the finer propellants don't sift their way inside the primer's "battery cup" to produce problems later.

After the likely load possibles are assembled, they're fired in a pressure barrel to determine pressure and velocity. The loads in the Winchester manual do not exceed 95 percent of SAAMI maximum in terms of pressure. This allows for slight variations in loading components which may be encountered by shooters in the field. The load must produce adequate velocity with allowable pressures, but it must also be uniform in performance.

The average pressure and velocity are important, but so are the high and low extremes; all are carefully considered. Further, the same criteria is applied to loads tested at 125 degrees Fahrenheit on the high side and zero degrees Fahrenheit on the low side. Wad performance is also checked at these temperature extremes. Noting whether the plastic wads tend to fracture at cold temperatures is particularly important.

When developing centerfire rifle loads, the people at Winchester again use readily available loading equipment (RCBS, Lyman, etc.) commonly used by the handloader. Again, a reference lot of powder and SAAMI reference ammunition are used to check the functioning of the pressure equipment. Pressure and velocity data are initially derived from ammunition fired at 70 degrees.

The criteria for developing metallic loads departs from shotshell criteria in several areas. For example, load data for Winchester Ball powder propellants consists of loads producing a minimum of 89 percent to a maximum of 98 percent loading density. All other loads are rejected.

In addition, pressure and velocity testing is conducted with variations in powder positioning within the case to simulate extreme uphill or downhill shooting. In other words, the cartridge is tipped up so the powder is very close to the primer and is then carefully chambered and fired. This information is compared with pressure and velocity data obtained with the propellant positioned next to the base of the bullet, away from the primer, during firing.

This aspect, which is greatly overlooked according to the people at Winchester, can have a great effect on pressure and velocity variations. It can be particularly critical with slow-burning propellants and cold temperatures.

The metallic cartridge loads are also checked at minus 40 and plus 140 degrees Fahrenheit. Regarding pressure, velocity, and accuracy, the acceptance criteria for the Winchester-developed handloads is the same as for the company factory loads. The criteria for rifle load data applies to handgun load development (except for the maximum and minimum loading density specifications).

If everything runs smoothly, about 100 rounds of ammunition are required to develop a single load. Questions occur frequently, and additional ammunition must be fired to verify the acceptability of the load for the load manual data. After hearing how data is developed, I gained a new appreciation for the loads listed in the loading manual.

The loads listed, at least in the Winchester loading manual, are not taken lightly by the people who develop them.

Benchrest Shooters Versus Ordinary Shooters

I'M OFTEN ASKED what can be done, beyond the ordinary, to ensure accurate ammunition. Sometimes a shooter has what he thinks is a superbly accurate varmint rifle and wants to be sure he's getting all the accuracy from it he can.

First you need to know what sort of accuracy you're talking about. For a coyote hunter, one-inch, five-shot groups at 100 yards from an off-the-shelf .22 centerfire sporter may be "accurate." For a prairie dog shooter who tunes his rifles, half-inch groups may be required before he calls the rifle accurate. A benchrest shooter today probably wouldn't call a rifle accurate unless it had the potential to produce an average of five five-shot groups, under ideal conditions, measuring under .2 inch. That means groups measuring somewhere in the "ones" – .1 inch to .2 inch.

Benchrest shooters can teach us a lot about accuracy. Keep in mind that some of their care in loading is wasted on the average varmint rifle simply because the rifle/shooter combination isn't accurate enough to realize the benefits from the fine-tuning techniques. A competition benchrest rifle is a highly specialized, refined machine, and few varmint rifles come close to having the care that goes into the manufacture or modification of a benchrest rifle.

If you're looking for the ultimate in accuracy, attend a registered benchrest match. You can see how these shooters load their ammo, and you can learn a lot just by looking at the equipment used and the loading techniques employed.

There is no higher level of competitive accuracy than benchrest shooting. Unlike other forms of competition shooting that try a shooter's skill in holding, more human error is eliminated in benchrest shooting. As a result, there is the possibility for a higher level of accuracy, and a seasoned competitor learns to discern accuracy levels more precisely.

In other words, most shooting sports competitors wouldn't know or care about the difference between a rifle that shoots .1-inch groups or one that shoots .25-inch groups. But to a benchrest shooter, that's a *lot* of difference. In large matches, it can mean the difference between winning and not placing in the top 20.

With that in mind, I'll look at how benchrest shooters prepare ammunition for competition. The first consideration is the case. A competitive shooter selects cases with care and may use only 20 to 100 during the lifetime of his barrel. From any given lot of virgin brass, cases are weighed, and those that weigh very close to the same are placed together. The thinking here is that weight equates to case capacity.

Primer pockets are then inspected and may even be miked for uniformity. Any that don't look like the rest of the cases are discarded. Flash holes should be on center. They are then reamed from the inside of the case to remove any burrs that may have been left by the punching process. A small drill bit will work, but there are tools made specifically for removing flash hole burrs. The reason such attention is directed at flash holes is that benchrest shooters are very concerned with uniform primer ignition.

One of the most important steps in case preparation is neck wall turning. This is done not so much to thin the neck as to produce a case with a uniform neck wall thickness. A neck that's thicker on one side than the other will cause the bullet of a chambered round to be off center or canted in the barrel. Variations in neck wall thickness on virgin brass are sometimes large and readily apparent. The neck-turning tool usually reveals how much the thickness varies by the amount of brass it removes from different portions of the case neck. There are many different tools designed for turning necks, but most of those in popular use by benchrest shooters have a pilot that fits inside the case neck, and there is a blade cutter that removes brass from the outside of the neck. Case neck wall thickness is checked with a tubing micrometer.

Benchrest shooters turn the case necks to a thickness so that the brass fits in the tight-necked chamber with very close tolerances when a loaded round is chambered. There is generally just enough room in the case neck area to allow the bullet to be released when the cartridge is fired. When the case is subsequently resized (if it is), there is little or no moving of the brass. In some instances, a bullet will seat with a friction fit in a fired case neck without resizing the case. Some shooters turn case necks only to the depth of a seated bullet. This way, there is a shoulder in the neck and bullets are seated simply by pressing them in with the fingers until they reach this shoulder stop, resulting in bullets being seated to the same depth. When case necks are turned this way, there's no case sizing at all (no working of the brass); for this reason, cases last almost forever.

Since you don't have a tight neck chamber in your production varmint rifle, your cases would best be turned just enough to "clean up" any eccentricities in the neck. In fact, if you turn your necks too thin, conventional sizing dies won't reduce the neck diameter enough to secure a bullet.

The benchrest shooter's brass is trimmed and deburred. It may be trimmed again after fireforming to fit the rifle's chamber precisely.

Rather than use a conventional bench-mounted press, benchrest shooters nearly always use handtools for loading. A hand mallet or arbor press is used to press cases into and out of dies. Loading dies are often custommade with the same reamer that chambered the rifle. While you probably wouldn't go to that trouble with your varmint rifle, RCBS Competition Dies are useful alternatives for the varmint shooter.

The bullet is considered to be perhaps the single most important component toward a high level of accuracy. Benchrest shooters usually employ bullets that are custom-made by hand in high-quality, expensive benchrest dies. There are relatively few of these bullets available for varmint hunters, and they're expensive. An alternative might be to select match bullets from the various major manufacturers. Some of these are quite good and cost a lot less than handmade benchrest bullets.

When a benchrest shooter finds a combination of powder and primer that shoots well in a particular rifle, he buys a large quantity of that particular lot. A varmint shooter can do the same.

Benchrest shooters often use hand-priming devices that allow the user to "feel" the primer seat in the bottom of the pocket. It's considered important to have the primer seated firmly at the bottom of the pocket without crushing the priming mix.

Most benchrest shooters dispense propellant with a measure and not a scale. In fact, many benchrest competitors don't even know the weight of the powder charge they're using. Instead, powder is thrown by volume or a particular measure setting. The measures are often modified to dispense a particular powder with a high degree of accuracy, but few benchrest shooters weigh each powder charge. Shooters have discovered that weighing every charge really has no advantage, even when it comes to fine benchrest accuracy. A varmint shooter would do well to use a powder that meters uniformly from his own measure and dispense loads by measure rather than by the time-consuming weighing process.

One thing a varmint shooter should never borrow from a benchrest competitor is load data. Competition shooters regularly use *hot* loads to achieve the highest velocity and best accuracy. A routine benchrest load is often in excess of what is considered to be maximum in a sporting rifle. Loads are often reported along with match results, but you should ignore them. Get your starting load data from data manuals published by the bullet and powder distributors.

The key to getting a high level of accuracy from ammunition is uniformity. Anything you can do to make your ammunition more uniform will contribute to a higher level of accuracy.

To apply this information to your varmint rifle, segregate cases by weight, deburr flash holes, turn case necks to a uniform wall thickness, use match bullets, employ straight-line handtools for handloading, and seat primers just so with handtools. This is all in addition to the usual experimentation with various components, such as the bullet, powder, case, and primer.

One last item: bulletseating depth. This one aspect has a direct bearing on accuracy, and it's one area that warrants experimentation.

After you've gone to all this trouble, your rifle might not shoot any better, but you'll have the knowledge that you're doing what you can to encourage a higher level of accuracy, and it just might pay off.

A Step Toward Ultimate Accuracy

SERIOUS SHOOTERS are forever striving to make their guns more accurate. This experimentation has brought about many improvements in firearms design, handload and loading techniques, shooting techniques, and shooting accessories that aid in making the bullet go precisely where you want.

Today's rifles, particularly those designed for precision shooting, are the culmination of all these refinements. But there are still experimenters—shooters who go a step beyond with the hope they'll obtain an even greater accuracy edge, no matter how slight.

Due to the high degree of precision shooting their sport requires, bench-rest shooters are known for the extremes they'll go to in order to obtain even very slight improvements in accuracy. For a number of years, these competition shooters have been turning or thinning the neck portion of cartridge cases in order to make brass thickness more uniform.

Most shooters know the barrel or bore axis must be perpendicular with the rifle's boltface and the chamber must be concentric with the bore in order to obtain a high level of accuracy. These relationships within the rifle are maintained with very close tolerance by machinists who are familiar with benchrest rifle building. The idea behind this relation-ship is to hold the bullet in near-perfect alignment with the bore prior to firing. A problem arises with brass cartridge cases because they are drawn rather than machined.

Even though it's more practical and less expensive, drawing brass is not as precise a machining. The result is that slight irregularities occur in the thickness and uniformity of finished brass cases. For example, it's not uncommon for .22-caliber case neck brass to vary by .002 inch in thickness as it comes from the box. If the thinnest and thickest parts of the case neck are on opposite sides, it's not difficult to understand how a chambered round might position the bullet out of alignment with the rifle's bore. When the cartridge is fired, the bullet would be jammed into the rifling offcenter. The results of such a misaligned bullet are likely to show up on the downrange target.

In benchrest rifles, the chamber necks are cut undersize (when com-pared to a factory chamber), which makes it necessary to thin the brass case neck to correspond with the rifle's tight chamber neck. With today's best neck-turning tools, brass is machined from the case neck so the resulting thickness is very uniform. As a result, the uniform case neck and the tight chamber hold the bullet in near-perfect alignment with the axis of the bore.

In recent years, many shooters besides benchrest competitors have become interested in case neck turning, and many varmint shooters are turning case necks with the thought that any potential accuracy improvement is worthwhile.

Though case neck turning is considered mandatory in a competitive benchrest situation, I've often wondered just how much advantage could be gained by turning necks on cases to be used in an off-the-shelf varmint rifle. Some shooters report as much as a 30 to 50 percent improvement in varmint rifle accuracy simply by turning case necks; others report there isn't any noticeable improvement.

Paul Marquart (Marquart Precision Co.) makes one of the finest neck-turning tools on the market. Paul claims his tools will turn brass uni-formly within .0001 inch. I was in his shop when a shooter came in and asked how much accuracy improvement could be expected by using a neck-turning tool on his cases for a particular rifle.

"I don't know," Paul said.

Somewhat confused, the shooter asked, "Can I expect *any* improvement in accuracy?"

Paul's reply: "I don't know."

Paul was just being honest. There is no question a neck-turning tool produces a more uniform neck thickness. How much more uniform can be measured with a ball or tubing mike. Unlike tight-necked benchrest rifle chambers, however, production-rifle chambers are cut with more room in the neck area to accommodate differences in case neck wall thickness of factory ammo. Consequently, when the brass of a case neck is thinned and made more uniform, there is a lot of room in the neck of the rifle's chamber for the case neck to move around in.

I wondered if most varmint rifles would reveal a higher level of accuracy from case neck turning. There's no question about advantages of a theoretical nature, but it's possible these advantages might not be significant from a practical standpoint.

A discussion of the pros and cons could go on forever, and I wanted some hard-and-fast test shooting evidence. I had never experimented with neck turning before in a varmint rifle. Most of the neck turners on the market are precision tools operated by hand that remove brass from the *outside* of the case neck; they are not to be confused with other types of tools that are actually boring bars and remove brass from the *inside* of a case neck.

Most of the benchrest-type tools (like Marquart's) consist of a pilot that goes inside the case neck and controls the length of the cut surface. The cutting portion of the tool is held in alignment by this tight-fitting pilot, which is ground to close tolerances and then rotated around the outside of the case neck using hand pressure.

Neck turning, unlike other forms of case improvement, needs to be done only once. Granted, a considerable amount of time is required to turn a large quantity of case necks, but unlike case trimming, it doesn't have to be repeated.

Sizing and trimming cases before neck turning them is important since the pilot shoulder and cutter are stopped by the case mouth. Consequently, case neck length regulates the length of the cut. Only remove enough brass to "clean up" the neck; otherwise, the case can be ruined by turning the neck too thin and may not hold a bullet securely.

One lot of new factory cases I measured with the tubing mike varied by as much as .002 inch in neck thickness. New, unfired cases are quite soft when compared to sized brass. Consequently, once-fired cases can be thinned more uniformly. After turning a number of new cases and miking them, I found neck wall thickness varied by as much as .0005 inch (still considerably better than factory brass), while neck wall thickness of once-fired brass cases varied by less than .0002 inch after turning.

If new cases varied a lot in neck wall thickness, case neck turning would be more likely to show accuracy improvement than if factory cases were initially uniform. The .22-250 Remington cases miked were very uniform as they came from the factory, showing the .002-inch variation mentioned earlier.

I decided to use a production varmint rifle as it came from the factory (with the exception of adjusting the trigger pull to two pounds) and fire a variety of loads with both turned and unturned case necks to see if any noticeable improvement in accuracy could be obtained by neck turning.

The most accurate production rifle I have is a Remington Model 700 Varmint Special chambered in .22-250 and fitted with a Weaver Varmint T scope in Redfield mounts.

I selected five different bullets and five powders without developing any of the loads for accuracy. The plan was to fire three five-shot groups with each load using turned case necks; the same loads would then be fired with unturned case necks for a total of 30 shots per load. This initial testing involved 30 five-shot groups or a total of 150 shots fired for accuracy.

The Remington Model 700 was fired from a benchrest at 100 yards; with the aid of a Custom chronograph, I clocked velocity simultaneously with accuracy testing. (In order to avoid interruptions between shots to record velocity, I enlisted the assistance of Kevin Duffield to keep track of velocity.) The results can be seen in the accompanying table.

CASE NECK TURNING DATA

Bullet	Powder (Type)	(Grs.)	Primer	Case	Velocity** (Average)	Accuracy (Inches) Turned Cases	Accuracy (Inches) Unturned Cases
Hornady 50-gr. spirepoint	IMR-3031	35.0	Rem. 9½	R-P	3539	1.13*	.73
Sierra 52-gr. HPBT	H380	39.0	Rem. 9½	R-P	3572	.56	.96
Speer 52-gr. HP	H4895	35.0	Rem. 9½	R-P	3688	.80*	.70
Remington 55-gr. P-L HP	W760	40.0	Rem. 9½	R-P	3530	.93	1.20
Nosler 60-gr. Solid Base	H414	38.0	Rem. 9½	R-P	3356	1.73	1.76
Sierra 52-gr. HPBT***	H4895	35.0	Rem. 9½	R-P	3633	.84	.92

NOTES: *Included in this average was the smallest group fired at .4 inch.
    **Velocities are an average of 20 shots at 10 feet from the gun's muzzle taken with a Custom chronograph.
    ***Accuracy is an average of three five-shot groups for all loads except this one, which is an average of five five-shot groups.

The cases with the turned necks came up with the smallest group averages in three of the five cases. The best 15-shot average was fired with the Sierra 52-grain hollowpoint boattail benchrest bullet and 39 grains of H380 powder. The average was .56 inch. The smallest group of the entire test was fired with turned case necks, the Speer 52-grain hollowpoint bullet, and 35 grains of H4895. But when the entire 30-group series was averaged, the turned case necks came up with such a slight edge as to be of little significance. The turned case necks came in with a 1.03-inch group average, while the unturned necks showed a 1.07-inch average.

With one exception, the turned case necks came in with the most consistent velocities. The most uniform velocity was produced by the Speer 52-grain hollowpoint bullet ahead of 35 grains of H4895. This load varied only 40 fps in 10 shots, while the unturned case necks came up with a 56 fps variation. Once again, all this shooting didn't really prove there was any advantage to turning case necks—at least not in this particular rifle at this accuracy level. Perhaps one-inch accuracy is not good enough for the slight advantages gained from neck turning to be realized on the target.

This thought plagued me since there are a good number of factory .22 centerfire rifles that will better the one-inch class with a bit of load development and tuning on the shooter's part. Another curious factor: Case necks of new brass are not turned as uniformly as necks from once-fired brass. For convenience, I had used new brass.

For these reasons, I decided to conduct additional shooting, utilizing what I hoped would be an extremely accurate combination using the consistent-velocity H4895 powder with the Sierra 52-grain boattail hollowpoint benchrest, the bullet that turned up the best group. Instead of three five-shot groups, I decided to fire five five-shot groups to hopefully obtain a more valid sampling. And I decided to utilize once-fired brass throughout this second test in order to obtain the most uniform case neck thickness possible.

In order to obtain the smallest groups possible, I was hoping for calm shooting conditions late in the evening, but the wind was a bit brisk. Since testing time was limited, I had to proceed with the shooting.

Considering the brisk wind, I was pleased with the group sizes. As can be seen in the table, there was a slight advantage to the turned case necks. The average of the five five-shot groups fired with the turned case necks came in at .84 inch; the unturned case necks produced a larger .92 inch average. This amount of shooting cannot be considered conclusive, but five five-shot groups generally provide a beginning for accuracy comparisons.

Despite the expenditure of 200 rounds, this testing was limited, as any test of this type must be. Only one rifle was used, and there are other areas where variations are possible — not the least of which are shooter error and variations in conditions. Your particular rifle in a specific situation may show greater improvement in accuracy with turned case necks. There is no question case necks can be made more uniform; the question is whether this will make a difference in your situation with your rifle.

The shooter in Paul's shop did decide to purchase one of Marquart's neck-turning tools. The fact that it *might* help was reason enough to try it. I think most shooters would agree trying anything which might possibly improve the accuracy of a favorite varmint rifle is worthwhile. After all, that's what seeking the ultimate in accuracy is all about.

Shooting/Handloading "Truths"

I T'S INTERESTING how shooters, both newcomers and veterans, accept without question some of the beliefs about shooting and handloading which have been passed around for years. There are some old-timers who've done more shooting than I ever will, and there's been a lot of tedious, time-consuming experimentation that has taught me a lot about shooting and handloading. Still, a fair amount of the "information" available is never questioned, and I think some of it could use additional examination.

Rifle bore cleaning is a good example. I've heard a number of shooters make this claim: "If a rifle is shooting good, don't mess with it. Don't run a brush through its bore!" On the other hand, benchrest shooters who really know what's what about accuracy have proven accuracy can deteriorate noticeably after the fouling from as few as 20 shots in a .22-caliber centerfire rifle.

Case length is another area which could use closer scrutiny. I've heard experienced shooters curse cartridges designed with short case necks. I've yet to figure out why.

One bullet diameter is repeated as the absolute minimum case neck length for any cartridge. In other words, it would be a .224-inch-long case neck for a .22, .257 for a .25, and .308 for a .30-caliber cartridge. Two of the more popular cases that don't cut it are the .223 Remington and the .300 Winchester Magnum. The .223 has a nominal .203-inch neck; the .300 Winchester has a .264. The .308, at .305, almost makes it. A few of the less popular short-neck rounds are the 6.5 Remington Magnum, .264 Winchester Magnum, .284 Winchester, and the .300 Savage. The .300 Savage, with a *very* short .192-inch nominal neck length, is the leader when it comes to short necks.

One reason given for a short case neck causing problems is because the bullet must be seated so deeply into the case that it intrudes on the case's powder capacity. While this explanation might sound good on the surface, it simply makes no sense. The .284 Winchester and .300 Winchester Magnum are often offered as prime examples. True, bullets must be seated deeply in these cases with most rifles, but this isn't due to cartridge design—it's because of the *rifles*.

The .284 was designed for maximum powder capacity in short-action rifles, while the .300 Winchester was made for standard .30-06-length actions. Magazine length and/or throating, not case design, are what determine how deeply a bullet must be seated. Lengthen rifle magazines and throat the guns longer, and bullets can be seated farther out so they don't take up powder space.

Another myth: A long case neck is necessary to produce the best accuracy. A long neck reportedly holds the bullet securely and concentric with the rifle's bore. But any shooter who mikes case neck thickness soon realizes how much neck thickness can vary around its circumference. Actually, case necks are more likely to produce a misalignment with the rifle's bore, which is the reason for the increased popularity of case neck turning tools. Benchrest shooters learned long ago to rely on a tight rifle chamber neck to align the bullet rather than a brass case, which can vary considerably.

Neither the short-necked .223 nor the .300 Winchester Magnum is inaccurate. The latter has been popular among 1000-yard competition shooters for years, while the former is a popular chambering in accurate varmint rifles.

My benchrest rifle is chambered for the long-necked .222 Remington cartridge, which has a reputation second to none for accuracy. However, the long case neck has nothing to do with the cartridge's accuracy potential. My rifle is throated so bullets are seated only about ⅛ inch inside the case mouth! Though the .222 case has a long neck, it's not used in many super-accurate benchrest rifles.

If a case neck were so short on a heavy-recoiling cartridge that its neck tension and overall bullet contact area were inadequate to secure a bullet under recoil, then a case neck could be called too short. I know of no commercially manufactured cases with this problem.

I think all this fretting over a long case neck versus a short one boils down to looks. We've had it drilled into us through years of reading gun books that cases of .25-06, .270, .30-06, etc., proportions are right. Anything appearing different in proportion just doesn't *look* right. How can you argue with this?

Controlling Headspace

S HOOTERS HAVE probably been concerned about headspace since the invention of the metallic cartridge. In the early years, headspace was a major concern primarily because rifle actions weren't as strong as today's and because cartridge brass was of poor quality both in design and brittleness.

However, there have been a lot of major advances in both areas. Today's actions are built with stronger materials and improved designs. And in some cases, the same action design that had a reputation for being weak 50 years ago has a very solid design today.

Case head separations were once common; now they are unusual. Yet, even today, excessive headspace can cause problems in terms of reloading difficulties, shortened case life, and less-than-the-best accuracy. The handloader who understands the subject thoroughly, however, has nothing to worry about because he can do something about it. He *can* control headspace completely. That means there should be no such thing as excessive headspace if you're a handloader.

A lot has been written on the subject, and a lot of it has been confusing. There's no doubt that a detailed description of headspace can be difficult for the uninitiated shooter to follow. But all headspace actually is is the fit of a cartridge in a chamber (i.e., the distance from the rifle's bolt or breechface to the part of the chamber which stops the cartridge's forward movement). Insufficient headspace hinders complete chambering; excessive headspace permits case stretching or separations.

To the firearms and ammo manufacturers, headspace is a matter of specific tolerances that are needed so any gun in a specific caliber will safely accept any factory ammunition of the same cartridge designation. Gun manufacturers have certain tolerances to which they must cut chambers; ammunition manufacturers have certain tolerances to which they must manufacture ammo. These manufacturers are concerned with their particular problem. The shooter, however, is concerned with the combination of both because the gunmaker's maximum chamber tolerances and the ammomaker's ammunition tolerances come together in his rifle.

Ideally, the ammo fits the chamber precisely. But due to the nature of tolerances and manufacturing difficulties, it can't. There will always be gaps around the factory cartridge as it rests in the chamber. The effect these gaps have when the cartridge is fired is partially dependent on where they are located. The most serious gap is between the cartridge case head or base and the boltface or breechblock when the cartridge is chambered in its forwardmost position and the action is locked (i.e., headspace).

Prior to actual firing, when the firing pin strikes the primer, it may drive the cartridge as far forward as possible in the chamber and away from the boltface prior to primer ignition. Then, when the powder ignites and builds pressure inside the case, the thinner case walls and neck will be forced tight against the chamber walls, while the thicker base portion of the case will be driven rearward as far as possible until it contacts the boltface with a pounding force.

In order to do this, the case must elongate, resulting in the brass just ahead of the thick base portion stretching and thinning. Normally, this is all that happens. But if a large gap exists at the rear of the case and/or if the brass is brittle, a case separation could occur at this point. This is why headspace specifications were developed with the idea of keeping the base of the case pressed against the boltface.

Headspace measurements are taken at different points for different cartridges, depending on design, but measurements are taken to make sure excessive space doesn't exist at the head of the cartridge. For a rimmed cartridge like the .30-30 or .45-70, the headspace measurement is taken from the rifle's boltface to the point in the chamber where the forward face of the case rim rests. In a belted case, such as a 7mm Remington Magnum, the forward face of the belt is used; in a rimless or rebated bottleneck design, such as a .30-06 or .284, the measurement is to a point on the chamber's shoulder. With a straight, rimless case like the .30 Carbine, the measurement is to the case mouth. Semi-rimmed rifle cases like the .220 Swift generally headspace on the shoulder (like a rimless case).

Fortunately, new cartridge brass is ductile and has a surprising ability to conform to the gun's chamber. Once the cartridge is fired, it will fit that particular chamber perfectly, even though there were gaps prior to firing it. But if the handloader wants to use these fireformed cases in another gun, he may have to turn the sizing die down in the loading press until it contacts the shellholder on the raised press ram. This will reduce the dimensions of the brass almost to its original size, just like it was in a factory load; as a result, the case will be small enough to fit any gun.

However, complete sizing like this does two things: First, each pass through the sizing die workhardens the brass a little more so that it is made progressively more brittle; secondly, the portion of the case wall that thinned on the initial firing will still be there—it is not made thicker by sizing. Consequently, when the case is fired a second time, it will become even thinner in the same place.

Eventually, if the case is sized and fired enough times, the brass will separate at this weak point, and high-pressure gases may leak back through the rifle's action. And in the event of a complete head separation, the portion of the case remaining in the rifle's chamber may be difficult, if not impossible, to remove while you're in the field.

The number of reloadings a case will hold up to before it separates depends on several things—like the brittleness of unfired brass, the size of the original cartridge and chamber, and the amount of headspace remaining after every case sizing. Remember: The more headspace that exists, the quicker and more completely the case will separate.

Factory-loaded rimmed and belted cases are frequently more susceptible to case stretching than rimless cases, particularly when the case is fully sized every time. This has nothing to do with the case itself; it has to do with the headspace measurements and manufacturing tolerances. Since, in both of these instances, the headspace measurement is taken only to the forward edge of the rim or belt, the rifle's chamber portion ahead of this—the distance to the chamber shoulder—may be excessively long.

As I mentioned, there's nothing wrong with this "problem" in factory loads; ductile brass will conform to the rifle's chamber—just like a wildcatter's cartridge does when he "improves" it by fireforming. (This is an example of excessive headspace to the extreme.)

The judicious handloader uses separate brass for each particular gun—even those in the same caliber. He also sizes the cases no more than necessary to ensure smooth functioning. And above all else, he makes certain the neck portion of the sizing die compresses the brass no farther than the junction of the neck and shoulder. Under no circumstances does he set the shoulder back. There won't be any excessive headspace if the handloader takes special care not to alter the case any more than necessary when reloading, no matter what the headspace situation was with factory ammo.

In most cases, neck sizing alone is enough to allow smooth cartridge chambering. Cases can actually last almost indefinitely if very little sizing is applied to them. For hunting applications, some working of the brass is necessary. However, the less sizing you do, the better.

I have a couple of old cartridge guns with weak actions which have been "set back" through years of use. In order to fireform factory ammo without case wall thinning in this excessive headspace situation, I simply pull the bullets from the factory ammo, size the case necks, and reseat the bullets far enough out to bear against the rifling lands when the round is chambered.

By going through this procedure, the excessive headspace is controlled with the bullet in order to hold the base of the case tight against the bolt-face for the first firing. After the first firing, the case has conformed to the rifle's chamber with very little thinning ahead of the web. Then, as long as I am careful not to set the shoulder back in sizing, each subsequent loading produces a properly headspaced cartridge, and the projecting bullets are no longer needed.

Even in modern guns, this technique has proven worthwhile. For instance, I recently miked samples of a wide variety of belted cases. With the aid of a depth mike and a special collar (designed by Paul Marquart) machined with parallel sides, I measured the distance from the forward edge of the belt to the base of the case.

Specifications call for this measurement to run .220 inch maximum on the more popular belted cases like the 7mm Remington and .300 Winchester. But in one particular box of ammo, I found a number of the cases measured only .211 inch, and the variation ran as great as .011 inch. Considering that maximum headspace allowance for a case/chamber relationship like the .338 Winchester Magnum should be no more than .009 inch (minimum cartridge; maximum chamber), the .011 inch variation in the belted cases is a lot, yet it is almost never considered.

In a nutshell, separate cases by rifle. For a bottleneck case, back off the sizing die so that it will size only the case neck and body slightly.

This can be easily accomplished by watching the burnish mark on the case neck where it has been sized. Alternately turn the die down in the press, raise the ram, and then check the amount of sizing. Do this until you've sized most of the neck. Then chamber the empty case to see if the bolt closes on it easily. If it does, then this is enough sizing; if not, try a little more sizing until the bolt closes easily.

If you follow this procedure, your custom-formed cases will not only last longer, but you will have produced zero headspace in your particular rifle.

Bullet Selection:
Tips On Testing For The Best

S HOOTERS IN the U.S. are loaded with luck. They have some of the top bullets in the world at their fingertips. In addition to some of the best hunting bullets available in factory ammunition, there's also a wide selection of bullet diameters, weights, and designs available to the handloader. Projectiles from Nosler, Hornady, Speer, Sierra, PMC, Barnes, and others are made with very uniform materials and in specially designed dies; as a result, the lot-to-lot performance received from each bullet is consistent.

As far as the hunter is concerned, matching up the proper bullet with the task at hand is what counts. In my experience, the problem many hunters encounter – "failure" with hunting bullets – has been primarily a result of improper bullet selection. A bullet that "failed" might have worked very well in another cartridge at a faster or reduced velocity, or when shooting over a longer or shorter distance, or at larger or smaller game.

It's not uncommon for a shooter to think a bullet failed if it opened up too fast, with its jacket possibly disintegrating or separating from the core, but the shooter might do well to consider whether the failed bullet would be more suitable for use in a lower velocity cartridge. If a bullet penetrates too deeply before opening or doesn't expand with a large enough frontal diameter, the hunter should perhaps consider that bullet to be better suited for deeper penetration in larger game.

There's no question bullet selection is important in terms of the game being hunted and hunting conditions (terrain, vegetation, etc.) which dictate the expected shooting distance. Even a sportsman's style of hunting or preference for shot placement will be important.

While these considerations might seem obvious, I'm amazed at the number of shooters who are using rapidly expanding varmint-class bullets for deer hunting. Many hunters avoid using the large-capacity magnum-class cartridges, saying these "ruin too much meat." Tissue destruction, however, is primarily a result of bullet performance – even more than velocity. If bullets are selected properly, magnum-case cartridges aren't any more destructive than lower velocity cartridges.

One year, I bagged a good-sized mule deer. I shot this buck with a .300 Winchester Magnum loaded with Nosler 180-grain Partition bullets, and there was perhaps an ounce or two of meat destroyed. The result of this experience was more than chance. This particular gun/cartridge/load/bullet combination was determined to be an excellent selection from the results of shooting a number of game animals; however, the combination was first tested by shooting into an artificial expansion medium.

I've previously mentioned the use of artificial expansion mediums like water, clay, wet newspapers, or wet phone directories. Wet newspapers can be bundled into eight- or 10-inch stacks; large phone directories can be used as they come. Immerse either in water overnight. When you're ready for testing, stack them horizontally on a plank. I generally shoot into a four-foot-thick stack of the wet newspapers or directories when testing rifle calibers. There are few expanding-type hunting bullets which will penetrate half this thickness.

This type of medium has the advantage of being large enough to be fired into from any distance, allowing the shooter to check the performance of his potential hunting rifle/cartridge at all reasonable ranges. Bullets can be easily recovered. Information like the amount of penetration and the size of the destruction cavity at various points along the bullet's path can be measured. And when the bullet is recovered, weight retention, percentage of weight retention, and frontal diameter can be checked. By taking notes, the shooter can predict how a particular type of bullet will perform compared to other bullets fired into the medium under identical conditions.

The artificial medium is strictly a convenient way of checking bullet performance. Such testing shows various hunting bullets do perform differently. Among the most obvious differences is the one between bullets designed for big game and those for varmints. This difference is readily apparent in calibers like the 7mm and .30, where there's a wide weight dispersion.

The shooter will also discover that, depending on the impact velocity, any given bullet can perform differently. For example, when the medium is fired into from a short distance, say 30 yards, the bullet's expansion performance will be different than if the same rifle and cartridge are used to fire into the expansion medium at 400 yards. Similarly, if different cartridges having widely varying velocities are used, the bullet performance varies drastically. For example, compare the performance of a 150-grain bullet fired at normal pressure in a .300 Savage rifle to the same bullet fired at normal pressure in a .300 Weatherby Magnum. By performing such bullet expansion experiments, the shooter can readily see how important matching a bullet to an individual hunting situation can be.

I've often heard about why this or that projectile is a "good" hunting bullet; what I don't hear about are factors like the muzzle velocity, the size of the cartridge, or the expected impact velocity or range. The hunter comparing bullet expansion in an artificial medium knows how critical these factors are.

Take the time to section various hunting bullets, and you'll clearly see why they perform differently. Sectioning involves cutting a bullet in half (from tip to base) so the inside of the bullet can be examined. This operation is not as easy as it might sound, and I went through several trial-and-error experiences without any success, trying to get a good sectioning job. Finally, Joe Callahan at Remington suggested casting the bullets in an epoxy block. The hard block could then be clamped in a milling machine, and the milling tool could be used to cut away one side of the bullet, epoxy and all.

I asked Tom Houghton at H-S Precision for assistance in trying to section bullets as Joe described. Tom offered to try the process on a large number of .30-caliber bullets.

First, a small mold was designed, the bullets were laid inside, and epoxy was poured around them and allowed to harden. Each block was approximately two inches high, one inch wide, and one inch thick. The blocks were clamped in a milling machine, and the top halves were milled away with a very sharp cutter. Finished surfaces were polished with 400-grit wet-or-dry paper for an excellent sectioning job. The epoxy supports the outside of the bullet jacket. As a result, the jacket and core don't have the tendency to "smear" the way they do when using an unsupported bullet and dressing it with a file.

By carefully examining sectioned bullets, I made some interesting discoveries. For example, Speer's Grand Slam bullets are said to have a core of two separate hardnesses, and the base core is said to be harder than the frontal portion of the core. I've often wondered about the length of the base core compared to the softer frontal core, wondered if the cores were fused together or if there were perhaps air pockets or tiny voids between the two, and wondered about the straightness of the joint between the two core hardnesses.

By sectioning the bullets, I could see the two different core alloys simply by noting the different colors in sectioned bullets. The two cores were joined very well and very squarely in relation to the jacket. Firing the Grand Slam bullets into the newspaper expansion medium, I found they performed consistently and penetrated deeply. Before shooting game, I already knew how well the Grand Slam bullets would perform, providing good penetration with a high percentage of retained weight.

Besides revealing jacket thickness and jacket tapering, examining sectioned bullets can also reveal base thickness and the effects of canneluring (insofar as pressing the jacket into the core). Studying a section of the Hornady InterLock bullet revealed just how much the interlocking jacket protruded into the core.

Sectioning does not show everything. It does not reveal jacket skiving or fracture lines which are built into the nose to cause the jacket to expand more readily, nor does it reveal the ductility of the metal.

You are probably familiar with the Nosler Partition bullet that utilizes two cores, one in the nose and one in the base. The two cores are separated by a partition of what is now gilding metal. At one time, the jacket metal in the Nosler Partition bullet was bronze, which is not nearly as ductile as the drawn gilding metal jacket. Shooters occasionally reported the old bullet would mushroom in the frontal portion and the jacket walls would break off when they reached the partition. This was reportedly a rare happening, but the older jacket was definitely more brittle, and the more ductile gilding metal is reported to eliminate the problem.

Knowing a bullet will do its job before the hunt is important. A hunt might only last a week or two; the shooter has the rest of the year to experiment with different bullet combinations. For the serious hunter/-

handloader, sectioning bullets or recovering them from an expansion medium to see what they'll really do can ensure more success than picking bullets at random and hoping they'll do the job. Your best bet is going to be the bullet you've tested and tailored to the task.

The Best Hunting Bullet Is...

THE .30 CALIBERS are by far the most popular of the big-game centerfires. The .30-06, for example, has not only withstood the test of 80 years of hard use, but continues to top the list of most popular hunting cartridges. The .308 Winchester is likewise right up there in cartridge popularity, allowing the use of a very short, compact rifle action if that's what the shooter wants. And if it's more steam you want, the .300 Winchester Magnum fills the bill for higher velocities than can be obtained in nonbelted cases.

These three rounds are the most popular .30-caliber bolt-action rifle cartridges, while the .30-30 Winchester holds the lead in the lever gun lineup. The .30-30 is used more often than the .308 and .300 Winchester Magnum, though both the rimmed cartridge and its blunt-tipped bullets are primarily used in lever-action rifles.

There are other less frequently used .30s. One of these, the .300 Savage, is currently chambered in the popular Savage Model 99 rifle, a lever gun with a rotary magazine allowing the shooter to use pointed bullets. There's also the .300 Weatherby Magnum and other less popular or defunct .30s like the .300 Holland & Holland Magnum, .308 Norma Magnum, and .30 Remington to name a few.

One of the best things going for the .30s is the wide selection of bullet weights and designs. Bullets are readily available in weights ranging from 100-grain Speer "Plinkers" or Hornady "Short Jackets" to the 220-grain heavyweights. Their intended uses range from popping pests with rapidly expanding lightweights to deep penetration on the largest game with controlled expanding heavies.

The most popular hunting bullet weights for use in bolt-action rifles can be distilled down to three basic numbers—the 150-, 165-, and 180-grainer. The 150 is popular for lighter species of big game (like deer and antelope), and the 165 is accumulating a larger following, but the 180-grain bullet is the standard by which others are judged. This is the one selected as the all-around best in most cartridges for game ranging from deer to moose.

It's a general consensus that a hunter can't go wrong if he selects the 180-grainer, no matter what he uses it for. This bullet offers a relatively high initial velocity and good velocity retention at extreme ranges, resulting in flat trajectory and high impact energy for larger game at long range. At the same time, the 180-grain bullets generally offer good expansion characteristics even on the smaller species of big game like deer and antelope.

Though the 180s can work well in any of the top three bolt-action .30s— the .308, .30-06, or .300 Winchester—few shooters consider the differences in bullet performance each of these cartridges might produce.

For example, a load may clock 2500 fps with the 180-grain bullet in a .308 Winchester, while the .300 Winchester Magnum will turn up nearly 3100 fps with the same bullet. It's a proven fact that a given bullet is going to perform differently depending on the impact velocity. Additionally, there are a great many different bullet shapes, brands, and construction types in this single 180-grain weight.

Taking all these facts into consideration, comparing a variety of 180-grain bullets in several rifle calibers to see just how each one stacked up for performance in terms of expansion, penetration, weight retention, etc., seemed like an interesting project.

It made sense to me that a hunter could gain several advantages by using only one bullet weight. First of all, he wouldn't have to sight-in his rifle every time he changed bullet weights for a different species of game. Secondly, he could learn what to expect from the performance of a single loading and bullet weight through continued field use; as a result, he'd become more effective with his gun and load. If different brands of bullets turned up different terminal ballistics, he could also select a bullet ideally suited to his particular hunting task without switching bullet weights.

In order to check the practicality of these ideas, I wanted to test a variety of 180-grain .30-caliber bullets. I came up with nine: the Speer Grand Slam, Speer Mag Tip, Speer roundnose, Hornady spirepoint, Nosler solidbase, Nosler Partition, Sierra flatbase spitzer, Sierra boattail spitzer, and Norma Dual Core.

For cartridges, I decided to go with the three most popular .30s designed to be used with pointed bullets in bolt-action rifles: the .308 Winchester, the .30-06 Springfield, and the .300 Winchester Magnum.

Next, I selected the rifles. The .308 cartridges would be fired in a Winchester Model 70 with a 22-inch barrel; the .30-06 was a Browning Model 78 with a 26-inch barrel; and the .300 Winchester Magnum was a Howa rifle with a 24-inch barrel.

To keep the tests as uniform as possible, I settled on a single load for firing all bullets from a given cartridge. Though each bullet produced a slightly different velocity average, this velocity difference was small enough that the terminal ballistic comparisons are valid.

The .308 load consisted of 48 grains of Winchester W760 with a CCI 200 primer in a Federal case. For the .30-06, I used 54 grains of IMR-4350 with a CCI 200 primer in a Frontier case. The .300 Winchester Magnum bullet was propelled by 76 grains of H4831 ahead of a CCI 250 primer in a Remington-Peters case.

All powder charges were dispensed with a Quinetics Mobile powder measure. And, as is the case when using most powder measures, the ball powder charges are probably more uniform than some of the coarse stick propellant charges. But considering the quantity of the stick powders used—76 grains and 54 grains—the percentage of charge weight variation is negligible for my purposes.

All cartridges were assembled with RCBS dies and an RCBS Rock Chucker press.

Once the loads were ready, the next step was to fire the bullets into a wet newspaper medium from a distance of 50 yards to see what sort of bullet performance would be received in terms of penetration, retained weight, frontal diameter, etc. The loads were chronographed at the same time they were fired into the expansion medium.

Once this phase of the testing was completed, the bullets were fired from 100 yards to determine group size and possible point-of-impact shift with two rifles, the .30-06 and the .300 Winchester Magnum. I was particularly interested in the point-of-impact shifts to see whether different brands of bullets could be interchanged without altering point of impact excessively. The results of this testing are summarized in the accompanying table.

.30-06
GROUP SIZE, POINT-OF-IMPACT DATA

	Group Size (Inches)	Point of Impact (Inches)
1. Speer Grand Slam	2.1	1.0 High, .6 Left
2. Speer Mag Tip	1.7	2.0 High, 1.9 Left
3. Speer roundnose	.7	2.2 High, 1.5 Left
4. Hornady spirepoint	1.6	1.0 High, 1.0 Left
5. Nosler Solid Base	1.1	2.3 High, 1.4 Left
6. Nosler Partition	1.5	4.4 High, 1.1 Left
7. Sierra spitzer	2.2	3.8 High, 1.1 Left
8. Sierra boattail	.9	4.5 High, 1.3 Left
9. Norma Dual Core	3.4	1.7 High, 3.0 Left

.300 WINCHESTER MAGNUM
GROUP SIZE, POINT-OF-IMPACT DATA

	Group Size (Inches)	Point of Impact (Inches)
1. Speer Grand Slam	1.3	.1 High, .1 Right
2. Speer Mag Tip	1.2	1.3 High, .8 Left
3. Speer roundnose	1.4	0 High, .6 Left
4. Hornady spirepoint	1.4	1.4 High, .5 Left
5. Nosler Solid Base	1.1	2.5 High, .5 Left
6. Nosler Partition	1.2	1.0 High, .5 Left
7. Sierra spitzer flatbase	1.0	1.7 High, 0
8. Sierra spitzer boattail	1.5	1.4 High, 0
9. Norma Dual Core	1.3	2.0 High, 0

Basically, my testing revealed that the more bullet speed attained, at least within the hunting cartridge velocity limits, the greater the bullet expansion of frontal diameter. Also, a greater speed (energy) results in less retained weight. Extremely high velocity has a tendency to make a bullet come apart, and the test of its ability to hold together is more severe at the higher velocities.

Another important item found in the accompanying table is that the higher the velocity, the less the penetration. The shock (energy) is apparently transmitted to the expansion medium much more rapidly and in a shorter distance, possibly due to the greatly increased bullet frontal area.

Both point of impact and velocity are somewhat laws unto themselves (depending on vagaries in individual rifles and loads), yet both are within very limited parameters. In many cases, the point of impact of various bullet brands is extremely close together—enough so bullet brands can be used interchangeably without altering sight settings.

As shown in the accompanying table, the Nosler bullets, both solid-base and partition, consistently provide the greatest penetration, which would possibly be an asset when hunting very large game. On the other hand, the more rapidly expanding bullets—like the Norma Dual Core—would probably be more effective at quickly dispatching deer-sized game. Or it's possible that one of the bullets falling somewhere in between these two performance extremes might be the best choice for an all-around application.

.308 WINCHESTER BULLET PERFORMANCE DATA

Rifle: Winchester Model 70, 22-inch barrel
Load: 48.0/W760/CCI 200/Federal cases

Bullet	Velocity (fps)	Penetration (Inches)	Retained Weight (Grains)	Percentage of Retained Weight (Grains)	Expanded Diameter
1. Speer Grand Slam	2550	17	145	80	.575
2. Speer Mag Tip	2551	17.5	153	85	.575
3. Speer roundnose	2541	18.5	123	73	.515
4. Hornady spirepoint	2529	15	154	85	.650
5. Nosler solidbase	2545	19	117	65	.460
6. Nosler Partition	2560	20	133.5	74	.500
7. Sierra spitzer	2547	15	121	67	.515
8. Sierra boattail	2568	15	111	62	.500
9. Norma Dual Core	2470	13	129.5	72	.565

.30-06 BULLET PERFORMANCE DATA

Rifle: Browning Model 78, 26-inch barrel
Load: 54.0/IMR-4350/CCI 200/Frontier cases

Bullet	Velocity (fps)	Penetration (Inches)	Retained Weight (Grains)	Percentage of Retained Weight (Grains)	Expanded Diameter	Remarks
1. Speer Grand Slam	2645	15	140.5	78	.625	
2. Speer Mag Tip	2657	16	143.5	80	.575	
3. Speer roundnose	2629	17.5	150.5	84	.540	
4. Hornady spirepoint	2606	14.5	143.5	80	.575	
5. Nosler solidbase	2546	17	108	60	.435	One core and jacket separated
5. Nosler Partition	2702	19	130	72	.485	
7. Sierra flatbase spitzer	2693	14.5	113.5	63	.500	
8. Sierra spitzer boattail	2708	15.5	110	61	.450	
9. Norma Dual Core	2615	12.5	124	69	.575	

By studying the tables, it's possible for you to better select a bullet for your next hunting task. You may want to pick two or even three different bullets for different hunting applications, matching bullet performance to the hunting situation. Or, after considering the game to be hunted, your hunting style, etc., it's possible you can select a single bullet that will perform best for all your hunting needs.

.300 WINCHESTER MAGNUM
BULLET PERFORMANCE DATA

Rifle: Howa, 24-inch barrel
Load: 76.0/H4831/CCI 250/R-P cases

Bullet	Velocity (fps)	Penetration (Inches)	Retained Weight (Grains)	Percentage of Retained Weight (Grains)	Expanded Diameter	Remarks
1. Speer Grand Slam	3020	14	108	60	.625	
2. Speer Mag Tip	3070	16	129	72	.695	
3. Speer roundnose	3000	14	86	48	.550	Jacket and core separated
4. Hornady spirepoint	3006	15	126	70	.695	
5. Nosler solidbase	2983	19	94	52	.460	
6. Nosler Partition	2980	19	128.5	71	.550	
7. Sierra flatbase spitzer	2947	16	97	54	.550	
8. Sierra spitzer boattail	2980	13	99	55	.525	
9. Norma Dual Core	3024	14	95.5	53	.575	

NOTES: A Custom chronograph with Ambient Light screens was used for clocking velocities. Velocities are instrumental at 10 feet from the rifle's muzzle.

For example, if you will be hunting deer exclusively, possibly from a stand where a shot can be placed precisely and usually into the lungs on a broadside-standing animal, the most rapidly expanding 180-grainer might be the best choice. If you prefer to stalk your game where it might be jumped from its bed and a poor angling shot taken, a slower expanding bullet with more penetration would be in order.

In other words, if the game you intend to hunt is mostly deer (but with an occasional elk), your bullet selection might be a little different than if you are hunting primarily elk and moose, with only a remote possibility for deer.

If you're using one of the high-velocity magnums, your bullet choice should be a bit different than it would be for the slower velocity .300 Savage or .308 Winchester.

These are some of the variables to be taken into consideration so you can more effectively select the best bullet for your purpose *before* going into the field after game. It has helped me make the right choice and ought to do the same for you.

The Obsolete Cartridge Alternative

MANY SHOOTERS HAVE inherited interesting old cartridge rifles, and as long as they are in good condition, there's no reason why such guns can't still be fired. The catch is whether or not you can obtain ammo for these old guns.

You might be fortunate enough to have a commercial cartridge still being manufactured for the rifle. The .45-70 and the .32-20 are two good examples. Most of the current factory calibers originally chambered in older rifles are still loaded to very low chamber pressures; as a result, they are suitable and safe for use in the older guns in good condition. (If there's any doubt about the condition of the rifle, check with a competent gunsmith before doing any shooting.)

If your gun is chambered for an obsolete cartridge like a .405 Winchester or .40-82 Winchester, however, there are no factory cartridges available, and you'll have to form your own cases and load your own ammo. There aren't any deep secrets required to assemble ammunition for these old cartridge guns; a bit of information is all you'll need. Most of the older rounds were originally loaded with blackpowder, and they still can be. If you prefer, smokeless propellant can be used.

Two or three numbers were originally used to designate blackpowder cartridges like the .45-70 Government or the .45-70-500 Government. The first number is the bullet diameter or caliber, the second is the charge of blackpowder in grains, and the third is the bullet weight in grains. A departure from this, however, was a second number which sometimes indicated case length. The Sharps Rifle Co. was known for this and called the .45-70 the .45-2.1-inch Sharps.

I have a Winchester Model 1886 rifle with the barrel stamped ".40-65 WCF." This indicates the cartridge case was a size holding 65 grains of blackpowder and fired a .40-caliber bullet. Marlin used the same size cartridge case but loaded it with only 60 grains of powder; this cartridge was called the .40-60 Marlin. Despite their different designations, the cartridges are nearly identical and interchangeable. Winchester also introduced the .40-60 WCF, which is a shorter case than the .40-60 Marlin.

Shooters loading older guns can use these original designations as guides for inserting charges of blackpowder or equivalent volumes of Pyrodex. They can be used *only* as a guide, however, because modern cases are different. Today's solidhead cases are thicker and stronger, particularly in the head or web section, than the old balloon or folded cases generally used with blackpowder. For this reason, internal case capacity of the newer cases is considerably less than the old blackpowder cases, and not as much propellant can be used. Many of these folded-head or balloon-head cases are still around, but due to their weak design and/or corrosion and possible brittleness, I would avoid using them.

The new cases offer an added safety margin besides the increased strength of the case. Their reduced capacity also makes them more suited to loading with smokeless propellant. Smokeless powder has a higher energy content per volume or is more dense than black; as a result, it occupies less space in the case. Many of the old cartridge cases are quite large by today's standards and most of them have more than enough space inside to contain any smokeless powder charge you'll want to use.

Most shooters will have these old guns for nostalgic reasons and will want to reproduce blackpowder ballistics even when using a smokeless propellant. Attempting to produce modern velocities is a losing proposition, however, and can be unsafe. There's no need to exceed the original ballistics.

I generally prefer using smokeless powders in the old guns. It's imperative to disassemble and clean your gun after a firing session with blackpowder. If this isn't done, the residue will attract moisture and rust any metal it comes in contact with, ruining a fine old gun in no time. I like to fire the old repeating Winchesters, and the old repeaters are a pain to disassemble and reassemble after each shooting session.

I also think smokeless propellant is much safer to use. For example, I feel comfortable dispensing smokeless powder through a conventional powder measure, but I wouldn't do this with blackpowder due to the possibility of static electricity causing an explosion.

Once you get the components and loading dies, loading an obsolete cartridge is no different than loading any other round. Powder and primers are no problem since standard labels work in both areas; cases and bullets are another matter.

Either jacketed or cast bullets can be used. There are many jacketed bullet diameters available for modern cartridges which also work well in the old guns. Make certain you're using the correct bullet diameter for your rifle. A chamber cast and bore slugging will help ensure your bullets fit. Many of today's jacketed bullets are designed to be fired at higher velocities than were possible in some of the old cartridge guns, and they might not perform well at the lower velocities received in your old rifle. If you want proper bullet expansion, for example, select a .45-70 type, not a bullet designed for the .458 Winchester Magnum.

In some instances, you might be able to use a modern jacketed magnum handgun bullet in your old rifle. These can perform well in terms of expansion at the lower rifle velocities. If you'll be taking game with your gun, proper bullet expansion characteristics are important.

If suitable bullets aren't available from the major manufacturers, try custom bulletmakers like Barnes Bullets. This firm has a number of bullets which are not carried by the large firms. Even so, a selection of jacketed bullets might be very limited in some calibers, and you'll need to use cast bullets. Bullet molds are available from Lyman, RCBS, and NEI for nearly any cartridge you'll want to load.

As mentioned earlier, obtain solidhead cases for loading. Assuming your rifle is chambered in an obsolete caliber, there are two ways you can obtain such cases for shooting. You might be able to purchase them readymade, or you can make the desired cases from another case.

Responding to the recent interest in the old cartridge guns, a few firms are supplying reloadable solidhead cases. Brass Extrusion Laboratories Ltd. has done a great service to the shooter of obsolete and European cartridges by making new brass cases available for some of these older calibers. In addition, RCBS furnishes a .45 Basic case from which many other cases can be formed. This case is 3¼ inches long, and a lot of the older cartridge cases can be formed by shortening, necking down, or both. If either of these sources don't fit your needs, you can form your own cases from another existing case. I found I could easily form .40-65 cases from .45-70 brass with the aid of RCBS forming dies. RCBS also makes forming dies for many of the other obsolete cartridges.

Once you have all the components and dies, you'll still need loading data. You can find data for some of the older cartridges in some of the newer manuals, but there are others you won't find in the manuals. One of the best sources of data I've come across for old cartridges is *Cartridges of the World* by Frank C. Barnes. This book doesn't list a lot of data (sometimes only one blackpowder and one smokeless powder load per cartridge), but loads are listed for many different cartridges, and the data does offer a starting point. In a nutshell, the text outlines how to go about loading an obsolete cartridge.

So much for the generalities. Perhaps how I obtained ammo for my .40-65 Winchester will be helpful.

I decided to see if I could find loading data for the old cartridge and whether making cases was practical. Information in Barnes' *Cartridges of the World* indicated the .40-65 cases could be made by reforming .45-70 brass. The book gave two handloads and factory ballistics which indicated a 260-grain bullet was fired from a factory load at 1420 fps muzzle velocity. I also found an article on loading the .40-65 Winchester in a back issue of *Handloader*. The magazine article outlined all the details about loading the old cartridge and supplied a number of loads. I learned assembling ammunition for the obsolete .45-65 cartridge was feasible.

The next step was to order forming and loading dies from RCBS. I also ordered cast bullet mold designs from both RCBS and Lyman. The forming and loading dies were the first to arrive in the mail, and I was soon forming .40-65 cases from newly acquired .40-70 Winchester brass.

The process involved passing a well-lubed .45-70 case to the initial forming die, which reduced case mouth diameter and applied some taper to the case. The case was formed about halfway between .45-70 and .40-65 with this initial die. After the cases had been through this initial die, they were pressed into the trim die for additional sizing. The excess protruding from the top of the trim die (about .05 inch) was filed off flush with the top of the die. The cases were then deburred, inside and out, and run through a full-length sizing die, completing the operation. I found the newly formed cases would easily chamber in my Model 1886 Winchester.

I decided to slug the bore first. Forcing three lead slugs through the barrel, I found a .4075- to .408-inch bullet would be much better suited to my rifle than .406-inch bullets I had tried earlier. I couldn't get the rifle to group five shots inside *six* inches with those bullets! Since the as-cast bullets came out .409 inch in diameter with the linotype metal, I decided to manipulate as-cast bullet diameter by varying alloy. I'd previously caused .44 Magnum bullets to vary in as-cast diameter by .002 inch simply by varying alloy composition.

I added pure lead to the .40-65 alloy until bullets began dropping out of the mold measuring .4076 inch in diameter. Instead of sizing these bullets, I decided to shoot them as cast, lubing by standing them in a shallow pan, pouring molten alox lubricant around them, and allowing it to harden. I then used a .44 Magnum lube cutter from a Lee kit to cut the bullets out of the lubricant. I traveled to the range with the softer bullets of larger diameter. I was quite pleased when my initial five-shot group clustered into 1.5 inches at 50 yards!

The two molds finally arrived. One was a Lyman No. 403169, which casts a nominal 245-grain bullet resembling the original Winchester mold design with three grease grooves. I also received an RCBS mold casting a 300-grain flatnose design; it had two grease grooves and a crimping groove. Both bullets were of the plainbase design. In addition, I received a previously ordered sizing die designed to squeeze cast bullets down to .406-inch diameter. From experience, I knew I wouldn't be able to use the lubricator/sizer until I had the sizing die polished out to .4075 inch; I'd also found I had to cast harder alloys with both molds in order for them to cast large enough. By controlling the alloy, I could ensure good performance with the .40-65 Winchester.

When seated into cases formed by the RCBS dies, these larger diameter bullets produce cartridges with pronounced bulges to the depth where the bullets are seated. This means I have to polish out my bullet-sizing die and my case-sizing die.

I'm looking into the possibilities of obtaining a sizing die to squeeze .41 Magnum pistol bullets down to .4075 inch. The .41 Magnum bullets mike .410 inch, and I don't anticipate any problems in reducing their diameter this much. I should receive excellent expansion since the .40-65 Winchester exceeds most .41 Magnum handgun velocities by only a marginal amount. I think adequate expansion on deer-sized game can be expected with such a bullet.

As you can see, making ammo for the .40-65 Winchester turned out to be more involved than I thought. Still, the effort was worth it. I find the enjoyment in plinking tin cans at 50 or 75 yards with the old Model 1886 can't be matched by a modern gun.

An obsolete cartridge can be a lot of fun. Just getting everything together and getting the old rifle to shoot is an interesting process. If you have an obsolete cartridge gun in good condition, don't hesitate to load for it. You'll have more fun than you thought possible.

Make Cases From Other Cases

TAKE A LOOK at the long line of commercial cartridges, and you'll see there's no need for any additional chamberings. Standard chamberings in American production rifles shooting centerfire rounds range from a 25-grain .17-caliber bullet at better than 4000 fps to a 500-grain .45-caliber belted magnum at more than 2600 fps (for nearly four tons of energy at the muzzle).

There are chamberings available for anything from ground squirrels to elephants. There are long-range "plains" cartridges, short-range "brush" cartridges, cartridges for dangerous game, and cartridges for varmints. There is an American cartridge ideally suited to bring down any animal.

The American rifle manufacturers have been so thorough in introducing new chamberings that gaps in the line of American cartridges have almost been eliminated.

This wasn't always the case. Metallic cartridges were initially designed around blackpowder. When smokeless powder came into vogue, cartridges began taking a different shape, with a movement toward smaller, faster bullets. These cases were called "bottleneck." The H&H cases— the .300 and .375—with the long, gently sloping shoulders were designed around British cordite powder consisting of long strands of propellant rather than today's granules, flakes, or spheres.

Besides these motivating factors in cartridge development, America's riflemen have always been experimenters, and the standard head-size cartridges have been necked up, necked down, shortened, lengthened, blown out, and altered in just about every way imaginable. It's difficult to name a modern commercial cartridge that has not been preceded by several wildcat versions of virtually the same round in perhaps a half-dozen variations. The variations are in shoulder angle, body taper, or neck length and frequently bear no meaningful differences from the commercial chamberings.

Those who alter existing cartridges generally do so for higher performances or to adapt the cartridge to a specialized purpose or firearm. In the past, this has been one of the major reasons for making a new case from an existing case. Now there's little need for developing a wildcat cartridge to reach a higher level of performance, but wildcatting is still fun.

Besides wildcatting, shooters may be interested in making their own cases for any number of reasons. For instance, there might be a need for obtaining ammunition to fit a rifle chambered in an obsolete cartridge. Obsolete cartridges can sometimes be made from existing cases with only minor brass modifications. I've made cases for my old Savage Model 99 .22 High-Power from .25-35 Winchester brass, and all it takes is a simple sizing operation.

Being able to make a case from another case can sometimes be more economical. A friend of mine had a supply of .308 Winchester brass far in excess of what he would use in a lifetime. He recently obtained a .358 Winchester rifle; instead of purchasing expensive .358 Winchester ammunition or brass, he found necking the .308 cases up to take .358-inch-diameter bullets was very easy. The result was a sizable savings.

Another reason for making cases from other cases is that some ammunition is manufactured to different specifications than what we're used to. The brass in Weatherby cases, for example, is made in Sweden and has been somewhat softer than American brass in the past. Some American handloaders want all the pressure and velocity safely obtainable. As a result, they will make Weatherby-caliber cases from the harder Winchester or Remington brass.

Necessity can be another reason. A shooter in an isolated area might not be able to obtain a certain caliber case. Rather than travel 150 miles just to place an order, he can make a desired case from another with the loading dies he has on hand.

There is nothing mysterious or dangerous about making your own cases as long as ample knowledge and liberal common sense are applied. The most easily accomplished case-making technique is necking up or down for cartridges having the same body diameter and length but which fire bullets of different diameters. One example is the cartridge family consisting of the .243 Winchester, 7mm-08 Remington, .308 Winchester, and .358 Winchester. All that's necessary to make one of these cases from another is a simple necking (up or down) operation.

In general, the most important point to remember when making cases is that both cases must have the same head size or rim diameter – within a few thousandths at least. I've included a chart listing all the popular cartridges with the same rim diameters. The list is not complete, but it covers all the more common numbers.

When I made the .22 Savage High-Power cases from .25-35 brass, the rims were not exactly the same diameter. The High-Power has a nominal .492-inch rim, while the .25-35's rim lists at .506. However, most other case dimensions between the two cartridges (other than bullet diameter) are very nearly the same. I found there was no difficulty in using the homemade .22 Savage High-Power cases with the larger rims of the reformed cases. As a matter of fact, factory cases do not always mike the nominal diameter, and this can work to your benefit. If you're uncertain, mike them; they could be the size you need.

FAMILIES OF CASES WITH THE SAME RIM DIAMETER

.378-Inch Rim Diameter	.300 Winchester Magnum
.17 Remington	8mm Remington Magnum
.222 Remington	.338 Winchester Magnum
.223 Remington	.350 Remington Magnum
.222 Remington Magnum	.375 H&H Magnum
6x47mm	.458 Winchester Magnum
.473-Inch Rim Diameter	**.530-Inch Rim Diameter**
.22-250 Remington	**(Belted Cases)**
.243 Winchester	.257 Weatherby Magnum
6mm Remington	.270 Weatherby Magnum
.250 Savage	7mm Weatherby Magnum
.257 Roberts	.308 Norma Magnum
.25-06 Remington	.300 Weatherby Magnum
.270 Winchester	.340 Weatherby Magnum
7mm-08 Remington	.358 Norma Magnum
7x57 Mauser	**.506-Inch Rim Diameter**
.280 Remington	.25-35 Winchester
.300 Savage	.30-30 Winchester
.308 Winchester	.32 Winchester Special
.30-06 Springfield	**.440-Inch Rim Diameter**
8mm Mauser	.256 Winchester Magnum
.358 Winchester	.357 Magnum
.532-Inch Rim Diameter	**.408-Inch Rim Diameter**
(Belted Cases)	.218 Bee
6.5mm Remington Magnum	.25-20 Winchester
.264 Winchester Magnum	.32-20 Winchester
7x61 Sharp & Hart	**.514-Inch Rim Diameter**
7mm Remington Magnum	.44 Magnum
.300 H&H Magnum	.444 Marlin

It's possible to make case rims smaller by turning them in a lathe; it's even possible to swage on a belt, but this is quite a bit of work. The closer the original case is to the intended case, the better off you are.

A case is necked up to take a larger bullet diameter simply by forcing its neck over a larger expander ball in a conventional loading die. Case neck size can be increased by a caliber or two with a single pass over the larger expander. If a greater neck enlargement is required, successive passes of increasingly larger expander balls may be in order to achieve the properly finished neck diameter without ruining cases. Brass is quite ductile and will stretch a lot as long as the change is accomplished in small increments. If you attempt to do it too abruptly, the necks will buckle.

The same goes for necking-down operations. Successively smaller neck-sizing diameters may be necessary in order to prevent ruining cases by crumpling the brass. The importance of a proper lubricant for case-forming operations cannot be overemphasized. My own experiences revealed many of the popular sizing lubricants simply aren't up to the task. I have found two lubricants which work satisfactorily. LeClear Imperial Sizing Die Wax, which is distributed by LeClear Industries, and Dave Corbin's draw die lube, which is distributed by Corbin Manufacturing & Supply Inc.

At one time, necking up was generally considered better than necking down in order to achieve a given case neck diameter. The reason given was uneven brass neck thickness frequently results when necking down. With the current availability of neck-turning tools, however, evening up neck thickness after a necking-down operation is a simple matter. For this reason, I prefer to neck down. After the sizing operation is completed, all case necks can be turned to a uniform wall thickness.

Remembering to thin case necks after any appreciable sizing-down operation is important. When a case neck is reduced in diameter, the brass must go somewhere; consequently, the neck becomes thicker. A too-thick case neck can raise chamber pressures to dangerous levels.

A case length trimming may also be in order after any necking (up or down) operation. The brass might become longer when a neck diameter is altered. More importantly, a case length trimming will square up case mouths.

As mentioned, cartridge brass can be altered greatly. For example, I have made .22-250 cases from .30-06 brass with only a couple of passes through different dies. This results in a .22-250 case neck which is about ⅞ inch long. Also, since the new case is considerably shorter than the original case, the new neck is derived from the original case's body.

As most shooters know, brass cases are generally tapered in wall thickness, becoming thicker at the base and thinner toward the mouth. Whenever a reformed case neck is developed from a preexisting case body, the new necks will be too thick and must be thinned besides being trimmed. One example is in making .30 Herrett handgun cases from .30-30 Winchester brass.

Remade cases sometimes end up shorter in neck length than specifications for the finished case indicate. In this situation, seat the bullets farther out of the case to attain the proper overall cartridge length. I have never found a short neck creating any problems. The important tolerance is the bullet-to-land relationship, not how far the bullet protrudes from the case mouth.

If an original case has a smaller body or a different shoulder angle than the desired case, the case body must be formed outward rather than sized downward. This type of "blowing out" operation is popular with wildcatters who shoot "improved" case designs with straight bodies, sharp shoulders, and short necks.

Forming a case outward is generally accomplished by one of two methods: fireforming the case in the rifle's chamber to make it larger or forming the case larger hydraulically. The hydraulic method involves filling the case with a liquid (usually water), inserting it in a die, and then placing pressure on the trapped liquid to force the case sides outward against the die's interior.

Fireforming in a rifle is accomplished by placing the undersized case in the rifle's chamber; generally using a light charge of quick-burning powder, the case walls are then blown out to conform to the rifle's chamber. There are other methods. Fireforming is sometimes accomplished with a normal charge and a bullet inserted, particularly if a very minor forming operation is required, or without a bullet and using (as mentioned earlier) a very quick-burning propellant like Bullseye or Unique with nothing more than a case of filler material (such as Cream of Wheat).

The important thing to remember in fireforming cases outward is to keep the base of the case next to the rifle's boltface during firing so the case forms properly and an excessive headspace situation does not occur in the finished cases. One way this can be accomplished is to seat bullets out to jam into the lands when the round is chambered. Another method is to form a step or extra shoulder in the brass near the case neck so it jams into the chamber shoulder when the action is locked.

When looking at the listing of cases, you might be surprised to find there really are many cases having identical rim diameters which serve as potential for making other cases. Remember, it's important to make a case that's as close to the desired case as possible. Cartridge dimension drawings in the loading manuals are excellent guides.

Cartridge nomenclature in no way indicates a potential candidate for a case-forming operation. For example, I can think of six different 6.5mm cartridges, none of which have the same rim diameters. The 6.5 Japanese has a .466 rim diameter; the 6.5 Carcano, .449; the 6.5x54 Mannlicher, .453; and the 6.5x55 Swedish Mauser, .476; the 6.5x57, .470; and the 6.5mm Remington Magnum, .532.

Although the Winchester, Remington, and H&H belted magnums are listed separately from the Weatherby and Norma belted magnum cartridges, both groups could be considered as having identical rim diameters because the variation is only .002 inch (as it is with the body diameters). The list of .30-06 head-size cartridges includes some rounds with body diameters that vary just ahead of the extractor groove. The variation generally runs between .471 and .470 inch. However, the .22-250 is listed with a nominal .467 inch at this point, and the 8mm Mauser is .469. These slight variations are of no consequence; as mentioned earlier, .22-250 brass can be made from the other cases. The .22-250 was originally a wildcat cartridge, and making cases from .250 Savage brass was common practice.

As can be seen (with few exceptions), American cartridges have three basic head sizes: the .222/.223 class, the .30-06 class, and the .300 Winchester Magnum class. Other cartridges from these families can be considered variations on these head sizes.

The Mauser or .30-06 cases are generally considered the ones that gave rise to the .30-06 family of cartridges, while the .375 H&H Magnum is the father of most belted magnum cases in use today. The .375 H&H Magnum was introduced in 1912 and, as such, was the first commercially chambered belted magnum cartridge in the U.S.

If you have a reason for making your own cases, don't hesitate. Use common sense and have some fun.

Altering Old Brass

ALTERING EXISTING cases or brass to be used in an entirely different case shape or cartridge design is sometimes necessary. Shooters of wildcat cartridges routinely do this in order to obtain cases for ammunition which is not available commercially.

Some of the more simple operations involve nothing more than reducing or expanding the case neck for a different bullet diameter. In addition, the case body can be expanded by firing in a larger chamber with a "forming load," or it can be reduced by sizing in a sizing die. The case shoulder can be altered so it's farther forward, consuming part of the case neck, or forced rearward to decrease case body length.

Shooters who utilize wildcat cartridges aren't the only ones who perform such operations. For example, suppose you have purchased a .358 Winchester and have everything you need for your loading except the brass case (which, incidentally, is the most expensive component). It just so happens that another shooter has given you 10,000 rounds of once-fired 7.62mm NATO brass (.308 Winchester) which you supposedly have no use for. All you have to do is expand the case mouths by using sizing dies with successively larger expander balls, forcing the case mouths out to the final desired diameter.

If you want to load the .243 Winchester, cases can be made from the same .308 brass by reducing the neck diameter in small stages until the desired size is reached.

On the surface, this seems simple, but there's a lot more to it. If the handloader isn't careful, there will be a high case loss. One way to reduce this case loss is to anneal or soften the case mouths by heating prior to any expansion or reduction. When this is done, there's much less chance of necks splitting or buckling under the stress of reforming.

There are several methods used to anneal cases. The point to remember is that the base of the case must not be softened because strength is required here. You can insulate the base of the case while exposing its mouth for heating by standing the case in a pan of shallow water with the base immersed and the case mouth protruding. After the mouths have been heated, tip the cases over to quench them. Take care to heat the case mouths uniformly.

Another method, one preferred by many shooters, is to dip the case mouth in oil and then into a molten lead alloy. The temperature of molten bullet alloy is generally under 800 degrees Fahrenheit, and this temperature is reportedly low enough that it will not destroy the grain structure in the brass.

According to some reports, the torching method can allow the brass to get too hot. If the dipping method is used, you must hold the case mouth immersed for a few seconds to allow the brass to come up to the temperature of the alloy before withdrawing the case from the melt.

Once case mouths have been annealed, you'll find reforming them is much easier and can be accomplished with a greatly reduced brass mortality factor.

Another factor which has a direct bearing on the number of case failures during reforming is the lubricant used. Some shooters have experienced great difficulty in any case-forming operation simply because they've made a poor selection of lubricant. During my many years of handloading, I've used everything from STP to lanolin hydrous, from water-soluble lubricants to waxes, for all sorts of sizing and forming operations. In short, there is a great deal of difference in lubricants and the ways they perform.

As mentioned earlier, annealing softens the brass. However, any drawing or working of the brass has a tendency to reharden it. When the case mouth or shoulder area is reformed, you'll find it has regained much of the spring and toughness it lost during the annealing process.

Some shooters have experienced problems with case necks splitting and have blamed it on too-hot loads. Actually, a hot load is seldom the culprit for a longitudinal case neck split. The culprit is generally brass rendered brittle by too many reloadings and refirings or brass that has been excessively sized without being annealed. Case necks can become brittle after they're reloaded many times, and a simple annealing operation can prolong brass life.

Contrary to popular belief, age does not make brass brittle. Brass becomes brittle from exposure to various chemicals and fumes. Mercury and ammonia are two examples. If your brass cases are exposed to the ammonia sometimes found in cleaning solvents, they could be ruined. In these instances, annealing brass may not help. Storing your brass away from any type of cleaning solvents is a good idea.

Whenever a forming operation is conducted, the displaced brass must go somewhere. If a case neck is expanded, it becomes thinner; if case neck diameter is reduced, brass in the neck portion of the case becomes thicker. To avoid potential high-pressure problems, case neck wall thickness should be reduced.

There are several devices available for thinning case neck walls. One type is an attachment that fits a case-trimming tool (Forster makes one). Lee packs a type of boring bar with its target model loading tool that reduces case neck wall thickness by scraping it from inside the neck. Benchrest shooters usually use a type of neck-turning tool that removes brass from the exterior of the case neck wall.

This latter type of tool is becoming more popular with silhouette shooters and varmint shooters. A pin that has a close-tolerance fit inside the case neck is slipped into the case mouth, and an adjustable cutter arrangement rotates about the exterior of the case mouth with the central pin as a pivot point. The cutter removes brass in a curl from the exterior of the case mouth to a uniform neck wall thickness.

Use of the case is made safer by thinning the neck, and with the neck-turning tool, the brass becomes much more uniform in wall thickness and more concentric with the rifle's chamber and bore. This is doubly important because when a case neck is reduced to a much smaller caliber, the process has the effect of causing the neck wall thickness to be even less uniform. The brass seems to "bunch up" in spots around the neck. A good tool can alleviate this situation.

Make sure the case neck wall isn't too thin. If it is, the case mouth will not hold a bullet firmly when it's resized and reloaded.

One way to determine approximate case neck wall thickness is to compare it with a factory-loaded round. If you're working with a SAAMI-standard chamber, a factory-loaded round should provide a good basis for comparison. A one-inch micrometer can be used to measure the outside diameter of the case neck with a bullet seated in both instances. Then the measurements can be compared, giving you a rough idea about how much your case necks need to be turned.

Determining Groove Diameter

ONE OF THE biggest factors in cast bullet accuracy and whether a bullet leads a barrel is bullet size in relation to the interior dimensions of the barrel. In most instances, the best results are obtained with finished bullets somewhere in the neighborhood of groove diameter to .0015 inch over groove diameter—not bore diameter. The term "bore diameter," as implied, is the distance from the top of one rifling land to the top of another directly opposite from it, the inside diameter of the barrel after it is bored and before it is rifled. Groove diameter is the distance from the bottom of one groove to the bottom of the other opposite from it. Bore diameter is smaller than groove diameter. How much smaller depends on the depth of the grooves.

There are several methods of determining groove diameter in a firearm. Slugging the barrel is one method. It basically involves forcing a slightly oversize soft billet of lead through the barrel and then using a micrometer to measure the groove dimensions left on the billet. This provides the smallest dimension inside the barrel.

A telescoping gauge can be used to measure the groove dimensions near the muzzle and sometimes the breech of a barrel, and a chamber cast (with cerrosafe or a similar material) can be used to acquire the same measurements.

Once groove diameter has been determined, the object is to produce cast bullets of the proper size. But there's a little more to it. My experiments have shown the amount the bullet is reduced by sizing, after it is cast, is critical. Too much sizing causes billet distortion that shows up on target.

In general, the less sizing there is, the better. If the bullet is reduced by .001 inch during sizing, fine. That's just enough to true up the bullet and clean up the mold marks where the two halves of the mold blocks meet. If the bullet is sized .003 or .004 inch, however, accuracy frequently suffers. Some of the most accurate cast bullets I've fired are those shot "as cast," with no sizing. They were lubricated by standing nose up in a pan and pouring molten lubricant around the bases.

Various molds in a given caliber cast bullets of different diameters.

Sometimes a particular mold will be suited for a particular firearm due to the diameter of the bullet it drops in relation to groove diameter. You can alter the diameter of the as-cast bullet by changing the composition of the alloy. It apparently has to do with the amount the bullet shrinks when it cools. A bullet with a high antimony content apparently shrinks less.

In one experiment with an Ohaus .44-caliber mold which was labeled for a 250-grain nominal weight, I was able to vary the average diameter by as much as .0033 inch just by changing the alloy. The alloys used were lead, tin, and antimony. I was also able to vary the as-cast weight by 113.86 grains, from 162.75 grains for an average of 10 bullets to 276.61 grains. In a given mold, the more lead that's used in the alloy mix, the heavier the bullet and the smaller the diameter.

There is another factor that can be as important as barrel groove diameter in determining the optimum cast bullet diameter. In revolvers, the front of the cylinder is sometimes considerably smaller in diameter than is barrel groove diameter. Your revolver may shoot best with finished bullets measuring the same size or .001 inch larger than this dimension.

All of this is a guide for getting the best possible accuracy. There are other factors that enter into the accuracy and barrel leading issues, such as the lubricant, ambient temperature, and interior barrel finish. You'll just have to shoot certain combinations in your gun and see what performs best for you.

Handloading Safety

WHILE I DON'T have any statistics on handloading accidents, I'd be willing to wager that loading ammunition is safer than skiing – or perhaps even riding a bicycle. Handloading isn't dangerous – if certain precautions are taken to ensure we don't make it dangerous.

When you think of reloading safety, you probably think about using too much propellant or the wrong kind of powder and about the resultant wrecked gun of the unknowing handloader. As a result, you probably check and recheck data and powder charges in carefully assembled handloads. This is certainly something to be concerned about, but there's a lot more to reloading safety than using the proper charge. In fact, there is an almost unlimited number of potentially dangerous situations. Although every situation can't be predicted, a little knowledge and precaution can go a long way toward preventing a disaster.

Primers are components that seldom get a second thought regarding potency. These tiny capsules, which ignite powder charges, have power out of proportion to their size. A friend of mind detonated a rifle primer on the loading bench, and the primer anvil was nearly driven through his free hand.

Taken collectively – and out of their factory cartons – lots of primers are like a bomb. As long as they're left in their original cartons, separated by partitions the way they are, primers are quite safe. Just remember to always store primers in their original cartons.

Powder is the other component that rates concern among handloaders. Smokeless powder is a flammable solid. A few one-pound containers sitting on the loading bench constitute no abnormal hazard; however, one should exercise the care he would with any flammable material. Never smoke around powder, never store it near any open flame, and if you have a large quantity of powder, store it in the original containers in some sort of magazine with a lock on the door.

If you don't use common sense and follow simple precautions, handloading can be dangerous. Here are a few points to keep in mind:

1. Wear safety glasses when handloading. If a primer does detonate accidentally, safety glasses could save your eyes.

2. Never hold your head above the top of a case while you're priming it. It's a natural position to assume in many instances, and you may have to make a conscious effort to avoid doing this. It's rare that a primer detonates while being seated, but it can happen. If you're using hand-priming tools, pay attention to where you point the case mouth.

3. Store powder and primers separately in a cool, dry place. If you have large quantities of either, make special provisions for storing them in a locked magazine.

4. Place only the powder you're currently using on the loading bench. All other propellants should be out of easy reach. When emptying a powder measure after use, check the type of propellant visually and with the label on the can. Empty the measure whenever you finish reloading. If time lapses and you aren't positive which powder is in the measure, dump it out. Never put a powder into a powder container if you aren't certain what it is.

5. If you change powder lots, be careful about maximum loads. What was maximum with one lot of powder may be beyond maximum with another lot of powder—even a powder of the same type. Reduce any maximum charge by 10 percent and then redevelop that maximum load.

6. Cross-check data in any loading manual with as many different loading manuals as possible. Typographical errors are possible in any printed material. Cross-checking data can help eliminate a potential problem. Cross-checking data also gives you a better idea about what sort of load performance to expect.

7. Never mix bullets in a box or place bullets in a box with the wrong label for the bullet. You could load an overweight bullet, which is no different than a too-heavy powder charge. The result is the same. If there's any doubt about a bullet, weigh it and mike it.

8. If you're using a progressive tool, make sure the primer magazine shield is in place (if the tool is designed for one). Make sure the area over the top of the tube is safe in the event of a primer magazine tube detonation.

9. Whenever you charge cases with a powder measure, use a loading block. Charge all cases in the block and then carefully look inside each case to check the powder level. Look for uncharged cases and for overcharged cases. An uncharged case can be as dangerous as an overcharged one. Imagine an uncharged cartridge in a revolver during a rapid-fire situation. When the hammer falls on the uncharged cartridge, the primer will drive the bullet into the barrel, obstructing it; a subsequent loaded round may cause the barrel or cylinder to burst.

10. It's a good idea to use a powder charge that fills the case. As a result, the powder will overflow the case if a double charge is thrown. This is a factor of choosing a powder with the proper burning rate.

11. Never use a coarse, extruded powder in a progressive loading tool. "Bridging" can occur too easily, causing one case to be undercharged and another to be overcharged. Beware of bridging whenever you use a coarse, extruded powder with any powder measure. Just to make sure, weigh every charge after it's measure-thrown.

12. Never simply reduce powder charge weight or use a slow-burning rifle powder to achieve reduced-velocity loadings in a rifle. Use only the quicker burning powders in conjunction with load data from a respected source.

13. Never use a load someone has given you without checking it first in a recognized loading manual.

14. Never substitute powder from one manufacturer with powder from another manufacturer without first reducing a maximum charge by 10 percent and redeveloping the maximum load. This holds true even if both brands of propellant have the same number. For example, 4227, 4198, 4895, 4350, and 4831 are powders distributed by both DuPont and Hodgdon. Don't assume these powders are interchangeable. When using 4831, remember that there are different burning rates with different lots of this propellant. Some of it was made many years ago; some was made more recently; some of it was made in different manufacturing facilities. It's always better to err on the conservative side and be safe.

15. Keep cleaning fluids and other solvents away from loading components. Many reloaders aren't aware that even the fumes from some cleaning solvents can cause cartridge brass to become brittle.

16. Never clean loaded rounds in a case vibrator or tumbler. The abrasive action of the powder granules could destroy the deterrent coating on the powder, altering the burning rate of the propellant. Clean only fired, empty cartridge brass.

17. Never try to improve powder ignition by enlarging a flash hole. Use the brass as it comes from the factory, with the exceptions of trimming, neck reaming, and deburring.

18. Never use pistol primers in a rifle cartridge. Most pistol primers are made with a thinner cup and are not designed to withstand the pressures developed by some rifle cartridges.

19. Never smoke while handloading or allow anyone else to smoke around your handloading area.

20. Always devote your full attention to the loading task at hand. Do not talk, read, watch television, etc., while loading ammunition.

Observing these 20 safety tips won't guarantee you'll never be injured as a result of handloading, but they're sound practices to follow. Just remember that using common sense and staying alert are the best ways to prevent a handloading accident.

Hunting

Hunting In The U.S.

S ELECTING A CENTERFIRE rifle battery that handles all game
depends not only on the species hunted, but on terrain and vegetation and the sportsman's hunting style. It's been said a number of times
that a hunter can simply pick a bolt-action .30-06 and be prepared to go
after anything in North America. Broadly speaking, this is true, but there
are other caliber and action types better suited to specific game animals
and hunting circumstances.

To provide guidelines about a centerfire rifle battery, the contiguous
U.S. has been divided into the Northeast, Southeast, Midwest, and West.

These sections have different types of game, hunting conditions, methods of hunting, etc., so the various hunting conditions in each region are also outlined along with a discussion about why a certain shooting combination is chosen. Not only are rifle/action types and cartridges covered, but sighting equipment and accuracy requirements are discussed as well.

Localized hunting conditions are often the same in all sections. To avoid redundancy in repeating preferred rifle choices in all sections, I have emphasized a class of firearm in only one section. For instance, jackrabbits are hunted in both the West and Midwest under similar conditions, but the jackrabbit rifle is outlined in detail only in the section on the West. Deer are hunted under thick timber conditions in all regions, but the timber rifle is covered in detail only in the section on the Northeast where this rifle is tradition. So, if you're looking for a "brush gun" to use in Missouri, you'll want to read the section on the Northeast, where the "brush gun" is outlined in detail.

And I haven't forgotten shooters in those areas where shotguns are required for deer hunting, and at the end of the regional sections, I will cover the smoothbore.

Northeast

T HE NORTHEAST, in general, is characterized by a high population density. True, some areas in the Northeast, such as Maine and upstate New York, are not heavily populated, but for the most part, the deer hunter will be contending with other hunters in the woods, and the 'chuck hunter will be watching which direction his long-range rifle is pointing so as not to offend several neighboring farmers. Much of the northeastern terrain is hilly, the woods dense.

The game hunted with a centerfire range from woodchucks and crows on the small end of the spectrum to deer and black bear.

First, the varmint rifles. Since the shooting distances and ballistic performance requirements are basically the same for both woodchucks and crows, the shooter will be able to use the same rifle for both species. However, depending on where the hunter is, the requirements in shooting can differ. I have hunted woodchucks in sections of southern and western Pennsylvania where the fields are large, the country open, and shooting distances are on the long side. On other occasions, I've hunted sections of Maryland where the fields are small, farmhouses are hardly more than a quarter mile apart, and the vegetation is heavy. Here, a 250-yard shot is a long one.

When shooting at a varmint the size of the woodchuck (sometimes only the top of its head), a rifle with a high degree of accuracy is mandatory. The general rule of thumb is groups no more than one-inch at 100 yards. The smaller the groups, the better. Since rapidity of fire is of little importance in most varmint shooting situations, a bolt action or finely tuned single shot is a good choice. Either produces acceptable accuracy levels.

These varmints usually aren't stalked, but rather are shot from a fixed position, with the rifle resting on sandbags, a bipod, or a benchrest. Since the rifle won't be carried much, the hunter doesn't need to worry about keeping things lightweight or compact. A heavy barrel generally shoots better with a variety of loads than a light one. It also has a greater affinity for keeping all shots in a tight cluster, even under the heat of many rounds. Most woodchuck shooting won't keep a barrel hot all day, but it doesn't take many rounds from a big-case .22 or 6mm to warm up the tube enough to cause a point of impact shift with a sporter-weight barrel.

For the open areas where disturbing a landowner's neighbor is no problem, any of the long-range varmint or varmint/deer cartridges from the .22-250 through .25-06 are well suited. The scope for this outfit would be something on the order of an 8X or 10X for plenty of target definition at long range. The rifle could be a heavy-barreled Remington Model 700, Winchester Model 70, Ruger 77, etc. I lean to the .22-250 or .220 Swift rather than the larger calibers because I don't like recoil when shooting from a prone position, particularly if a lot of rounds are fired. Since a high level of accuracy is required, there's no room for a shot-pulling flinch from the kick of a .25-06.

In heavily populated sections where ranges are short, the shooting conditions demand a different approach. The same type of rifle mentioned earlier, but chambered in .222 or .223, will cut noise somewhat, but you might find the .22 Hornet cartridge provides more challenge at these shorter ranges while it markedly reduces shooting noise. Since the ranges are shorter, the limited-range Hornet brings the excitement of bullet drop and wind doping back into the game.

The deer rifle of the Northeast has long been characterized as a short, fast-handling carbine capable of quick followup shots. In much of the area I've hunted in the Northeast, shots longer than 50 yards are the exception rather than the rule. The levers, pumps, and semiautos best fit into this traditional deer gun category. The thinking is that since ranges are short, a high level of accuracy is not required, but getting the gun up quickly—on a rapidly disappearing deer—is. And since deer are frequently driven past a hunter's stand on the run, there is a chance that the first bullet might not connect the animal. Hence, the need for followup shots.

There are many hunters in most of the northeastern woods, and for this reason, I also want the traditional deer gun to be chambered for a cartridge that drops a deer in its tracks, results in a profuse blood trail, and has a bullet that will completely exit the animal. Let me explain.

Many years ago I was deer hunting in central Pennsylvania. The roadsides through the deer woods were like the side streets to the county fair. Cars were parked everywhere, people were in the roads, and the smog from campfires would rival Los Angeles on a calm summer day.

It takes a lot more than that to discourage a determined hunter on the eve of opening day. As I was making my way up the mountainside in the pre-dawn darkness, I was thinking I would beat the crowd into the woods, where I would wait on stand while they drove the deer to me.

I quietly moved forward, hearing sticks cracking occasionally—I knew from previous scouting trips that there were lots of deer around. It was getting light enough to see when someone coughed a few feet to my left, and I could distinguish two hunters moving up the mountain ahead of me. I stopped a minute to determine which way to proceed in order to avoid the other hunters when I noticed a third hunter a few feet to my right.

The eager deer hunter from the Midwest was beginning to taste a bit of discouragement already. Not wanting to wander around in the dim light with so many hunters in the woods, I sat down against a tree, laid the lever-action .243 Winchester Model 88 across my lap, and waited.

It was barely light enough to shoot when I heard crackling in the brush above and swung my head around just in time to see a beautiful 10-point buck come crashing down the hillside. He was only 30 yards away and would pass no more than 20 yards from my position. I raised the Winchester and quickly had the 4X Weaver crosshair on the deer. My first shot put the deer down on his knees, but he regained his feet as I levered a second round into the chamber. The deer ran away at an angle, almost going out of sight in the heavy cover when I fired again. The big buck staggered, but kept going with obvious difficulty.

I had no doubts about being able to recover that buck—I knew he wasn't going far. Magazine articles always said to wait a bit before pursuing a wounded deer so it would lay down. Having hunted primarily in the West, and without the experience borne of having grown up in the heavily populated Northeast, I simply glanced down for my empty brass. Barely had I looked at the forest floor when I heard a volley of shooting 100 yards or so below. Following the tracks of the deer downhill, I found three hunters gathered around the big buck, eyeing its magnificent antlers.

I looked at the deer's body, finding not two but several bullet holes. At that point, it was hard to tell where the 100-grain Hornady from my .243 had impacted the buck. It quickly became apparent that these hunters would have no part of any suggestion that I had shot the buck twice from my uphill stand. Looking carefully in the buck's backtrail, I could see no sign of blood for proof of a hit.

Rather than make the hunt an unpleasant experience by starting an argument, I decided to go after another buck. Besides, I wasn't really ready to quit hunting so early in the season. Three days later I got my deer, a four-pointer that in no way approached the size of the earlier trophy. In fact, after looking at deer in many other camps, I began to realize how large the buck I had given up really was. I never did see a deer with a rack as large as his.

The incident taught me a lesson. I now use a bullet of relatively large diameter that expands rapidly and exits to produce a profuse blood trail. I carry an iron-sighted slide-action Remington chambered for the .35 Remington cartridge. The first deer shot through the lungs with that rifle ran about 30 yards and left a blood trail that could be seen from some distance and followed at a fast walk. The .358 Winchester with 200-grain bullets in the Savage Model 99 is probably an even better choice for deer hunting under these conditions. Scopes of low magnification, certainly no more than 3X, offer the field of view needed for this fast, close-range shooting.

I have also participated in deer drives which are popular in Pennsylvania. A line of hunters or "blockers" assembles somewhere in the forest, depending upon wind direction and the lay of the land, while another line of hunters or "drivers" assembles at a distant point. The drivers move toward the stationary blockers in order to flush the deer out. Sometimes a hunter at either end of the drivers carries a cowbell to keep all moving hunters on line.

This method of driving deer is employed in dense cover situations where the shots are close. Not only are shooting ranges short, but any deer coming back through the line of drivers is apt to be moving very fast. Safe hunting practice dictates hunters cannot shoot toward the blockers, but rather must wait until the deer runs through the line and then shoot as the animal runs away. Thus, half the shooting time is eliminated. Here again, a fast-handling, quick-pointing carbine is an advantage.

Although these situations typify shots encountered in the dense northeastern woods, there are times when game can be spotted along the far side of a field, along a powerline right-of-way, in a clear cut section, etc., where a shot exceeding 200 yards is offered. Here, the hunter is better served by a flat-shooting round typified by the traditional western deer cartridge—a .25-06, .270 Winchester, .280 Remington, etc., might be ideal. Rather than a semiauto pump or lever gun, a bolt action and 4X scope capable of producing 1½-inch, three-shot groups at 100 yards is best suited to the task.

Whether to go with the dense-cover gun or the open-country rifle depends on the hunting area and a hunter's methods. If the hunter likes to take a stand in dense timber, the short-range carbine would be the one to choose. If he prefers to watch a greater area by sitting along the edge of a clear-cut area, field, or powerline right-of-way, the long-range rifle would be the choice.

Black bears in the Northeast are frequently taken as incidental to deer hunting, and in this case, the rifle used on black bears is dictated by the choice for deer. In other instances, bears are taken either with the aid of dogs or by shooting over bait. Either instance is generally a short-range shooting proposition. The short, light carbines that work ideally for dense-country deer hunting are also good for bears. When following a pack of bear dogs over hill and creek bottom, the shortest, lightest carbines, such as the now discontinued Ruger .44 Magnum semiauto or the Browning 92 in .44 Magnum, can make the carrying easier. If you feel you need more energy than the .44 Magnum delivers, go with a lever action in .375 or .358.

Basically, four centerfire rifles could fill all hunting requirements in the Northeast: two varmint and two big-game guns. For varmints, use the .22 Hornet rifle with a 6X scope at shorter ranges dictated by heavily settled areas, small fields, and heavy undergrowth. The accurate, heavy-barreled .22-250 or .220 Swift with an 8X or 10X scope is ideal for long-range shooting in more open country.

For big game, pick a light, fast-handling pump, semiauto, or lever-action carbine chambered for a cartridge capable of putting either deer or bears down quickly. A .35 Remington, .358 Winchester, .375 Winchester or, possibly, .44 Magnum will work well. And iron sights or a low-magnification scope works well for these dense cover situations. For the more open country deer hunting, carry a bolt-action .25-06, .280 Remington, etc., with a 4X scope.

Southeast

A NIMALS HUNTED IN the Southeast are much the same as those sought in the Northeast—with the exception of wild hogs. Hunting these large critters has become quite popular in certain sections of the Southeast. As with bears in the Northeast, both bears and wild hogs are hunted primarily with the aid of dogs in the Southeast. Much of the country where these hogs are hunted, particularly in the Carolinas, consists of mountainous terrain. A lightweight carbine can make gun carrying a whole lot easier. (A handgun is even better for some of this dog-following hunting, but in many states its use for hunting is not allowed.)

Because the hogs are taken at very short ranges, sometimes measured in feet rather than yards, a high level of accuracy is not required. However, the cartridge should have plenty of punch—a big boar can exceed 400 pounds in weight, and its thick, often calloused, shoulder hide can be tough to penetrate. It's important to have enough stopping power to do the hog in quickly so he won't chew on the dogs—or the hunter—before he dies.

Some boar hunting is done in the flat, swampy, tall grass areas, particularly in the lower South. Sometimes the dogs are followed by boat in open water, then once the hog is bayed by the dogs, the hunters move in with the aid of hip boots for the kill. The light, handy carbine has an obvious advantage here; it can be difficult to walk in grass-choked waters, much less carry a long, heavy rifle. Also, when the hog-and-dog fighting gets fast and furious, the hunter may need to maneuver his rifle quickly and get the shot off at a critical instant.

Something on the order of the Ruger semiauto .44 Magnum Carbine, Browning Model 92, or Marlin Model 1894, also in .44 Magnum, is considered ideal.

The Southeast in general is not quite as heavily populated as the Northeast. Hunting woodchucks, in particular, is done a bit differently. Some hunters go after woodchucks in mountainous country where ranges are incredibly long. Hunters frequently shoot from benchrest and have a friend along to spot the hits with the aid of a spotting scope. It's important to be able to tell, sometimes from a great distance, where a bullet strikes the woodchuck.

The grassy sod in these areas almost eliminates the .22 centerfires, for they don't kick up enough sod to spot easily from such a distance; the varmint cartridge must kick up a good-sized chunk of grass and dirt, even 400 or 500 yards downrange. In this case, the larger varmint cartridges that are actually varmint/deer cartridges are the first choices. A 6mm Remington is okay, and a .25-06 is considered to be just right. And the hunter isn't as concerned about recoil, for there are relatively few shots during a day's hunt.

A very high level of accuracy *is* a requirement, however. Heavy-barreled bolt actions capable of one minute of angle (MOA) or less allow the shooter to live up to the hunting requirements of the sport. Scopes of high magnification, even up to 20X, can be an advantage, particularly during cooler hunting conditions when mirage is no problem. When the heat waves start building during the middle of the day, a scope of lesser magnification, such as 10X or 12X, could be a better bet.

The shooter will want a streamlined bullet, possibly a boattail design, with a very high ballistic coefficient. Its velocity retention capabilities offer a flatter trajectory for easier hitting at extreme ranges. Since the hunter won't be carrying the rifle, weight and length are of no consequence. A long, heavy barrel can be an advantage in terms of consistent accuracy, steadier holding, and higher velocity. Deer hunting rifles that best equip the hunter in the Southeast are similar to rifles best suited to hunting conditions in the Northeast. Since hunting conditions are similar, sighting equipment and cartridges also remain much the same.

Refer to the Northeast section for the deer rifles and cartridges used.

Midwest

MIDWESTERN DEER hunting conditions differ from conditions farther east because the Midwest is a bit more open, due to flatter terrain and farming. The Dakotas, Nebraska, Kansas, and parts of Oklahoma are quite open, vegetation-wise, except for heavily timbered sections in river bottoms and isolated woodlots. In this open country, the deer hunter has the opportunity to take much longer shots than is generally the rule in the East.

There are sections of the Midwest—southern Missouri, Arkansas, Louisiana, etc. —that are heavily timbered, and the hunting conditions are similar to the more dense sections of the East. However, the bulk of the Midwest consists of farming country interspersed with isolated woodlots.

Deer frequently bed down in thickly timbered areas, brush patches, or even weed patches during the day, then venture into cornfields, alfalfa fields, or bean fields during the night to feed. Those who hunt the farming country know nothing tastes better than a corn-and-alfalfa-fattened buck. Deer in these areas can be very heavy bodied with excellent antler structure.

For most of these farming areas, a flat-shooting, bolt-action rifle is the best bet—a .25-06, .270 Winchester, .280 Remington, etc., would be ideal. The rifle should also be quick-pointing for bucks jumped in heavy cover. Winchester's Model 70 Featherweight, Ruger Model 77, and Sakos are excellent choices. A 4X glass would be just right, offering plenty of magnification for deer-sized game at any reasonable range, yet its field of view isn't so limited that it can't be easily used at close range. Most of this farming country is privately owned, and there won't be as many hunters as in the Northeast.

For heavily timbered sections, a traditional lightweight, quick-pointing brush gun with a low-magnification scope, or even iron sights, might be a better choice.

A Browning BAR or Remington Model 7400 or Model 7600, which are offered in several flat-shooting chamberings, may be good compromise rifles for both situations.

There is some black bear hunting in heavily timbered portions of the upper Midwest. Rifle/cartridge selection follows the same logic as for bears hunted in the East, whether you intend to take them by coursing with dogs or by shooting over bait.

By fall, a black bear has accumulated a lot of fat. Some hunters believe this fat is the reason bears don't leave much of a blood trail. And since bears are soft-footed, they can be difficult to track without one. This is why I prefer a cartridge with plenty of punch and with a bullet that penetrates well enough to exit with most shots. A bullet that exits generally produces a better blood trail, because the exit hole is usually larger than the entrance hole. I've had excellent results with the .358 Winchester and the 250-grain Speer HotCor bullet, and the .300 Winchester Magnum with 180-grain Nosler bullets.

Though there are groundhogs and woodchucks in the Midwest, hunting them is not nearly as popular as in sections in the East. In most portions of the Midwest, crows have been the traditional varmints.

Because of the high pelt prices in recent years, predator hunting for foxes and coyotes has become increasingly popular. It's great sport in some sections of the upper Midwest to glass for distant foxes napping in the snow under the midday sun. The hunter then plans his stalk, sometimes on snowshoes, to get within rifle range. All this demands a high level of hunting, stalking skill, and shooting ability. Here, an accurate bolt-action rifle is the correct choice. A lightweight or sporter-weight barrel is also an advantage because of the walking involved, sometimes through snow.

Many of the high-velocity varmint cartridges pack too much energy and are too destructive to fox pelts. The .17 Remington cartridge may be the best bet for this job. Or, in areas where it's legal, a .22 or 6mm using a full metal jacket (FMJ) bullet can help preserve the pelts. I generally don't recommend a nonexpanding bullet, but a fox-sized animal generally expires in a few seconds with a lung hit from one of these projectiles. A predator can travel a good distance in those few seconds, but in the wide-open prairies where foxes are often taken, they are seldom lost. However, forget using FMJs in brush country.

Coyotes are larger and usually much more difficult to stop. I prefer the larger case .22 centerfires from the .222 Remington up. The .22-250 and .220 Swift are excellent for these larger predators.

Fragile bullets at high velocity frequently do not exit coyotes, making them ideal for pelt hunting. I do not use FMJ bullets for coyote hunting because these prairie wolves are tenacious and require the effectiveness of an expanding bullet.

The same rifle used for coyotes or foxes can be used on crows as well.

Summing up, a rifle battery for the Midwest consists of a rifle typical of the traditional brush gun and an open-country deer gun, depending on where you hunt. A compromise gun may be one that carries a little of both rifle qualities—such as a Browning BAR, or a Remington Model 7400 or 7600—chambered for a flat-shooting cartridge and topped with a 2½X to 4X scope.

When it comes to varmints, a bolt action, like the .17 Remington Model 700 or .17 Sako with an 8X scope, will work very well for fox hunting on midwestern plains. This rifle would also be the first choice for crow shooting. The fragile .17 bullets are ideally suited to hunting in farming country because they'll disintegrate on impact.

If you plan to hunt coyotes by calling them in, a .22-250 or .220 Swift in an accurate bolt-action rifle, with a 2½-7X or 3-9X variable, would be the choice. There is a good reason for using the variable scope on a coyote rifle. In most calling situations, the coyote will be very close and frequently moving fast. The wide field of view afforded by the lower magnifications is ideally suited to these conditions. At other times, coyotes are sighted at long range in open country so the higher magnifications offered in 7X or 9X is better for these 300- or 400-yard shots.

If you're hunting coyotes and foxes at the same time, you may wish to go with the .17 Remington and top it off with a variable scope, or you can use the high-velocity .22 centerfire coyote rifle and simply load FMJ bullets when it comes time to hunt foxes.

West

HUNTERS IN THE West have the greatest variety of hunting conditions—from tabletop level, wide-open plains to near vertical ruggedness above the timber line. The vegetation ranges from short-grass prairie to hard-to-get-through rain forest.

The choice of game is also widely varied in the West, encompassing deer, bears, antelope, goats, sheep, elk, javelina, and moose. The varmint hunting spectrum includes crows, prairie dogs, gophers, rockchucks, and jackrabbits. Furbearing predators include coyotes, foxes, and bobcats.

There are certain sections of the West, such as the Olympic Peninsula in western Washington, where a shot beyond a few yards is the exception. And there are other areas, such as on the Wyoming flats, where a long shot is the rule. But when hunting timber-country game—deer, elk, bear, etc.—the hunter runs into situations that are a combination of those hunting styles. Most of the deer and elk country in the West consists of densely timbered areas, but they are rugged, with steep mountain slopes, canyons, ridges, etc. The hunter can break out of a flat, timbered area where a 100-yard shot is a long one, to the edge of a canyon where game will be spotted 300 yards across the abyss.

Whitetails of the East are frequently hunted by sitting along a game trail, and the shooting range is somewhat determined by where you sit. The western mule deer or elk hunter soon learns these animals migrate during the winter and are likely to meander over a wide section of real estate. One day they'll be in green timber and aspen forest at 10,000 feet, and a few days later they'll be in semi-open brushy areas at 5000 feet. This is another reason why the hunter has about a 50/50 chance of getting a shot at short range in dense cover, or from ridge to ridge, or across a canyon at several hundred yards. It's usually best to be prepared for the most difficult shot—the long one.

In some states, it's popular to hunt deer and a larger species of game at the same time. For instance, during Colorado's late-season hunt, deer, bear, and elk can all be taken at the same time. In this situation, the .270/.30-06 class of cartridges should be considered the minimum, and the 7mm Remington Magnum, or one of the .30 belted magnums, is an even better choice as a combination deer/elk cartridge. The Weatherby cartridges, which emphasize high velocity, are also suited to western hunting.

For most western hunting, a scope is the best choice in sighting equipment. For big-game hunting, I have found no need for magnification greater than 4X, and for the hunter going after game predominantly in the timbered areas, a 2½X or 3X would be an excellent choice.

I don't think the scope is the cure-all some would have us believe. I vividly recall three occasions when I lost shots at game because I had an optic sight. None of the occasions involved scope fogging, which many believe is the primary downfall of scopes.

One incident happened while I was elk hunting in the Colorado mountains at about 11,000 feet. During the second day of the hunt, a heavy, wet snowfall began while I was hunting in thick green timber, just below timberline. I found myself on the track of a bull, and after following his trail for a couple of hours, I jumped him. The bull's bed was uphill from my approach, and he was watching his backtrail. I had been moving slowly and carefully and was watching intently ahead. I caught the antler flash as the elk rose to his feet; simultaneously, I shouldered my .300 Winchester Magnum. Evidently, the bull wasn't certain what I was, as he paused for a look back as my rifle came up.

To my disgust, the lenses were coated with wet snow, and I couldn't see anything. I quickly lowered the rifle, flicked the snow off with my hand, and shouldered it again just as the bull disappeared into the timber. Had I been using "irons" that bull would have been mine.

On two other occasions while deer hunting, I jumped bucks but moisture on the scope glass prevented me from getting a killing shot off in time. In both cases, I'm certain the bucks would have been brought to bag had my vision not been obscured by the wet lenses.

Under these hunting conditions, I prefer to use an iron-sighted rifle, and I like the aperture, or peep sight, best. It's faster to use and provides more precise aiming in a rush than open sights.

Any time fog moves in with the possibility of rain or snow, I'll slide my scope-sighted magnum back into the case and pull out an iron-sighted rifle chambered for something like the .358 Winchester.

In the fall, when most of the hunting seasons are open, the western section of the U.S. is at the brink of a severe winter in the high country. The weather is ready to change and can do so in a matter of hours. Therefore, even though you may leave for the hunt under bright, sunny conditions, it's a good idea to take a second iron-sighted rifle along just in case.

I prefer the second rifle to be an easy-to-carry, quick-pointing brush gun; the iron sights limit its effective range, anyway. Also, this iron-sighted backup rifle is perfect for stalking the flatter, heavily timbered sections. By switching to the iron-sighted rifle in such conditions, a hunter can be much better prepared for that shot in heavy timber. And I have both rifles chambered for cartridges powerful enough for elk or moose.

Open-country hunting, whether it's antelope on the plains or sheep above timberline, is a different proposition. Here, 400-yard shots are commonplace, and the rifle must be capable of producing consistent long-range accuracy. The cartridge must also be flat shooting for easier long-range hitting—the .25-06, .270 Winchester, .270 Weatherby Magnum, 7mm Remington Magnum, 7mm Weatherby Magnum, etc., are considered ideal for shooting smaller species of big game at long range.

The hunter after such quarry is best equipped with a 4X or 6X scope, possibly with a bipod attached to the rifle's front sling swivel stud. The reason for the bipod is that in many sections of flat, short-grass antelope country there is nothing the hunter can use for a rifle rest. The use of a bipod can considerably increase the hunter's odds under such conditions. If you're hunting deer in open country, the same long-range rifle can be used.

The variety of varmint hunting in the West may necessitate the hunter having two rifles, much like in the Midwest, but for different reasons. I prefer the traditional heavy-barreled bolt-action varmint rifle with a high-magnification scope for prairie dogs, gophers, and rockchucks. The hunter generally shoots from a stationary position, and in some prairie dog hunting situations, he has the opportunity to fire several hundred rounds in a day's time. The heavy-barreled rifle can be an asset because it usually maintains its original point of impact after heating up, and this is something a sporter-weight barrel may not do. Also, due to the great number of rounds that can be fired at prairie dogs, I prefer one of the .22 centerfires to the larger .24s or .25s.

These larger calibers generally have a reputation for being better wind-buckers, but most of this lack of .22 centerfire wind-bucking ability is more imagined than real. The .22-250 and .220 Swift generally start bullets out so much faster than the larger calibers that there is no significant difference in wind drift at reasonable shooting ranges.

Additionally, the .22 centerfires have less recoil. Most people do not consider any of the varmint cartridges to have much recoil, but those same people probably haven't fired 500 rounds from the prone position in a day's prairie dog shoot.

A few weeks ago, I fired nearly 750 rounds in a single day's prairie dog shooting with a heavy-barreled Model 70 Winchester chambered for the .243 Winchester. Even with the heavy rifle and lightweight 80-grain bullets, shooting became painful toward the end of the day and gave me a bruised shoulder. Besides being chambered for a high-velocity .22, the prairie dog/rockchuck/gopher rifle would ideally be topped with an 8X or 10X scope.

Jackrabbits, a frequently hunted varmint in the West, offer a unique varmint shooting experience. These large hares are generally taken by walking up and jumping them out of their hiding places. The usual ranges run from 50 yards to as far as you want to shoot. This type of hunting usually requires some amount of walking, and shots are taken from the shoulder. A lightweight rifle is the obvious best choice. Also, the game will be moving, and consistent benchrest accuracy isn't a prerequisite. A 4X scope offers plenty of magnification for this running game.

If the hunter is selecting a rifle specifically for jackrabbits, he'll probably want one producing less recoil than a big-game rifle. Though he generally won't have the opportunity to fire as many shots at jackrabbits as at prairie dogs, he may fire 50 or so rounds in a short period.

I consider a good jackrabbit hunting rifle to be in the same class as a coyote calling rifle, and the same rifle can be used for both types of hunting. More important than a high level of accuracy is a shooter's ability to get on target fast and be a good running-game shot. Also, fast repeat shots are a definite advantage. One of the lever-action .22-250s, such as the Savage Model 99 or Browning BLR, is an excellent choice for this type of hunting. Or, a semiauto, such as the Remington Model 7400 in .243 or 6mm or the Browning BAR in 6mm, would also be a very satisfactory choice. (However, rifles chambered for the 6mm cartridges would not be as ideally suited to coyote calling because with most loads they're excessively damaging to pelts.) Even a bolt-action rifle can work well for jackrabbit shooting, and the practice will teach you to be faster with this action type.

Whether selected for coyotes, jackrabbits, or both, the rifle should produce one MOA accuracy and be topped with a variable 3-9X scope. The scope would be turned down to 3X for coyote calling or for walking up jackrabbits, and would be turned up to 7X or 9X when driving between coyote calling stands or whenever spotting jackrabbits at long range. Generally, game at extreme range isn't likely to be spooked by the shooter, so you have time to change scope magnification prior to taking the shot.

All these rifle/cartridge, scope/accuracy recommendations can be confusing. Certainly, a hunter could select a .30-06 and be adequately prepared for any big-game hunting in the U.S., and the varmint shooter can pick a .22-250 and be prepared for any varmint. But the hunter can be much better prepared by selecting his shooting combination with something specific in mind. Besides, it's more fun to own a lot of different rifles.

Varmint Hunting

V ARMINT HUNTING offers unequaled opportunities. There are usually no bag limits, no permits to obtain, and little or no competition from other hunters. Varmints can be found virtually anywhere in the U.S. Your quarry could be the groundhog and crow in the East or prairie dogs, ground squirrels, rockchucks, crows, and jackrabbits in the West. Some shooters include furbearing predators like red and grey foxes, coyotes, and bobcats on their lists of varmints. And certain regions have their own specialized species (like the armadillo of southwest Texas).

Some regions offer more wide-open shooting opportunities than others. In the wide-open spaces of the West, where there are vast tracts of public Forest Service or Bureau of Land Management lands, it's not necessary to gain permission to hunt. It's simply a matter of finding the quarry.

At the opposite extreme, some eastern areas are so heavily populated that, regardless of the number of chucks or groundhogs, no hunting is allowed or you can't fire a "loud" rifle.

In some sections of the Great Plains, the pursuer of prairie dogs is welcomed with the red carpet treatment. In fact, the prairie dog is an expensive pest in many of these areas. The sod poodles dig deep holes and eat or cover up a lot of grass. Prairie dogs are also carriers of plague in some regions.

In the plains states, some farmers and ranchers have spent thousands of dollars in efforts to control these pests. In states like Kansas, allowing prairie dog populations to expand can be against the law; a landowner can be held directly responsible for keeping prairie dog populations in check. In other words, prairie dogs are not merely pests—they're serious, expensive troublemakers.

It's surprising to me more shooters haven't taken advantage of this valuable hunting opportunity. Most hunters think nothing of traveling across a state or two to go after deer or even pheasants. But offer an animal with practically unlimited shooting opportunities at times of the year when nothing else can be hunted, and most of these same sportsmen think it's absurd.

So much the better for those who like to hunt varmints.

Finding a place to shoot varmints can range from simply asking a neighbor for permission to writing to a state game department to find locations of varmint concentrations. In many instances, state game departments are eager to provide assistance due to the fact that varmints are a problem. Even intense shooting offers little hope of holding large populations in check.

In addition to game departments, agricultural extension services can provide valuable information regarding the locations of particularly troublesome pests. I have also had excellent success locating prairie dog towns in agricultural areas by checking with grain elevator operators. Vendors of agricultural pesticides are another excellent source of information. These people know if someone is thinking about initiating a poison program for the pesky critters.

The equipment to be used for varmint shooting depends primarily on what you plan to shoot and the specifics regarding where you plan to shoot. In most instances, varmint shooting involves small targets at extreme ranges. For such long-range small-target shooting, accuracy is the name of the game. To derive the most from the sport, the rifle chosen should be capable of keeping its shots within a killing area of the varmint-sized animal over all shooting distances.

For all practical purposes, the bolt-action rifle is the No. 1 choice. Though a heavy barrel is frequently preferred for such shooting, many lightweight barrels have the accuracy capability for long-range varminting. The performance of the trigger is extremely important for such riflery, and serious shooters either have their factory triggers adjusted by a competent gunsmith or replace them with a custom trigger. The latter can be adjusted to a crisp, reliable few ounces if desired.

Most varmint shooting action involves stationary targets at long range, so a high scope magnification of 8X to 20X is generally preferred. Not too many years ago, scopes in the 8X to 10X range were about tops in hunting scope magnification. During more recent years, however, scopes of higher magnification have become available.

One of my favorites for such long-range varminting is the Leupold 6.5-20X. This scope offers high magnification for excellent target definition at extreme range. At the same time, however, I can reduce the magnification for a wider field of view to engage varmints at a shorter distance or to locate additional varmints after a shot is made.

I find locating another varmint is quicker with a scope having a wider field of view. Generally, there will be several prairie dogs in a given location, although you might be able to see only one. When a shot is fired, other prairie dogs will scurry to a nearby den, then hesitate for a few seconds before diving in. The shooter with a wide field of view scope (8X or 10X) will be ready for another shot. Shooters with a narrow field of view scope (20X to 25X) won't even be able to see them because they'll be out of the field of view.

For varminting situations like crow shooting that generally offer single-shot opportunities, the high-magnification scopes can produce better target definition. However, high-magnification scopes also emphasize heat waves and mirage, which can reduce target definition.

Flat-shooting calibers are the rule for most varmint situations. The .22-250 Remington, .220 Swift, .243 Winchester, 6mm Remington, and .25-06 Remington are top choices for long-distance shooting. The type of varminting you do will have some bearing on the caliber you choose.

For example, some areas get a lot of rainfall to create a grassy sod, making it difficult to determine where the bullet impacts if the varmint is missed. In this situation, larger calibers like the 6mm Remington or .25-06 Remington are preferred. These will kick up a chunk of sod if a shot is missed. A companion "spotter" can then advise where to hold for a hit on the next shot. In other areas, the smaller, faster .22 calibers are preferred due to their lower noise and recoil levels.

Though most shooters don't consider recoil to be a factor in varminting situations, hundreds of rounds fired from the prone position can cause a shooter's firing shoulder to become tender and possibly prompt the development of a flinch. You just have to fit the caliber to the situation.

In some types of varminting—western ground squirrel or prairie dog shooting, for example—the varmint hunter should be prepared for fast shooting and lots of it. He should have plenty of ammo, and his gun should be capable of holding its point of impact and grouping ability even after the barrel gets hot. It's a great idea to take two guns along, alternating them when one of the barrels gets hot. For the same reason, some shooters prefer milder cartridges like the .222 Remington or .223 Remington due to the fact that the milder cartridges cause the barrel to heat up slower (which means it will also last longer).

Crows or groundhogs do not generally offer as many shots. A half-dozen groundhogs in a morning's shoot might be great. In this latter instance, larger calibers like the .25-06 might be preferred. In yet another situation, the tiny .22 Hornet might be the preferred choice in heavily populated areas or where there is concern about alarming neighbors when high-noise calibers are fired.

In some areas, the shooter might not be able to take the tiny targets at extreme range due to the terrain. I once hunted one section of Maryland where small fields and the hilly, wooded surroundings made it difficult to take even a 200-yard shot.

For varminting in this situation, a shooter can add to the challenge by picking one of the "lesser" cartridges, the .22 Hornet, .17 Remington, .222, .223, etc. A smaller cartridge like the Hornet can add to the drop and wind-doping challenge which would be lost if the shooter were trying one of the fast and flat .22-250 or .220 Swift numbers.

Not all varmint shooting involves stationary targets at extreme range. Jackrabbit hunting in the Midwest and West can involve walking the rabbits up and shooting them "on the run." In these instances, the larger hares are taken at distances frequently no greater than 200 or 300 yards. A lightweight, easy-carrying rifle would be ideal for this action-packed sport. A short-barreled number like the Remington Model Seven in .222 is ideal. Since the target will be relatively close and frequently moving, scopes of a lower magnification are the most effective due to the wider field of view they offer. A 4X or 6X scope works just fine.

This type of shooting offers excellent preseason practice for the big-game hunter, and any rifle normally used for deer or other big game can be fine for a jackrabbit shooting tuneup. However, using ammunition with lightweight, high-velocity, explosive varmint bullets to prevent as many ricochets as possible is a good practice.

If selecting a rifle specifically for running jackrabbit shooting, I prefer a cartridge producing a very mild report. I like to hunt jackrabbits without the use of hearing protection because a hare can often be detected by the sound of its scurrying out from a hiding place. Hearing protection can prevent such sounds from being heard. For this reason, a cartridge with a low noise level is best. The .17 Remington is ideal, as are the .222 Remington and .22 Hornet. Larger calibers with reduced loads can also produce a mild report and recoil.

The hunter after predators may also do well to select a slightly different shooting rig. Basically, the furbearer or predatory varmints are taken in one of two manners; they're either shot at extreme range or called in close with the sound of a prey species in distress. Entirely different shooting rigs are appropriate for each hunting situation. Any of the long-range rigs mentioned could be ideal for the long shots. For the calling situations, the outfits described for jackrabbit shooting would be best. This includes rifle type, sighting equipment, and cartridge.

If the hunter wants to preserve the valuable pelts of the predatory varmints, he'll have another requirement. The ammunition should dispatch predators cleanly and without excessive pelt damage. The best selections for such shooting will be different, depending on whether the animal is a thin-skinned, seven-pound fox or a thick-skinned, 40-pound coyote.

When it comes to big-cased .22 or 6mm cartridges, full metal jacket bullets are generally better for the small foxes, or you may have success with the .22 Hornet. For coyotes and bobcats, high-velocity, rapid-expanding .22-caliber bullets may not exit, particularly when the range is short. This is a perfect situation for the pelt hunter.

Besides the shooting rigs, the varmint hunter will find a need for accessories like a Harris bipod or other types of rests for zeroing-in on tiny targets at extreme range. A good sling is always handy, particularly when walking long distances over unproductive terrain with a heavy-barreled rig.

A partner with a good set of binoculars or a spotting scope can add to the hunt. The shooter frequently loses sight of the target when the rifle fires and recoils, but the "spotter" can report if a hit was made. He can also tell where a miss impacted by the puff of dirt or fling of sod, allowing the shooter to adjust accordingly for the next round.

The important thing when hunting varmints is to relax and enjoy it. At the same time, it'll sharpen your shooting eye, hone your wind- and mirage-doping skills, and give you practice at range estimation. In short, it'll make you a better shot. There's nothing quite like connecting with a prairie dog or groundhog while holding three feet over and two feet into the wind. Only a varmint shooter knows the thrill. Once you've connected on your first one, you'll know what I mean.

What's Perfect On Predators

F LUCTUATING PRICES of predator pelts have spurred interest in hunting large varmints at different times during the last decade. It's not surprising. When prices are high, one bobcat pelt can pay for a new gun. A coyote or fox brings the price of a scope. With that kind of return, it's not hard to justify buying a rifle just for predator hunting. Unfortunately, a lot of first-time fur hunters have no idea what goes into a good pelt hunting rifle and load. And using an unsuitable cartridge can take a good chunk out of a fur check.

Through experience, I have found the .22 centerfires provide the best balance between killing power and minimal pelt destruction. The .17 Remington is on the light side in killing power on coyotes and bobcats, while calibers larger than .22 centerfire are overly destructive with standard loads.

Loading nearly any caliber down in velocity to the 2000 fps range reduces pelt damage for a suitable close-range load, but there's considerable sacrifice in long-range effectiveness. The rainbow-like trajectory resulting from this low velocity makes long-range hitting more a matter of luck than shooting skill. And hunting predators, even when trying to call them in, demands that a cartridge perform well at all reasonable ranges.

It's true that the shot will generally be less than 100 yards in most calling situations. Sometimes, however, a wary old coyote, particularly toward the end of the season, may be hesitant to come in to the sound of an imitation rabbit. In this case, the hunter may have to be content with a 300- or 400-yard shot. In addition, there are other hunters who prefer to glass their game from a distance and then stalk as close as possible for the shot. The open terrain required for spotting predators this way generally means the hunter still won't have ample cover to stalk closely. For this type of hunting, the long shot remains the rule.

Add to this condition the fact that a coyote is only six or seven inches from the top of the shoulders to the bottom of the chest, and it's not difficult to see why high-velocity cartridges give hunters a definite advantage: They reduce the degree of precision required in estimating range for a hit. All it takes is a glance at a ballistics table to see that the *faster* a bullet moves, the *flatter* it shoots over a given range.

Another advantage to higher velocity is less wind drift. The quicker a bullet arrives on target, the less its course is affected by wind (because wind drift is a result not only of bullet weight, but also of time). In some shooting circles, the .22 CFs have a reputation of drifting more in wind than the heavier bullets in larger calibers. What is generally overlooked is the fact that .22-250 and .220 Swift cartridges have the potential to propel bullets much faster than most larger calibers, negating the apparent wind drift advantage with heavier bullets.

These are the main reasons why the .22-250 and .220 Swift have the edge on other .22 centerfires like the .222 and .223 Remingtons. Though high velocity provides an edge in connecting with game, it is also noted for its destructive potential. In big-game calibers, high velocity, with its attendant high energy, generally contributes to greater tissue destruction. However, for pelt hunting, I'm not concerned about the internal damage or meat—just the hide.

The .17s and .22 CFs are unique in that when bullets are chosen for proper expansion characteristics and fired at velocities in the 3600 to 3800 fps range, they won't generally exit a coyote or bobcat, assuming a solid hit. (Foxes are not included in this category because of their small size and fragile skin.)

Even though the two hottest .22 CFs form the basis for the best shooting combinations, just any loads won't do; it takes a precise recipe for the best performance on pelts. But first, I'll offer my ideas on why the improper choices don't work.

All sorts of remedies have been tried by handloading hunters to prevent pelt damage (big holes). Indeed, the demand from fur hunters has been the primary impetus behind the introduction of the full metal jacket (FMJ) bullets in .22 CF and 6mm calibers. However, a good number of pelt hunters are finding the FMJs are not the solution some would have us believe. The FMJs can be fired at high velocity, and they don't generally expand, meaning pelts aren't damaged excessively. However, neither are the coyote's innards, which could result in losing the coyote.

I have experienced a considerable lack of killing power with the FMJ bullets, even in the larger .30 calibers. I shot one called-in coyote through the lungs while he trotted broadside about 30 yards, using a 172-grain FMJ .300 Winchester Magnum. The coyote took off at the shot as if its tail were on fire and went out of sight over a ridge 200 yards away. Not thinking I'd missed, I walked over the ridge and found the coyote piled up just out of sight from my calling stand.

The coyote apparently expired in 10 or 15 seconds, but these animals can travel a good distance in that time. And had I been in brushy country, I would probably have assumed it was a miss and never found the coyote because upon backtracking from where the predator dropped, I found no sign of a blood trail.

I've experienced this problem several times using FMJs. It seems there isn't enough energy and shock transmitted by pointed FMJs to stop the coyotes quickly, and soft-footed predators don't leave much of a track. That's one reason why it's important to drop them instantly.

If the .30-caliber FMJs won't work consistently, how can the smaller 6mm and .22s be expected to?

Coyotes are not large in the Southwest, averaging close to 25 pounds. During a 19-day hunt several years ago, I weighed 77 northern Arizona coyotes, and they ranged from 17 to 34 pounds. But they're amazingly tenacious to life. Biologists have documented evidence to show that many coyotes have lived years after surviving damage which would kill most animals quickly. In most cases, the FMJs don't do enough damage, and that spells problems for the hunter.

At other times, the FMJs which penetrate the animal completely produce another sort of problem. The last coyote I shot with an FMJ was with the Hornady 80-grainer in 6mm Remington. The coyote was trotting towards me at a quartering angle about 25 yards away when the FMJ entered the predator just in front of the near shoulder and exited the opposite shoulder. The result was a six-inch hole in the off-side of the pelt. Most likely, this was due to secondary bone fragments and not necessarily a result of the FMJ bullet design. However, this type of excessive damage can be prevented with a proper choice of cartridge and load.

Some hunters who have tried FMJs with poor success have decided to go to the opposite extreme and use the Hornady SX or Sierra Blitz bullets. These bullets are designed to expand violently upon impact when fired at .222 Remington velocities. Hunters figured these bullets would enter a predator, disintegrate, and not exit. This is *sometimes* the case, but you can encounter problems. First, these fragile bullets cannot be loaded to maximum velocities in order to reach the same levels as the .22-250 or .220 Swift. Hornady packs a note with the SXs saying the bullets cannot be depended on to perform properly at velocities in excess of 3500 fps. This means they cannot be fired at maximum velocities in the .22 CFs. And there's nothing more frustrating than to assemble a batch of hot loads and then discover they're disintegrating as they're fired.

I'll never forget trying to zero-in a rifle using this type of bullet. I couldn't figure out why the bullets wouldn't print a group on paper. After shooting into a plowed field, I saw that each bullet was patterning like a 12-gauge skeet gun with ⅛-ounce of No. 9s! Even if these fragile bullets are loaded down to a velocity where they can be fired without coming apart, severe entrance holes (up to five inches) may result when they impact a coyote.

The FMJ bullets and the fragile Blitz and SX bullets have to be eliminated from competition, leaving the vast group of in-between .22 bullets. By selecting any of these expanding bullets in the .22 CF calibers, the hunter can't really go wrong.

Still, I have discovered a few choices that have worked ideally for me on coyotes and bobcats. Bullets like the 52-grain Speer hollowpoint or the 55-grain Remington Power-Lokt hollowpoint work very well. When fired at .22-250 or .220 Swift velocities in the 3600 to 3800 fps range, they will seldom exit a coyote, particularly at close, varmint-calling ranges. At the same time, they almost never produce a large entrance wound. The .22-caliber entrance holes they put in pelts are very small. Best of all, they'll stop a coyote or bobcat in its tracks, even with a poorly placed hit in some cases.

On occasion, the bullets will exit broadside-standing coyotes at longer range. However, due to their rapid expansion characteristics, most of the energy is apparently expended by the time they completely penetrate a coyote. When bullets exit, they leave only golf ball-size holes. I have shot broadside-standing coyotes (at ranges up to 100 yards) just behind the shoulder, where there are no bones larger than ribs, without bullet exit.

Some hunters might question the suitability of the blunt Speer 52-grain hollowpoint for velocity retention at long ranges. But remember: Bullet shape or its form factor is a component of ballistic coefficient (B.C.); the other components are weight and diameter. All this can get complicated, but it's nothing more than a mathematical measure of a bullet's ability to overcome air resistance and retain velocity. The higher the B.C., the better the bullet's long-range velocity retention.

.22-250 LOAD DATA

Remington Model 788, 24-inch barrel

Bullet	Powder (Type)	(Grs.)	Primer	Case	Muzzle Velocity (fps)
Hornady 50-gr. spirepoint	IMR-3031	35	Fed. 210	R-P	3710
Sierra 50-gr. spitzer	IMR-4064	36	Fed. 210	R-P	3660
Sierra 50-gr. spitzer	H380	39	Fed. 210	R-P	3615
Speer 52-gr. HP	H4895	35	Fed. 210	R-P	3656
Speer 52-gr. HP	IMR-4064	36	Fed. 210	R-P	3775
Speer 52-gr. HP	IMR-4320	36	Fed. 210	R-P	3643
Remington 55-gr. P-L HP	H4895	34	Fed. 210	R-P	3672
Remington 55-gr. P-L HP	IMR-4320	36	Fed. 210	R-P	3698
Nosler 60-gr. Solid Base	IMR-4320	35	Fed. 210	R-P	3543
Nosler 60-gr. Solid Base	H414	38	Fed. 210	R-P	3409
Nosler 60-gr. Solid Base	IMR-4350	39	Fed. 210	R-P	3461

NOTES: Velocity is instrumental at 10 feet.

.220 SWIFT LOAD DATA

Ruger Model 77V, 26-inch barrel

Bullet	Powder (Type)	(Grs.)	Primer	Case	Muzzle Velocity (fps)
Hornady 50-gr. spirepoint	IMR-4064	37	Rem. 9½	Super-X	3715
Sierra 50-gr. spitzer	IMR-3031	34	Rem. 9½	Super-X	3642
Remington 50-gr. P-L HP	IMR-3031	34	Rem. 9½	Super-X	3650
Speer 52-gr. HP	IMR-3031	34	Rem. 9½	Super-X	3595
Sierra 63-gr. semipointed	IMR-4350	39	Rem. 9½	Super-X	3480

The 52-grain Speer hollowpoint with a ballistic coefficient of .225 is not the most efficiently shaped bullet. For instance, the 55-grain Hornady spirepoint carries a B.C. of .246, while the 60-grain spirepoint is rated at .269.

At one time, I used the higher B.C. bullets and chose a 63-grain Sierra with a .300 B.C. However, initial velocity was nearly 200 fps less with this heavier bullet. And as a result of the heavier bullet starting slower, there was no apparent advantage in terms of long-range trajectory, even though it retained its velocity better.

The 63-grain bullet, even though it was accurate and retained velocity and energy well, exited coyotes much more frequently than the more fragile, lighter weight bullets. That's why it's not ideally suited for pelt hunting. In my experience, all heavier .22 bullets performed similarly. Mass and energy are apparently too great and velocity too low, causing less violent expansion and excessive penetration (i.e. an exit).

Obviously, there are a lot of .22 bullets besides the 52-grain Speer HP and 55-grain Remington P-L HP that will perform well on coyotes. I have tried a good number of them, but I don't feel I've given them a valid test.

For instance, when I first began using the Sierra 63-grainer, I experienced good success on 20 or 30 coyotes. The bullets were from an older lot I purchased 10 or 12 years ago. When those bullets were used up, I bought new ones and loaded them with the same powder charge I used before—41.0 grains of Norma's MRP for 3440 fps from a Remington Model 788. To my surprise, these bullets exited completely on the first six coyotes I bagged, producing severe exit holes in several of them.

I immediately (and erroneously) decided these new bullets were different, possibly in jacket design. I continued using them, however, and later found those six instances of poor results were nothing more than the result of chance. Performance on subsequent coyotes indicated the new bullets performed just like the old ones.

No one bullet will perform perfectly every time. If the bullet hits a coyote "around the edges" at a glancing angle (when he's coming in or going away), a long rip in the pelt will often result, no matter what bullet or cartridge is used.

The key to obtaining rapid bullet expansion is adequate velocity. What powders produce high velocity in these .22 centerfires? Traditionally, extruded propellants in the burning range of 3031 to 4064 have been considered ideal for these cartridges with lighter bullets. Slow-burning powders are frequently used with the heavier bullets like MRP, 4350, or even 4831.

Hodgdon's 4895 has accounted for a good portion of the predators I've taken with a .22-250. I use this powder because it produces excellent accuracy in my Model 788 Remington with many different bullets. Additionally, the 52-grain Speer HP performs well in the Model 788 with a wide range of powders. This indicated to me that a combination of the two was in order. My preferred .22-250 load is 35.0 grains H4895 with the 52-grain Speer HP, producing 3650 fps from the 24-inch barrel with a .75-inch, five-shot group average at 100 yards.

A .220 Swift load that works quite well in this same velocity category is 35.0 grains of DuPont's 3031 with either the 52-grain Speer or 50-grain Remington P-L HP bullets. A heavy-barreled Ruger Model 77 groups this load around .5 inch at 100 yards with the Remington bullets.

Spherical or ball powders like H380, H450, W760, or H414 also perform well in the big-case .22s while metering very uniformly from any powder measure. But there is such a wide choice of both powders and bullets now available that it's impossible to try all the combinations.

There is one problem in loading any "overbore-type" case (with a large powder capacity in relation to bullet size). The .22 centerfires are extremely sensitive to variations in primer, case, case neck thickness, etc., at maximum velocity. If you're shooting maximum loads and alter any component of the load, back off a few grains and work up again slowly. I've found that pressures can become dangerously excessive with seemingly insignificant load alterations. For the same reason, the handloader should progress in charges only one-half grain at a time as he works up to maximum loads. Watch closely for any indicators of high pressure and stop immediately when they're reached.

Several years ago, I was progressing a grain of powder at a time developing a .22-250 load. There were no visible signs of high pressure at one charge level—but adding only one more grain blew a primer and froze the rifle's bolt shut. In other words, I was on the ragged edge of danger, and I was still a couple of grains *below* the maximum loads listed in several reloading manuals.

For some reason, that particular rifle would not accept charge levels most other rifles would. I could have prevented the incident by going a half grain at a time and miking case head expansion as well. And if you're not familiar with miking a case to determine maximum loads, you can find an explanation in the *Nosler Reloading Manual*.

Getting a load to shoot accurately enough to drop coyotes and bobcats is not difficult. Most off-the-rack .22-250 or .220 Swift rifles have the accuracy potential to put three shots in one inch at 100 yards. I consider this to be plenty good for coyotes. If your centerfire .22 doesn't match that, a bedding job or other tinkering might be in order to get the accuracy you need.

Experience has shown me what works best most of the time. By using the foregoing guidelines in velocity and bullet selection, it shouldn't be difficult to develop a load that shoots well in your rifle, has good velocity, and doesn't damage pelts excessively. About the only thing a good load won't do is hit the coyote for you!

The Best Bullet For Coyotes

R ELOADING OFFERS a shooter loads of versatility in terms of performance of his handloads. Even though there is a wide range of factory loadings available, this variety does not even come close to the handloader's flexibility in loading most cartridges. Not only is there a wide range of primer and propellant types, but the bullet—the most important element in hunting situations—comes in a vast array of weights and terminal performance characteristics. The handloader can select a bullet to match almost any hunting purpose, range, velocity, etc.

A few years ago, I would not have included "almost" with that statement. Only when the price of predator pelts skyrocketed did a need for a new bullet to meet specialized requirements develop. The major requirement was to dispatch a predator cleanly at both short and long ranges without doing excessive damage to the pelt.

Coyotes are generally taken in one of two ways: they're called in close and shot at under 100 yards, or they're spotted moving fast in open country and shot at long ranges. Both instances show why it's important to have a coyote rifle and load that will perform well at all ranges.

I have hunted coyotes for many years, even when pelts brought next to nothing. In those days, the best cartridge was one that shot fast and flat with bullets which expanded rapidly. My favorites for such coyote work were the 6mm and .25-06 Remingtons with fast-expanding bullets. Coyotes were taken effectively, but the exit wounds destroyed a large portion of the pelt. Not the best method for preserving predator pelts . . . .

During this period, I began to realize a coyote's tenacity. In terms of energy, cartridges generally used on coyotes are all out of proportion to the size of the animal. If cartridges deemed adequate for elk hunting were scaled down pound-for-pound proportionately for coyote hunting, they would be inadequate. I know of no game animal which comes close to matching the coyote's tenacity. This physical capacity of the coyote compounds the issue when pelt hunting. The projectiles must do the job internally but only perforate the pelt (as if using a pencil).

Like many other shooters, I began trying different cartridges and loads when pelt prices increased. For bullets, I went from lightweight varmint bullets in large calibers to heavyweight big-game slugs and low-velocity cast lead. I even tried the then-new FMJs. For cartridges, I went from the mighty magnum .30 down to the tiny .22 centerfires.

The varmint bullets in 6mm and larger calibers frequently left gaping exit holes. The heavy big-game bullets always exited. If a heavy enough bullet were fired (like the 220-grain .30-06), the velocity generally wasn't great enough to cause excessive expansion before the bullet exited. Sometimes, however, they did leave gaping exit holes. The next step was the low-velocity cast bullets. A blunt projectile would do the job with a relatively small exit hole, but due to the blunt shape and low velocity, it was strictly a short-range proposition.

The reason I'm concerned with exit holes is that even one two inches in diameter can decrease a coyote's pelt value by 50 percent. Furthermore, skinning such an animal becomes more difficult when pelt and flesh damage is extensive. In short, exit holes should be avoided.

The best compromise in commercial calibers was to use a .22 centerfire. The bullets still exited, particularly at long range where expansion was reduced, but the exit holes were small. Further experimentation turned up some fragile .22 bullets which expanded more rapidly than others yet didn't blow up on impact. Several of these projectiles would not exit even a broadside-standing coyote as long as the distance was under the 50-yard mark. A select few bullets, such as the gaping-nosed Speer 52-grain hollowpoint, would generally stay inside a broadside-standing, lung-shot coyote out to 100 yards. Beyond this distance, velocity decreased enough so expansion was reduced; consequently, the bullets penetrated more and generally exited.

I had already done a considerable amount of terminal or bullet expansion performance testing with big-game bullets in an artificial expansion medium, but I'd never tried it with varmint bullets, so I began experimenting with bullets for pelts.

It's generally believed fragile varmint bullets expand violently on contact and there are relatively few differences among them regarding terminal performance. I had experienced inconsistent bullet expansion on coyotes, but I suspected the inconsistencies were a result of different bullet impact situations rather than differences in bullet performance. At any rate, I decided to shoot a variety of .22 bullets into an expansion medium to see what happened. I found their expansion and penetration characteristics were inconsistent.

The hydraulic effect of body fluids entering the hollow cavity promotes rapid and reliable bullet expansion, particularly with hollowpoint bullets. Even if an animal were hit where there was not ample body fluid to initiate immediate expansion, there would still be some variation in expansion.

If body fluids initiate immediate, reliable expansion, why not insert a fluid into the nose cavity of a hollowpoint bullet prior to shooting? I corresponded with Dave Corbin at Corbin Manufacturing and Supply and related the bullet requirements to him. He offered several suggestions and supplied special bullet core punches so I could experiment.

A jacketed bullet is generally made by first drawing the jacket cup out of sheet material. The jacket wall thickness must be uniform around its entire circumference. Jacket thickness should also be consistent among all bullets. Once jackets are obtained in a proper diameter and length, a core of lead is produced by casting, swaging, or cutting a small billet to fit inside the jacket. Keeping the insides of the jacket and the lead clean and free of swaging or drawing lubricant is important.

The lead billet is pressed down inside the jacket under pressure by means of a precisely fitting core-seating punch. This pressure forces the lead tight against the jacket and prevents voids. Then the jacket and core are forced into a nose- or point-forming die which shapes the ogive, closes the mouth opening, and leaves a hollow tip on the bullet. The ogive or shape is a result of the interior shape of the die. The diameter of the nose opening is determined by the extent the bullet is pressed into the point-forming die

My initial experiments involved seating cores in jackets and then punching various types of cavities down into the lead cores. One experiment involved punching a circular cavity deep into the soft-lead core, which formed a lead "post" in the center of the bullet core. Then the fluid was poured to fill the cavity and jacket. Next, a tiny steel ball (of the proper diameter for a sharply pointed tip) was dropped into the jacket and supported in the fluid by the central "post" of lead. When the bullet was forced into the nose-forming die to close the jacket mouth opening, the steel ball formed the bullet tip and served as a seal for the fluid. As a result, the fluid was trapped inside the core cavity and bullet nose.

When the die was adjusted properly, the finished bullet looked like it would work. In practice, however, there were problems. The jacket mouth did not form a perfect seal around the steel ball, and cooking oils used for the fluid seeped out. The steel ball in the tip also acted as a penetrator; it would penetrate several inches beyond the point where the bullet jacket and core stopped in the expansion medium. Such a tiny sphere would probably not damage the exit side of a coyote pelt excessively, but I still did not like the idea. Finally, these bullets were as inconsistent regarding expansion as conventional bullets.

The next step was to experiment with different nose-capping devices.

I tried using spent pistol primers with the anvils removed. The primer cup was dropped open end down inside the bullet on top of the core. When the bullet was forced upward into the nose-forming die, it caused the primer cup to form into a silver-colored bullet tip looking something like Winchester's Silvertip.

I also tried using lead or copper-coated BB shot to do the same thing. The shot was a bit harder than the soft lead core, but it would produce the sealing effect while allowing the jacket mouth to be left open. I hoped this would lend a good exterior pointed shape to the bullet for long-range shooting while still leaving a gaping jacket mouth for rapid expansion. However, variations in the size of the shot prevented me from making consistent bullets. If the shot had too much lead in it, the excess would extrude into the bullet ejection punch hole. This resulted in a spitzer bullet with a tiny "post" projecting from the tip.

I thought the fluid core was a good idea, but I needed something that wouldn't seep. I began working with alox, the cast-bullet lubricant. Besides the circular core cavity, I tried another variation by punching a cylindrical cavity in the center of the bullet core with a punch having a rounded end. I tried bullets with cavities of varying depths and cores of various lengths. I conducted extensive expansion testing in a wet newspaper medium.

The test results indicated fluid does lend a degree of consistency to the expansion performance. One of the best-performing bullets was made with a long bullet jacket and a relatively short core. After the core was seated, the cylindrical nose punch was pressed down into the center of the core, and molten alox was inserted inside the jacket and cavity. The alox was melted to prevent air pockets from forming. The bullets were filled to the jacket mouth with alox, and the lube was allowed to harden. Then when the bullet nose was formed, the excess alox squirted out the bullet's nose. The alox did not have a tendency to seep out of the tiny hollow tip as long as temperatures were mild. For this reason, no nose-capping or sealing device was needed.

At the time, I was conducting the shooting tests at ambient temperatures of 60 to 70 degrees and getting excellent results at ranges from 20 feet to several hundred yards. Some of the best-performing bullets penetrated about three inches of the expansion medium at a distance of 25 yards.

The next step was to try it on coyotes. Carrying a .22-250 Remington Model 700, I dropped coyotes at distances ranging from 15 feet to nearly 300 yards. After bagging 10 coyotes, I had not had a single bullet exit. Even finding the bullet entrance point was frequently difficult. What could be better for the pelt hunter? After skinning the coyotes, I discovered the bullets had fragmented inside the rib cage. The largest fragment remaining was generally a disc-like wafer of the bullet's base. In a few instances, tiny fragments exited the opposite side of the coyote, but in all cases these were no larger than the size of a pin head. After the coyotes were skinned and the pelts stretched, the holes could not be noticed without close scrutiny.

Next, I gave some of these bullets to several friends for more extensive field testing just as cold weather and fur season began. That's when I had a rude awakening. At cold temperatures, I found the bullets produced excessive penetration and extreme pelt destruction on exit. I learned alox can change its consistency drastically with ambient temperatures, getting as hard as a rock at temperatures below zero. No wonder these bullets penetrated more in colder temperatures than they had during warmer weather.

I abandoned the use of alox as the interior fluid. I contacted a specialist in the lubricant field, and he produced a fluid which had the consistency of alox at approximately 70 degrees yet held this viscosity through all ranges of ambient temperatures. This fluid also melted at about 250 degrees for insertion into the bullet. He would not tell me what the material was, but he assured me it was nontoxic.

I used the material and swaged a very sharp tip on the bullets for a good shape. With the fluid core, a gaping bullet tip opening for rapid bullet expansion is not necessary, meaning very streamlined bullet configuration is possible.

I had produced an extremely accurate-shooting bullet. The bullets shot very well in a number of rifles from a .222 Remington through a .22 wildcat cartridge with a case capacity on the order of the 6mm Remington. Half-inch, five-shot groups were not uncommon at 100 yards. I had previously experienced difficulty obtaining groups this small with other bullets.

During a discussion with the people at Sierra Bullets, they indicated the fluid possibly had some sort of a gyroscopic effect on the bullet which tends to counterbalance any out of balance a bullet might have. They also said base-heavy bullets generally shoot more accurately than nose-heavy bullets. This was a surprise to me, but my bullets supported this.

Another interesting item came out of the bullet expansion performance testing: different rifle barrels produce different bullet-expansion characteristics among varmint bullets. Since the jackets of varmint bullets are quite thin, and some barrels perhaps have deeper grooves, rougher lands, narrower lands, etc., this tends to increase the fragility of the jacket so more rapid expansion results from some barrels than from other barrels.

Even so, I believe the fluid-core principle has applications, even for big-game bullets, because of the consistency of expansion. The fluid could possibly provide this even at the very reduced velocities of extreme range. And any improved accuracy characteristics would accompany bullets of any diameter made on this principle.

We'll certainly be seeing continued improvement in bullet design, and I think we're on the brink of designs which are more innovative than anything before.

Hunting Bullets:
How To Match Them To The Game

O VER 300 hunting bullets are available from the four major manufacturers. As a result, there are bullets to fit any hunting situation for any species of game. The problem, in some cases, is selecting the proper bullet for a specific task. With the variety being provided, how does the handloading hunter select the perfect projectile?

There are three important factors involved in selecting a hunting bullet. It must be right for your rifle—not too long, too blunt, or lacking a flat tip, a cannelure, or whatever your rifle requires. A hunting bullet must also provide proper terminal performance. A varmint bullet should expand rapidly for maximum tissue destruction and minimal penetration with a greatly reduced danger of a ricochet; a fur-hunting bullet should dispatch the animal cleanly while doing minimal damage to the pelt; a big-game hunting bullet should penetrate deeply enough but not destroy an excessive amount of meat. Finally, hunting bullets must be reasonably accurate. Hunting bullets from the major manufacturers are all capable of the accuracy needed for their intended applications.

Since most hunting rifles have a wide latitude of acceptance regarding the function of a particular projectile, and since accuracy is generally not a problem, the terminal performance of a bullet should be the number one criterion for the selection of any hunting bullet.

The hunter must know the intended purpose of a particular bullet. The cartridge and/or initial velocity produced for a given bullet is also something to consider because velocity has a direct bearing on terminal bullet performance. Other considerations include the gun, the expected range, size of the game, the shooter's hunting habits, and the shot placement.

One of the best sources when determining the application of a bullet is the manufacturer. Sierra, for example, has adopted a system for its extensive line of bullets which specifically indicates the purpose of each. "Varminter" indicates bullets which are exceptionally accurate and lightly constructed to provide explosive expansion and minimize ricochets; they're also lightweight to attain high velocities and flat trajectories. "Pro-Hunter" is applied to Sierra bullets built for all-around big-game hunting, bullets with tapered jackets that will expand well and retain a high percentage of weight for deep penetration. "GameKing" indicates bullets designed for hunting at long range. These bullets feature a boattail design for added long-range shooting advantages.

As a general rule, Hornady rolls a cannelure onto bullets designed for game hunting. Bullets without cannelures are usually designed for varmint shooting. Hornady also publishes a list of optimum specific usage and performance criteria for each bullet. In addition to indicating the intended game for each bullet, the company provides a published range of impact velocities which reveals a specific impact velocity/use area at which the bullets are expected to perform well.

Speer bullet literature indicates whether each bullet is suited for hunting varmints or big game. Some are dual-purpose bullets (also indicated).

In general, the lightest bullets in any given caliber (.308 and below) are designed for varmint shooting. Specific varmint bullets are not usually supplied for larger calibers like the .338 and .375. When fired at reduced velocities, full metal jacket bullets in the smaller calibers are used for pelt hunting or for edible small game. FMJs and slower speeds reduce tissue and pelt damage. Among the game bullets, the heavier weights in any given caliber are used for the larger species of game; however, these should be used only as a guide.

There are a multitude of other factors which enter into the selection of a proper hunting bullet. One of the most important factors affecting terminal performance is impact velocity. Impact velocity varies considerably, depending on the cartridge, the load, and the shooting distance. A second major consideration regarding terminal performance is bullet construction. The basic design of the bullet can influence terminal performance considerably.

Both impact velocity and bullet construction affect the manner in which a given bullet expands. I have conducted extensive bullet expansion tests with both varmint and big-game bullets and found a number of interrelated factors regarding penetration, tissue destruction, etc. For example, as the impact velocity increases, so does the likelihood a given jacket will peel back. A higher impact velocity generally means a shorter shank will remain on the bullet; sometimes this means more weight will be shed as the soft lead core dissolves from the frontal portion when the jacket sides peel back. This peeling back can also mean greater frontal diameter – up to a point. If you increase velocity beyond this point, more mushrooming generally means a smaller frontal diameter since the jacket will fold back closely to the sides of the bullet. The larger frontal diameter means greater tissue destruction but less penetration.

Heavier bullets are generally constructed with thicker jackets and are fired at slower velocities. Penetration will be increased via more controlled expansion and reduced velocity producing less expansion of bullet frontal diameter, particularly when the bullet initially impacts the game or expansion medium.

How does all this information apply to hunting? Suppose a hunter is extremely conscientious and will take nothing but a broadside lung shot. Suppose he's hunting deer. Since a bullet passing through the ribs of a deer destroys almost no meat, no matter how much tissue is destroyed, the hunter will probably select a lighter bullet producing relatively rapid expansion for little penetraton but a great degree of tissue destruction.

If a shooter is a trophy hunter and frequently shoots deer in thick cover, a bullet which expands with a small frontal diameter is the preferred choice because more penetration is needed to pass through the animal at a raking angle and penetrate deeply into the lungs. Furthermore, if a hind quarter is hit, the bullet with a small frontal diameter will not produce nearly as much tissue/meat destruction. For this type of shooting, a heavy bullet at a slower velocity will penetrate more and destroy less meat.

The shooter taking lung shots would not use a deeply penetrating bullet with a small frontal diameter. Conversely, if the rapidly expanding bullet were used on a raking shot, it might not penetrate deeply enough to reach the vitals and would destroy an excessive amount of tissue.

Many handloaders unknowingly shoot bullets at extremely high velocities originally designed for much lower intensity cartridges. For example, it's not uncommon for 7x57 bullets to be loaded in the 7mm Magnum case or for 8x57 bullets to be loaded in the 8mm Remington Magnum case. These bullets expand too rapidly and destroy an excessive amount of tissue. The magnum cartridge is usually blamed when the problem is the handloader's poor bullet selection. Take a bullet which expands with a small frontal diameter, and this bullet will destroy very little tissue.

The factors influencing bullet performance are interrelated. Bullet penetration depends on mushrooming; mushrooming depends on impact velocity; impact velocity depends on the load, the cartridge, and the impact distance. Since all of these are variables, indicating which bullet is ideally suited to a specific species of game is impossible. There are simply too many variables.

Only guidelines can be provided. For example, the heavier bullets in any given caliber are generally for larger game. If you are using a .30-06, bullets weighing less than 150 grains are generally varmint bullets; 150- to 165-grain bullets would be considered deer/antelope bullets; 180- to 200-grain bullets would be considered best for elk-sized game; and 200- to 220-grain bullets would be used for the large grizzly and brown bears, Alaskan moose, etc.

Another general rule: hollowpoints are frequently – but not always – varmint bullets. The Sierra .25-caliber 120-grain HPBT, for example, is considered a game bullet, as is the Hornady 120-grain hollowpoint of the same diameter.

There are factors besides terminal performance. For example, the best long-range bullets are pointed and streamlined (spirepoints or spitzers). Such shapes, with either flatbase or boattail designs, are generally considered best for long-range shooting. If the bullet has the boattail configuration, a slight advantage for long-range velocity retention and slightly flatter trajectory is provided. Flatnose or roundnose bullets are poor choices for long-range shooting, but there are times when the hunter has to use a flatnose or blunt roundnose bullet. One example is the bullet loaded in a cartridge for a tubular magazine. The tip of this bullet will be resting against the primer of the next cartridge.

In some cases, bullets must have cannelures. Tubular magazines require them to prevent bullets from being pressed deeply inside the case by the force of magazine spring tension. Many bullets are designed for specialized purposes, such as the flatnosed bullets with cannelures designed for tubular magazines.

Some shooters don't like battering the tips of sharply pointed spitzer or spirepoint bullets when cartridges are housed in a box magazine. Shooters who fire bolt-action rifles producing heavy recoil know all about the battering of bullet tips. Speer and Nosler make bullets specifically designed for such use. Speer bullets are designed with a tough, flattened tip called the "Mag-Tip"; the Nosler version, called the "Protected Point," is similar.

The lightweight roundnose .30-caliber bullets designed for use in semi-auto .30 Carbine rifles are special-purpose bullets. The blunt roundnose is required for smooth feeding, and the bullets are designed to expand reliably at low .30 Carbine velocities.

There are other limited use bullets designed with specific calibers in mind. Hornady manufactures several of these: the 200-grain .338 bullet for the .348 Winchester cartridge, the 200-grain .338 flatpoint for the .33 Winchester, and the .227-inch-diameter 70-grain softpoint for the .22 Savage Hi-Power cartridge.

I've prepared a bullet application chart which lists the hunting bullets from the four major manufacturers – Hornady, Nosler, Sierra, and Speer – and, based upon the manufacturers' recommendations, it illustrates which bullet to select for a specific application. Save this for future reference. Choose wisely. After all, it's the bullet that brings the game to bag.

MY HUNTING BULLET APPLICATION CHART

.22-Caliber Bullets (.223 and .224 Diameter) For The .22 Hornet (Varmints)

Sierra 40-gr. .223 Hornet
Speer 40-gr. .223 spire softpoint
Hornady 45-gr. .223 Hornet
Sierra 45-gr. .223 Hornet
Speer 45-gr. .223 spitzer softpoint
Sierra 40-gr. .224 Hornet
Speer 40-gr. .224 spire softpoint
Hornady 45-gr. .224 Hornet
Nosler 45-gr. .224 Hornet
Sierra 45-gr. .224 Hornet
Speer 45-gr. .224 spitzer softpoint

(Prewar Hornet rifles accept .223 bullets. Use .224 diameter bullets only in late Hornet rifles. If there are any questions, have your rifle checked.)

.22-Caliber Bullets (.224 Diameter) For Extremely Rapid Expansion At .222 Velocities (Varmints)

Hornady 50-gr. SX
Nosler 50-gr. Expander
Sierra 50-gr. Blitz
Hornady 55-gr. SX
Sierra 55-gr. Blitz

.22-Caliber Bullets (.224 Diameter) For Varmints

Speer 40-gr. spire softpoint
Sierra 45-gr. semipointed
Sierra 45-gr. spitzer
Speer 45-gr. spitzer
Hornady 50-gr. spirepoint
Nosler 50-gr. spitzer
Nosler 50-gr. hollowpoint
Sierra 50-gr. semipointed
Sierra 50-gr. spitzer
Speer 50-gr. spitzer
Nosler 52-gr. spitzer
Nosler 52-gr. hollowpoint
Speer 52-gr. hollowpoint
Hornady 55-gr. spirepoint
Hornady 55-gr. spirepoint with cannelure
Nosler 55-gr. spitzer
Sierra 55-gr. semipointed
Sierra 55-gr. spitzer
Sierra 55-gr. boattail
Speer 55-gr. spitzer
Speer 55-gr. spitzer with cannelure
Hornady 60-gr. spirepoint
Hornady 60-gr. hollowpoint
Nosler 60-gr. spitzer
Sierra 63-gr. semipointed

.22-Caliber FMJ Bullets (.224 Diameter) For Edible Small Game Or Pelt Hunting At Reduced Velocity

Hornady 55-gr. FMJ boattail with cannelure
Sierra 55-gr. FMJ boattail with cannelure
Speer 55-gr. FMJ

.22-Caliber Bullets (.224 Diameter) For Antelope/Deer-Size Game

Speer 70-gr. semipointed

6mm Bullets (.243 Diameter) For Varmints

Sierra 60-gr. hollowpoint
Hornady 70-gr. spirepoint
Nosler 70-gr. hollowpoint solidbase
Hornady 75-gr. hollowpoint
Sierra 75-gr. hollowpoint
Speer 75-gr. hollowpoint
Speer 80-gr. spitzer
Nosler 85-gr. spitzer
Sierra 85-gr. spitzer
Hornady 87-gr. spirepoint
Hornady 87-gr. hollowpoint boattail
Speer 90-gr. spitzer
Speer 100-gr. spitzer boattail

6mm Bullets (.243 Diameter) For Antelope/Deer-Size Game

Sierra 85-gr. hollowpoint boattail
Speer 85-gr. spitzer boattail
Speer 90-gr. spitzer
Nosler 95-gr. spitzer Partition
Hornady 100-gr. spirepoint
Hornady 100-gr. spirepoint boattail
Hornady 100-gr. roundnose
Nosler 100-gr. spitzer solidbase
Nosler 100-gr. spitzer Partition
Sierra 100-gr. spitzer
Sierra 100-gr. semipointed
Sierra 100-gr. spitzer boattail
Speer 100-gr. spitzer boattail
Speer 105-gr. roundnose
Speer 105-gr. spitzer

6mm Bullets (.243 Diameter) For Edible Small Game Or Pelt Hunting At Reduced Velocities

Hornady 80-gr. FMJ
Sierra 90-gr. FMJ boattail
Speer 90-gr. FMJ

.25-Caliber Bullets (.257 Diameter) For Varmints

Hornady 60-gr. flatpoint
Hornady 75-gr. hollowpoint
Sierra 75-gr. hollowpoint
Hornady 87-gr. spirepoint
Sierra 87-gr. spitzer
Speer 87-gr. spitzer
Speer 100-gr. hollowpoint
Speer 100-gr. spitzer
Speer 100-gr. spitzer boattail

.25-Caliber Bullets (.257 Diameter) For Antelope/Deer-Size Game

Sierra 90-gr. hollowpoint boattail
Hornady 100-gr. spirepoint
Nosler 100-gr. spitzer solidbase
Nosler 100-gr. spitzer Partition
Sierra 100-gr. spitzer
Speer 100-gr. spitzer
Speer 100-gr. spitzer boattail
Hornady 117-gr. roundnose
Sierra 117-gr. spitzer boattail
Sierra 117-gr. spitzer
Hornady 120-gr. hollowpoint
Nosler 120-gr. spitzer solidbase
Nosler 120-gr. spitzer Partition
Sierra 120-gr. hollowpoint boattail
Speer 120-gr. spitzer boattail
Speer 120-gr. spitzer

6.5mm Bullets (.264 Diameter) For Varmints

Sierra 85-gr. hollowpoint
Hornady 100-gr. spirepoint
Sierra 100-gr. hollowpoint
Speer 120-gr. spitzer

6.5mm Bullets (.264 Diameter) For Game

Nosler 120-gr. spitzer solidbase
Sierra 120-gr. spitzer
Speer 120-gr. spitzer
Nosler 125-gr. spitzer Partition
Hornady 129-gr. spirepoint
Hornady 140-gr. spirepoint
Nosler 140-gr. spitzer Partition
Sierra 140-gr. spitzer boattail
Speer 140-gr. spitzer
Hornady 160-gr. roundnose

.270-Caliber Bullets (.277 Diameter) For Varmints

Sierra 90-gr. hollowpoint
Hornady 100-gr. spirepoint
Nosler 100-gr. spitzer solidbase
Speer 100-gr. hollowpoint
Speer 100-gr. spitzer
Hornady 110-gr. hollowpoint

.270-Caliber Bullets (.277 Diameter) For Game

Sierra 110-gr. spitzer
Hornady 130-gr. spirepoint
Nosler 130-gr. spitzer solidbase
Nosler 130-gr. spitzer Partition
Sierra 130-gr. spitzer boattail
Sierra 130-gr. spitzer
Speer 130-gr. spitzer boattail
Speer 130-gr. spitzer
Speer 130-gr. Grand Slam softpoint
Hornady 140-gr. spirepoint boattail
Sierra 140-gr. hollowpoint boattail
Hornady 150-gr. spirepoint
Hornady 150-gr. roundnose
Nosler 150-gr. spitzer solidbase
Nosler 150-gr. spitzer Partition
Sierra 150-gr. spitzer boattail
Sierra 150-gr. roundnose
Speer 150-gr. spitzer boattail
Speer 150-gr. spitzer
Speer 150-gr. Grand Slam softpoint
Nosler 160-gr. semispitzer Partition

7mm Bullets (.284 Diameter) For Varmints

Hornady 100-gr. hollowpoint
Speer 115-gr. hollowpoint
Hornady 120-gr. spirepoint
Hornady 120-gr. hollowpoint
Speer 130-gr. spitzer
Speer 130-gr. spitzer boattail

7mm Bullets (.284 Diameter) For Game

Nosler 120-gr. spitzer solidbase
Sierra 120-gr. spitzer
Speer 130-gr. spitzer
Speer 130-gr. spitzer boattail
Hornady 139-gr. spirepoint
Hornady 139-gr. spirepoint boattail
Nosler 140-gr. spitzer solidbase
Nosler 140-gr. spitzer Partition
Sierra 140-gr. spitzer boattail
Sierra 140-gr. spitzer
Speer 145-gr. spitzer boattail
Speer 145-gr. spitzer
Nosler 150-gr. spitzer solidbase
Nosler 150-gr. spitzer Partition
Hornady 154-gr. spirepoint
Hornady 154-gr. roundnose
Nosler 160-gr. spitzer Partition
Sierra 160-gr. spitzer boattail
Speer 160-gr. spitzer boattail
Speer 160-gr. spitzer
Speer 160-gr. Mag-Tip softpoint
Speer 160-gr. Grand Slam softpoint
Hornady 162-gr. spirepoint boattail
Sierra 170-gr. roundnose
Hornady 175-gr. spirepoint
Hornady 175-gr. roundnose
Nosler 175-gr. semispitzer
Sierra 175-gr. spitzer boattail
Speer 175-gr. Mag-Tip softpoint
Speer 175-gr. Grand Slam softpoint

.30-Caliber Bullets (.308 Diameter) For Varmints And Hunting Small Game At Extreme Reduced Velocity

Hornady 100-gr. Short Jacket
Speer 100-gr. Plinker

.30-Caliber FMJ Bullets (.308 Diameter) For Edible Small Game Or Fur Hunting At Reduced Velocity

Hornady 110-gr. FMJ
Sierra 110-gr. FMJ
Hornady 150-gr. FMJ boattail

.30-Caliber Bullets (.308 Diameter) For Varmints

Hornady 110-gr. spirepoint
Sierra 110-gr. hollowpoint
Speer 110-gr. spirepoint
Sierra 125-gr. spitzer
Hornady 130-gr. spirepoint
Speer 130-gr. hollowpoint

.30-Caliber Bullets (.308 Diameter) For Game

Sierra 125-gr. spitzer
Hornady 150-gr. spirepoint
Hornady 150-gr. roundnose
Nosler 150-gr. spitzer solidbase
Nosler 150-gr. hollowpoint solidbase
Nosler 150-gr. spitzer Partition
Sierra 150-gr. spitzer
Sierra 150-gr. spitzer boattail
Sierra 150-gr. hollowpoint boattail
Sierra 150-gr. roundnose
Speer 150-gr. roundnose
Speer 150-gr. spitzer boattail
Speer 150-gr. spitzer
Speer 150-gr. Mag-Tip softpoint
Hornady 165-gr. spirepoint
Hornady 165-gr. spirepoint boattail
Nosler 165-gr. spitzer solidbase
Nosler 165-gr. spitzer Partition
Sierra 165-gr. spitzer boattail
Sierra 165-gr. hollowpoint boattail
Speer 165-gr. roundnose
Speer 165-gr. spitzer boattail
Speer 165-gr. spitzer
Speer 165-gr. Grand Slam softpoint
Nosler 168-gr. hollowpoint solidbase
Hornady 180-gr. spirepoint
Hornady 180-gr. roundnose
Nosler 180-gr. spitzer solidbase
Nosler 180-gr. spitzer Partition
Nosler 180-gr. Protected Point Partition
Sierra 180-gr. spitzer
Sierra 180-gr. spitzer boattail
Sierra 180-gr. roundnose
Speer 180-gr. roundnose
Speer 180-gr. spitzer boattail
Speer 180-gr. spitzer
Speer 180-gr. Mag-Tip softpoint
Speer 180-gr. Grand Slam softpoint

Hornady 190-gr. spirepoint boattail
Nosler 200-gr. spitzer Partition
Sierra 200-gr. spitzer
Speer 200-gr. roundnose
Hornady 220-gr. roundnose
Sierra 220-gr. roundnose

.30-Caliber Bullets (.307 and .308 Diameter) For Varmints And Tubular Magazines (.30-30 Bullets)

Speer 110-gr. flatnose hollowpoint
Sierra 125-gr. flatnose hollowpoint
Speer 130-gr. flatpoint

.30-Caliber Bullets (.307 and .308 Diameter) For Deer-Sized Game And Tubular Magazines (.30-30 Bullets)

Sierra 125-gr. flatnose hollowpoint
Speer 130-gr. flatpoint
Hornady 150-gr. roundnose
Nosler 150-gr. flatpoint solidbase
Sierra 150-gr. flatnose
Speer 150-gr. flatpoint
Hornady 170-gr. flatpoint
Nosler 170-gr. flatpoint solidbase
Sierra 170-gr. flatnose
Speer 170-gr. flatpoint

.30-Caliber Hunting Bullets (.308 Diameter) For The .30 Carbine

Hornady 110-gr. roundnose
Hornady 110-gr. FMJ
Sierra 110-gr. roundnose
Sierra 110-gr. FMJ
Speer 110-gr. hollowpoint
Speer 110-gr. roundnose

.303-Caliber And 7.7mm Bullets (.311 and .312 Diameter) For Game

Sierra 125-gr. FMJ (edible small game and fur hunting)
Hornady 150-gr. spirepoint
Sierra 150-gr. spitzer
Speer 150-gr. spitzer
Hornady 174-gr. roundnose
Sierra 180-gr. spitzer
Speer 180-gr. roundnose

.32 Special Bullets (.321 Diameter) For Game

Hornady 170-gr. flatpoint
Speer 170-gr. flatpoint

8mm Bullets (.323 Diameter) For Game

Hornady 125-gr. spirepoint (varmints)
Hornady 150-gr. spirepoint
Sierra 150-gr. spitzer
Speer 150-gr. spitzer
Hornady 170-gr. roundnose
Speer 170-gr. semispitzer
Sierra 175-gr. spitzer
Nosler 200-gr. spitzer Partition (8mm Rem. Mag.)

Speer 200-gr. spitzer (8mm Rem. Mag.)
Hornady 220-gr. spirepoint (8mm Rem. Mag.)
Sierra 220-gr. spitzer boattail (8mm Rem. Mag.)

.338-Caliber Bullets (.338 Diameter) For Game

Hornady 200-gr. spirepoint
Hornady 200-gr. flatpoint (.33 Win.)
Speer 200-gr. spitzer
Nosler 210-gr. spitzer Partition
Hornady 225-gr. spirepoint
Hornady 250-gr. roundnose
Nosler 250-gr. spitzer Partition
Sierra 250-gr. spitzer boattail
Speer 250-gr. Grand Slam softpoint
Speer 275-gr. semispitzer

.348-Caliber Bullets (.348 Diameter) For Game

Hornady 200-gr. flatpoint

.35-Caliber Bullets (.358 Diameter) For Game

Speer 180-gr. flatpoint
Hornady 200-gr. spirepoint
Hornady 200-gr. roundnose
Sierra 200-gr. roundnose
Hornady 250-gr. roundnose
Speer 250-gr. spitzer

.375-Caliber Bullets (.375 Diameter) For Game

Hornady 220-gr. flatpoint (.375 Win.)
Speer 235-gr. semispitzer
Hornady 270-gr. spirepoint
Hornady 270-gr. roundnose
Hornady 300-gr. roundnose
Hornady 300-gr. FMJ
Sierra 300-gr. spitzer boattail

.44-Caliber Bullets (.430 Diameter) For Game

Hornady 265-gr. flatpoint

.45-Caliber Bullets (.458 Diameter) For Game

Hornady 300-gr. flatnose hollowpoint
Sierra 300-gr. flatnose hollowpoint
Hornady 350-gr. roundnose
Speer 400-gr. flatpoint
Hornady 500-gr. roundnose
Hornady 500-gr. FMJ

NOTES: Do not use varmint bullets for game. Pointed bullets are best for long range. Boattail bullets offer *slight* increased long-range advantage. Roundnose bullets are poor choices for long range. The heavier bullets in any given caliber are for larger species of game.

Deer Rifles & Cartridges

DEER HUNTERS HAVE more choices than ever when selecting a rifle. The selections vary from short-barreled, 5¾-pound synthetic-stocked flyweights to the long-barreled, nine-pound belted magnums.

Why so many choices? Because hunting conditions vary. In order to narrow the choices, terms like "Eastern Deer Rifle" and "Western Deer Rifle" have come along. The former is for whitetails in thick cover; the latter is for mule deer in open country.

I've hunted deer from Oregon to Maryland, from Pennsylvania to Arizona, and one thing I've learned is that the geographic region doesn't dictate the denseness of the vegetation or the shooting distance. I've had plenty of thick-cover, "get-'em-off-quick" short-range shooting in the West, and I've had some extremely long-range shots in the East.

Besides the many different deer hunting conditions, there are countless personal preferences in hunting style. And there are several species and sizes of deer.

So what makes a deer rifle? Is there such a thing as a perfect deer rifle?

The answer is yes, but the making of a good deer rifle is not universal for all types of hunting. The perfect deer rifle for you may be about as useful as a crowbar to the next guy. The key to selecting your deer gun is defining the type of hunting you do. Only after you've done this can you match the hunting with the rifle and the cartridge.

Deer country, whether it's an Idaho wilderness, a midwestern farming region, a southern swamp, or New England woods, offers variety. Thickets, brush patches, and swamps are accompanied by meadows, fields, and clear cuts in all these regions. What governs hunting conditions is your hunting preference and style. Do you like to still hunt thick cover, stand hunt open forest, or glass a vast expanse? Perhaps you like to do a little of all three—with a few other styles of hunting thrown in. Most of us simply like to hunt where the deer are and go after them in a way that has produced success and brings a measure of pleasure to the pursuit.

Some families have had success for generations in large tracts of dense forest where still hunting and jump shooting whitetails is what deer hunting is all about; others derive endless hours of pleasure from glassing vast sagebrush flats for a solitary trophy and then stalking close enough for a shot. And some deer hunters do both.

This brings up three basic categories of deer rifle: 1) the thick-cover, quick-shooting rifle, the true hunter's rifle for the person who gets up close; 2) the open-country, accurate rifle for the hunter who prides himself in spotting game at long range and doping the shooting distance and bullet drop; and 3) the combination rifle for the person whose hunting style means that he's likely to get a shot at any distance.

If you like to still hunt dense cover, whether it's spruce timber at 10,000 feet in Colorado or a low-country cedar swamp in New York, you're going to get shots at short range. The range is short because you can't see any farther than short distances. If you're still hunting, you're going to be jumping deer, which means the target will be moving. Often all you get is a quick look at a buck before he's out of sight. The gun has to come up effortlessly and point and shoot fast. Quickly getting on target for the first shot is of utmost importance.

A lightweight rifle comes up quicker, and a short barrel doesn't snag on brush. A short, light rifle doesn't tire your arms as much, so your reflexes are faster at the "surprise" moment. The swing is faster with a light rifle, and it's easier to follow the target and align the sights. By "light rifle," I mean one weighing less than seven pounds. One closer to six pounds is best. By "short barrel," I mean 20 inches or less. The buttstock has to be short enough not to snag on clothing—usually a lot more clothing than you'll have on when you practice-swing the carbine in a sporting-goods store. Keep this in mind.

If the first shot slams into an oak, you'll need a fast second. This means a quick-to-cycle action. It also means you can't waste precious split seconds recovering from the recoil of a big round.

The sights have to be on-target almost naturally when the gun meets the shoulder. Any scope needs to have a very wide field of view for close-up moving targets.

Which rifles fit this category? The pumps and semiautos have the fastest cycling actions going, with the lever guns close behind. Unfortunately, with a couple of exceptions, the semiautos and pumps currently available are generally long and heavy. A couple of today's top choices remain the traditional lever gun favorites. I'm thinking of the Winchester Model 94 .30-30, weighing in at 6½ pounds for the standard carbine with a 20-inch barrel or 6⅛ pounds for the Trapper version with a 16-inch barrel. The latter carbine is also available in a .44 Magnum variation that weighs only six pounds.

Marlin offers a 336 lever-action variation called the 336LTS that features a 16¼-inch barrel and weighs only 6½ pounds. The chambering is .30-30. The company also has a six-pound .44 Magnum with a 20-inch barrel called the 1894S.

Those are perhaps the top contenders in this category. If you want a faster action, more power, or both, you can get it, but you'll have to trade a little of the lightweight advantage for it. Take a look at the Remington semiautos and pumps. Remington has a .30-06 carbine with an 18½-inch barrel in either the 7400 semiauto or 7600 pump. The only drawback is a little extra weight (at 7¼ pounds), but it's still a good choice, and the extra weight allows a quicker recovery from the larger round's recoil. If you also hunt elk or some other species of large game, it's probably the very best choice in a close-cover firearm.

Ruger has a semiauto carbine with not nearly the power of the Remingtons in its Mini-Thirty 7.62x39. It sports an 18½-inch barrel and weighs 7¼ pounds. While the power is down, so is recoil. It's about like shooting a .223, and for this reason, you can get back on target as fast as you can aim it.

Browning offers a lever gun with a little more weight and a lot more power in the BLR. It's chambered for such convincing and flat-shooting rounds as the .257 Roberts, 7mm-08 Remington, .308 Winchester, and .358 Winchester. These lever guns have 20-inch barrels and weigh in at seven pounds. They also have detachable-box magazines that allow the use of pointed bullets. The BLRs I've shot are quite accurate. They are good choices if you plan to hunt in dense cover but have a possibility for a longer shot.

If you rely on your first shot and don't mind sacrificing just a bit of speed in action cycling, there are a lot of mighty fine bolt actions that fill the bill nicely in every other way.

Ruger makes a series of lightweight bolt-action carbines with 18½-inch barrels. Deer cartridges include the .250-3000, .270, .308, and .30-06. The Model 77RL Ultra Light has a black forend tip and the Model 77RSI carries a Mannlicher stock.

Weatherby, a firm known for good-sized bolt actions and long barrels, has a lightweight, wood-stocked Vanguard VGL and synthetic-stocked Fiberguard. Both have 20-inch barrels and weigh about 6½ pounds, depending on the chambering. Deer cartridges include the .270, 7mm Remington Magnum, .308, and .30-06.

Remington came out with one of the lightest guns going when it fitted the Model Seven with a fiberglass stock. Guns in 7mm-08 and .308 weigh only 5¼ pounds. Barrel length is 18½ inches, making them ideal for thick-cover hunting. A wood-stocked Model Seven weighs 6¼ pounds in the same calibers.

An ideal sighting arrangement for a short-range woods carbine is a scope with no more than 2X magnification. A 1X is even better, and I like the electronic sights like the Aimpoint. They're very fast to get on target. A peep sight is another excellent choice and offers an advantage over optical sights because there is no lens to become moisture coated in the rain or snow.

Getting a long shot requires some open country, or at least an opening, whether it be grassland, cornfield, cross canyon, or just a gap in thick cover. If you almost always hunt the type of terrain and vegetation where the shots are long, entirely different criteria enter into the picture.

The bolt action is a frequent choice for this type of hunting because it can be chambered for any cartridge made and because such rifles generally shoot well. However, other action types are fine if they produce the necessary level of accuracy and are chambered for high-intensity cartridges.

There are so many quality bolt-action rifles and single shots in this category that it's difficult to list them all. The Ruger 77, The Remington 700, the Savage 110, the Winchester Model 70 series, the Sako, the Browning A-Bolt, the Weatherby Mark V, KDF's K-15, and the Interarms Mark X are some of the more popular choices in bolt actions. The Browning 1885, Ruger No. 1, and Thompson/Center single shots are also top choices.

The primary deciding factor here is the rifle's chambering rather than gun size, and there are many cartridges from which to choose. Traditional favorites are the .270 and .30-06; you can't go wrong with either one. Belted magnum rounds like the 7mm Remington or .300 Winchester will really reach out for the big bucks. If recoil is a consideration, you might lean toward something like the .25-06, a round I deem minimal for long-range deer shooting. A longer barrel only adds emphasis to the downrange performance.

For this type of hunting, you'll want at least a 4X scope. A 6X or 8X will offer better target definition. A 4-12X variable offers even greater magnification for a really long shot.

This type of deer hunting encompasses by far the bulk of hunting situations. Most hunters go after deer wherever the deer are—and they can be practically anywhere. By selecting one rifle for all hunting, the hunter sacrifices a bit in speed on one extreme and a bit in range on the other. With a little discretion on long shots and a lot of practice at shouldering, pointing, and swinging, however, he'll find a rifle in this category can prepare him to effectively meet a wide variety of hunting conditions.

This category eliminates all but high-intensity bottleneck cartridges. Short-range flatnosed rounds like the .30-30 or .44 Magnum just don't have the punch at long distances. Heavy guns and high-magnification, fixed-power scopes are a hindrance for the short-range shot.

Any action type is suitable; personal preference and chambering are more important considerations. The top chamberings in this category are identical to top choices in the long-range category. Remember, a long-range cartridge is just as effective for short-range shooting, but the reverse is not true.

All the bolt-action and single-shot rifles listed in the long-range category are suitable, but they're not necessarily ideal. The hunter who goes after deer in various types of vegetation and terrain is often covering a lot of ground. That's the reason for the variety in shooting conditions.

In this instance, light weight is an important consideration. Therefore, some of the short, light bolt-action rifles listed in the dense-cover category would also be good choices.

OPEN-COUNTRY RIFLES, MAXIMUM RANGE

(Accuracy and caliber selection are the primary factors)

Ruger M77 Bolt	.270 Win., .30-06, 7mm Rem. Mag., .300 Win. Mag.
Remington M700/78 Bolt	.270 Win., .280 Rem., 7mm Rem. Mag., .30-06, .300 Win. Mag.
Savage M110 Bolt	.270 Win., 7mm Rem. Mag., .30-06
Winchester M70 Bolt	.264 Win. Mag., .270 Win., .270 Wby. Mag., .280 Rem., 7mm Rem. Mag., .30-06, .300 Win. Mag., .300 Wby. Mag.
Sako Bolt	.270 Win., 7x64 Bren., .30-06, 7mm Rem. Mag., .300 Win. Mag.
Browning A-Bolt Bolt	.270 Win., .280 Rem., 7mm Rem. Mag., .30-06, .300 Win. Mag.
Weatherby Mark V Bolt	.257 Wby. Mag., .270 Wby. Mag., 7mm Wby. Mag., .30-06, .300 Wby. Mag.
KDF K-15 Bolt	.270 Win., 7mm Rem. Mag., .30-06, .300 Win. Mag.
Interarms Mark X Bolt	.270 Win., 7mm Rem. Mag., .30-06, .300 Win. Mag.
Browning M1885 Single Shot	.270 Win., 7mm Rem. Mag.
Ruger No. 1 Single Shot	.270 Win., .270 Wby. Mag., .280 Rem., 7mm Rem. Mag., .30-06, .300 Win. Mag., .300 Wby. Mag.
Thompson/Center TCR '87 Single Shot	.270 Win., .30-06

Fortunately for today's hunter, rifles are getting lighter, and stable synthetic stocks are becoming more readily available; even the bore-wearing and nonrusting qualities of stainless steel are becoming available on some bolt-action rifles.

TOP LONG-RANGE DEER CARTRIDGES

1. .300 Weatherby Magnum	6. 7mm Remington Magnum
2. .300 Winchester Magnum	7. .264 Winchester Magnum
3. 7mm Weatherby Magnum	8. .30-06 (handloads only)
4. .270 Weatherby Magnum	9. .280 Remington
5. .257 Weatherby Magnum	10. .270 Winchester

TOP SHORT-RANGE DEER CARTRIDGES

1. .358 Winchester	7. .444 Marlin
2. .356 Winchester	8. .45-70 Government
3. .35 Remington	9. .375 Winchester
4. .307 Winchester	(availability problem
5. .30-30 Winchester	for new rifles)
6. .44 Remington Magnum (very short range only)	10. 7.62x39

Aside from custom and semicustom rifles, one of my top choices in this general category is the Browning Stainless Stalker. The rifle features an entire barreled action of stainless steel and synthetic stock to boot. Weighing in at a mere six pounds, 11 ounces, the rifle is available in .270 and .30-06, two flat-shooting favorites with plenty of punch for any deer. A-Bolt rifles (the Stainless Stalker included) are exceedingly accurate, on the average, and the price is right. This rifle offers a 22-inch barrel length.

Remington offers a good synthetic-stocked firearm in the Model 700

FS. Best caliber choices include the .270, .308, and .30-06 with a 22-inch barrel and 6¼ pounds of weight.

Winchester's Model 70 Winlite is a synthetic-stocked rifle in the 6¼- to 6½-pound weight range with chamberings in .270 Winchester, .280 Remington, and .30-06. You can get a wood-stocked lightweight in .308 that weighs six pounds.

THICK-COVER RIFLES, SHORT RANGE

(Short length, light weight, fast action cycling, and quickness to point are primary factors)

Lightweight Lever Actions

Winchester M94 Lever	.30-30 Win., .307 Win., .356 Win., 20-inch barrel, 6½ pounds
Winchester M94 Trapper Lever	.30-30 Win., 16½-inch barrel, 6⅛ pounds
Winchester M94 Trapper Lever	.44 Mag., 16½-inch barrel, six pounds
Marlin M336LTS Lever	.30-30 Win., 16¼-inch barrel, 6½ pounds
Marlin M1894S Lever	.44 Mag., 20-inch barrel, six pounds

More Weight, Fast Actions

Remington M7400 Semiauto	.30-06, 18½-inch barrel, 7¼ pounds
Remington M7600 Pump	.30-06, 18½-inch barrel, 7¼ pounds
Ruger Mini-Thirty Semiauto	7.62x39, 18½-inch barrel, 7¼ pounds
Browning BLR Lever	.257 Roberts, 7mm-08 Rem., .308 Win., .358 Win., 20-inch barrel, seven pounds

Short, Lightweight Bolt Actions

Sako Carbine Bolt	7mm-08 Rem., .308 Win., 18½-inch barrel, 6¾ pounds
Ruger M77RL Bolt	.270 Win., .308 Rem., .30-06, 18½-inch barrel, six pounds
Ruger M77RSI Bolt	.250 Savage, .270 Win., .308 Win., .30-06, 18½-inch barrel, seven pounds
Weatherby Vanguard VGL Bolt	.270 Win., 7mm Rem. Mag., .308 Win., .30-06, 20-inch barrel, 6½ pounds
Weatherby Vanguard Bolt	.270 Win., 7mm Rem. Mag., .308 Win., .30-06, 20-inch barrel, 6½ pounds
Remington Model Seven FS Bolt	7mm-08 Rem., .308 Win., 18½-inch barrel, 5¼ pounds
Remington Model Seven Bolt	7mm-08 Rem., .308 Win., 18½-inch barrel, 6¼ pounds

The Savage Model 110F is chambered in .270 and .30-06; it comes with a DuPont Rynite stock and a 22-inch barrel. It weighs 6¾ pounds. A wood-stocked version is called the 110E and weighs the same.

I would fit my all-around rifle with a 4X scope and be ready for anything. Some hunters prefer a little more magnification for the long shots and a little less magnification for dense cover. In this case, a 2-7X or 3-9X would be the ticket.

Whatever you choose, become familiar with the safety and trigger. You shouldn't have to think about how to release the safety, and you should be able to do it quietly. The trigger should release the shot more by your will than by a conscious finger squeeze. I'm not talking about a light trigger. I'm talking about the trigger breaking at the precise instant you want it to.

No matter which rifle you choose, you'll become a lot more effective with it if you shoot it a lot, particularly under hunting conditions or simulated hunting conditions. A poorly chosen rifle in the hands of a hunter that's experienced can still be an effective performer.

The categories mentioned are my guidelines. If you have a specialized purpose, use commonsense in the selection of your deer rifle. If you hunt from horseback, for example, a slab-sided lever action offers some advantage. If you hunt rugged country, a lighter rifle is a better choice. If you hunt in the rain a lot, an aperture sight might be a better choice than a scope. And stainless steel doesn't rust like chromemoly. You'll want more downrange wallop if the ranges are long and the deer large.

Apply the guidelines, use commonsense, practice shooting your rifle a lot, and when that moment of truth arrives, you'll be ready.

Elk Rifles, Calibers & Loads

A FEW YEARS ago, I was guiding an elk hunter who was carrying a Model 70 Winchester in .375 H&H Magnum loaded with Hornady 270-grain spirepoint bullets. After about three hours of hunting, we spotted a five-point bull elk across a small canyon. It was grazing away from us at a quartering angle. I motioned to the hunter; he rested his rifle on a boulder and fired, placing the big slug just behind the animal's diaphragm. The bullet angled forward through the chest cavity and lodged in the far shoulder. At the shot, the elk jerked its head up and walked uphill. It traveled about 40 yards, showing no sign of being hit—and then suddenly collapsed.

On another occasion, I was after elk in Colorado with another hunter. He was sitting quietly against an aspen tree when a spike bull came walking through the aspen grove about 75 yards away. My companion raised his custom-barreled Remington Model 721 .25-06 and sent a Sierra 117-grain bullet into the elk's neck, breaking the spine and dropping the animal on impact. These two examples illustrate clean, one-shot kills with widely varying calibers, showing the extremes in cartridges that can be used for elk. Some shooters consider the .25-06 to be too light for elk, while others consider the hunter with the .375 H&H Magnum to be "overgunned." Even within these cartridge extremes, however, there is considerable disagreement about what it takes to make a good elk gun and load. In the instances mentioned, each hunter considered his particular selection of rifle and cartridge to be ideal for the task at hand.

Like elk hunters, well-known and respected gun writers often disagree on what it takes for a cartridge to be suitable for elk. The writings of Elmer Keith represent the "big case, fat bullet" point of view when he recommends nothing less than a 275-grain bullet of .33 diameter traveling at least 2400 fps when hunting elk. Jack O'Connor, in many of his writings, held the opposite point of view, saying the .270 Winchester with a 130-grain bullet at 3000 fps was all anyone needed for elk. In his book *The American Rifle*, Colonel Townsend Whelen said three considerations are imperative when it comes to selecting a cartridge for hunting any game: killing power, accuracy, and trajectory. Accuracy and trajectory requirements, among many modern cartridges and guns, are easily fulfilled. However, the term "killing power" brings about considerable disagreement.

All three writers mentioned had elk hunting experience. When Jack O'Connor wrote *The Art of Hunting Big Game in North America*, he mentioned that he had taken almost 20 elk. I have taken about 12 and don't believe this sampling, even with diligent bullet recovery and wound examination, to be adequate by itself for basing any assumptions on what it takes to make an effective elk cartridge and load. I have utilized this information—along with bullets recovered from game taken by others—to form a comparison with a bullet expansion test program. A consistently uniform expansion medium forms the basis for a valid relative bullet and cartridge performance comparison. Using all this information—performance on elk compared with more extensive tests of performance in an expansion medium—I believe that some relative cartridge and load performance comparisons can be made. At the same time, I believe another source of information is professional guides who have extensive practical experience in the form of seeing hundreds of elk taken by their clients with all types of cartridges and loads. For this reason, I solicited the assistance of 17 guides and outfitters located throughout the western states. Taken cumulatively, these professionals hunt elk under all types of terrain and climatic conditions. Their ideas on what it takes to make an excellent rifle, cartridge, and load for elk proved very interesting.

A total of 31 questions regarding elk hunting and elk guns, scopes, and loads were presented to the professional guides. Subjects ranged from the average range at which most elk are shot and the number of shots fired to the type of terrain hunted and the amount of competition from other hunters. All this data was then tabulated in an effort to determine what the shooter can expect when he goes elk hunting.

I'll readily admit that your individual elk hunting circumstances may demand something a bit different from what the questionnaire norm suggests. But on the other hand, the responses from the individual guides were surprisingly similar when it came to gun and cartridge preferences.

According to the survey, the *average* elk hunting situation goes something like this: The animal will be standing at a quartering angle, facing away from you. You'll be taking a shot averaging 187 yards. If you end up taking him, your first shot will be into the shoulder area and you'll end up firing 3.2 rounds, one of which will penetrate the animal's lungs. The animal will travel 164 yards before he goes down.

If you're the average guided hunter, you probably took the elk with a Remington Model 700 rifle topped with a 3-9X scope and chambered in 7mm Remington Magnum.

When questioned about what they considered to be the *ideal* elk rifle outfit for the average hunter, the guides overwhelmingly favored .30 calibers, 180-grain bullets, 4X scopes, and bolt actions. More specifically, the Winchester Model 70 was the top choice in rifles, followed closely by the Ruger 77 and Remington 700. A Weaver 4X got the nod in scopes. Nosler Partition and Remington Core-Lokt bullets were top picks. The .30-06 came highly recommended for the *average* hunter, and most of them considered the .270 Winchester to be the minimum cartridge acceptable for most elk hunting situations.

When questioned about recoil, it was evenly split among those guides who considered recoil to be a major factor when selecting an elk rifle and those who considered it unimportant. The guides who considered recoil to be a factor thought the .270 Winchester and .30-06 Springfield were adequate for elk while "not kicking too much"; the same guides indicated they thought cartridges on the order of the .300 Magnums kicked too much for most elk hunters.

Most guides considered a rifle that would fire two-inch groups from a benchrest at 100 yards to be the minimum acceptable accuracy for elk hunting.

It was interesting that nine of 17 professional guides considered the .270 Winchester to be only marginally acceptable for elk and then most recommended only *150-grain* bullets. Two didn't respond to the question, three listed larger cartridges as being minimum, and only three listed less potent cartridges as being minimum.

When questioned about what they considered to be ideal elk cartridges, the guides were evenly split among standard and magnum chamberings. The preferred chamberings were the .270 Winchester, .308 Winchester, .30-06 Springfield, 7mm Remington Magnum, .300 Winchester Magnum, and .338 Winchester Magnum.

Perhaps the reason there is so much disagreement about killing power is because hunter techniques and hunting conditions differ. The overwhelming majority of professional guides indicated there is little or no competition from other hunters in their hunting areas. There's little doubt that the hunter who goes after elk under these conditions (no competition) is far more likely to get a standing shot at an elk. He's also more likely to take his shots when the animal is standing at a more ideal angle or can at least wait until the elk moves into a better position for a shot.

Most elk hunters, on the other hand, pursue their quarry on readily accessible public land without the assistance of a guide. Very often, there are a great many other hunters in the area. I fit into this latter group. I have yet to enlist the services of a guide for an elk hunt, and from experience I know any elk seen after the first couple of hours of opening day are wary because they've probably already been spooked by rifle fire. In this situation, I believe that the standing shot is the exception rather than the rule. Elk encountered usually offer either a rapidly departing backside shot or are driven past one hunter by another hunter. These vastly different hunting conditions should be considered by the would-be elk hunter. Will you take a rear end or angling shot, or will you pass it up until you have an animal standing broadside?

The requirements for a load placed between the ribs call for a more rapidly expanding bullet to cause a lot of damage with little penetration. The bullet/load requirements for a going-away shot demand deep penetration to reach the animal's vitals.

Colonel Townsend Whelen summed it up in *The American Rifle*:

"Most any rifle would kill if one got a fair, standing, broadside shot and could aim accurately so as to reach the heart, but the game cannot always be found standing in this position. Indeed, the usual target one has will be a rear shot at game running away; what is wanted is a bullet with a charge behind it that, in such a position, will plow right through into the chest vitals without being deviated or stopped by striking a heavy bone."

Jack O'Connor indicated that one reason he preferred the light .270 Winchester was that he had the opportunity to place his shot where there was little resistance to the bullet before it met the vital lung organs. He even wrote in *The Art of Hunting Big Game* that "The big bores (.338, .375, .358 Norma Magnum, .416, and such powerful medicine) have two advantages over rifles of smaller bores with lighter bullets when used on elk and moose. They have strong, heavy bullets that will generally break the shoulder blade whereas lighter bullets will not." He also indicated that these lighter bullets cannot be depended on to penetrate even a considerable amount of paunch to reach the lungs. In other words, though O'Connor highly touted the .270 Winchester with 130-grain bullets and is largely responsible for so many elk hunters taking up this cartridge, it cannot be emphasized enough that O'Connor always had precise shot placement.

This is, indeed, an admired and sportsmanlike trait. However, my own experience indicates that there are a good many more sportsmen who go after elk without the assistance of a guide on public land where there is an extreme amount of hunting pressure. My experience, like the guides', indicates most elk offer angling-away or rear-end shots. Furthermore, even on a broadside-standing elk, I think it's important to remember that an elk's leg bone and shoulder blade cover up a large portion of the vital area. The hunter should not aim in line with the shoulder or leg, but just behind it. But again, experience indicates that the hunter can't always shoot precisely where he wants.

Visualize watching the large antlers of an elk passing through an opening in a forest. As you bring up your rifle, the bull stops so that only his shoulder and leg are visible. Would you pass up the shot? I believe a good elk cartridge and bullet combination should have adequate penetration qualities to break through any major bones. Similarly, I don't want to be forced to pass up less-than-ideal shots or wound an animal because my equipment is marginally acceptable only for ideal shots. I want a cartridge and bullet capable of penetrating a large portion of paunch or breaking bones in order to reach the vitals if necessary.

Some hunters believe bullet diameter and the size of the case are the only factors in penetration. Shooting tests have shown that bullet performance is a *major* criteria in penetration. It's common knowledge that lightweight varmint-type bullets expand violently and penetrate very little. But even among big-game bullets, there is considerable difference regarding how they expand. Some expand to produce a large frontal area; others expand with a small frontal area. Large bullet expansion destroys more tissue but penetrates less; smaller expansion destroys less tissue but penetrates more. The hunting conditions should dictate which type is best for you.

Bullets that will expand with a small frontal diameter are the Nosler Partition and, in some instances, the Speer Grand Slam. Bullets in 7mm diameter weighing 160 or 175 grains or in .30 caliber weighing 180 or 200 grains are excellent in this penetration category.

The Nosler Partition bullet has two cores—one in the bullet's nose, the other in the bullet's base. They're separated by a partition of jacket material. The nose portion of the bullet expands rapidly, and this frontal core is usually gone in recovered bullets. The ogive portion of the bullet folds inside out, in a conventional manner, but stops at the partition. The rear core nearly always remains intact. The Nosler Partition bullets don't generally retain a great percentage of weight as some other conventional bullets do because of the bullet's loss of the frontal core. The "petals" of the Partition bullets generally fold back close to the bullet shank for a small frontal diameter.

It is true that a broadside-standing animal, lung-shot with a bullet that expands with a small frontal area, generally does not drop as quickly as an animal lung-shot with a more rapidly expanding bullet that has a large frontal area to destroy a large portion of lung tissue immediately. Also, a long bullet having more weight will generally penetrate deeper, all else being equal.

Bullet velocity also has a direct bearing on bullet performance – the higher the velocity, the more violent the bullet expansion usually is. This sometimes produces less penetration due to a larger bullet frontal area resulting.

A large portion of bullets in a given caliber manufactured by a particular manufacturer have identical jacket thicknesses. The exceptions generally come with varmint bullets and extremely heavy big-game bullets. Varmint bullets are sometimes made with thinner jackets, while heavy big-game bullets are sometimes made with thicker jackets. Also, the heavy bullets are generally fired at a lower velocity. All this works to produce less expansion or frontal area, and when combined with a higher sectional density, the heavy bullets are more likely to penetrate deeper.

Larger calibers, heavier bullets, and higher velocities mean more recoil. There is a limit to the recoil a hunter can tolerate and still shoot well. At the same time, however, any rifle suitable for elk is going to kick. That's the nature of a heavy bullet, high velocity, and flat trajectory. If you can shoot the larger calibers, such as an 8mm Remington Magnum, .338 Winchester Magnum, .358 Norma Magnum, or even .375 H&H Magnum, there's no question they all have the bone-smashing power needed. But if you're recoil sensitive, use a .270, 7mm Remington Magnum, .308, or .30-06 and select your bullet carefully in line with your hunting conditions.

My preference in an elk gun is really not that different from the guides' choice – it's a .300 Winchester Magnum bolt gun topped with a 4X scope. The bullets I use for elk are generally 180- or 200-grain Nosler Partitions.

When it comes to selecting an elk cartridge, the thing to do is consider hunting conditions, your hunting technique, and your tolerance for recoil. Only then, can you make a valid judgment about the elk cartridge that is best for you.

Make A Practice Of Packing Two Rifles

I STOPPED and wiped the wetness off my brow before cautiously moving ahead. Mixed rain and snow in the cold early morning light limited visibility to little more than 75 yards. No amount of inclement weather would have dampened my outlook. It was opening day of deer season.

Trudging quietly through junipers in the bottom of a wide canyon, I spotted movement 30 yards away. A doe mule deer trotted through an opening in the trees and was followed by a nice buck. Both were out of sight before I could shoulder the rifle, but there was another opening ahead that would offer a chance for a shot. I knelt down, shouldered the rifle, and flicked the gun's safety while I concentrated on the second opening, hopefully in the buck's line of travel.

Peering over the top of the scope, I watched the doe trot through first as I had expected; the buck had to be right behind. Dropping my line of sight to the optics, I expected to see a sharp, magnified image of the spot where the buck was to appear. Instead, there was only a blurred form moving across the field of "view." I couldn't make out antlers or even be certain the indistinct shape was a deer. Lowering the rifle for a better look, I spotted a long-tined three-pointer disappearing into dense undergrowth.

Upset about the lost shot, I looked down at the scope to determine the problem. Water droplets covered the scope's lens, and they wouldn't shake off. Wiping the glass, I found water still remained, but I was able to distinguish objects through the scope. Within a few minutes, however, the rain once again obliterated my efforts. Try as I might, I couldn't keep the optics protected from the rain enough to provide a constantly clear sight picture.

Disgusted with the unfortunate circumstances, I tried to console myself by reasoning it was too early to end the hunt. But the fact remained: As long as there was foul weather, I had a rifle that might not be operable when a buck jumped again. My iron-sighted .30-30 would have been the ticket for this type of close cover hunting, but a lot of good it did me in a closet at home—50 miles away.

Flip-up scope caps probably would have cured the rain problem, but thinking back, I began remembering other incidents which put guns out of use. There was the time a friend leaned his rifle against the four-wheel-drive vehicle. The gun fell, knocking the scope out of alignment. And I once took a bad spill while crossing a rockslide, banging the scope and snapping the crosshairs.

The problem isn't just scopes. A broken extractor once ended a .244's usefulness on a coyote hunt. A separated case had the same effect on another occasion. Scope mount screws have vibrated loose a couple of times. Precautions can prevent most of these situations from recurring, but after considering all the other countless possibles that can put a gun out of commission, not to be prepared with a backup rifle just in case seems foolish.

The unlucky incident with the three-pointer happened many years ago. I now pack two guns, even when preparing for a single day's outing. I always have a backup.

Guns are generally well made, and the times one will be broken are few. Since I began taking the backup rifle, however, I find it gets used much more often than just when the primary gun breaks. There are times when I'll spend half a day hunting in heavy cover. The short, light, iron-sighted carbine backup rifle is more comfortable to carry and quicker to point, making it more suited to the hunting at hand than the scoped primary gun.

I have a Gun Guard case by Doskocil that is big enough to hold two rifles of nearly any type, scoped or not. With this case, packing two guns in the vehicle is no more trouble than one, and it's reassuring to have the backup available.

If you're thinking you can't afford a new $400 or $500 rifle for a backup, look more closely. The second gun need not be a top-of-the-line sporter, and it doesn't have to be expensive. Just because a rifle is less expensive doesn't mean it's less effective. The used market is where the real bargains are found. Many used rifles in excellent condition are sitting on dealer shelves, and they usually sell for a fraction the cost of a new gun. For instance, the very strong Remington bolt-action Models 721 and 722 are no longer manufactured, yet they are quite plentiful, and the plain-looking stocks have kept their prices down. I've seen several tagged in the $200 price range—and these included serviceable scopes.

There are other action types on the used market that are reasonably priced. One is the slide-action Remington chambered for .35 Remington, .270, .308, and .30-06. I bought an excellent bolt-action .30 Remington Model 30S for less than $100. The caliber is obsolete, which lowers the price, but this poses no serious problem for the handloader.

Buying one of the older quality rifles is an investment and not an expense. Take your time, look around, and buy wisely. Prices of some of these classic rifles have soared in recent years; unlike many investments, a gun can be used while it appreciates in value.

For some shooters, price won't be as important as serviceability, and they can be more selective when buying a gun. Selection of the caliber and action type for a second rifle depends on a number of considerations, including the intended quarry and personal preference.

The backup rifle can take any one of several forms. For example, many hunters in the West hunt deer and elk in the same area during the same season. As most hunters know, however, some areas are better for elk, while others are better for deer. If you're hunting an area strong on elk, a rifle in a heavier caliber may be in order. If you bag an elk, or if you move to a second area better for deer, you may want to carry a smaller caliber rifle with lighter recoil.

The hunter after antelope in the wide-open spaces has different requirements entirely. He will want both rifles to be scoped and flat shooting as well.

Due to all the variables involved with the hunter's individual situation and his personal preference, there is no way any specific second gun can be recommended. In fact, practicality doesn't enter the picture as much as the pride or pleasure a hunter derives from carrying a backup rifle.

I have departed from carrying my usual rifle just for the fun of carrying something different. This is one of the reasons I sometimes switch to an iron-sighted carbine; I'm not tired of carrying the heavier scoped rifle, but I like the variety the carbine offers.

A few years ago, I bought an old Winchester Model 1886 rifle in .40-65 caliber. When fully loaded, it is muzzle heavy from the cartridges in the long magazine tube and heavier overall than most scoped rifles, but I've derived hours of pleasure from carrying it in the field. The cartridge has a rainbow trajectory, and the energy from the round is not appreciably more than a .44 Magnum handgun.

RECOMMENDED DEER CALIBERS & SIGHTING EQUIPMENT

Primary Rifle	Backup Rifle
4X scope	
2-7X variable scope	Iron sights
3-9X variable scope	
.257 Roberts	.30-30 Winchester
.25-06 Remington	.300 Savage
.270 Winchester	.35 Remington
7mm-08 Remington	
.280 Remington	
7mm Remington Magnum	
.308 Winchester	
.30-06 Springfield	

RECOMMENDED BEAR CALIBERS & SIGHTING EQUIPMENT

Primary Rifle	Backup Rifle
3X scope	
4X scope	
1.5-5X variable scope	Iron sights
2-7X variable scope	
3.9X variable scope	
.270 Winchester	.308 Winchester
.280 Remington	.358 Winchester
7mm Remington Magnum	.444 Marlin
30-06 Springfield	.45-70 Government
.300 Winchester Magnum	

RECOMMENDED ELK CALIBERS & SIGHTING EQUIPMENT

Primary Rifle	Backup Rifle
4X scope	
2-7X variable scope	Iron sights
3-9X variable scope	
.30-06 Springfield	.358 Winchester
.300 Winchester Magnum	.45-70 Government
.300 Weatherby Magnum	
8mm Remington Magnum	
.338 Winchester Magnum	

When I bag a big-game animal with this oldtimer, the satisfaction is far greater than if I'd bagged the same animal with my scoped, flat-shooting magnum rifle. Even if I don't get the opportunity to fire a shot, there is a certain amount of nostalgic satisfaction derived from carrying a rifle like this one.

Another reason for having a backup rifle is that perhaps you'll be in a hunting party when someone else has either broken his rifle or forgotten the ammo for his gun (believe me, it happens). If this does happen, the gun will most assuredly be chambered for a wildcat cartridge or another round that can't be bought at a local store. Your backup rifle will preclude a ruined hunt for another member.

RECOMMENDED ANTELOPE CALIBERS & SIGHTING EQUIPMENT	
Primary Rifle	
4X scope	
6X variable scope	
2-7X variable scope	
3-9X variable scope	Note: Primary and
6mm Remington	backup rifles would
.25-06 Remington	have the same
.257 Weatherby Magnum	requirements.
.264 Winchester Magnum	
.270 Winchester	
.280 Remington	
7mm Remington Magnum	

As can be seen, there are all sorts of reasons for having a backup rifle along on any hunt. A $200 auxiliary rifle can save a $2000 big-game hunt or bag your once-in-a-lifetime trophy when the old standby malfunctions. And it's a good hedge against inflation. Why be without one?

Straight Talk About Trajectory

W HEN MOST shooters talk about sighting-in a rifle or handgun for hunting, it's generally understood the sportsman will be trying to make the gun hit where he points it. For some, this means using a lever-action .30-30 to plink a tin can off a log at some unknown distance. For the hunter with a bolt-action rifle, this might mean leaning over the hood of a jeep to dust a rock of unknown size at an unknown distance. As long as you can make the rifle hit where you want it to, you're going to bag game. Then again, there's a lot more to sighting-in a rifle.

More sophisticated shooters use a paper target to see precisely where the bullets are impacting. The shooter will pace off 100 steps, set up a paper target, and try to punch the center hole out of the bullseye from his rest. This is immensely better than shooting at a target at an unknown distance where precise bullet impact points cannot be determined, but shooters who attempt to sight-in their rifle or handgun to hit point of aim at 50 or 100 yards still aren't utilizing the potential inherent in today's firearms.

In order to increase the range at which game can be taken without needing to hold over, some shooters sight-in to hit slightly high at 100 yards. Anywhere from one to three inches high is common with a big-game cartridge, no matter whether it's a .30-30 or a .300 Winchester Magnum. Such a high impact point is generally chosen with little regard to precisely what is to be accomplished by such a sighting-in procedure.

Still other hunters have approached the same shooting aspect differently. Rather than sighting-in their rifles to hit slightly high at a predetermined distance, they choose a longer shooting range, generally about 250 yards, and then attempt to make their rifles hit dead-on at that distance. Sighting slightly high at 100 yards or making the rifle shoot to point of aim at a distance much greater than 100 yards is a good idea and does extend the range at which game can be taken without a holdover. However, few hunters really get down to the nitty gritty of trying to obtain every possible advantage from a given rifle cartridge. Some cartridges shoot flatter than others, and various cartridges have trajectories that are different. A blunt, slow-moving bullet is going to drop more at a given distance than is a pointed, fast-stepping projectile from a magnum case.

Few hunters really analyze the trajectory of a specific load. Furthermore, few hunters really consider the game being hunted and how important this is to maximizing the potential of a rifle or handgun. Today's modern cartridges and bullets have the velocity and energy to take game at great distances, but the hunter must sight-in his rifle in order to take advantage of this potential.

Suppose you want to hunt deer. A deer might measure 18 or 20 inches from the top of the shoulders or whithers to the bottom of the chest line. If you take a center hold on the animal, halfway between the top of the back and the bottom of the brisket, a bullet impacting anywhere in an area nine inches high or nine inches low still produces a hit in the vital area. The question you should ask is how far away can a center-of-the-chest hold be used without undershooting and still not produce high shots at closer distances. This is where things can get complicated, and detailed ballistics tables listing trajectory, preferably in 50-yard increments, are a decided asset.

Using a center hold, the maximum range at which a game animal's vital area can be hit without midrange misses due to shooting over is called the "point-blank range." The maximum point-blank range of your rifle is probably farther than you think.

In the *Sierra Bullets Reloading Manual,* there is a table near the back of the book that clearly delineates maximum point-blank range. For most big-game calibers, the point-blank range is computed for 5.0 inches above and below line of sight in Sierra's manual. For example, suppose you're shooting a .30-06 with a 180-grain spitzer flatbase bullet. You've chronographed the load, and it produces 2500 fps from your rifle. A quick look at the Sierra manual will tell you the maximum point-blank range with the Sierra 180-grain flatbase at this muzzle velocity is 300 yards.

Still, maximum point-blank range isn't really what you need to know when you're sighting-in your rifle. What's more important is the range at which the rifle must be zeroed to obtain this maximum potential from it. Sierra anticipated this, and again, a quick look at the manual tells you the rifle should be zeroed at 250 yards to receive the maximum point-blank range of 300 yards.

Fire the same bullet at 2300 fps muzzle velocity, and the point-blank range is 280 yards; to obtain it, the rifle should be zeroed at 230 yards.

Suppose you're shooting a .300 Winchester Magnum with the same bullet, only now you're starting it at a muzzle velocity of 3000 fps. The maximum point-blank range will be 360 yards, and in order to achieve it, the rifle must be zeroed at 300 yards.

Suppose you're not interested in hunting big game; you want to hunt coyotes with your .22-250. You have loaded your brass with Sierra 55-grain spitzers and have chronographed the ammo at 3700 fps. From the top of the shoulders to the bottom of the chest, a coyote measures only seven or eight inches. This means the point-blank range for the big-game calibers (five inches above or below the line of sight) is going to cause undershooting at the extreme distances and overshooting at midranges. Again, the people at Sierra anticipated this. For the smaller calibers generally used on varmints, the point-blank range is computed for 2.5 inches above or below the line of sight. This clearly places calculations within coyote-killing capability.

A quick look at the Sierra tables for the .22-250 load mentioned earlier indicates the maximum point-blank range is 310 yards. To achieve it, Sierra says the rifle should be zeroed at 260 yards.

Take my word for it, the Sierra tables are accurate. I once conducted extensive long-range shooting tests using a world record-holding competition benchrest rifle topped with a Leupold 36X scope. By shooting when conditions were ideal, I found the Sierra ballistics tables consistently predicted downrange bullet impact. In fact, the tables were more precise than my ability and my equipment's ability to shoot at 400 yards. Such ballistic tables can be used with confidence.

It's really nice to know that you can simply take a center-of-the-chest hold and hit the target without worrying about holdover. I've found it's almost always best not to hold over a game animal as long as a modern flat-shooting cartridge is used. In my experience, I'll generally shoot over if I hold over. For one thing, today's cartridges are flat shooting, particularly if they are sighted-in to maximize the point-blank range as mentioned earlier. Secondly, the game is frequently not as far away as you think. Third, if the game really is so far off that you have to hold over, it's probably too far away.

About now, I can hear some experienced deer hunters saying a deer doesn't always present a perfect broadside-standing silhouette. This is true, and a deer in the forest may be somewhat obscured by fallen logs, limbs, boulders, etc. Plus or minus five inches is a lot of variation; all the maximum point-blank tables in the world won't help if the bullet impacts a tree limb before getting to the deer. Even though you may have a clear shot at the center of the chest, the bullet's trajectory may take it into a tree limb you may not have seen through the scope.

This brings us back to square one. You've got to use commonsense. If you're hunting deer in thick timber, and your shots are not likely to be more than 75 yards anyway, you'll be better off sighting-in your rifle to hit point of aim at about 60 yards. This way, you can place your bullet more precisely without worrying about hitting a tree limb or rock. If you're hunting deer or antelope in open country, however, take a look at the trajectory tables. You might be surprised at how effective your flat-shooting cartridge is. Perhaps you really haven't been taking advantage of its potential after all.

How-To

Check Out Your New Rifle

A GREAT THRILL for many avid gun buffs is obtaining a new rifle and then heading for the range to see how it will shoot before going hunting. The rifle is usually purchased with some ammo; if the gun buff is a real horse trader, he'll have talked the store owner into throwing in a box of factory ammo with the purchase. If he is a handloader, he'll assemble a few rounds from brass he already has on hand.

I guess this is only human nature. Though we would like to believe otherwise, new rifles frequently have bugs to be worked out as they come out of the box from the factory. Considering what it takes to make a rifle really shoot well, and considering how rifles are produced and assembled at the factory, assuming an out-of-the-box rifle will shoot extremely well in every instance is really assuming too much.

If everything works out the way it's supposed to, a new rifle can be a real shooter. But production techniques require the use of tolerances so that any number of stocks, triggers, safeties, etc., will mate with any number of barreled actions. Tolerances and machine inletting being what they are, this leaves room for potential problems. Though nearly all of these potential problems are minor and can be easily corrected, the shooter who doesn't look for them before traveling to the range may expend a large quantity of ammo before realizing there is a problem.

As a gunwriter, I have the opportunity to shoot many rifles just as they come from the factory, and I've found a preshooting checkout can save many rounds of ammunition, hours at the range, and frustrating experiences. In most instances, the preshooting checkup takes only a few minutes and can pay big dividends in immediate accuracy improvement.

The first step involves giving a new rifle a close visual examination. I begin by seeing how the stock fits around the barreled action. If the stock happens to be touching along one side of the barrel channel, I can detect the problem. Slipping a sheet of paper between barrel and forend to determine exactly where the stock bears on the metal is also effective. This will reveal whether the barrel is free floating, bedded all the way out, bedded only at the forend tip, bedded along the first two inches of barrel, touching on one side of the barrel, etc.

When a barrel is apparently contacting wood all the way out, I generally leave it alone and first see how the rifle shoots. If the barrel appears to be touching only at the forend tip, I leave it alone to see how it will shoot before making any changes. In general, however, a rifle should be able to shoot well with the barrel free floated. This way the wooden stock is not touching the barrel anywhere to impart pressure differences as a result of stock warpage from humidity changes.

Lightweight barrels on most sporting rifles will frequently shoot better with pressure at the forend tip. About the only time I'll make a change in the wood/barrel fit prior to shooting is when the forend is touching only one side of the barrel. In this instance, I'll use a scraper to relieve side pressure on the barrel.

Other steps include:

• Checking the sights to make sure everything looks proper; using a screwdriver to ensure sight screws are tight. If you decide to put a scope on the rifle, or if the rifle already has a scope, disassemble the mount so all scope base and mount screws can be checked with a screwdriver from the ground up. In addition, it's a good idea to daub Loctite or lacquer on the screw heads so they won't shoot loose from recoil.

• Checking the muzzle's crown to make sure it hasn't been nicked in shipment. A slight nick in the metal right at the muzzle can cause accuracy to suffer severely.

• Checking the function of the rifle's action while it's in the stock. Make sure the bolt isn't binding anywhere and that the mounted scope doesn't interfere with bolt movement.

• Checking the safety to make sure it operates in a positive manner and that its movement is not restricted by the way the safety is inletted in the riflestock.

• Checking the floorplate release to make sure it works and that everything functions properly while the barreled action is tightened in the stock.

The next step, the one I consider to be most important, is to remove the barreled action from the riflestock. This is the step that reveals many previously unseen problem areas. I believe the bedding of the barreled action in the stock holds most of the potential problems for the new rifle.

In some instances, the stock inletting may not be completely sealed; it should be sealed with some sort of epoxy or oil so it will not absorb moisture readily. In other instances, I have found wood chips under the action bedding areas; these also pose potential problems.

One of the biggest bugaboos with new rifles is that various portions of the trigger, safety, etc., are bearing on a surface where they shouldn't. Basically, an action should bear on the stock in the area of the recoil lug, tang, or where action screws thread into the action. Under no circumstances should action screw tension be absorbed by the gun's trigger or safety, nor should the magazine box or floorplate be put into a bind when the action screws are tightened.

If the barreled action is bedded or touching wood in the trigger housing or safety housing area, wood should be removed at these points until the pressure is relieved; then the newly exposed wood should be sealed. If the magazine box is in a bind, scrape wood from the inside of the magazine box mortise to relieve pressure. Again, seal the newly exposed wood so it will not readily absorb moisture.

Generally, a rifle's bedding can be given a rough check without a transfer agent like lampblack or shoe polish. A poorly bedded barreled action can generally be detected simply by tightening and loosening action screws. Place a thumb and forefinger along the barrel and stock at the forend tip so any movement between the two can be easily felt. With your other hand, alternately tighten and loosen each of the action screws to see if the barreled action produces excessive movement at the forend tip.

Any movement detected by your fingers is too much. This means there is an unevenness or binding in the action to cause it to rock or bind as screw tension is applied and released. The approximate location of the problem will generally be revealed by which screw is being tightened and how the barreled action moves.

A close visual examination of the stock inletting with the barreled action removed often reveals a burnish mark where the metal is bearing. A scraper or gouge can be used to remove wood at this point until the action rests perfectly flat in its recess and tightening or loosening of the action screws has no noticeable effect. If this sort of burnish mark cannot be detected with the eye, apply lampblack or shoe polish to the action and then insert the coated action into the stock mortise very carefully to reveal where the wood is touching metal. The shooter thus determines where wood should be removed in order to produce a better fit.

The action's recoil lug should usually bear only at the rear of the lug. Its forward surface, bottom, and sides generally are best left with a gap all the way around. This point is minor compared to other bedding maladies mentioned.

Once you have obtained a fit of the barreled action in the stock that appears to be good, seal all areas of the stock mortise that have been gouged or scraped; then replace the barreled action in the stock without undue tightening of the action screws.

It's best to tighten front and rear screws alternately so the action is pulled down parallel with the bedding surface. Tightening one screw at a time has a tendency to compress the wood excessively in the area where the first screw was tightened. Done to the extreme, the bedding can actually be ruined by the manner in which the screws are tightened.

I prefer to have "snug" pressure on the front recoil lug and tang screws while I generally like to leave the middle action screw with very little tension if it's a three-screw action. Excessive tension on this middle screw can place the action in a bind, and this can be detrimental to the best accuracy.

All this is not to say factory quality control is going to pot, but since these rifles are assembled in great numbers, and since hand craftmanship must be kept to a minimum in order to retain the lowest price possible, it is only natural that slight problems will crop up.

Remember: You're not paying $1000 just for the fitting of the stock to the barreled action (which is what many custom stockmakers would charge). I'd rather pay the going price for a mass-produced gun and then do the minor tuneup myself.

Sighting-In Your Rifle

I REMEMBER going deer hunting with a couple of friends many years ago. As we whizzed down a mountain road in an open jeep, one remarked to the other that it wouldn't be a bad idea to sight-in their rifles. We stopped, and they prepared to shoot at the "target," a limestone rock across a small canyon. All this surprised me because I'd sighted-in my rifle several days earlier and checked it again the day before we left.

One fellow said "That's about 100 yards, isn't it?"

"I think it's more like 150 or 200," replied the other.

I'm not too good at judging distance across a canyon, but I suppose the rock was somewhere between 150 and 300 yards away.

These guys sighted-in their rifles by having one of them blaze away at the rock while the other watched to see if the bullet kicked up white dust. The shooting positions ranged from offhand to elbows resting on the hood of the jeep. At an unknown distance, the rock was also of an unknown size. I figured it was probably two or three feet in diameter, but if farther away than it looked, the rock could have been even larger. They had no trouble hitting the rock and kicking up white dust.

Before long, the two hunters were satisfied their rifles were sighted-in. I hoped they would be hunting thick brush country and their shots would be close ones. There was no telling where those rifles were shooting . . . .

Little can replace positively sighting-in a rifle on paper. Paper illustrates exactly where each bullet impacts. It's much more precise than shooting at rocks, tin cans, or dirt clods. Perhaps this is the primary reason some shooters don't shoot on paper . . . it clearly reveals poor marksmanship.

Those who do sight-in their rifles with paper targets at a known distance frequently expend more time and expensive ammunition than is necessary. A little knowledge can make sighting-in quick, easy, economical, and, best of all, effective. After you've hunted days for a trophy and the chips are down, you'll know the rifle is capable of doing its part if you do yours.

There are three basic ways to sight-in a rifle, and I'll cover all of them. But before I get to the sighting-in procedure, here are some tips that will make the process go more smoothly.

First, you need some means of determining when the rifle is sighted-in, and to do this, you must be able to fire good groups. The sitting position, elbows over the hood of a truck, or other makeshift rests generally aren't good enough. A benchrest is the key to shooting a rifle consistently for tiny clusters of bullet holes.

You'll also need to support the rifle with something besides your arms and shoulder. Ideally, a front pedestal rest can form the basis for supporting the sandbags on which the rifle's forend rests. If you don't have the front pedestal, don't fret. A couple of catalogs, an old metal ammo box, or 4x4 blocks can do the job.

A lot of shooters dispense with the rear bag, which fits under the buttstock between the toe of the stock and the pistol grip. Those who use a rear bag, and use it properly, however, will get more consistent groups.

It's also important to know how to adjust your sights, whether they're iron or optical. Iron sights are all but obsolete, so nowadays you'll most likely be sighting-in with a scoped rifle.

If a scope is mounted properly, the windage turret will be located at the right side of the scope tube, and the elevation turret will be located on top. In a very few instances, scopes are rotated 90 degrees to the left to make ample clearance for the ejection port at the right side of the rifle's receiver. If you have one of these rigs, the windage turret will be located at the left side of the tube, and the elevation turret will be on top. This is an exception, however.

If the scope is mounted in a conventional manner, rotating the turret knobs will move point of impact in the direction indicated on the knobs. All scopes I'm aware of have the direction of point-of-impact shift marked on the turret knobs. Generally, only the right (or left) and up (or down) are marked on respective knobs. These coincide with an arrow to indicate turning the knob in one direction will move the point of impact that way. Conversely, rotating the knob the opposite direction will move the point of impact the opposite way.

This is all pretty basic and self-explanatory once you look at the adjustment knobs on your scope. But as basic as it might seem, a surprising number of shooters don't know how much each click, or increment, on the knob shifts the point of impact. Some scopes shift point of impact ¼ minute, others shift ½ minute, and still others shift ⅓ minute. (One minute of angle is approximately one inch at 100 yards.) This information might not be marked on the turret knob or turret cap. Some manufacturers mark it on the scope; some don't. If it's not marked inside the cap or on the turret, I'd suggest reading the literature received with the scope or literature in the scope manufacturer's catalog to determine the amount of impact shift with each increment or adjustment. Doing so will save you time and ammunition.

Adjusting iron sights is not usually as precise as adjusting a scope. Unless you have a fine receiver sight with micrometer-type adjustments, adjusting the iron sight is a matter of mechanically moving the rear sight notch or front sight post. Some have screws which loosen to allow adjustment. In this case, you make the adjustment and retighten the screw(s). Others have a notched wedge (of sorts) to allow vertical adjustment. Still others must be driven or drifted laterally in a dovetail slot. Sometimes, there aren't even witness marks on the rear sight, and the shooter simply taps the rear sight or front sight blade laterally and then shoots to see how much it moved.

Once you've determined how to adjust the sights and have a solid rest with a front and rear bag, there are three ways to zero-in your field. One way to get the rifle shooting on the paper at 100 yards is to collimate the sights, another is to bore-sight the rifle, and the third is to do the initial shooting at very close range.

To collimate a rifle means the sights are aligned to be coincident with the axis of the bore. This is generally done with an optical device featuring a stud which fits inside the rifle's bore at the muzzle. Various studs are available to match different bore diameters so the stud fits snugly. The optical device attached to the stud has its own crosshair, so when you look through a riflescope with the collimator in place, you see the scope's crosshair and the crosshair in the optical device.

The crosshair in the optical device is generally rotated 45 degrees so it bisects the quadrants formed by the crosshair in the riflescope. While looking through the scope and collimator, you should rotate the turret knobs on the scope until the intersection of the crosshairs in the riflescope match up with the intersection of the crosshairs on the collimator. Then the rifle will be shooting somewhere on the paper at 100 yards.

Collimating a scope can be done before going to the range, and it's quick, easy, and doesn't require any ammo. However, collimating a scope does not mean the rifle is sighted-in. Final sighting-in can only be accomplished by shooting.

Most shooters don't have access to a collimator, although most gunsmiths will collimate a rifle for a nominal fee. If you don't have a collimator and don't want to take your rifle to a gunsmith, try either of the next quick and easy methods.

The second method, bore-sighting, requires no collimator, but it does require the use of a rest, vise, or some other means for holding the rifle in a solid, stationary position while the scope turret knobs are rotated.

To bore-sight a rifle, first remove the gun's bolt so you can look through the rifle's bore. This technique generally applies to single-shot or bolt-action rifles and isn't always possible with slide, lever, or autoloading firearms.

After you remove the rifle's bolt or lower the breechblock for a clear view through the bore, place the rifle in a rigid device. A vice works very well; however you must be able to look through the bore and view a distant object, perhaps 100 yards away, and this might not be feasible with a vise.

I've used the rifle rests (front pedestal and rear bag) in order to bore-sight by simply seating the rifle in the sandbags. The rifle may shift slightly in the sandbags as the turret knobs are rotated, but it's a simple matter to realign the bore on the distant object and look through the scope again.

Once everything looks close, let go of the rifle so it's supported only in the rest. Without touching either the rifle or the rest, look through the bore to determine the exact center. Then, still without touching anything, raise your head to look through the scope and be sure the crosshair is precisely aligned on the same object. Much like collimating, this quick and easy method will get the rifle shooting on the paper at 100 yards, and you don't need any ammo.

The third method of sighting-in a rifle is to move the target closer to the shooter. After a scope has been mounted on a rifle, the rifle will generally print "on the paper" at 25 yards without any sight adjusting. If you fire a single shot and the bullet does not leave a hole somewhere in the paper, you can either move the target closer or determine where the bullet impacted by the dust it kicked up. In the latter instance, adjust the sight so the next shot will hit the paper.

What's the advantage in firing a close initial shot? The bullet is much more likely to hit the paper than it would be if the target were 100 yards downrange. Once a shot is fired, the shooter determines how many inches the point of impact must be shifted vertically and horizontally for the bullets to strike the target in its center at 25 yards.

Remember, four times as much sight adjustment is required at 25 yards than is required at 100 yards. If the scope has ¼-minute clicks, this means each increment of adjustment will move point of impact approximately ¼ inch at 100 yards. At 25 yards, however, the shooter will have to adjust the knob 16 clicks to receive the same point-of-impact shift at the closer distance. If the shooter knows how much an increment of adjustment shifts the point of impact and makes the adjustments properly, the second shot should impact the center of the target. I usually fire a third shot to verify this point of impact, then move the target back to 100 yards for the final sighting-in.

After a rifle has been collimated, bore-sighted, or roughly sighted-in by shooting at close range, the next step is to sight-in the rifle more precisely at a greater distance (usually 100 yards). I generally sight-in flat-shooting hunting rifles so bullets impact slightly higher at this distance. How high depends on the caliber, the expected hunting range, and the intended species of game. I'll sight-in 1½ inches high at 100 yards with varmint calibers like the .22-250, .220 Swift, etc.; with elk hunting cartridges like the .300 Winchester, .338 Winchester, or 8mm Remington, I'll sight-in to hit three inches high at 100 yards; for deer and antelope-size game, I'll go 2½ to three inches high. This high sighting-in makes maximum use of the cartridge's trajectory for the game being hunted.

I prefer to fire three shots initially at the 100-yard target. Take as much time as you need and concentrate on holding the rifle steady and getting each shot off without a flinch. I usually insert some sort of a pad or sandbag between the gun butt and my shoulder in order to avoid flinching. I also wear hearing protection and shooting glasses. This combination tends to prevent flinching.

After the initial three shots are fired, view them through your scope (if it's powerful enough) or spotting scope or go downrange and see where the bullets impacted on the paper.

Using targets with a one-inch grid pattern marked directly on them can be helpful. Leupold, Redfield, Remington, and others distribute targets with this grid pattern, which allows a shooter to quickly determine how many inches or fractions of an inch the bullets impact from the aiming point.

When you determine the center of the group, go back to the benchrest, make the necessary turret-knob adjustments, and shoot another group of three shots. If the scope's adjustments are precise, and if you make them properly, the rifle should now be sighted-in. If it isn't, adjust the windage and elevation knobs accordingly and shoot again.

If the rifle has been collimated or bore-sighted carefully, it should require only six shots for sighting-in. Some shooters might want to fire additional rounds for added confidence or point-of-impact verification. If the rifle has been sighted-in by first shooting at a close target, two more shots would be required for a total of eight.

Still, firing six rounds to sight-in a rifle is a far cry from using a whole box of ammunition or more. These methods of sighting-in are fast and economical. If you do your part, you'll know your rifle will shoot where you want it to.

Sighting-In Varmint/Big-Game Rifles

I WAS AT the local rifle range recently testing some loads. A few benches down the line was a shooter firing a .30-06. We finished shooting about the same time, and I retrieved my targets and began clearing shooting equipment off the benchrest. He came over and started talking about the accuracy of his .30-06 while handing me his just-fired 100-yard target. Sure enough, five holes were clustered into a group no larger than an inch in diameter, all neatly centered on the target's bullseye.

"That's a good-looking group. Planning to go after deer with that rifle?" I asked.

"Yeah. The country where we hunt is pretty open, and I want to be ready for a long shot. With the rifle shooting right where I aim, I guess it'll do its part if I do mine."

What this shooter didn't realize was that "doing his part" for a long-range shot was going to be a lot more involved than he thought. If he'd sighted-in his rifle a bit differently, he would have been better prepared. He simply wasn't utilizing the flat-shooting capability offered by the trajectory of his .30-06. Instead of 100 yards, he should have been thinking in terms of 250 or 275 yards. And if a 250-yard range with a benchrest wasn't available, he could have sighted-in with a higher impact point at 100 yards. This would also provide point-of-aim hitting at the greater distance.

Let's assume a shooter is firing Sierra 150-grain bullets in his .30-06. Furthermore, let's assume he is getting a reasonable 2900 fps muzzle velocity from his rifle/cartridge combo. With the rifle sighted-in to hit the point of aim at 100 yards, the bullets—with a ballistic coefficient of .409—would be 3.4 inches low at 200 yards, 12.7 inches low at 300 yards, and 29 inches low at 400 yards. If the rifle were sighted-in to hit the point of aim at 250 yards, however, the projectiles would be 2.9 inches high at 100 yards, 2.4 inches high at 200 yards, only four inches low at 300 yards, and 17.3 inches low at 400 yards.

Many hunters would just as soon not bother discussing subjects like trajectory. They think knowing a cartridge pushing a bullet fast also shoots it flat is sufficient and will pass on the details of trajectory, the mathematics involved in extrapolation and interpolation, and the reading of fine print in ballistic tables.

One area which confuses a lot of shooters involves the seemingly contradictory statements about bullet drop. For instance, most serious shooters have heard a bullet drops from the moment it leaves the muzzle, and it does. However, illustrations of trajectory curves and ballistic tables generally show bullets being *above* the line of sight—and sometimes apparently above the line of bore—at various distances downrange. Since the line of sight (iron sights or scope) is above the line of bore, this is confusing.

All the shooter really has to remember is that a rifle's trajectory is meaningful only in relation to the line of sight; this is where he will be looking when he fires. The line of sight, unlike the line of bullet travel (trajectory), is perfectly straight and does not drop.

For this reason, the line of sight or the gun's sights must be adjusted so the line of the rifle's bore is canted upward slightly in relation to line of sight. This is the only way a bullet will still be reasonably close to the line of sight (aiming point) at distances downrange. Since the bore is canted upward, the bullet will cross the line of sight on its upward travel (in relation to line of sight) and again on its downward travel (in relation to the line of sight).

If the rifle and load mentioned earlier were sighted-in for 200 yards with a scope, the line of sight at the muzzle would be approximately 1.5 inches above the line of bore with most scope mounts. In other words, the bullet starts out 1.5 inches low. By the time the bullet gets to 100 yards, it is 1.7 inches above the line of sight, meaning the bullet crossed the line of sight before getting to 100 yards. With such a sight adjustment, the bullet will have generally crossed the line of sight about 30 or 40 yards from the muzzle; it will reach its highest point (in relation to line of sight) at 140 yards or so and will then cross the line of sight again at 200 yards since the rifle is sighted-in for that distance.

Again, bullet trajectory is important primarily in relation to line of sight. The 250-yard sighting-in distance is not always the best. What's important is adjusting the sights to position the bullet's trajectoral curve along the sight path to maximize its potential.

In order to determine the optimum sighting-in distance, first consider the intended hunting application. I'll use a deer as an example because measurements have been taken from a lot of deer, and the average size is well established as being about 18 inches from the animal's withers to its brisket when standing broadside.

When the deer is standing broadside, a behind-the-foreleg hold is used by most astute riflemen. This hold will result in a downed deer if the bullet impacts anywhere between the top of the deer's back and the lower portion of its chest. If the bullet impacts a bit high, it will hit the deer's spine; if it impacts slightly lower, it will destroy lung tissue in addition to transmitting shock to the spine. If the bullet hits low in the animal's chest, it will destroy the heart or the main arteries leading from the heart.

If maximum utilization is derived from the bullet's trajectoral curve, a center-of-the-chest hold should produce a hit without undershooting or overshooting. This is commonly referred to as the "point-blank" range of a gun. Point-blank range is the maximum distance from which a shooter can hit an intended target with a center hold without overshooting at shorter distances.

In my experience, it's always best to avoid holding over an animal. With today's flat-shooting cartridges, holdover isn't necessary if the rifle is sighted-in to make maximum utilization of its potential. Its point-blank range will be around 300 yards, and this is a long way. By simply holding high on the deer (not over it) at the longer distances, the hitting range can be increased to nearly 400 yards. The reason for this thinking is that ranges are often misjudged, particularly in broken country. A deer thought to be 400 yards away frequently turns out to be 250 yards away. Often as not, the hunter who holds over his game will shoot over.

Remember the shooter who sighted-in at 100 yards? You'll recall that his 150-grain bullet will be 3.4 inches low at 200 yards. With an 18-inch deer and the center-of-the-chest hold, he will not undershoot the animal. When the range is increased to 300 yards, however, the bullet will be 12.7 inches below point of aim. If he does not hold high on the animal, he will undershoot because there's only nine inches of latitude above or below point of aim on an 18-inch deer. If his bullets are impacting 12.7 inches below the line of sight at 300 yards, he will be shooting more than three inches under the deer's belly with a center-of-the-chest hold.

Let's assume, as we did earlier, that the rifle is sighted-in for 250 yards. With this arrangement, the bullets are only 2.9 inches high at 100 yards; even with the center-of-the-chest hold, there is no danger of overshooting at the closer distance. The bullet is still 2.4 inches high at 200 yards—still no danger of overshooting—and, as mentioned earlier, is right on target at 250 yards. At 300 yards, the bullet is only four inches low, and the shooter has a point-blank range for his rifle of something beyond 300 yards (probably on the order of 350 yards). At 400 yards, the bullet is 17.3 inches low. With the relatively mild (by today's standards) .30-06, the deer hunter has a maximum point-blank range of about 350 yards with the Sierra 150-grainer if he utilizes the potential in his rifle's trajectory. This compares to a point-blank range of less than 300 yards with a 100-yard sighting-in.

Following this line of thinking, a hunter will probably decide 2.9 inches high at 100 yards is not quite enough for deer hunting. Why not sight-in the rifle at six inches high at some midrange point to increase the rifle's point-blank range even more?

There is a practical limit to this line of thinking. For example, there's not always going to be a fully exposed broadside-standing deer. Shots taken through the trees offer only a part of deer to aim at. If the bullet is allowed to stray too far from the line of sight, impracticality begins to creep in.

In addition, I see no reason for having a point-blank range beyond about 350 yards because of the other shooting variables in the field. Most shooters are unable to hold well enough beyond this distance under field conditions. If a shooter thinks he's up to the shooting necessary to connect at such distances, he can move up to a magnum cartridge with a bigger case for a faster bullet and flatter trajectory; this will increase his point-blank range.

In my opinion, 400 yards is farther than most hunters should be shooting at big game. Hits can sometimes be made at greater distances, but animals will frequently be wounded and lost at these shooting distances for a couple of reasons. The major one is the hunter's inability to hold precisely on such targets. Also, big-game bullets can lose much of their stopping power at extreme distances in terms of energy and the velocity which produces the mushrooming effect and tissue-destroying characteristics.

So how does a shooter go about finding the optimum sighting arrangement for his rifle's trajectory? As mentioned earlier, he can get some idea by studying the ballistic tables. To simplify matters, I've found three inches high at 100 yards is a good rule of thumb to use for big-game animals when using one of the flat-shooting high-velocity cartridges on the order of the .270, .30-06, 7mm Express Remington, .25-06, etc. If I'm after smaller big game like deer, I generally sight-in 2½ to three inches high; if I'm after elk, I'll go for a good three inches high. This arrangement offers a very long point-blank range without allowing the bullet's arc to stray too far from the line of sight at the shorter distances.

When shooting woodchucks and prairie dogs, a different sighting-in arrangement is necessary due to the smaller size of the targets. If the three inches high at 100 yards rule of thumb is followed, the hunter will constantly be overshooting varmints at the shorter distances. For this reason, my varmint rifles, the .220 Swift, .22-250, 6mm Remington, etc., are sighted-in to hit 1½ inches high at 100 yards. This 100-yard distance is convenient because 100-yard shooting ranges with benchrests are easier to come by than those with 275-yard ranges.

By following these rules, the hunter can be set for animals from varmints on up. By checking the trajectory tables, he will know the point-blank range of his cartridge/sighting-in setup; he will also know how far above or below the line of sight the projectile will be at certain points along its flight path.

I've conducted shooting tests comparing my results with the published data in ballistics tables, and I've found the bullet drop received in actual practice is exceedingly close to the tables, generally much closer than I can hold—even from a benchrest.

One of the best ways to see what your rifle is doing downrange is to take it out and actually shoot it at various distances to see what the rifle/cartridge/scope mount and scope setting situation produces. This is the only sure way to tell what your combination is producing in terms of the line of sight/bullet drop relationship.

If a deer is close enough you can hold the crosshair on it, it's probably close enough to be taken with a dead-on hold when you're using one of the modern flat-trajectory cartridges. This is not to say everyone needs flat trajectory. Hunters in the dense woods know they're not going to get a shot beyond 100 yards. For those who hunt the open country, however, long-range hitting can be made much easier by utilizing the rifle's trajectory.

The key is sighting-in your rifle.

The Clean-Cut Advantages Of A Clean Rifle

T HERE HAS BEEN a great deal written on the subject of rifle cleaning. Published in 1918, *The American Rifle,* a book by highly respected author Townsend Whelen, offered this advice: "The rifle is a piece of fine mechanism. It must be kept clean, free from rust, and well lubricated if it is to do good work, even passable work, and if it is to remain in serviceable condition." Whelen went on to discuss the method of cleaning a blackpowder gun using soap and water followed by oiling. "While this method of cleaning the bore will suffice for the old rifles using blackpowder only, such cleaning will positively result in the ruination of the bore of a smokeless powder arm."

Remember, this material was written prior to 1918, a time when primers were acidic, extremely corrosive, and had to be neutralized. Jacketed bullets were also prone to fouling. In addition, this was back when blackpowder rifles were still very much in use and had to be cleaned at the end of every shooting day.

Today, it's not uncommon to hear a shooter claim he cleans his rifles once a year whether they need it or not. Further, I've heard shooters warn against spoiling the accuracy of a good-shooting rifle by cleaning the bore. Other shooters insist the bore is not as important as keeping the action free of dirt and grime so it can function smoothly. On the other hand, benchrest riflemen say frequent cleaning is necessary for top accuracy. Competition benchrest shooters clean the bores of their rifles every eight to 15 shots, depending on the course of fire.

Is a regular cleanup of the average hunting rifle really necessary? Could all this fuss about bore cleaning just be a holdover from the days when primers were acid and cupro nickel bullet jackets were popular? Are shooters going through cleaning routines without deriving any real benefits?

If any type of action is left unattended, it will eventually begin to malfunction. Some of the more complex actions – semiautomatic, lever, or slide – may begin to malfunction long before a bolt, but any action can have problems if sand, weed seeds, etc., get inside the bolt, around the extractor, and along the lug raceways.

Does bore cleaning really lead to improved accuracy? Well, you can bet benchrest shooters wouldn't bother cleaning bores as frequently as they do if it didn't help. Though most hunting rifles won't produce the level of accuracy benchrest rifles do, there's no doubt frequent cleaning does produce a tendency for better shooting. Whether your particular rifle will show an accuracy improvement from a cleanup every 20 rounds instead of an annual cleanup remains to be seen. An improvement may not show up in your .30-06, but the tendency for better shooting would be there.

Data in the *Nosler Reloading Manual Number Two* also supports the view that bore cleaning improves accuracy. At the beginning of each load data section, the manual lists a "cleaning interval for match (or best) accuracy." This interval encompasses surprisingly few shots by most shooter standards.

I phoned Bob Nosler to see what the criteria was for establishing a cleaning interval. He indicated it was a result of firing many thousands of rounds and keeping detailed records on every single load fired through each rifle. In all cases, some degree of accuracy deterioration was consistently noted after firing a number of rounds. Bob also said most of the test barrels were match barrels that had been hand-lapped before being used at the Nosler plant. These barrels are naturally not as prone to foul as some other barrels.

Jim Hull of Sierra Bullets has also had considerable experience with barrels and detailed recordkeeping. The test barrels of rifle bullet manufacturers see many thousands of rounds, and extremely detailed records are kept on such barrels. Furthermore, Hull is a competition rifleman shooting primarily at 600 and 1000 yards. He says it's not uncommon for a shooter to report the barrel of a severely fouled rifle has been "shot out." According to Hull, bore scrubbing with an abrasive-type lap can restore such rifle barrels to a highly accurate condition.

So what method should be used to routinely clean a rifle barrel and action, and what method should be used to remove bullet metal fouling? As mentioned earlier, there's very little corrosive fouling with today's propellants and primers, but the residue from both of these will accumulate and can be highly abrasive. Bullet jacket fouling can be seen in many rifles simply by looking into the muzzle; it appears as copper- or brass-colored streaks in the barrel.

For routine barrel cleaning, I use a technique I learned during my benchrest shooting days and have found it to work just as well for any hunting rifle. In a nutshell, each shooting session is followed by a bore scrubbing with a tight-fitting brush and solvent. This is followed by a drying session with a number of patches. Severe bullet jacket fouling is removed via a good scrubbing with an abrasive-type bore cleaner. The action is cleaned by removing all the dirt, grime, and grit before applying a lubricant.

This nutshell introduction, applied literally by many shooters, is a gross oversimplification. There is a lot more to gun cleaning. A rifle's accuracy and lifespan can be aided by proper cleaning or damaged by an improper cleaning technique.

First, bore cleaning. It's one of the most important steps because a rifleman depends on the bore to direct the bullet in a consistent manner. While the rest of the rifle provides a means for introducing the cartridge to the chamber, denting the primer, and containing the pressure, the bore is what determines whether the rifle will shoot exactly where intended.

I prefer to use a nonjointed steel cleaning rod. Jointed rods collect abrasive grit at the joints, and slightly ill-fitting joints can scrape the rifling unnecessarily. I prefer not to use coated rods because abrasive grit can become imbedded in the coating and be transferred to the bore. Aluminum rods sometimes leave aluminum residue in the barrel. A steel rod can be wiped clean prior to each use. If I'm traveling, and a nonjointed rod is impractical, I'll carry a quality jointed steel rod.

The brush is also important. A tight-fitting brass-core brush with a looped tip is preferred. Some brushes have a core formed of twisted steel wire which is simply cut off at the tip; this produces a hard, sharp edge perfect for scratching rifling. If you can't find the softer brass-core brush and must use a steel one, select one with wire looped at the tip.

For the patch-holding tip, I prefer the jag rather than the loop because a jag tip won't contact the rifling the way a loop will. The jag tip also has a provision for accumulating fouling from the bore. With the jag, the patch can be pushed through the bore and out the muzzle; the patch will then drop to the ground when the rod is withdrawn. Or the patch can be passed back and forth inside the bore in a scrubbing motion, and as long as it's not allowed to exit the bore, the patch will stay in place on the jag tip.

For a solvent, I use Hoppe's No. 9. Though the formula for its manufacture has been guarded for all these years, its acceptance as a quality product is almost universal among shooters—even among the most serious competition shooters.

A cleaning rod guide is also an excellent accouterment for the cleaning kit. Resembling a rifle's bolt, this device has a hole through its interior to admit, center, and guide the cleaning rod into the rifle's bore. A guide also serves to keep abrasive cleaning compounds or solvents out of the trigger mechanism, and it can ease the introduction of a patch into the bore. Trying to get a patch and jag into the bore through the chamber can be an exercise in frustration at times, but the cleaning rod guide makes this a snap.

Like the cleaning rod, the best type of guide is made of steel. Unlike plastic, steel does not have a tendency to become imbedded with abrasive grit and powder fouling. Inexpensive plastic guides are available from MTM for a number of rifles, particularly big-game rifles which aren't fired or cleaned as frequently. For this application, the plastic guide has a place. If used with an abrasive cleaner, however, it should probably be discarded.

Remember, a rod guide is generally used with a bolt action, not with a slide, lever, or semiauto. Some of these other rifle action types must be cleaned from the muzzle; the rod tip should be carefully guided into the muzzle so the crown is not scratched.

The cleaning patch should be tight fitting. I like the tough ones made of DuPont Reemay and distributed by Hoppe's. For example, I use a square-cut .270/.35-caliber patch for a .22 bore. This makes for a very tight fit.

For routine cleaning, dip the brush into the jar of Hoppe's solvent and scrub the bore in a back-and-forth motion five or six times to loosen the fouling. This is followed by a series of clean, dry patches on the jag tip until one comes out relatively clean and dry. If the fouling is a bit more stubborn, the bore can first be cleaned in this manner and then left wet with Hoppe's solvent. Put the rifle away and clean it again the next day. You may be surprised by what will come out the next day. If necessary, this process can be repeated for several days.

If the bore is severely fouled with bullet jacket metal, an abrasive cleaner like Corbin's Benchrest Bore Cleaner may be in order. Basically, these liquids contain jeweler's rouge or refined silicon carbide that scratch away the fouling. They can be applied in a conventional back-and-forth cleaning action with a patch on a rod, but be sure to keep them out of the trigger or any other mechanism.

For a really tough job—a barrel plated with jacket fouling—a lapping compound used in conjunction with a lead lap may be the only solution. To make a lap, use a worn brush on a cleaning rod. Wrap a piece of cloth around the rod, just below the brush bristle, so it will stay in place and fit tightly in the bore. Slide the rod into the bore from the breech until the patch is positioned about five or six inches from the muzzle; then you must pour molten lead into the muzzle until it is almost full. The lead will soon harden and can be forced out the muzzle by pushing on the rod. Coat the lap with lapping compound and use a back-and-forth motion to scrape the bore. Don't overdo this, however, or your bore will become prematurely worn.

How often should a bore be cleaned? With Arizona's dry climate, I've found big-game rifles shot very little during a season may be cleaned once a year. On the other hand, I'll clean my .22-250 prairie dog rifle in the field several times during a full day's shooting. A rifle's bore should probably be cleaned every 15 to 30 shots to help prevent fouling buildup.

Concerning the action, I think it's a good idea to clean those parts exposed to dirt and grime on a regular basis, so I wipe the accessible parts with a rag. In a bolt-action rifle, a "lug recess cleaner" is a very handy item. This consists of a wooden dowel or fiberglass rod which approximates the diameter of the bolt body and has a ⅜-inch hole drilled laterally through one end. A gauze plug (the type used by dentists to absorb liquid) about 1½ inches long and ⅜ inch in diameter is inserted through this hole so either end of the gauze protrudes the same distance from the rod. The rod is then inserted into the bolt lug raceways; when the lug recesses are reached, the gauze is rotated to easily and thoroughly clean the bolt lug recesses as well.

I've also found the "canned air" used by photographers to blow dust from negatives can be extremely useful in blowing weed seeds and other grit from hard-to-reach areas in actions without completely disassembling them. There are times, however, when an action should be completely disassembled, dried, cleaned, and oiled.

These techniques will provide you with the basics on how to keep your rifle shooting accurately and lasting longer, but you should also remember that preserving a fine rifle involves more than just keeping it cleaned and oiled. Knowing how to store it for a long period of time or how to prepare it for cold or humid conditions, are also important lessons to learn.

Bedding Check

ONE OF THE most interesting – and sometimes most enjoyable – aspects of riflery is getting a poor-shooting rifle to group well. Frequently, an out-of-the-box gun just doesn't shoot as well as I'd like; even if a gun doesn't shoot all that badly, it's a satisfying feeling to fine tune a varmint rifle to squeeze out every bit of potential accuracy.

The handloader's approach to obtaining a greater degree of accuracy is to simply try a variety of different powders, primers, and bullet weights to determine if his rifle will drive "tacks" with one particular load. If the rifle still doesn't shoot well after you've tried a variety of different components, the next step usually involves tinkering with the bedding. The usual "fix-it" here is glass bedding, barrel channel relieving, or applying barrel up-pressure at the forend tip.

Besides mechanical defects like loose scope mount screws or bore blemish, improving a rifle's bedding can make the most dramatic improvements in accuracy. It's also one of the most frequent reasons why a rifle is shooting poorly. All the load variations in the world *won't* make a poorly bedded rifle consistently shoot well.

However, the basic problem is that a shooter must first be able to detect there is a bedding problem. Sometimes, the gun's barrel is obviously bearing more heavily on one side of the stock channel than the other. This can be detected by sliding a paper shim between the barrel and forend. A high point in the bedding can often be detected with lamp black, but this is a messy process, and scraping down a high spot is time consuming and almost impossible for the inexperienced person to make perfect. More frequently, the shooter finds it easier to glass bed the gun, and it's generally accepted that this will cure all the bedding ills. But as with load development, this is a trial-and-error process, and the hit-and-miss approach can consume a lot of time while possibly producing very few positive benefits. If glass bedding doesn't correct the rifle's poor shooting characteristics, the shooter still won't be certain whether the bedding was part of the problem.

Don't fret. There is a better way. Benchrest shooters commonly use a method of checking a rifle's bedding without firing a shot or even taking the rifle out of the stock. All you need is a dial indicator and a means for attaching the indicator base to the gun barrel while allowing the sensor to bear against the gun's forend.

Ideally, a rifle action should rest in the stock recess with uniform pressure and wood-to-metal contact on all bedding surfaces. The rifle will generally shoot best when there are no uneven stresses placed anywhere on the barreled action when the screws are tightened. Uniform tension should apply to all proper bedding surfaces. A high spot in the bedding area or action recess – depending on where it is – can place uneven stresses on the action when the screws are tightened. This can result in wild shots when the rifle is fired.

With a dial indicator, it is very easy to determine whether improper bedding is placing unnecessary tension on the action when the action screws are tightened. If there is irregular bedding, the stock forend-to-barrel relationship will change as the screws are tightened or loosened. This movement is particularly noticeable out at the rifle's forend tip, where the motion is magnified.

If the action screws are placing severe tension on the barreled action, the barrel's movement away from or toward the forend will be considerable—even to the point that it can be felt with the fingers when you place them touching both the barrel and forend. Loosening one of the action screws will result in a barrel/forend movement that can easily be felt in this area; however, the dial indicator offers a more precise means for checking bedding irregularities *and* for applying a quantitative measurement to them.

The first step when using a dial indicator to check for a bedding problem is to apply masking tape along the barrel to prevent the base of the dial indicator from marring the blueing. (I use a magnetic-base indicator which allows precise positioning anywhere along the barrel.)

Next, adjust the indicator so the pointer bears against the stock's forend and will move if there is any movement between barrel and wood. Loosen the forward guard screw while watching the dial indicator to see how much it moves.

The next step is to snug the forward screw back up and loosen the rear action screw while watching the indicator. If there are three screws to the action, it's a good idea to check the third one as well. Any movement over .002 inch is considered to be too great by many shooters; no movement at all may indicate that the action is binding in the stock; acceptable movement is anything less than .002 inch.

When loosening and tightening guard screws in order to check for bedding problems, make sure you don't tighten a screw too tight and aggravate a bedding problem by compressing the stock wood. For example, some gunsmiths recommend loosening the tang screw first when disassembling a Mauser-type rifle. They claim that if the forward screw is loosened first and the rear screw is tight, the bedding surface in the very narrow tang area can be compressed and distorted so that the very manner in which the guard screws are loosened can destroy the bedding.

This could make a significant difference. I do know, however, that too tight guard screws can cause a good-shooting rifle to go sour. Just snug them up firmly—there's no need to lean heavily on a big-handled screwdriver to get the job done.

Contrary to what some shooters might think, a glass bedding job is not a permanent cure for a rifle's bedding ills, nor is a conventional in-the-wood bedding job—particularly if a rifle is carried in areas where climates vary. Climate changes can cause the stock to change. An increase in humidity may cause expansion, or the stock may shrink if the climate is dry. Either change can cause accuracy to go sour. The bedding remains stable only as long as the entire (or the two different) bedding surface(s) remain in exactly the same relationship.

A rifle action is generally bedded in the recoil lug area and in the tang. These two points are separated by the gun's magazine cutout—meaning the stock dwindles in two thin layers of wood on either side of the magazine box. A shooter who expects such a rifle to stay perfectly bedded year after year is expecting something that's not in the cards, no matter how much epoxy is placed in the action recess.

On a number of big-game rifles, the expected accuracy level is not great enough that slight bedding shifts will be noticed. Even so, the discriminating varmint shooter can benefit with an occasional bedding check. It's not a bad idea to check a rifle's bedding prior to each varminting season, and the dial indicator makes this relatively easy. Then, if the bedding is irregular, an additional (thin) layer of epoxy applied to the existing bedding may make the rifle shoot accurately for another season.

Most shooters who have attained a high level of accuracy with a given gun and load expect the combination to continue to shoot that way. If the rifle begins to shoot poorly for some reason, they blame the ammunition or themselves when there could possibly be some other factor. Before you blame either, use a dial indicator to find out whether the bedding has gone bad.

Once the bedding is tested and found to be okay (with no unnecessary side tension on the barrel), and after you have checked to make sure all scope-mount screws are secure, you can begin a load development program with the confidence that your accuracy testing is meaningful and will lead to improved accuracy.

Refinishing A Riflestock

A HUNTING riflestock is bound to show signs of wear with a lot of use—a scratch from a barbed-wire fence, a dent from bumping a boulder, or a chip from an antler tip when recording a trophy on film. A scratch or chip may add character, but a stock will gradually lose its appeal over the years from normal wear and tear. Fortunately, these signs of wear are relatively easy to correct by refinishing the riflestock.

Unlike some gunsmithing or complete stocking jobs, most shooters can refinish their own stock, even if they aren't artistically or mechanically inclined. Many serious shooters have already attempted refinishing a rifle stock. Some of these facelifts have turned out okay, while others weren't as good as planned. Few refinished stocks ever end up as nice as the exquisite finishes applied by custom stockmakers.

Dan Martin is one shooter who produces custom stocks and completes them with a beautiful finish. A conservative-looking, nongloss finish, it has a satin appearance but wears like rhino hide. It's the type shooters want but can never seem to *produce*.

It's generally known that stockmakers' trade secrets aren't for public knowledge; after all, that's how Dan makes his living. But I decided to ask Dan how he does it. Not only did he let me in on the methods, but he helped finish my scarred old .22 (the first rifle I ever owned) and gave me permission to pass the techniques along.

Actually, putting one of Martin's finishes on the old .22 is a bit like putting a Rolls-Royce paint job on a bicycle. The difference is that Martin's finish doesn't normally cost more than others, and it doesn't take a lot more time. So why not go first class?

"Refinishing" a stock is something of a misnomer because 90 percent of the work consists of getting the old finish off and preparing the wood; only about 10 percent of your time is spent applying the new finish. How the old finish is removed depends on the type.

If the stock has an oil- or varnish-type finish, a quality furniture-stripping liquid does the trick. Be sure to remove all hardware—trigger guard, recoil pad, etc.—because the stripper can eat away at them. Also, the stripper's action on the old finish can be hastened by roughing up the surface with coarse steel wool or a Scotch Brite abrasive pad. This will cut the glaze from the old finish and allow the liquid to penetrate faster.

It's a good idea to use rubber gloves when applying most stripping agents because they can be hard on your hands. Simply brush the liquid on and, using the Scotch Brite pad, wipe it off after a few minutes. The finish will come off with it. You will need to apply two or three coats of stripper, but this step is still relatively fast and easy.

If the rifle has a space-age epoxy finish, however, you have your work cut out. About all a furniture stripper will do in this case is soften the finish; in some instances, it won't even do that. Though there are stronger solvents available, some of them are toxic and some can affect the wood. For the most part, you'll have to remove the epoxy finishes mechanically—by chipping, sanding, and/or scraping. Scraping may be the fastest, although it can also get the inexperienced person into trouble because gouges are easily made in the stock.

Once the bulk of the old finish is removed, it's time to sand the stock. There will still be some finish remaining in the pores of the wood, but the abrasive papers will remove it. Sanding is something practically everyone has done; as simple as it appears, however, there are still few who do it properly.

First, replace the buttplate or recoil pad and sand it along with the stock. That way it will have a precise fit when the sanding is finished. Start with 80-grit paper ("No Fil," a paper produced by 3M, works well because it won't clog with finish like some conventional abrasive-coated papers).

An old recoil pad works ideally as a sanding block on a gunstock because its curved surfaces will conform to the curves on the stock. It's also soft enough to "give" under pressure, so the original curvature of the stock is easily retained.

Sand with the grain and try to keep the original flat spots flat and the sharp edges sharp; it's a common tendency to round off corners. Pieces of new rubber gasoline line hose work very well for sanding the inside curves—like the underside of a cheekpiece. Avoid using the fingers or hands for sandpaper backing because this is where dished-out spots will originate. And if your stock has checkering, the best solution is to re-cut it after you're finished.

Use the 80-grit paper to remove the old finish and eliminate all the scratches and dents possible. A better looking surface will result if the scratches and gouges can be sanded out. Otherwise, they'll have to be filled with shellac stick or tinted wood putty, and this will usually leave a discolored spot—without grain—on the finished stock.

Dents can sometimes be steamed out with a hot iron and a damp paper towel. Just place the damp towel between the stock and the iron. But be aware that dents, even when removed like this, can show in the finished stock. If at all possible, it's best to remove wood to get all the blemishes out.

If you remove all the scratches and dents with the 80-grit paper, the sanding will be about four times easier than if some remain. Don't think the finer grit paper will take care of it. Remember: The coarse paper removes wood faster and easier. Each successively finer paper can then be used only to remove scratches of the previous paper grade.

After you've removed all the old finish and sanded out all the gouges and dents possible, go over the stock with 120-grit paper, then use 220.

Next, you need to "whisker" the wood. Moisten the stock with a wet paper towel or cloth, but don't get it sopping wet. Dry it quickly over a heat source like a radiator or an electric bathroom heater. (The sharply defined edges of the stock will burn easily, so be careful.) This process raises the wood fibers so they can be sanded smooth. After sanding (if an oil finish will be applied), follow with 400-grit paper. If an epoxy finish is to be applied, use 320 grit.

After getting the old finish removed, you may be disappointed by how the basic stock looks completely stripped. What you thought was walnut might turn out to be birch. Or, even if it is walnut, the wood may contain unsightly light or dark sections. Quality walnut is expensive and has become harder to get. For this reason, some manufacturers are putting a stain in the stock finish to make the wood appear more uniform.

The best remedy for these problems is to stain the wood (as I did with my light-colored birch .22 stock). Make certain the stain you use is compatible with the type of finish you want to put on the stock. Directions for applying stain are usually on the can. Apply the stain sparingly until you have the shade you want. With the birch stock, I used a walnut stain and applied it with a soft, lint-free rag.

If the stock looks good after the old finish is removed, you can skip the staining step and proceed with the finish. There are all sorts of finishes and finishing methods that can be applied to a gunstock. Most of them work; some have drawbacks (like getting sticky in hot weather or being difficult to apply). I've included two different finishes—oil and epoxy— that Martin used without any problems. He prefers a varithane plastic oil-type finish.

In general, an oil finish is *in* the wood; an epoxy finish is *on* the wood. It's best to stay away from furniture lacquers because some of them will chip and gun-cleaning solvents can damage them.

To apply the finish, the first step is to soak the wood with the varithane until it won't absorb any more liquid. This is done by brushing it on, setting the stock aside for a while, and then brushing more on. Once the wood surface is saturated, the excess is wiped off. Then the stock is placed aside overnight so it can dry thoroughly. The next day, apply another coat of finish and allow it to dry. This takes about two days, although the time will vary, depending on temperature and humidity conditions. After it's dry, sand the finish with 400-grit paper to the bare wood, repeat the process of applying finish and sanding until all the pores are filled and then brush on the last coat of finish. It's important to use a very fine camel hair brush to apply the finish because a stiff-bristle brush can pull the finish out of the wood pores.

After the last coat is applied, sand the stock with 600-grit paper and wax it. If you want a duller finish, rub it with pumice after the 600-grit sanding. For a really high-gloss shine, some stockmakers dampen their fingers with the finish and rub it on repeatedly until the stock acquires a plastic-like gloss.

If you prefer an epoxy finish, it's best to spray it on, thinning it first (50:50) with whatever solvent or thinner is recommended on the label. Most epoxies come too thick to penetrate the wood at all; they will later chip if applied without being diluted. Thinning allows the liquid a better purchase in the wood pores.

After the first coat hardens, sand away any roughness with 400-grit paper and repeat the process until all the pores are filled. Even though you're sanding only the finish – and not the wood – be careful to maintain the sharp corners, flats, etc.

You may not be able to produce the kind of finish a professional stockmaker gets the very first time; on the other hand, the results might pleasantly surprise you. Mine surprised me.

Assembling A Tool Kit For Emergencies

S EVERAL YEARS AGO, a friend and I loaded coyote hounds into the back of a pickup and headed for a section of brush country that was inhabited by a good many coyotes. The plan was to send the dogs through the undergrowth and hope they'd run coyotes out so we'd get a shot.

It had been some time since I'd fired my custom Douglas-barreled .244 Remington built on a Mauser action, and I decided to stop on the way out and check the rifle's zero. I held carefully on a distant beverage can and was pleased to find that the bullet punched a hole through the insignia on the label.

And then the trouble started.

When I worked the bolt to eject the case, I was dismayed to find that the case remained in the barrel. Rather than pulling the rim off the case with the claw-type extractor, the extractor had a piece broken off so it couldn't hook the case rim. This was the only rifle I had with me; without it, I'd have been out of the coyote-shooting picture.

I couldn't find anything in the pickup long and skinny enough to push the case out from the muzzle. My partner was a bit wiser. He had been in such a predicament before. Taking a sixteenpenny nail from the back of the pickup, he cut the head off with fencing pliers, then dropped the tiny rod into the barrel of the .244, held his thumb over the muzzle, and began shaking the rifle, holding the barrel in a vertical position.

The continually dropping nail eventually tapped the case out of the chamber.

With the chamber now free of any obstruction, there was still the problem of the broken extractor. We couldn't fix it, so I had to proceed on the hunt with what I had. At least I would get one shot; I just wouldn't be able to extract the empty case in a hurry. With a little foresight and preparation, however, I could have prevented such a predicament.

Many potential problems that come up in the field can put a gun out of use. A horse can slip and roll down a mountainside with the hunter's favorite big-game rifle still in the saddle scabbard. If this happened, it wouldn't be uncommon for the stock to break, the scope to be dented, or a lens broken or knocked out of alignment. A hunter can take a fall which can have the same effect. A rim can be pulled off a stuck case, mud can become lodged in the barrel, or a trigger can jam.

Admittedly, these things seldom happen. But remember Murphy's Law: "Anything that can go wrong, will go wrong."

It's better to be prepared just in case something does happen to your rifle. Even if it doesn't happen to your rifle, you may save the hunt for someone else in camp if you're properly prepared.

It's impossible to predetermine what's going to happen, and you can't prepare for everything. Carrying an entire gunsmith shop with you is definitely impractical.

If you are able to get your vehicle into hunting camp, it may be possible to take a good quantity of tools with you. If that's the case, though, I prefer to carry a backup rifle—or two—rather than a bunch of tools. Two rifles can require less room than a great quantity of tools, and the backup rifle is readily available. But when you have to pack into the back country where heavy and bulky equipment must be kept to a minimum, you'll probably only have one rifle with you.

You can't always be prepared for everything, but you *can* prepare for the most common problems—bore obstructions, stuck cases, a broken stock, a scope that's out of alignment, a broken extractor, etc. With a few tools, it's surprising what you can fix in the field. All sorts of tools will immediately come to mind when thinking about fixing a gun, but when you consider having to pack them into the back country, compactness becomes a factor. Following is a list I've compiled in order of importance.

First of all, I would have a screwdriver to fit any screw on my gun or scope. It doesn't take a lot of screwdrivers in order to meet this need. For example, Brownells distributes a hollow-handled screwdriver with interchangeable tips that can be stored in the handle. A screw cap keeps the extra tips in place. Tips are available for anything from a standard slotted-head screw to a Phillips head or a hex head.

Another item I'd have in my tool kit is a jointed steel cleaning rod which could be used to remove any sort of bore obstruction. Belding & Mull distributes a fine model that breaks down into short sections to fit in a carrying pouch, and it comes with cleaning tips and a handle.

Along with the cleaning rod and various tips, I carry a number of cleaning patches or, better yet, patch-making cloth. This way, larger pieces can be cut for cleaning the action. It's always a good idea to swab the bore out after removing any obstruction. In addition, a tiny bottle of solvent can be used to further clean and lubricate the bore or possibly lubricate bolt lugs, trigger, etc.

Another item I consider to be important on a pack-in-type hunt is a spare scope and rings. In using a mounting system like the Weaver Quick-Detachable, the small bases, each having two screws, are practically indestructible. With this type of mount, scope and rings can be removed from the bases and then returned to the bases while maintaining the rifle's point of impact amazingly close.

I prefer to first sight-in the rifle with the spare scope attached; then, without moving the scope's adjustments, I remove that scope and rings from the bases. The primary scope and rings are then attached to the rifle, and the combination is sighted-in for the hunt. If the need arises, scopes can be changed in seconds, and the hunter can use the second scope without having to sight-in, though a cursory sight check certainly wouldn't hurt. This second scope and set of rings will prevent many scope problems—a broken lens, a dented or bent tube, a broken ring, or a stripped screw thread, etc. By using one of the lower magnification scopes like a 2X or 3X, the size of the scope is small enough so that it really doesn't take much room for the added insurance provided.

An epoxy should also be included in a tool kit for stock repairs. I prefer the epoxy supplied in the dual-cavity syringe-type container, with the hardener on one side and the resin on the other. This way, the epoxy can be easily mixed in the field for any emergency repair. The bottom side of an aluminum beverage can makes a good shallow container for mixing epoxy.

If a stock breaks, it'll usually be in the wrist portion, and sometimes it breaks completely in two. Though epoxy has very little sheer strength, there are ways this type of a break can be repaired so that the rifle is usable for the remainder of the hunt.

First, coat the break surfaces with epoxy and then coat the exterior of the grip section with a liberal application of epoxy. A piece of canvas or burlap can then be saturated with epoxy and applied around the broken section. Now wrap it tightly with stout nylon cord (which can then be coated with epoxy). When this dries, you'll have a highly reinforced grip that will look ugly, but it will get you through the hunt. A stock that is broken completely through the wrist will eventually not be usable, so any added damage done by the epoxy generally won't matter. If you don't have canvas or burlap available, just use the epoxied string.

With these few items, in addition to an extractor and a means for replacing it, you'll be surprised at the number of rifle repairs you can make in the field. There are other specialized tools you might need, depending on the specific rifle. Most people feel more comfortable with a few more tools; I'll list some others that would be my next choices.

First is a set of pliers. This has all sorts of uses. A small set of punches with interchangeable tips can be important, depending on your particular rifle and trigger. For example, they can be essential in gaining access to broken trigger parts.

A small hammer or mallet can drive the pins with the punches, but a rock or piece of hardwood will also work. Files can have a variety of uses. Like pliers, you may not see the intended use until you actually need them. A hand vise can be handy for holding small parts while repairing them in the field, though pliers can also serve this purpose.

A collimator can also be useful, though it is a bit on the bulky side for the advantage it offers. It is a great little gadget to check a rifle's zero in the field without having to fire the gun and possibly frighten nearby game. If the number of rounds you've packed in is extremely limited, the collimator can be invaluable in preventing you from expending all your ammo while attempting to sight-in a rifle that has had a scope knocked out of alignment.

You can't be prepared for everything, but if the problem is so severe that it can't be corrected with this equipment, you're probably going to need the services of a gunsmith.

How To Invest In Guns

G UN PRICES ARE rising. While inflation accounts for some of this increase, you'll find many guns you bought a few years ago have escalated in value more than the annual inflation rate.

I first learned this lesson while I was still in high school. I wanted a handgun, but my parents said I couldn't have one until I was 21. When I had the opportunity to buy an Iver Johnson hand ejector from a friend, I jumped at the chance. The gun was chambered for the .32 Smith & Wesson Long cartridge, and it came complete with 50 rounds of ammo—all for $10. I remember keeping the gun in the barn and going out to dry-fire it when I fed hay or got grain. Finally, the day came when I was able to take the gun down into the woods. I shot the 50 rounds at bullfrogs, cottontails, and squirrels and never hit a thing!

I decided handguns weren't all I'd envisioned them to be, and after the ammo was gone, I sold the gun for $15—a tidy appreciation in value over a short term (less than a month).

A few years after that bargain buy, I attended a farm sale and discovered a Marlin Model 1892 was to be auctioned. Since I had wanted a lever-action .22 rimfire with an octagon barrel, I examined the Marlin carefully. I wasn't looking for a collector's piece, just a good-shooting .22. The Marlin appeared to be in excellent condition. I levered open the action, inserted a white piece of paper into the breech to reflect light into the bore, and examined the inside of the barrel as well as I could from the muzzle. Even the rifling appeared to be in good shape.

I made up my mind to go as high as $20 for the .22. Bidding started at $10, and it seemed like half the crowd was trying to buy the gun until the price went to $17.50. Then there were only two others in contention, and the price went to $20. The moment of truth had arrived. The other two fellows in the bidding must have had the same idea I had about the $20 because one offered $21 and the other declined to bid higher. The auctioneer looked at me, and I quickly hiked the bid to $22. The other fellow didn't top it, and I was the proud owner of the Marlin.

I could hardly wait to get home and shoot it. When I did, I was discouraged to find Long Rifle ammo made the case swell into a pit in the old gun's chamber, and I couldn't extract it unless I pried the rim with a pocket knife. I explained this situation to my father, and he said the affliction wasn't uncommon to the old rifles. He figured someone had probably fired a lot of corrosive .22 Short ammunition in the firearm without cleaning it. As a result, pitting occurred in the chamber just ahead of the mouth of the .22 Short case. My father thought the rifle would be fine if I only fired .22 Short ammunition through it.

I decided not to fire a rifle with such a pit in the chamber, and I left the gun in a closet for about a year. Then I came across a used .300 Winchester Magnum in a gunshop. At $125, I thought the gun was reasonably priced, but "reasonably priced" still didn't mean I had the money to pay for it. So I took my old .22 to the store and asked the owner what he would give me toward the purchase of the .300 Winchester. The owner was interested in the .22. I explained to him about the pit in the Marlin's chamber, thinking it still might be worth $10. He said my rifle was more of a collector's piece than a shooter, and he would be glad to trade the .300 Winchester Magnum for the old .22. There was a long pause as I waited for him to explain how much additional money was needed for the .300 Winchester Magnum. Then I realized he was willing to trade *straight up*! I immediately took him up on the offer.

In one year, the value of the old Marlin lever-action .22 had appreciated from $22 to $125. I walked into the gunshop a few days after the trade and found a $225 price tag on the old Marlin. The next time I was in the store the rifle was gone, which indicated to me the shop owner had also made a tidy profit on his investment.

Gun trading was becoming a lot of fun, particularly when I could use one for awhile and then sell it for more than I paid. What could be better?

Not long after the Smith & Wesson Model 53 (chambered for the .22 Remington Jet) was announced, I found a used one which appeared to be in excellent condition at the local store. The price was $90, and I bought it. I bagged a good number of coyotes and jackrabbits with the Model 53 but ultimately decided to trade it. At that point, I decided I needed a shotgun and traded the Model 53 straight up for a Browning "Sweet Sixteen" priced at $200. I was quite pleased the gun had appreciated more than 100 percent in the short time I'd had it. Even at $200, the handgun was a good buy for the gunshop owner; the same gun would be worth considerably more today (at least $475).

My gun-buying experiences seemed to get even better. Only a few years ago, a fellow walked into my office with a Winchester Model 54 chambered in .30-30. He said he needed money and asked if I was interested in buying the Model 54. At the time, Winchester Model 54s in the most common .270 or .30-06 chamberings and in reasonably used condition were selling for about $175. I'd always thought the Winchester Model 54 rifles were "sleepers" on the used gun market. It was interesting to me that pre-'64 Model 70s were selling at a premium, yet you could occasionally find Model 54s, the forerunner to the Model 70, which sometimes sold for a song.

I scrutinized the old Model 54, which appeared to be in practically new condition. I opened the bolt and noticed there was hardly even a bullet-jacket-rubbed streak on the feedramp. It didn't look like the rifle had been refinished, but I was skeptical that such an old rifle could be in such good condition. I asked the man what he wanted for it, and he said $175. I wrote him a check.

I wasn't really familiar with the value of a Model 54 in this chambering, so I started phoning collector friends. My sources said the Model 54 chambered in .30-30 Winchester was unusual and should be worth about

$300 to $350. I had another acquaintance who was a Model 70 collector, and perhaps two hours after I'd bought the Model 54, the Model 70 collector was looking at it. He asked me what I wanted for it, and I quoted $350. Without batting an eye, he sat down and wrote out a check. I thought it was strange that a horse trader of the first water would pay my asking price without question. I thought this fellow knew something I didn't, so I said, "Now that you own it, what do you think it's worth?"

"Around $700," he replied. I still felt $350 was a fair price, but it just goes to show you a collector's rifle is worth whatever someone is willing to pay for it. No doubt if someone were collecting Model 54s and needed a nice .30-30 to round out his collection, this unusual chambering might very well have been worth even $1000.

Guns don't have to be old to drastically appreciate in value. The .22 Remington Jet mentioned earlier was not a particularly old handgun (made from 1960 to 1974). Most people have heard of the escalated prices of the Ruger single-shot Hawkeye (made in 1963 and 1964) chambered for the .256 Winchester Magnum cartridge. Now these guns are worth $800 and up. In 1963, they cost $87.50 new.

It wasn't all that long ago (1955-56) that Remington introduced the Model 600 rifle with the laminated stock and chambered for the 6.5mm Remington Magnum ($144.95) and .350 Remington Magnum ($149.95). Both are highly prized today and are bringing premium prices—perhaps four or five times what they cost new.

The Model 88 Winchester in .358 Winchester caliber is another example. This is one example of an individual chambering worth a premium price (selling for $129.90 in 1956). Model 88 Winchesters in chamberings like .243 or .308, which are quite common, are not worth nearly what a good .358 is worth.

Anything unusual or odd about a gun can make it worth much more than its counterparts. For example, when the 6mm Remington cartridge designation was first introduced, Remington considered calling it the 6mm Remington Magnum. A few initial guns were stamped with this designation, and if you can find one, it's rare.

Another rifle I procured a few years ago was a Winchester Model 490 in .22 rimfire. I attended the Winchester seminar at which this rifle was introduced during the mid-'70s. The Model 490 is a semiautomatic which was intended to resemble the Winchester Model 100 semiautomatic centerfire rifle in appearance and weight. The rifle was made in Canada, and after it appeared in the Winchester catalog for a year or two, it was dropped. A few years ago, I found one still in its original carton with original tags and purchased it for investment purposes.

For the vast majority of the guns I've purchased, however, appreciation in value has been a secondary factor. I bought the guns because I liked them for one reason or another or because they were chambered for an unpopular caliber that I wanted to handload and test fire. Since the guns were already used, no value was lost in shooting them (if care is taken not to place any additional blemishes on the finish). This way, I can use my investment while it appreciates.

Collecting guns for investment can be an enjoyable pastime. Frequenting gunshops, garage sales, swap meets, and just talking guns can be fun. You'll eventually learn which guns are rare or seldom seen, and you'll soon learn the relative prices of various firearms. Then when you happen onto a jewel aging away on the gunshop owner's rack, you can take advantage of it. To aid you along the way, there are plenty of buyer's guides or value guides on the book market, and these can be excellent sources of information regarding guns. However, I have yet to see one I think reflects prices accurately, so take the listed prices with a grain of salt.

The gun sections in the want ads of large city newspapers can give some indication about pricing, but don't rely on this information without looking at the guns.

Also keep in mind there are more people collecting certain brands or types of guns than others. For instance, there are probably a lot more collectors of old Winchester lever-action rifles than Marlins. More people are interested in Model 70s than Model 54s, and this also establishes a price.

So far, I've been talking about buying individual guns on a small scale. This is something anyone can do on an occasional basis with a few dollars. Good buys come along so seldom that this is the best way to make the most of your dollar. Once you've bought and sold a few guns for a sizable, short-term profit, however, the wheels will start clicking, and you'll begin thinking about buying more guns and perhaps keeping them for a longer time period. I know another investor who purchased new pre-'64 Model 70 Winchesters. He bought them new and kept them unfired in the original cartons, complete with all the literature. About 10 years later, he sold 26 of these rifles to another investor for about $13,000. They cost him perhaps $5000 or $6000 new.

All is not so rosy when purchasing used guns for an investment. You could miscalculate whether a gun will appreciate in value and pay a premium price to get one in good condition. This particular model might not ever reach the state of desirability among collectors that it should. Or you could purchase a gun you thought was an original and then discover it's been altered or refinished. As a rule of thumb, most of the guns produced during more recent years can show very little wear and still be all original. Whenever I see a gun supposedly made around the turn of the century that looks new, I become cautious. If you find one of these, look carefully for signs of refinishing on the stock and on the metal. These guns sometimes have had severe pitting, but the pitting has been polished out and the gun reblued. Worn or pitted barrels may have been relined or replaced. Collector value has been destroyed for such guns, and the wise gun buyer should beware. Also, be careful to purchase firearms in good mechanical condition. Even collectors don't want a gun if it doesn't have all the parts or doesn't work.

You stand the best chance of latching onto a real "sleeper" in the field of collecting old and/or fine guns. Some of these guns are worth thousands of dollars. To keep things interesting, there are few people, even among collecting buffs, who know what some of the guns are worth. For this reason, huge profit is sometimes realized overnight. I once saw a collector buy an old Mauser for $200. The previous owner had valued it at no more than a modern centerfire rifle. The collector knew the rifle was worth upward of $2500 when he wrote the man a check.

Buying used guns as an investment is an enjoyable way to manage your money. Even if the gun doesn't appreciate, you've still had the opportunity to take the gun home, work its action, admire its mechanism, and perhaps shoot it just to see what it's like. If the gun doesn't appreciate a dime and is subsequently sold, you've still been enriched by the pleasure of using it and the knowledge you've gleaned from it.

Mixed Bag

The .22 For Beginners

I N 1920, MY father, at the age of 15, saved $15 for a new slide-action Winchester .22 he'd been eyeing for weeks. The gun was chambered only for the Short cartridge, but he didn't care to own a rifle chambered for the "outrageously priced" Longs because Shorts were expensive enough at 15¢ a box.

He had been sent to town with the wagon team for a load of corn, and it wasn't mere coincidence the rifle could be easily hidden in the shelled corn for the trip past the house on the way to the barn.

You see, he didn't have his father's permission. So, with both delight and fear, he plunked down the money for the rifle he'd soon be using for Sunday afternoon rabbit hunts.

At age 12, I asked whether I could own a .22 rifle. My father refused, saying I needed to wait until I was 15 like he had.

When I was 13, I visited a brother-in-law who asked me what I wanted for my grade school graduation. I traveled back home with the bolt-action

Stevens Model 86C, a gun chambered for Shorts, Longs, or Long Rifles and sporting a tubular magazine, wondering what my father would say. I was afraid he would demand I put it up until I turned 15, but he only said, "You be careful with that." However, he said it with a stern look I will always remember because what went *unsaid* was the most important.

Six months later, I bought my first shotgun, a bolt-action 20 gauge.

When most youngsters start shooting, their first gun is frequently a BB or pellet gun. It's generally thought BB and pellet guns are good first guns for a youngster since they are not considered lethal. However, my father and older brother still impressed upon me a BB gun is nothing to fool around with. I was to treat it as though it were lethal, because how I handled it would determine how soon I would own a .22 rifle.

BB and pellet guns offer valuable shooting practice to the supervised youngster. Even in the city, a safe basement or other indoor range can be easily constructed.

When it's time for a youngster to own a real hunting gun, parents are sometimes undecided about which one is best suited to the beginner—a .22 or something on the order of a .410- or 20-gauge shotgun. Selection is sometimes based on whether the father is an avid wing shooter, small-game hunter, or big-game hunter. If he hunts quail five or six times a year without going after small game at all, the beginning shooter will have more hunting opportunities with his father if he begins with the small-bore shotgun.

There are advantages, however, in starting the new shooter with the rifled long gun. And there is no contest for choice of caliber: the .22 rimfire is the obvious one. Its low noise level and almost nonexistent recoil are decided pluses, but the best part of the .22 is the cost of the ammo. All-important practice is more affordable with this cartridge than with any other. In addition, deliberation and shooting precision are important attributes for the shooter to acquire, and these are learned with the rifled long gun, not the scattergun.

The single shot is the preferred action for the beginning shooter. It requires the youngster to reload the gun completely for every shot, which is a definite safety advantage. It also encourages proficiency at shot placement because the shooter knows there is no fast followup shot.

On the other hand, these desirable attributes can be taught with other actions, and once a shooter progresses beyond the basics, he will most likely want a repeating rifle. However, it is best not to obtain a semiauto. It takes a while to become familiar with gun handling, and an autoloader instantaneously prepares another cartridge for firing without giving the new shooter time to think.

Initial steps to introduce the new shooter to the sport should not be taken lightly. It's important to build confidence right from the start, and certain measures will ensure a more positive and satisfying beginning.

First, make certain the rifle fits the new shooter well. A too-long stock makes the rifle feel heavy and hard to hold steady—something the new shooter will have enough problems with without having to overcome an ill-fitting stock as well.

The length of pull, or the distance from trigger to butt, is too long on most factory-dimensioned stocks. This makes the gun muzzle heavy and extremely hard to steadily support with the forend.

Shortening the stock and possibly even a barrel-cutting job can help matters tremendously. Some manufacturers supply boy's versions of various .22 rifles, which is a definite plus.

To check the length of pull, have the new shooter rest the buttstock on his arm just inside the elbow while pointing the gun muzzle up. He should be able to comfortably grasp the pistol grip and still be able to place the pad of the first joint of his index finger around the trigger. If he cannot do this easily, the stock probably needs to be shortened.

Once the gun is fitting properly, thoroughly explain the use of the iron sights to him. This is particularly important if he has not had a BB or pellet gun.

Draw a picture to illustrate how the front sight blade and rear notch should be aligned at the instant of firing. You might also draw examples of sights out of alignment and explain the probable point of bullet impact; for example, if the front sight blade is sticking up too high in the notch at the instant of firing, the shot will impact high, and if the front sight blade is too far left in the notch, the shot will impact left.

Next, draw a picture of the rear sight notch and let the new shooter sketch in the front sight bead to show the proper position in the notch.

Have the new shooter demonstrate he can actually align the sights properly on target. This can be done with his rifle, preferably with the bolt removed, resting in "V" notches cut into a cardboard box. Let the new shooter adjust the box until the sights are aligned perfectly on a bullseye target. Then take a look yourself to see whether everything is right.

This sounds like a lot of time is spent explaining sight picture and the use of the sights. In many cases, however, a new shooter has difficulty understanding the precise alignment of the sight unless it is thoroughly explained. If he commences shooting before he understands how the sights should be aligned, he'll be disappointed when the rifle doesn't shoot where he wants. Again, building confidence from the start is extremely important.

Although a scope sight is simpler for the new shooter to use in terms of sight picture (because he doesn't have to keep so many different points in alignment), factory iron sights are the usual equipment for the new shooter and require the most explanation.

Establish a very close range with a large bullseye target for the new shooter. I'm talking about a ridiculously close range—like 10 feet.

Before the actual shooting, spend a few minutes dry firing to make the new shooter a little more familiar with rifle holding. This will also indicate the relative steadiness of various shooting positions and show what a rest can do to calm the wobbles.

Once the new shooter becomes fairly comfortable with the shooting positions, it's time to begin shooting—assuming he has handled the rifle in a safe manner during the dry-firing tests. Above all else, *safety* must be constantly stressed.

Use hearing protection, even with the .22 rimfire. Although the .22 rimfire report is very mild, its sudden crack is unfamiliar to the new shooter, and any precaution to prevent a flinch is definitely worthwhile.

Allow the shooter to begin firing, preferably from one of the more stable positions, either sitting or kneeling. Keep the initial shooting session short so the shooter doesn't tire. Holding a rifle up is physically taxing to a new shooter though he probably won't admit it. An eager beginner will want to continue firing, but as he begins to tire physically, his groups will become poorer. It's best to quit on a positive note and leave the shooter wanting more.

Once the shooter becomes proficient at hitting large, close bullseyes, allow him to try different positions until he's relatively confortable with each. Then gradually increase the shooting distance until he can shoot at most reasonable ranges from all positions.

Paper targets are, by nature, extremely unforgiving. They show the beginner and instructor precisely where each and every bullet impacts.

But plinking tin cans is often more fun for the beginner and a refreshing change during the practice session. Hitting a tin can anywhere is a hit—regardless of precise point of impact. Again, this helps inspire confidence.

The next step in shooting preparation for hunting is to go after small game like cottontail rabbits or squirrels. Stress using any available rest and placing the shot precisely. You'll never forget the gleam in his eye when your beginner bags that first cottontail.

The Benchrest Advantage

"**W**HY SHOULD I learn to shoot from a benchrest? I won't have one with me when I'm hunting."

The answer is simple. Your shooting ability in the field is important, but you first need to have confidence that your gun and load are up to delivering what you expect of them.

What can be accomplished with a benchrest can't be done any other way, from any other shooting position. A benchrest or shooting table offers the average guy an insight into the accuracy characteristics of his gun and load. A benchrest can help determine which load of five or 10 shoots most accurately and how much more accurately. It can reveal whether a rifle shoots better with forend pressure on the barrel or with the barrel floated. It can reveal whether a new rifle shoots like a dream or needs a little tuneup. It can even indicate how productive tuneup work is.

While a benchrest or shooting table offers the answers in all these situations, it doesn't ensure that you will receive all the accuracy of your rifle and load. Even a benchrest used haphazardly is better than any other shooting position, but you'll really know what your gun and load are doing if you bring proven techniques to a benchrest.

It wasn't until I got seriously involved in benchrest competition that I learned how to use a shooting table and "sandbags." The benchrest boys have refined the use of this equipment to the nth degree. In order to consistently shoot five-shot groups that aren't much larger than a single bullet hole, they've had to. Since competition benchrest rifles are so accurate, a shooter *knows* if he holds the rifle incorrectly or errs in trigger squeeze.

The key words in benchrest shooting are solidity and uniformity. The benchrest and rifle rests must be solid and the shooting technique uniform, shot after shot. The top of a solid shooting table should be about 34 inches above the ground. A shooting stool should be high enough to allow the shooter to sit chest high to the tabletop when his back is straight; this arrangement will also allow him to put his feet comfortably flat on the ground with his thighs parallel with the ground.

Besides the shooting table, two rests, front and rear, are needed to support the rifle. The front rest or pedestal should be solid and adjustable for forend height. It should also conform to the curvature of the rifle's forend, allowing the rifle to track fore and aft during recoil without sideways play. Making an adjustable pedestal would be one approach. You can also make do with two or three sandbags. Just make sure that the forend support is stable and that the stack of bags is secure.

The best rear bag is a "rabbit ear" type, which consists of a base bag about 4x6 inches square and 2½ inches thick (filled with sand). Two upright "ears," also filled with sand, are attached to the base and designed for the stock to track between them. A simple sandbag at the rear will suffice, but it should be high enough to prevent the toe of the buttstock from contacting the benchrest during recoil.

To check the height of the two bags, first make sure your rifle is unloaded, with the bolt or action open. Then, with the rifle resting in the bags, look through the scope. When the rifle is rested solidly in the bags, you should be able to align the crosshair just above the aiming point. If not, adjust the height of the front rest. You can adjust horizontal crosshair alignment some by sliding the rear bag fore or aft to lower or raise the buttstock.

If there's a sling on the rifle, take it off to get it out of the way and adjust the rests so the swivel studs don't dig into the bags. A competition benchrest shooter generally positions his front rest far forward to gain distance between rests for gun stability. Benchrest rifle actions are bedded very well in their stocks and the barrels are generally floated. Your sporter isn't bedded as well and may shoot better with the front rest under the recoil lug area.

Once the rests are positioned, slide the rifle back and forth in the bags with a firm downward pressure to conform the bags to the curvature of the stock. The rifle should track fore and aft very smoothly. Benchrest shooters use talcum powder or Teflon tape to reduce gun/bag friction and allow the rifle to recoil smoothly. A benchrest rifle that catches the bags during recoil has a tendency to throw fliers. A sporting rifle may have forend checkering that drags on the front bag or a rear swivel stud may be positioned so you can't avoid the bag with it. Just do the best you can.

Make sure you have the proper hearing protection and shooting glasses. Be sure to observe the range rules. Always keep the muzzle pointed downrange with the action open when you're not shooting. Cease fire, open the action, and step back from the bench if anyone is going downrange. When you're ready to shoot, position the stool so that you sit comfortably with the rifle shouldered.

The trigger on a benchrest rifle is very light and crisp. Pull weight is measured in single-digit ounces rather than pounds, so it's easy to squeeze off a shot with a very light grip on the rifle. Most benchrest shooters prefer almost no body contact with the rifle. There's little or no cheek contact with the rifle, the shoulder is there only to meet the rifle when it comes back, the left hand (assuming a right-handed shooter) is on the rear bag, and there's just enough grip with the right hand to get the trigger squeezed. Some benchrest competitors fire the rifle by placing the index finger on the trigger and the thumb on the rear of the trigger guard and then squeezing the two together. With less body contact, there is less chance that a shot will go where it shouldn't.

With sporting rifles, the light-touch technique is good only for a heavy-barreled varmint rifle chambered for a light-recoiling caliber. Don't try it with anything that kicks much. The rifle may jump off the front rest, and you could get a scope cut on your brow.

As you look through the scope, the crosshair should be aligned just above the aiming point, as mentioned earlier. Squeeze the rear bag to raise the buttstock and lower the crosshair onto the target. In benchrest shooting, the rifle is aimed entirely with left-hand bag squeeze (assuming a right-handed shooter). The crosshair should then hold on the aiming point without moving as you squeeze the trigger with the index finger of the opposite hand.

When the gun fires, it should recoil straight back and the crosshair straight up. After the shot, pushing the rifle forward in the bags will align the rifle on target if the rifle is tracking as it should.

If you're shooting a rifle that kicks harder than a 10-pound .243, you're probably going to have to hang onto it a little. The more a rifle kicks, the tighter you'll have to hold it and pull it back into your shoulder. Just remember that consistency of hold becomes very important when you grip the rifle. You need to grip and shoulder the rifle with the same pressure, rest the gun in exactly the same position, and cheek the stock in exactly the same manner for every shot in the group. A change in any of these could cause one of those "unexplained" fliers.

As recoil increases, one's tendency to flinch escalates. Sandbag rests, solid as they are, won't prevent a flinch from throwing a shot out of the group. There are several steps that can be taken to prevent flinching. The obvious solution is to do something about recoil.

If I'm shooting anything that kicks harder than a .22 centerfire, I use a shoulder pad. I strap on a PAST Recoil Shield, which consists of what feels like stiff foam rubber covered with leather. The pad comes with a nylon shoulder harness and fastens with Velcro. Inside this pad, I insert a Recoil Shock Eliminator, another pad made of Akton. The Recoil Shock Eliminator comes in several thicknesses and can be suited to recoil level. The one I use most is a half-inch thick. The best way I can describe this unusual material is to say you can place a half-inch thick pad of it against a brick wall and strike it without hurting your hand. I've never seen anything like it, and it really takes the sting out of recoil. If you don't have one of the commercial pads, you can improvise with a folded towel.

Pads can prevent a bruised shoulder, but they don't prevent the recoil. You can reduce the ft-lbs of recoil by increasing the effective weight of the rifle. The heavier the rifle, the less the recoil, all else being equal.

A bag of sand or shot placed between the gun butt and your shoulder means the rifle has to accelerate the added weight before it kicks you.

This helps, but the length of pull becomes too great and it's difficult to reach the trigger if the bag is too thick. Also, the bag must be repositioned constantly because it shifts during shooting and has a tendency to fall out.

In addition to recoil, noise is a major contributor to a flinch. I wear double hearing protection: inserts in my ear canals and muffs. If I could add a third type, I would do that as well.

Besides having a consistent benchrest technique, you should pay attention to ambient conditions. If you can, do your load work at daybreak, when there's not a breeze to ruffle a feather or drift a bullet. In lieu of that, try to shoot when the wind conditions are exactly the same for each shot. Shoot when the breeze blows a hanging strip of cloth exactly the same each time or when the blowing leaves in the trees sounds exactly the same. It helps to hang wind flags at several points along the range. Watch these and shoot only when the combination of all flags is the same.

If you've shot a lot of different rifles from the benchrest, you've probably noticed that each has idiosyncracies about how it groups with various types of resting positions. Some rifles shoot better with a tight hold; others shoot better with a less firm grip. Rifles with two-piece stocks often shoot better when the front rest is positioned on the frame immediately in front of the trigger guard. Because of such quirks, you will want to check the zero of your rifle by shooting from positions you might use in the field. These quirks generally aren't significant enough to be noticed except from the stability of a benchrest.

Remember, the key to shooting from a benchrest is solidity and uniformity. Do everything the same, time after time, and you'll shoot tight groups—if your gun and load have it in them.

Downrange Bullet Drop

N OT TOO MANY years ago, a wildcatter with a just-developed hotshot cartridge could present shooters with the fat-bodied, sharpshouldered case and quote some astronomical velocity figure the round supposedly churned up. This velocity was generally based on the wildcatter's computations, and naturally, it always sounds more impressive to lean toward the higher velocity figures.

Even rifle and ammunition manufacturers were eager to have the hottest commercial round on the market. Of course, no mention was made of the fact that the loads were fired in a 28-inch-barreled pressure gun, even though all the rifles available had only 20- or 22-inch barrels. And if the round produced only 2740 fps, no shooter wants to be concerned with details, so what's the harm in "rounding it off" to 2800 fps? In short, velocity figures were sometimes a bit optimistic.

This is like getting automobile mileage estimates from the automobile manufacturer—without the benefit of the EPA. Still, all this ballistic information was entered into the advertising literature and was consumed by millions of shooters (sometimes with a grain or two of salt).

There was no convenient way to pin down actual velocities at that time. Then came the widespread availability of inexpensive chronographs.

The average shooter now has a way to determine exactly what velocity a particular brand of ammo produces in a particular rifle.

Loading data is much the same way, though for a different reason. Anyone who has done much handloading and chronographing soon realizes the load and velocity data found in the loading manuals is hardly more than an approximation. The velocity listed with a given load can vary considerably depending on the rifle's barrel length, chamber, bore diameter, land width, the bullet brand, powder lot, primer type, case structure, etc. The shooter doesn't really know what velocity his particular ammunition is producing until he chronographs it.

Bullet drop is another area where the shooter and handloader have traditionally relied on the tables supplied by the manufacturers. It's common to sight-in a rifle at 100 yards, say two inches high at that distance, and then simply refer to the loading manual or drop table supplied by the ammunition manufacturer. This information provides some idea about bullet drop in case game is seen at extreme range. In some cases, the shooter tapes the information to his rifle's buttstock for quick reference in the field if a long shot is needed.

Like many shooters, I've always memorized published drop figures for any hunting load. I've rarely checked actual bullet drop by shooting at various distances. It's a pain in the neck to check a bullet's point of impact in 100- or 50-yard increments all the way out to 400 or 500 yards. But I recently began wondering if a bullet manufacturer might lean toward the "optimistic" side in terms of bullet drop, much like the wildcatter used to do with his cartridges. And there does seem plenty of room for optimism in this area.

For example, nearly all bullet drop tables are developed by the use of a mathematical formula. I won't even attempt to get into all the ballistic mumbo-jumbo. Basically, a numerical figure is applied to a bullet's shape which mathematically describes its ability to overcome air resistance. This information is then fed into a computer (along with a lot of other numbers) to derive a theoretical bullet drop downrange. Since any velocity or distance can be fed into the computer, it isn't all that difficult to quickly get a neat-looking table.

Situations in the real, practical world don't always relate to the theoretical situations the computer comes up with. For these reasons, I decided it would be an interesting project to check bullet drop at a variety of ranges to see how close *actual* drop figures came to those published in the load manuals.

I chose .22-caliber bullets for several reasons. First, .22 bullets are used in hunting situations primarily for varmints. Bullet drop here is more critical than any other aspect of hunting because the target is small and the ranges are long. To make consistent hits at long range, the varmint shooter needs to know as closely as possible how much his bullet will drop. When it comes to bullet drop, the big-game hunter normally has greater room for error than the varmint shooter.

Another reason I decided to go with the .22 bullets is that the test required an accurate shooting rifle, and .22-caliber rifles are the only really accurate rifles I currently have on hand. For instance, it's a bit difficult to determine there are seven inches of bullet drop at 300 yards if the group measures 15 inches.

Tom Houghton, benchrest shooter and owner of H-S Precision in Prescott, Arizona, offered the use of his .22 PPC Heavy Varmint competition rifle in the bullet drop tests. I knew Tom had won a number of benchrest matches with it, so it had to be capable of producing ¼-inch groups at 100 yards.

The .22 PPC cartridge was developed by Dr. Louis Palmisano and Ferris Pindell especially for its accuracy potential in benchrest shooting competition. The cartridge consists of a short, fat case based on the .220 Russian round. It utilizes a Small Rifle primer rather than a Large Rifle type for its reported ability to produce more consistent ignition.

Houghton's rifle carries a 1:15 twist barrel built by Bill Atkinson in the H-S Precision shop.

Dave Hall designed the gun's action especially for benchrest shooting competition. The action has extremely thick walls housing the turnbolt. There is a very small ejection port and no magazine cutout to provide maximum stiffness.

A Remington trigger was modified by Ben Burns of Morenci, Arizona; it releases consistently under three or four ounces of pull.

The riflestock is an H-S Precision Fiberthane stock designed with a wide, flat forend for benchrest competition. It has a mating sandbag in a Wichita pedestal rest. The rear rest I used consisted of the standard rabbit-ear leather bag.

For sighting equipment, the rifle was topped with a 36X Leupold scope with parallax correction in the objective lens.

In addition to this competition gun, I decided to use a rifle similar to what the varmint shooter would carry into the field. The most accurate rifle I have on hand is a Remington Model 700 Varmint Special chambered for the .22-250 Remington cartridge. I fitted one of the Weaver 10X "Varmint-T" scopes onto this rifle with Redfield mounts. This scope also has a parallax-correcting adjustment in the objective lens. This particular rifle is capable of producing 100-yard, five-shot groups measuring less than one inch.

The next step was to assemble a variety of handloads with bullets ranging from the lightweight Speer 40-grain spirepoint to the heavy Speer 70-grain semispitzer. Seven different bullets were tried in the .22-250, and three match bullets were fired in the .22 PPC.

The plan was to sight-in the rifles as closely as possible to hitting point of aim, at 100 yards. Then, with this same sight setting, the rifles would be fired at 200, 300, and 400 yards to determine the amount of bullet drop. I knew from past benchrest shooting experience that the wind has a noticeable effect on bullet drop as well as lateral drift, and I knew that either a headwind or a tailwind could cause a bullet to impact high or low.

In order to keep group size as small as possible and to avoid as much mirage as possible, particularly with the 36X scope, I decided to fire the drop tests at the crack of dawn. The air would be absolutely calm, and there would be no mirage to distort sighting through the optics.

The first step was to find a range. For shooters in some parts of the country, finding a 400-yard range can be difficult, but I'm living in an area where even a 2000-yard range would be no problem. I drove a few miles outside of town and began measuring off the distances and marking them with stakes.

A few days later, I had the benchrest assembled at the firing point in preparation to fire the initial test strings. I wanted to check velocity while doing the drop testing to make certain I applied the proper velocity to a given bullet. The Custom Chronograph Model 900 with the Ambient Light screens made this simultaneous testing possible.

Though the aforementioned shooting equipment is capable of producing excellent accuracy, I was still concerned about the variables that could crop up in the drop testing. I was wondering, for instance, what effect the line of sight above line of bore had on the drop figures. Most of the drop tables list a standard 1.5 inches line of sight above line of bore, which is a close approximation for most scoped rifles. Measuring this on an individual rifle, however, can be difficult.

A second area of discrepancy can result from barrel flip (how the barrel vibrates when the bullet exits the rifle's muzzle). While this factor would be much more apparent with a light or sporter-weight barrel than the heavy-weight barrels I was using, it could still be a factor.

Third, I was wondering if the accuracy produced with my equipment would be good enough to determine bullet drop at the various distances. I also wondered how difficult establishing a dead-on 100-yard bullet impact point would be. Even though bullet impact might be off just a quarter or one-half inch at that distance, there could be a considerable difference downrange. In fact, I found this was one of the biggest problems in the testing.

.22-250 BULLET DROP/VELOCITY TABLE

Bullet	Powder (Type)	Weight (Grs.)	Actual Chronographed Velocity (fps)	Actual Drop In Inches (100-yard zero) 200 Yards	300 Yards	400 Yards
40-gr. Speer spirepoint	W748	38.0	4001	-2	-9	-23
45-gr. Sierra H.V. spitzer	W748	38.0	3952	-¼	-7½	-16½
50-gr. Hornady spirepoint	IMR-3031	35.0	3749	0	-6	-17
55-gr. Nosler Solidbase	H4895	34.0	3639	-½	-3½	-13
60-gr. Hornady HP	H414	38.0	3402	-1	-6½	-18
60-gr. Nosler Solidbase	H414	38.0	3420	-3¼	-9	-24
70-gr. Speer semispitzer	H414	37.0	3283	-2¼	-9	-26

.22 PPC BULLET DROP TABLE

Bullet	Powder (Type)	Weight (Grs.)	Actual Chronographed Velocity (fps)	Actual Drop In Inches (100-yard zero) 200 Yards	300 Yards	400 Yards
52-gr. Sierra HPBT Benchrest	H322	26.0	3343	-1¼	-9	-23
52-gr. Speer Gold Match	H322	26.0	3204	-2¾	-12¼	-31
53-gr. Hornady HP (Match)	H322	26.0	3232	-2	-9	-23

NOTES: R-P cases and Remington No. 9½ primers were used in the .22-250 shooting; Sako cases and and Remington No. 7½ primers were used in the .22 PPC shooting. Velocities are an average of 10 shots at 10 feet from gun's muzzle.

The shooting results are summarized in the accompanying table. I was amazed at how close my actual drop tests came to the figures listed in the ballistics tables. For example, the 52-grain Speer Gold Match bullet fired from the .22 PPC rifle at 3204 fps impacted 31 inches low at 400 yards. The Speer manual suggested this bullet at 3200 fps should impact 31.1 inches low at 400 yards. At 300 yards, I was 13¾ inches low while the Speer manual suggested 12.6 inches. There was a bit more discrepancy at 200 yards. While I received 2¾ inches drop, the Speer manual showed 3.1 inches.

Though some of the drop testing is not this precise, all of it is surprisingly close. Due to the practical shooting problems mentioned earlier, I believe the slight discrepancies were the result of my technique.

The greatest discrepancy at 400 yards, for instance, was 5.9 inches. It occurred with the 60-grain Hornady hollowpoint bullet at 3402 fps. The actual drop was 18 inches, while the Hornady manual suggested 23.9 inches of drop at this distance. I suspect my initial sighting-in might have been erroneous, for I only received one inch of drop at 200 yards, while the tables listed 2.4 inch drop. My bullets were 6½ inches low at 300 yards, while the manual listed 9.8 inches.

Even though the drop I received was less than the drop listed in the manual, it was consistently less at *all* distances downrange. A very slight point of impact error at 100 yards can make a big difference downrange, and this would explain the discrepancy.

Of course, it's always better to test your particular rifle/scope/cartridge combination by actual shooting tests after it's sighted-in to determine drop. But as long as you know the velocity your particular combination is turning up, you can rely on the published tables.

My shooting seems to indicate that the computer-derived drop figure is the least likely alibi for missing that chuck.

Accuracy Isn't Everything

A FEW YEARS AGO, I met an old acquaintance at the range. He had come out to work up a load for a .308 bolt-action rifle he intended to use for elk and had a variety of different types of ammunition loaded with different bullets and powders. All were carefully labeled. He had come to the range in order to determine, by shooting, which would be the best. I talked with him briefly and saw that most of the test loads carried bullets weighing 180 grains.

As he began his testing, I continued my shooting down the firing line. After a couple of hours, I checked to see if he had discovered anything about his rifle's preference in elk ammo.

"Did you find any good loads?" I asked.

"I've got it narrowed down to these two, and the next series of groups will decide which one I'll take."

I looked at his load data labels and saw that one was a spitzer and one was a roundnose. I'm familiar with .308 loads, and the roundnose load appeared to be a mild one. I decided to stay and see how everything turned out.

He fired the 180-grain spitzer load first. The initial five shots clustered into a nicely rounded group which measured 1.6 inches. The next two groups measured 1.7 and 1.4 inches.

He cleaned the rifle and changed targets while the barrel cooled. The roundnose loads were next. The first group measured a scant .8 inch, a beautiful cluster. The next five shots went 1.4, and the final group measured 1.2 inches. The average for the spitzer load was only 1.6 inches; the roundnose averaged 1.1 inches.

"I guess that decides it," he said, eyeing the targets from both loads. "The 180-grain roundnose is it."

"You've got a few loads left. Let's try running them over my chronograph screens," I suggested.

He was delighted to be able to chronograph his ammo, and we soon found his chosen load was a mild one, turning up only 2267 fps at 10 feet from the muzzle. The spitzer load averaged a healthy 2558 fps. But the velocity figures didn't make the same impression on my friend the accuracy results did. He thought the roundnose bullet was still the best choice.

If I'd been the one judging those elk loads, there would have been no contest. My selection would have been the spitzer.

For many years, shooters, riflemen and handgunners alike, have sought the highest level of accuracy. It has long been the primary—if not the only—criterion for judging a load's worth. Accuracy is something easily seen and measured by anyone. No special equipment is necessary. But I think the importance of accuracy has been emphasized—and over-emphasized—for so long that it is ingrained in many shooters beyond reason. They don't even feel confident about their loads and shooting equipment unless the level of accuracy delivered is what they think is the best.

All this is admirable, to an extent. Yet it seems the importance of velocity and energy is often lost in the quest for accuracy. When it comes to group sizes, there is no such thing as too much accuracy. More is always better. However, it can be beneficial to evaluate what sort of accuracy is really necessary for the task at hand. How much accuracy can you really use?

Shooting from a benchrest at the range in no way compares to the type of shots presented in the field. Most of the big game I've encountered at any distance has been taken with the aid of some natural rest. A rock or a tree has helped me bag many head of game. I'll often use a sitting position in open country; on rare occasions, the vegetation is such that I can use a prone position. On shots I've taken up close, say 50 yards and less, offhand is probably the preferred position simply because there usually isn't time to look around for a rest at such close range— the game is either alerted or already trying to make a fast getaway. Of all the positions I've mentioned, the prone position is the most accurate of the unaided shooting positions. The amount of steadiness gained by leaning against a tree or a rock depends on the shape and position of the object used.

In any event, it's unlikely that I'll be able to hold even two inches of accuracy under field conditions on the average, even in the better situations. For offhand shots or other shots taken in a hurry, I wouldn't even be able to hold three inches of accuracy in the field at 100 yards.

Without detracting from the significance of accuracy, we may benefit from putting it into perspective and by examining some of the other variables involved in hunting with either a handgun or rifle.

I've often heard it said that high velocity or energy does no good if you can't hit what you're aiming at. Most shooters include the ability to hit what they're shooting at in the definition of accuracy. As a practical matter, however, the accuracy of a good many loads is easily up to hitting what we're shooting at. With today's excellent ammo, components, load data, and firearms, hunting accuracy for most species of big game is not at all difficult to achieve. The shooter really has a lot more to do with hitting game than the load does.

Given that several loads are accurate enough for the task at hand, let's examine two other factors which should be considered in the making of a good hunting load: velocity and energy.

Higher velocity makes for a flatter trajectory. A flatter trajectory means range estimation becomes less critical. If you misjudge the range and the quarry is farther than anticipated, you're more likely to make a good hit rather than missing or wounding. From this standpoint, high velocity is an aid to accurate, effective shooting in the field since it improves your ability to hit what you're shooting at.

Higher velocity also means reduced wind drift. Since the time of flight is shorter, there's less time for wind to act on the bullet. There's also less opportunity for the quarry to move between the time the trigger is squeezed and when the bullet arrives.

These factors are seldom realized while shooting groups because most shooters fire at relatively short distances (and fixed targets) when they're checking accuracy. The advantage in wind drift and drop are apparent only on long shots, but that's also where a higher level of "accuracy" is often needed.

While these advantages are directly related to velocity, other advantages are intertwined with both velocity and energy. The two are interrelated since the higher the velocity, the higher the energy. A higher velocity and energy means a bullet will hit harder and transmit more shock to the game. And shock is a major factor that contributes to anchoring game in its tracks.

When a bullet is going faster when it hits, there's also a greater assurance of adequate bullet expansion. This becomes very important at long ranges with rifle cartridges and at any range with handgun cartridges. It is easily possible for the velocity and energy to be so low that there is little or no bullet expansion, resulting in decreased shock, energy, and tissue destruction transmitted to the game (i.e. killing power). With equal bullet expansion, higher velocity means deeper penetration—all else being equal. Deeper penetration can make the difference between a bullet reaching or not reaching the vitals. It can mean the difference between an exit wound which produces a good blood trail and no exit wound and almost no blood trail.

A higher muzzle velocity means a higher bullet rotational velocity, another type of kinetic energy. A bullet which exits a muzzle at 3000 fps from a 1:12-twist barrel, for example, is rotating at 180,000 revolutions per minute (rpm). A bullet which exits the same barrel at 2000 fps is rotating at the rate of 120,000 rpm—or with a third less kinetic energy due strictly to rotation. Few shooters even consider rotational velocity,

IMPORTANCE OF MUZZLE VELOCITY WITH A GIVEN BULLET
(HORNADY 180-GRAIN SPIREPOINT, .431 BALLISTIC COEFFICIENT)

Muzzle Velocity	Muzzle Energy (ft-lbs)	Wind Drift: 10-mph Crosswind (Inches)				Drop From Line Of Bore (Inches)				Retained Velocity (fps)				Retained Energy (ft-lbs)				Time of Flight (Seconds)			
		100	200	300	350	100	200	300	350	100	200	300	350	100	200	300	350	100	200	300	350
2100 fps (.30-30 Win.)	1763	1.1	5.0	12.0	16.8	4.2	17.8	42.6	60.0	1920	1758	1610	1540	1473	1235	1036	948	.150	.313	.492	5.87
2300 fps (.300 Savage)	2114	1.0	4.4	10.7	15.1	3.5	14.8	35.4	49.8	2108	1921	1768	1690	1776	1492	1249	1141	.136	.285	.448	.534
2500 fps (.308 Win.)	2498	.9	3.9	9.6	13.6	3.0	12.5	29.8	41.9	2298	2109	1931	1846	2111	1778	1490	1362	.125	.262	.410	.490
2700 fps (.30-06)	2914	.8	3.5	8.6	12.2	2.5	10.7	25.5	35.7	2489	2289	2097	2006	2476	2094	1758	1608	.116	.242	.379	.492
2900 fps (.300 H&H Mag.)	3362	.7	3.2	7.7	11.0	2.2	9.2	22.0	30.8	2680	2470	2267	2170	2871	2439	2054	1882	.108	.224	.351	.419
3100 fps (.300 Wby. Mag.)	3842	.6	2.8	7.0	9.9	1.9	8.0	19.1	26.8	1872	2653	2440	2337	3297	2813	2380	2183	.101	.209	.327	.390

IMPORTANCE OF BULLET SHAPE AT A GIVEN VELOCITY
(180-GRAIN .30 CALIBER AT 2700 FPS MUZZLE VELOCITY AND 2914 FT-LBS OF MUZZLE ENERGY)

Bullet Type	Wind Drift: 10 mph Crosswind (Inches)				Drop From Line of Bore (Inches)				Retained Velocity (fps)				Retained Energy (ft-lbs)				Time of Flight (Seconds)			
	100	200	300	350	100	200	300	350	100	200	300	350	100	200	300	250	100	200	300	350
Hornady 180-grain roundnose .239 ballistic coefficient	1.6	7.2	18.6	26.9	2.6	11.7	29.8	43.2	2327	2987	1688	1556	2164	1578	1139	967	.120	.259	.423	.516
Speer 180-gr. spitzer flatbase .500 ballistic coefficient	.7	3.0	7.2	10.1	2.5	10.5	24.8	34.7	2517	2343	2175	2094	2532	2194	1891	1753	.115	.239	.372	.443
Speer 180-gr. spitzer boattail .540 ballistic coefficient	.6	2.7	6.5	9.2	2.5	10.4	24.5	34.2	2530	2369	2212	2136	2559	2243	1956	1824	.115	.238	.369	.438

which is separate from linear velocity. Rotational kinetic energy is not only an additional amount transmitted to the target, it's likely a factor in aiding bullet expansion due to the increased centrifugal force and stability imparted by the spin.

All my friend considered in load selection was 100-yard group sizes. If he had considered the velocity and ballistic coefficient difference between the two loads, it might have made a difference in his choice. The differences? His slow load (2267 fps) was topped off with a Hornady 180-grain roundnose, which has a reported ballistic coefficient of .239. The spitzer was a Speer bullet; it clocked 2558 and has a .500 ballistic coefficient.

The slow "accurate" load would arrive at the 300-yard mark with only 1403 fps of velocity remaining, which may very well not be enough speed to promote adequate bullet expansion. The energy remaining at that distance is a puny 786 ft-lbs. By comparison, the fast load arrives at the 300-yard mark with 2053 fps of velocity and 1685 ft-lbs of energy. Those velocity and energy figures are mighty significant when the game is elk.

So what about the guy who says velocity and energy are no good if you can't hit what you're shooting at? Let's examine my friend's loads a little closer. Elk rifles are often sighted-in three inches high at 100 yards. Suppose both loads were sighted-in in that manner. The slow load would be shooting dead-on at 180 yards; the fast load would be on point of aim at a little over 220 yards. At 250 yards, the fast load is 1.9 inches low, and the slow load is 8.9 inches low; at 300 yards, the fast load is 7.2 inches below the line of sight, and the slow load is 19.8 inches below the line of sight.

Isn't it ironic that my friend, who decided his load based upon a half-inch accuracy advantage, is now *disadvantaged* to the tune of *12.6 inches* at 300 yards—just because of his choice in loads. Three hundred yards is still within the realm of a possible shot for many elk hunters.

With such examples, it becomes abundantly clear that accuracy is not the only important factor. In fact, higher velocity actually *aids* one's ability to hit what he's shooting at. While 100-yard group sizes should be within reason, there are other considerations in a hunting load which are perhaps more important.

It's no secret that higher energy and velocity are usually achieved with additional recoil and muzzle blast. Again, this is another factor which needs to be kept in perspective. There are a lot of variables to felt recoil besides the speed of the bullet. The amount of powder used, the shape of the rifle's stock, the type of buttpad, and whether the rifle has a muzzle brake are all factors that bear more significance regarding felt recoil than 200 or 300 fps in bullet velocity.

While we have used rifles as examples on several occasions, everything regarding velocity and energy said about rifles holds true for handgun hunting cartridges and loads as well. In fact, handgun velocities are so low, in many instances, that adequate velocity and energy are even more critical. Velocities are often critical regarding bullet expansion with handgun cartridges. Like velocity, energy is sometimes marginal, and so these two factors bear even greater importance.

Don't throw accuracy out the window—but don't overlook other important factors in your quest for the best load.

How Hunters Can Track Trajectories

I T WAS AN exceptional rack by anyone's standards. Ron, my hunting partner, figured the deer was too far away, but this was the last day of the season, and from the lack of deer where we were hunting, it was unlikely I would get another shot.

I was trying to figure out how to get closer as we watched the buck through binoculars. The deer was bedded down under a juniper bush and didn't know he was being watched. Owing to the surrounding terrain, however, all we had to do was raise up, and he would be hightailing it over the far hill. There was no cover around the big deer, and he had a good vantage point.

"How far do you think he is?" I asked as I pulled off my gloves, stacked them on a rock, and laid my rifle on top of them.

"You need the kind of gun that comes on wheels," Ron said with a grin.

I didn't know how far away the deer was. I did know a bedded deer looks smaller and seems farther away than he actually is. But I also have a tendency to underestimate range.

Just then, the deer stood up broadside. He was far away, but my rest was as good as a benchrest, and I found I could keep the crosshairs on him. I wanted to hold over the deer but fought the urge, held high on the body, and squeezed the trigger on the .300 Winchester Magnum. The deer bolted—but his reaction was too late. He was dead inside 50 yards with a bullet through the heart.

Ron thought it was a great shot. It might have been an exceptional shot had I not had the rest that I did or had I sighted-in with the traditional 100-yard zero. With my rifle zeroed at 270 yards (2½ inches high at 100), I was confident of a hit in the vitals; the heart shot was luck. Under the circumstances, taking the shot was reasonable.

There are many facts to consider before a long-range shot becomes a reasonable proposition. A hunter needs a flat-shooting caliber that has plenty of downrange punch to produce proper bullet expansion and penetration for a clean kill. The rifle must have the accuracy, and the sighting equipment must be adequate for the shot in question. A shooter needs to be familiar with the trajectory of his rifle and know how to use it. If a shooter sights-in his rifle to make optimum use of the trajectory, he can forget about range estimation up to 350 yards or so.

The term "trajectory" is burdensome to spell, onerous to pronounce, and downright difficult to understand. One thing to remember is that if a rifle barrel is held horizontal to the ground, any bullet fired from it starts dropping the moment it leaves the muzzle. Unlike the bullet, which drops, your line of sight is straight. If the sights were adjusted to make line of sight parallel with the bore, a bullet fired from the barrel would never cross the line of sight. The farther the bullet traveled, the farther it would be from the line of sight.

To make a sighting arrangement more practical, simply tip the barrel up toward the line of sight. Actually, adjust the sights to make yourself tip the barrel up. This way, the bullet travels upward slightly to cross the line of sight when it is "rising" and then crosses the line of sight again when it's "falling." We can tip the barrel up as far as we want to make a bullet hit wherever we want. Thousand-yard shooters do this all the time. But what works on targets doesn't work for hunting. Since we never know what distance we'll be shooting in a hunting situation, we can't forget about the shorter distances.

The peak of the arc the bullet travels along (in relation to line of sight) is an important aspect to consider when it comes to sighting-in a hunting rifle. The peak of the arc should not be too far above the line of sight. If you're shooting a big animal, it's allowable to have the peak of the arc farther above the line of sight than if you're shooting at a small animal. If the bullet rises too much from line of sight, and if the animal is standing at the distance where the bullet's arc is at its peak, you could overshoot.

For a varmint rifle, I like the peak of the arc to be no more than 1.5 inches above the line of sight. For a big-game animal, I like it to be no more than three inches above the line of sight. A hit three inches above the line of sight is usually of no consequence on a deer, but it could cause a complete miss on a standing prairie dog. By the same token, the distance at which the bullet drops to 1.5 or three inches *below* the line of sight is what we'll consider to be "point-blank range" for the purpose of this story. In more conventional terms, it's the maximum distance at which you can hit a big-game animal's vitals with a center hold, without overshooting at shorter distances. If you can put up with a four- or five-inch bullet departure from sight line, as some hunters do for elk, then you'll have a longer point-blank range.

Again, I stay with plus or minus three inches for a deer or antelope rifle. It is true that one of these animal's vitals is larger than six inches in diameter, but I don't think it's a good idea to stretch things to the outside limit. What if your rifle's muzzle rises slightly just as you fire or drops slightly? What if you have to place the bullet between two horizontal tree limbs before it reaches game? With the right cartridge, plus or minus three inches allows for an easy hit on a big-game animal as far away as anyone should be shooting at it.

I performed an experiment on life-size game targets, placing them at various distances and shooting them with various calibers. I discovered a few things I had been doing in the field without realizing it. For one, whenever a big-game animal appears to be on the near side of the 200-yard mark, I hold low in the chest. If the animal is around 200 or a little farther, I take a center-of-chest hold. And if the animal is really far away, I hold high on the chest—but never over. That's all anyone ever needs to know about trajectory for shooting big game at long range. As long as you have a flat-shooting cartridge and it's sighted-in as mentioned, you'll kill game with consistency.

I learned never to hold over the hard way—and had the experience repeated several times before it stuck. I found that, almost without exception, whenever I held over, I shot over the game. If you can't hold the crosshairs or sights on a big-game animal long enough to get a shot off, you shouldn't shoot. Try standing a life-size deer target at a distance where it's necessary to hold over to hit and see if you can hold on its vital area from any shooting position that can be assumed in a hunting situation. The animal will also appear to be too far away to be shooting at it.

There are those hunters who consider a 400-yard shot to be reasonable, but let's look at how impractical it really is. The Winchester 180-grain Silvertip fired from my .30-06 is 14.9 inches below the line of sight at 350 yards, even when it's sighted-in 2.8 inches high at 100. At 400, it's 24.8 inches low; at 450, it's 37.3 inches low. Out at 500 yards, it's 52.8 inches below the line of sight. At these distances, you've got to be able to judge range within 50 yards or less to make a hit. That's impractical to say the least.

I once asked a group of shooters how far away an object was over level ground. Estimates ranged from 175 to 450 yards. The object proved to be 320 paces away. Those wide-ranging estimates are not unusual for the average hunter. You can apply all the "football field increments" you want, but as distances become greater, an accurate range estimate becomes more difficult. The problem is, when range estimation errors become larger, the accuracy of their estimation becomes more critical. Add broken terrain or a canyon between the shooter and the target, and range estimation is usually even worse.

Besides the problems encountered with bullet drop, there's also wind drift. The Winchester 180-grain bullet would drift 19.6 inches in a 10-mph crosswind at 400 yards. There is usually some wind in big-game country, and a 10-mph gust variation is common. Besides this, the wind drift changes dramatically with the distance. The bullet drifts nearly twice as much at 400 yards as it does at 300. Remember, you can't normally judge range that accurately.

Terminal energy is still ample at 400 yards with the .30-06 for deer; it has 1315 ft-lbs remaining. However, the 400-yard velocity of 1814 fps does not necessarily promote adequate bullet expansion. It depends on the bullet. One major bullet manufacturer told me he wouldn't expect his .30-caliber big-game bullets to expand all the time at less than 2000 fps. A poor hit at close range often does enough damage to slow down an animal for a finishing shot, but a poor hit at long range (which is more likely) often does not inflict extensive damage. To compound the problem, many shooters who try a long shot across rugged country or up a steep slope are reluctant to go see if there is evidence of a hit. Just because the game took off at the shot and disappeared in the brush doesn't mean there wasn't a solid hit. The bullet may not expand much, and a fatal hit may not be a quick kill at that distance. No matter how large the canyon is, no matter how steep the mountain, if you risk a shot, you owe it to the game and other hunters to go up and look for signs of a hit. If you're not willing to do that, don't shoot.

I have a nephew who is a guide in Wyoming. He once put four 150-grain .270 bullets through an elk's chest at long range. The elk did not move or show any sign of being hit until several seconds after the fourth shot. The elk finally toppled. All four entry holes, low in the chest, could be covered with the palm of a hand. Normally, an elk would have run after the first hit, even though it is fatal. The low-velocity (at that distance) bullets just punched through. Again, a 300-yard shot is a long one, but when a flat-shooting cartridge is properly sighted-in, it becomes a reasonable one—under the right conditions.

I've decided that a three-inch maximum bullet departure from line of sight is correct. It's easy enough to sight-in three inches high at 100 yards, but this doesn't necessarily mean that's where peak trajectory occurs. In fact, it usually occurs beyond the 100-yard mark. How do you determine how high to sight-in the rifle at 100 yards or zero at some other distance to obtain the three-inch maximum bullet departure from line of sight?

The way you sight-in a rifle to achieve this varies, depending on the cartridge, the weight and shape of the bullet, and its speed. If a bullet has a flat nose or a blunt round nose, it's going to slow down faster due to air resistance. Since it slows down faster, it drops more over a given distance than a more streamlined bullet. A bullet's ability to overcome the resistance of air is mathematically described by a number called "ballistic coefficient" (BC). The more streamlined the bullet, the higher the BC.

The BC for handloaded bullets can be determined by looking at the data in manuals from bullet manufacturers. Ballistic coefficients for factory loads can be derived from "Extended Ballistics for the Advanced Rifleman," which is available from Pachmayr Inc.

If you know the BC of the bullet you're shooting and the muzzle speed your load produces (most accurately determined by chronographing it or determined approximately by examining data tables), you can determine your bullet's drop at various distances by looking at data tables or by mathematic computations. I use a computer program called "Load From A Disk" to determine trajectory. The program is available for Apple, IBM, Commodore, and CP/M computers.

You can also use the drop tables supplied by ammunition manufacturers, but I consider this source to be the least desirable. Muzzle velocity figures from the ammo companies are traditionally optimistic when compared to the velocity received in hunting rifles. Consequently, their downrange figures are optimistic.

Contrary to factory ammo ballistic figures, I've found the data in the loading manuals is close to the mark as long as you know the true velocity being produced by your firearm and load and the true BC for the bullet you're using. For those who are skeptical about the accuracy of ballistics tables in load manuals, I've spent a lot of time with competition benchrest rifles in an effort to determine how accurate the published drop tables (in handloading manuals) are. In my experience, they are more accurate than most shooters can sight-in and shoot, even from a benchrest situation.

Let's look at the trajectory (curve) of a Winchester 180-grain Silvertip bullet fired from a .30-06. This bullet chronographs 2674 fps from the muzzle of my Thompson/Center rifle. This figure is derived by chronographing the load at 10 feet (2659) and then computing muzzle velocity, based on the BC of the bullet. The BC of the bullet is listed at .383.

The bullet drops 26.6 inches from line of bore over 300 yards. By allowing a plus-or-minus three inches bullet path sighting arrangement, however, the bullet will cross the line of sight on its way up at just under 24 yards. It will be one inch above the line of sight at 43 yards, 2.8 inches high at 100 yards, three inches high (or at the peak of its arc) at 123 to 129 yards, 2.8 inches high at 150 yards, and will cross the line of sight on the way down at 222 yards. The bullet won't be three inches below the line of sight until it reaches 260 yards; at 300 yards, it is only 7.4 inches low. Compare this with an often-used 100-yard zero. The bullet is below the line of sight until it reaches 56 yards, where it crosses. It's dead-on at 100 yards and three inches low at 180 yards; at 300 yards, it is 15.8 inches low.

In addition to comparing drop table results with actual shooting results on conventional targets out to 400 yards, I used life-size deer and fox targets to make point-of-impact comparisons with a variety of calibers in both the varmint and big-game classes. Although the fox was close to standard size, the deer target I used represents a very small deer with a 12-inch back-to-bottom-of-chest measurement. My current shooting again indicates the computer-derived drop figures are close to that realized in the field—closer than one can hold as a practical matter.

Published drop tables are very complete nowadays. But if perusing long columns of drop figures isn't your idea of a relaxing Saturday afternoon, there is an alternative. As a rule of thumb for a flat-shooting big-game rifle, sight-in 2.5 to three inches high at 100 yards and you'll come pretty close to making the best use of the rifle's trajectory. For a flat-shooting varmint rifle, sight-in one to 1.5 inches high at 100 yards.

After you've done that, set targets up at 150, 200, 250, 300, and 350 yards and fire groups to see where your bullets hit at various distances. This is an excellent idea, even if you've derived precise downrange figures. The actual shooting not only tells you how much the bullets drop from line of sight, it also illustrates how large your groups become at various distances. Try it from the same shooting positions you use in the field. It'll make you more aware of your capabilities, and you'll become a better shot because of it.

So far, I've discussed only flat-shooting big-game rifles. What about those that aren't so flat, like the .30-30 Winchester or .444 Marlin? I've included tables on a variety of cartridges, including these latter two, which illustrate that the 2½ to three inches high at 100 yards sighting-in isn't a bad idea with even these rounds. The difference is that the point-blank range is much shorter. However, considering that this type of cartridge is generally selected for use in a heavy cover situation where a shot as long as 150 yards would be unusual, I think I would opt for a 100-yard zero or close to it rather than the high-at-100 rule of thumb. These are short-range cartridges anyway, having neither a flat trajectory nor high energy at long distances. When you're hunting in thick brush country, it helps to have the bullet impacting close to the line of sight so that you can slip a bullet between sticks a little easier if you have to. It's also satisfying to be able to put a bullet *exactly* where you want it without needing to think about trajectory.

Some of the statements about shooting big game don't hold up when it comes to varmint shooting. Since the maximum allowable bullet departure from line of sight is much smaller, the point-blank range may be shorter, depending on the cartridge. It's also generally acceptable to shoot varmints at extreme ranges. Unlike a big-game animal that can escape wounded with a hit that's not in the vitals, a hit anywhere in the torso of a varmint results in a quick kill with most varmint loads. This means that a hunter's attitude about a "reasonable" shot is not the same

Downrange Load Performance Comparison

Cartridge/Loading	Muzzle Velocity (fps)	Muzzle Energy (ft-lbs)	Published Ballistic Coefficient	300-Yard Velocity (fps)	300-Yard Energy (ft-lbs)	300-Yard Bullet Drop (from line of bore)	300-Yard Wind Drift (10-mph crosswind)
.222 Rem. (Norma 53-gr. SP)	2968	1037	.218	1793	378	25.2	18.4
.223 Rem. (Hornady 55-gr. SP)	3216	1263	.220	1979	478	21.1	16.1
.22-250 Rem. (Federal 55-gr. SPBT)	3629	1608	.275	2527	780	15.2	9.8
.22-6mm CG (Nosler 55-gr. SB)	3924	1880	.282	2797	995	12.7	8.3
6mm Rem. (Rem. 80-gr. P-LHP)	3239	1864	.255	2143	816	19.8	13.0
6mm Rem. (Rem. 100-gr. SPC-L)	3045	2059	.355	2263	1137	20.6	9.2
7mm Rem. Mag. (Hornady 139-gr. SPBT)	2954	2694	.425	2305	1640	21.2	7.7
.308 Win. (Norma 180-gr. PPC)	2573	2646	.450	2015	1623	27.9	8.7
.30-06 (Win. 180-gr. Silvertip)	2674	2858	.383	2007	1610	26.6	10.1
.300 Win. Mag. (Rem. 180-gr. C-L)	3058	3738	.437	2412	2325	19.6	7.0
.356 Win. (Win. 200-gr. Power-Point)	2355	2463	.238	1456	941	39.8	22.3
.444 Marlin (Rem. 240-gr. SP)	2256	2713	.146	1037	573	56.0	46.5

Trajectory With Optimal Sighting-In

Cartridge/Loading	Muzzle Velocity (fps)	Published Ballistic Coefficient	Muzzle Energy (ft-lbs)	Optimum Sighting-In Distance (Yards)	Maximum Point-Blank Range* (Yards)	50 Yards	100 Yards	150 Yards	200 Yards	250 Yards	300 Yards	350 Yards
Varmint Loads (plus or minus 1.5 inches)												
.222 Rem. (Norma 53-gr. SP)	2968	.218	1037	180	207	+ .6	+1.5	+1.0	-1.0	-5.0	-11.2	-20.2
.223 Rem. (Hornady 55-gr. SP)	3216	.220	1263	194	223	+ .4	+1.4	+1.3	- .3	-3.4	-8.3	-15.5
.22-250 Rem. (Fed. 55-gr. SPBT)	3629	.275	1608	224	258	+ .3	+1.3	+1.5	+ .7	-1.1	-4.1	-8.4
.22-6mm CJ (Nosler 55-gr. SB)	3924	.282	1880	242	279	+ .2	+1.2	+1.5	+1.1	- .3	-2.6	-6.0
6mm Rem. (Rem. 80-gr. P-LHP)	3239	.255	1864	199	229	+ .4	+1.4	+1.3	0	-2.8	-7.2	-13.5
Big-Game Loads (plus or minus three inches)												
6mm Rem. (Rem. 100-gr. SPC-L)	3045	.355	2059	248	289	+1.1	+2.6	+3.0	+2.1	- .1	-3.9	-9.4
7mm Rem. Mag. (Hornady 139-gr. SPBT)	2954	.425	2694	246	288	+1.1	+2.6	+3.0	+2.1	- .2	-4.0	-9.5
.30-30 Win. (Win. 170-gr. Power-Point)	2050	.254	2050	166	194	+1.9	+3.0	+1.2	-3.8	-12.6	-26.0	-44.5
.308 Win. (Norma 180-gr. PPC)	2573	.450	2674	217	254	+1.4	+2.8	+2.7	+1.0	-2.6	-8.1	-15.7
.30-06 (Win. 180-gr. Silvertip)	2674	.383	2858	222	259	+1.3	+2.8	+1.2	+1.2	-2.1	-7.4	-14.9
.300 Win. Mag. (Rem. 180-gr. C-L)	3058	.437	3738	255	298	+1.0	+2.5	+3.0	+2.3	+ .3	-3.1	-8.0
.356 Win. (Win. 200-gr. Power-Point)	2355	.238	2463	186	230	+1.6	+3.0	+2.1	-1.2	-7.6	-17.5	-31.5
.444 Marlin (Rem. 240-gr. SP)	2256	.146	2713	165	190	+1.9	+3.0	+1.2	-4.4	-14.9	-31.8	-56.5

Trajectory With a 100-Yard Zero

Cartridge/Loading	Muzzle Velocity (fps)	Ballistic Coefficient	Maximum Point-Blank Range* (Yards)	50 Yards	100 Yards	150 Yards	200 Yards	250 Yards	300 Yards	350 Yards
Varmint Loads										
.222 Rem. (Norma 53-gr. SP)	2968	.218	157	-.2	0	-1.2	-4.0	-8.7	-15.6	-25.3
.223 Rem. (Hornady 55-gr. SP)	3216	.220	167	-.3	0	-.9	-3.1	-6.9	-12.6	-20.4
.22-250 Rem. (Fed. 55-gr. SPBT)	3629	.275	191	-.4	0	-.4	-1.8	-4.3	-7.9	-12.9
.22-6mm CJ (Nosler 55-gr. Solid Base)	3924	.282	206	-.4	0	-.3	-1.3	3.2	6.1	10.1
6mm Rem. (Rem. 80-gr. P-LHP)	3239	.255	171	-.3	0	-.8	-2.8	-6.3	-11.3	-18.3
Big-Game Loads										
6mm Rem. (Rem. 100-gr. SPC-L)	3045	.355	199	-.2	0	-.9	-3.0	-6.6	-11.6	-18.4
7mm Rem. Mag. (Hornady 139-gr. SPBT)	2954	.425	197	-.2	0	-1.0	-3.2	-6.8	-11.9	-18.6
.30-30 Win. Win. 170-gr. Power-Point	2050	.254	147	+.5	0	-3.2	-9.7	-20.1	-34.9	-54.9
.308 Win. (Norma 180-gr. PPC)	2573	.450	177	-.1	0	-1.5	-4.7	-9.6	-16.5	-25.8
.30-06 (Win. 180-gr. Silvertip)	2674	.383	180	-.3	0	-1.4	-4.4	-9.1	-15.8	-24.7
.300 Win. Mag. (Rem. 180-gr. PSP C-L)	3058	.437	203	-.3	0	-.8	-2.8	-6.1	-10.7	-16.9
.356 Win. (Win. 200-gr. Power-Point)	2355	.238	159	+.2	0	-2.3	-7.1	-15.0	-26.3	-41.8
.444 Marlin (Rem. 240-gr. SP)	2256	.146	147	+.4	0	-3.3	-10.3	-22.4	-40.7	-67.0

*(For varmint loads, a maximum 1.5-inch departure from line of sight is used; for big-game loads, a maximum three-inch bullet departure from line of sight is used.)

Rifles Used For Testing

1. .222 Remington TCR '83, 23-inch barrel
2. .223 Remington, Kimber Model 84, 22½-inch barrel
3. .22-250 Remington, Savage Model 110, 25-inch barrel
4. .22-6mm CJ, Remington Model 700, 24-inch barrel
5. 6mm Remington, Ultra Light Arms Model 20, 22-inch barrel
6. 7mm Remington Magnum, Sako, 24½-inch barrel
7. .30-30 Winchester, Winchester Model 94, 20-inch barrel
8. .308 Winchester, Remington Model 78, 22-inch barrel
9. .30-06 Springfield, TCR '83, 23-inch barrel
10. .300 Winchester Magnum, KDF K-15, 25½-inch barrel
11. .356 Winchester, Marlin Model 336ER, 20-inch barrel
12. .444 Marlin, Marlin Model 444SS, 22-inch barrel

with varmints as it is with big game.

Varmint shooting is a hit-or-miss proposition to tax the skills of the most advanced rifleman. It helps if you can see your bullet impact through the scope on your varmint rifle. A miss can easily be a hit on the next shot if you can see where the first bullet impacts so you can allow for bullet drop and drift.

With a lot of experience shooting in the field, you will eventually know exactly where a bullet will hit at most any distance without having to think about it. One problem is that if you change calibers, the trajectory curve may change also. Another factor is that today's hunter almost never gets enough shooting at big game to really learn much about trajectory. I've found it works great to select varmint and big-game rifles with near-identical trajectory curves (in relation to line of sight), and this isn't difficult to do.

Some of the varmint cartridges are really flat shooting and have point-blank ranges which compare favorably with flat-shooting big-game rifles, even though the varmint rifle sighting requirements are more stringent. For example, the .22-250 loading in the accompanying table is 4.1 inches below the line of sight at 300 yards with the optimum 1.5-inch sighting-in. The .300 Winchester with a 180-grain bullet is 3.1 inches below line of sight—with a three-inch sighting-in. An inch difference at 300 yards isn't much, and my hard-earned bullet drop knowledge, acquired all summer while shooting at hundreds of rockchucks and prairie dogs at all ranges, carries over for big-game hunts during the fall and winter.

The accompanying tables serve only as a guide. There are many variables in downrange performance. Change rifles or brands of ammunition and the muzzle velocity can change. Change bullets and the ballistic coefficient could be different. Different barrels result in different velocities, even with the same loads. To really know what your load is doing in your rifle, you need to chronograph it.

If you're developing a long-range load by handloading, first select sleek bullets (spitzers and boattails) with high ballistic coefficients. Next, load them to produce the highest velocity possible, within reason. Then select a high-velocity loading that produces excellent accuracy.

When you have your load, fit your rifle with a quality scope of ample magnification with good definition and sight-in your rifle to maximize its potential relevant to the game you'll be hunting. With that out of the way, your equipment is up to the task, but you're still a long way from becoming an effective long-range shot. You need to practice from hunting positions, know your limitations, and acquire the ability to pass up shots that you know aren't reasonable.

Don't waste any more time. Take the guesswork out of hunting. Find out right now how your rifle and load perform at various distances.

R-E-C-O-I-L...

A LOT HAS been written about recoil, but the bulk of this information has been contradictory.

There is no questioning the fact that guns which fire cartridges with bigger cases and heavier bullets at higher velocities produce more recoil. Articles on the subject of recoil frequently incorporate graphs and tables which clearly show larger cartridges produce more "kick" with a given rifle. But there's more to the subject of recoil than immediately meets the eye. The shooter in the field doesn't get kicked by a ft-lbs figure pulled from a graph; it's the feel of the gun butt on his shoulder and the blast in his ears that makes the difference.

Writers who specialize in producing technical articles on the subject of shooting and reloading generally fire more ammunition than just about anyone. And these same people are the ones responsible for implanting ideas into the minds of thousands of shooters. If John Q. Hunter owns nothing more powerful than a .30-30 and is contemplating buying a gun chambered in a larger caliber for an elk hunt out West, he will probably base his choice of an elk cartridge on what he has read in the gun magazines.

While he might follow the advice of an experienced friend, I'd say the average hunter generally believes what he reads over all else.

I was once such a believer. If Jack O'Connor or Warren Page said something was true, then it *had* to be true. I finally realized, however, that O'Connor and Page didn't always agree—and other gunwriters didn't have the same viewpoints as either of these two experts. Gunwriters are human, and, as with anything which can't be quantitatively measured, there are going to be differences of opinion. This is simply human nature.

There's one gunwriter I've talked with who probably shoots as much as anyone, if not more than most. He feels nothing larger than a .308 Winchester is really needed for anything up to and including elk. The primary reason the shooter feels this way is due to the recoil of some of the larger cartridges.

At the opposite extreme, I know another gunwriter who also fires a lot of ammo in load testing and development and he maintains that the problems with recoil, developing a flinch, etc., are nothing more than a state of mind. He says good shooting (and avoiding a flinch) is a matter of concentration; by concentrating intensely, a person can successfully shoot even the heavy-kicking rifles.

Shooters who argue that big cartridges have too much recoil usually point to "the tables," which show guns of equal weight produce more kick if the cartridge size (powder weight), bullet weight, and velocity are increased. It's this type of shooter that advocates using something on the order of a .243 Winchester or 6mm Remington for deer, maintaining the .30-06 produces more energy than is needed and more kick than a deer hunter should have to tolerate. I've also noticed this type of hunter usually thinks nothing of firing half a box of duck loads in his 12-gauge shotgun during a morning's waterfowl outing and fails to realize his duck gun is turning up just as much recoil (in ft-lbs) as the .30-06.

The person who says recoil really doesn't matter and that good shooting requires nothing more than absolute concentration is the same guy who likes his coffee strong, has a hairy chest, and sleeps on nails. There are a few shooters around who wouldn't admit their guns kicked even if their heavy-recoiling firearms broke their collarbones.

I suppose I fall somewhere between these two extremes. While I don't sleep well on nails, I don't feel the kick of a .30-06 or .300 Winchester Magnum is too much to handle well for big-game hunting. I'm the first to admit that guns chambered for big cartridges can kick.

I have fired the .510 Wells Express—a cartridge larger than the .458 Winchester Magnum or .460 Weatherby Magnum. The .510 Wells is a .460 Weatherby case necked up to .50 caliber and, when loaded with 104 grains of IMR-4064, moves a 750-grain bullet out at nearly 2200 fps. The 100 ft-lbs (or more) of recoil produced by the 12-pound rifle is enough to make a shooter take a step back to stay on his feet when firing from the offhand position. I would like to see anybody fire 50 rounds from this rifle off the benchrest without developing some sort of a flinch or complaining about recoil.

Since most of us aren't going to be hunting in Africa, I'll wager that most of you are not terribly concerned about the recoil of an elephant gun. But you may be interested in rounds like the 7mm Remington Magnum or .300 Winchester Magnum. These are the rounds generally considered for North American elk or moose hunting.

In my experience, the recoil from any of the popular elk cartridges is noticeable. If a cartridge is adequate for elk-size game, it's going to kick. A certain amount of bullet weight, diameter, and speed is required for it to be consistently effective on elk-size game.

Forget head shots with cartridges like the .243, 6mm Remington, or even .25-06 on elk. They just don't occur under today's hunting pressure. Any shot offered at an elk is a good one, but the hunter should never go after such animals with a cartridge incapable of producing clean kills, even with angling shots that must penetrate a great deal of tissue, and possibly bone, to reach the vital zone.

Cartridges almost universally considered to be adequate for elk begin with the .270 Winchester or .308 Winchester at the light end and go upward from there to the .300 Winchester Magnum, .338 Winchester Magnum, or 8mm Remington Magnum. The recoil tables clearly indicate that the cartridges on the top end of the list, even in this limited range, do kick much harder than those at the bottom end—if the rifles are otherwise the same. However, a great deal is overlooked if a hunter considers *only* ft-lbs of recoil.

In my experience, I've noted that there is a much more noticeable difference between individual rifles and stock designs when it comes to recoil than there is in the size of the cartridge.

Nearly all popular rifle models chambered for both standard and magnum calibers generally come with thick recoil-absorbing pads on the magnum-chambered guns. This alone is enough to make a big difference. A bit of added rifle weight will also dampen recoil; the magnum-chambered guns usually have barrels that are two inches longer. And stock design has a much greater effect on felt recoil or recoil sensation than most people are willing to admit.

There are two types of recoil—actual and felt. Actual recoil is the computed recoil in ft-lbs that is turned up with a given cartridge and load in a given rifle and to which a mathematical figure (in ft-lbs) can be applied. Felt recoil is how the recoil feels to the shooter.

The subject of felt recoil can really make a difference, but this is difficult to measure or put into universal terms everyone understands. Only a shooter's experience can guide him.

I became interested in shooting a muzzleloading rifle because I wanted to hunt elk during the special Colorado muzzleloader-only season. Shortly after I acquired a rifle, I was at the range sighting it in with elk loads. All the literature I had read indicated 100 grains of FFg behind the 370-grain Maxi slug would be adequate elk medicine in the .50-caliber Thompson/Center Hawken rifle. I hadn't taken very many shots from the benchrest with those loads before being convinced this big-bore muzzleloader kicked harder than any elk rifle I'd ever fired. The kick seemed even worse than my .375 H&H.

In order to see just how hard the muzzleloader was kicking, I chronographed the loads, weighed the rifle, and did a few calculations. My Hawken tips the scale at eight pounds, 10 ounces—the same weight as my custom .300 Winchester Magnum with the scope attached. After completing the recoil calculations, however, I had a real surprise. The muzzleloader was producing *less* recoil (in ft-lbs) than my eight-pound .30-06!

The reason this recoil seemed so bad was due to the extreme drop in the stock and high center of bore in relation to the buttstock. In other words, I was taking a lot of the kick in the cheek rather than in the shoulder. The muzzleloader stock is exaggerated in drop when compared to any centerfire rifle, but the instance does explain why ft-lbs figures for recoil should be taken with a lot of salt.

Dan Martin, a stockmaker for custom rifles, explained that a straight stock generally seems to kick less because the recoil is absorbed straight back and prevents the muzzle from climbing and keeps the comb from rising into the shooter's face. Martin prefers the classic-styles stock with a straight line to the comb.

On some factory rifles, the top line of the buttstock rises at a distinct angle from front to rear. And even though there is some drop to the stock at the butt (high line of bore in relation to butt) causing the muzzle to climb, there is so much relief at the forward portion of the comb that this prevents the stock from crashing into the shooter's cheek.

To some shooters, a kick exerting some of its energy in raising the gun's muzzle is much more pleasant than the forces of a kick directed straight back into the shooter's shoulder. Here again, we're dealing with opinions and preferences.

Some shooters are more sensitive to recoil than others, and some shooters prefer different types of rifles over others. Still, there are factors which aren't easily measured in a quantitative manner, but they still hold true regardless of the shooter.

Remember that a flinch is developed more through noise and muzzle blast than through recoil. There is no faster way to develop a flinch than to fire a number of rounds from a modern centerfire without hearing protection (not to mention that a shooter's hearing can be permanently damaged by the practice). I suggest using both earplugs and muffs.

I recall one instance when I developed a terrible flinch shooting a 10½-pound .222 Remington rifle. As any shooter knows, the recoil of such a cartridge is almost negligible when compared to a cartridge large enough for elk. But I was firing the rifle at a benchrest match under a sheet steel roof. Unfortunately, I'd gone up to the line to begin my timed string of shots before I realized I had forgotten my hearing protection. Instead of going back for my muffs, I decided to go ahead and fire the group. I learned a valuable lesson.

The shooting position employed also makes a considerable difference. Prone is the most painful position from which to fire a heavy-kicking gun. Probably the second most painful position is from the benchrest, particularly if the tabletop is a bit low in relation to the stool so you're leaning forward into the buttstock. Lowering the stool will help considerably in such a case. A standup shooting bench can also help dampen recoil a lot.

Offhand is probably the most comfortable position from which to shoot a heavy-kicking gun since the shoulder has plenty of "give" when the shooter is in this position. Kneeling and sitting positions aren't bad either. Fortunately, these latter three positions are commonly employed in any hunting situation. The prone position is impractical and seldom used because of problems with rocks, brush, etc.

Also, the big-game hunter will be firing relatively few shots in the field – possibly only one during a season. In addition, the trees, grasses, hills, etc., have a tendency to dampen the rifle's noise. Hearing protection, impractical in a hunting situation to begin with, isn't really needed.

When you spot a big-game trophy, you're not going to be thinking about a rifle's kick, and you're not going to flinch – unless the flinch was developed in practice or unless you've been conditioned to be afraid of the rifle by what you've heard or read.

Even though recoil probably isn't going to bother you in a hunting situation, you still have to sight-in your rifle from the benchrest with your hunting loads. To help dampen the kick at the shooting bench, a bag of shot can be placed between the gun butt and the shooter's shoulder. As mentioned earlier, adding weight to a rifle decreases recoil considerably. In effect, weight is added to the gun by placing a bag of shot between the shoulder and the gun butt.

The double-hearing protection and bag of shot, along with sitting up straight at the bench, can help a lot. Even so, you'll still have to concentrate and talk yourself into proper hold and trigger squeeze so you don't flinch the gun off the point of aim.

Despite what some gunwriters would have you believe, I'm not certain a shooter can become inured to recoil. No matter how many times the rifle is fired, the kick may still be a problem. This is why silhouette shooters prefer the lightest calibers that will consistently knock down the targets over some of the flatter shooting high-velocity rounds. As a practical matter, however, the average hunter won't be shooting many rounds.

It is true that the best shooter in the field is the one who becomes thoroughly familiar with his hunting rifle, and there is no better way to become comfortable with a rifle than by actual shooting practice. This is where the handloader has an edge, for reduced loads produce very mild recoil and can be fired all day long with no pain.

For reduced-load data, I have applied cast-bullet data from the *Lyman Cast Bullet Handbook* to jacketed bullets with complete success. My chronograph data indicates that the velocity with jacketed bullets is similar to cast bullets when using the same charges Lyman suggests for cast bullets.

Higher performance cannot be achieved without some increase in actual recoil, but this doesn't necessarily have to be *felt* recoil, depending on the individual rifle and shooter preference. Don't let the sight of a belted cartridge scare you into fear of recoil. Just take the above precautions and use a lot of common sense before you shoot those high-performance cartridges.

Casting Bullets Increases Your Savings

LIKE EVERYTHING ELSE, shooting grows increasingly more expensive. Fortunately, handloading is one way to cut costs and do more shooting. The brass cartridge case is usually the most expensive component in a round of ammunition. And reusing this expensive case when handloading is the primary reason handloading saves you money. After the case, the bullet is the most expensive item. But casting your own bullets saves a considerable amount, and you can have fun in the process.

Some shooters think there are a lot of drawbacks to cast bullets. Everybody knows the stories: they're inaccurate; they lead bores; they can't be fired at high velocities; they really aren't much good for anything, certainly not for hunting. But if thought and care are exercised during the casting and loading process, none of the "drawbacks" will hinder your shooting success.

It has been proven time and again that cast bullets can provide all the accuracy needed for nearly every shooting task. And in most instances, they'll offer more accuracy potential than you can use. The "secret" to cast bullet accuracy is in their manufacture and loading. *You* are solely responsible for quality control. (But don't let this spook you. Fact is, you can produce amazingly accurate cast bullets with surprisingly little effort.)

Bore leading with cast bullets can be a problem—particularly if a poor alloy or an improper lubricant is used or if the bullet is not the proper diameter. Lead bullets have been saddled with this reputation in part from attempts to load the soft-lead, commercially swaged bullets at velocities higher than the soft slugs were intended. Unlike swaged bullets, it is possible to produce a harder bullet when casting your own. Cast bullets are ideal for handgun shooters because they can be fired at top velocities with little or no leading—*if* a suitable alloy and lubricant are used and the bullet is the proper diameter. In fact, it is possible to fire cast bullets in excess of 2000 fps without appreciable leading.

Cast or lead bullets have been used for hunting everything from rabbits to elephants. After all, before jacketed bullets came into wide use, lead bullets were all that was available. Jacketed bullets do have advantages for hunting big game with modern rifle cartridges at high velocity, but cast bullets are ideally suited for other hunting applications. I've taken dozens of rabbits and squirrels with handguns that fired my own home-cast slugs. Anything from the .38 Special to the .44 Magnum can be a good small-game gun when cast bullets are fired in the neighborhood of 1000 fps or less. The moderate velocity helps to reduce meat damage—an important consideration for game intended for the pot.

Handguns aren't the only hunting applications for lead bullets. There's nothing more satisfying than using a high-velocity varmint or deer rifle with reduced loads and cast bullets of your own making to hunt squirrels. I'll never forget one afternoon when I was hunting squirrels with a .257 Roberts and cast bullets fired at about 1400 fps. I had another memorable day calling coyotes and dropping them with cast bullets from a .30-06. A lever-action .358 Winchester and inexpensive cast bullets have provided many enjoyable hours of jackrabbit shooting.

In my opinion, the common flinch is the major reason that many hunters have difficulty shooting big-game rifles well. It is also my experience that a flinch is developed during practice shooting—not in the hunting field. The effects of the gun firing are usually not noticed during the excitement of the hunt. Cast bullet loads usually have a very mild report and recoil, allowing the hunter to get plenty of inexpensive preseason practice without developing a flinch. With them, you can get in lots of shooting inexpensively and become thoroughly familiar with your deer or elk rifle so that using it becomes almost second nature by the time the big-game season opens. When you get ready to go after big game, simply switch loads and resight your rifle.

Casting bullets isn't a lot of trouble. To get set up for bulletcasting, you need a pot for melting the alloy. Several fine electric furnaces are available, but you'll probably be satisfied, at least to start, with a simple cast iron pot. (And it's a lot less expensive.) You'll need a bullet mold, a dipper with a pour spout for filling the mold, and some means of sizing and lubricating the bullets. As the name implies, sizing means making the freshly cast bullets perfectly round and of the proper diameter. Lubricating is necessary to reduce bore leading. The use of a mechanical lubricator/sizer that mounts on the loading bench is the most convenient way of accomplishing this process. With it, each bullet is forced into a die by means of ram force activated by cycling the operating handle, much like a loading press. Lubricant is forced into the bullet grooves at the same time that it is sized. These tools are also capable of installing a gascheck, a hard copper alloy cap that fits onto the bullet's base.

If you don't want to go to the expense of a lubricator/sizer, lubricating/sizing kits are available.

For load data, when it comes to cast bullets, the *Lyman Cast Bullet Handbook* is the best source I've found. The book has a wealth of information on bulletcasting and is practically a must for the cast bullet shooter. (Probably the best advice I can give you is to get the Lyman manual and read it. Then decide how you're going to handle bulletcasting.)

There are various firms that supply bullet alloys. This makes producing a good, nonleading load easier, and your results will be consistent. As long as we're on the subject of shooting for less, however, you might be interested to know that various scrap lead alloys work well. I recommend wheel weight alloy and linotype alloy. Unfortunately, the latter is very hard to obtain today because linotype typesetting machines are practically a thing of the past. Wheel weight alloy can vary somewhat in composition, but I've had excellent results with the alloy I've used — as long as the velocities are held around 1000 fps or less. For faster speeds, I use linotype. If you can't find linotype, make the wheel weight metal more suitable by adding tin.

Cast bullets are sometimes larger in diameter than jacketed bullets, and they're softer. This means you'll have to apply a generous mouth-belling to cases so cast bullets seat smoothly. If you're loading a handgun cartridge with a three-die set, you should have no problem applying enough belling with the standard expander die. However, standard rifle dies frequently don't apply enough expansion at the mouth. A heavy inside chamfering to the case neck helps, but it's better to purchase a special cast bullet case-mount expanding die for this purpose.

One last point: be sure to conduct your casting operations where there is plenty of ventilation. The fumes are hazardous to your health. If you're doing it inside the house, putting the lead pot under an exhaust fan is a good idea.

Of course, this doesn't include everything you'll need to know. It's only an introduction, but it hits the high points regarding equipment.

Distances Bullets Travel

E VER WONDER how far your gun fires a bullet? While looking through the *Lyman Reloading Handbook,* 46th edition, I noticed tables on pages 448 and 449 which provide information regarding the maximum distance for popular rifle and pistol cartridges.

The tables assume the use of jacketed bullets with a tangent ogive nose of eight caliber radius, cylindrical bearing, and a flat base. Thirty degrees is assumed to be the optimum angle of departure for a maximum horizontal range. If muzzle velocity or bullet shape is altered from what's listed in the tables, a change of maximum range will also occur.

If you're shooting a .243 with a 100-grain bullet at a muzzle velocity of 3070 fps, the Lyman tables indicate a maximum range of approximately 4000 yards (about 2.3 miles). If you're shooting a .264 Winchester Magnum with a 140-grain bullet at 3200 fps, the distance is listed at 4666 yards (about 2.6 miles). A milder cartridge like the .30-30 Winchester with a 170-grain bullet at 2200 fps muzzle velocity is said to travel 3666 yards.

Some of the figures for handgun cartridges might surprise you. For example, a .38 Special with a 150-grain bullet at 1060 fps muzzle velocity will travel 2100 yards (about 1.2 miles). The .44 Magnum with a 240-grain bullet at 1470 fps is listed at 2500 yards (about 1.4 miles).

Rifle Cartridges...Handguns...Handrifles

W HEN COLT WAS planning its Frontier sixshooter in 1878, there wasn't a lot to consider regarding which cartridge to chamber it for. Central-fire cartridges were the coming thing, and the .44 Winchester Center Fire, or .44-40, had already proven itself in a rifle. Colt was in the business of making guns, not cartridges, and the use of the rifle round in the revolver was a natural course to take.

In 1880, shortly after the .38-40 rifle cartridge came out, Colt added this one to the single-action line. These cartridges were widely known for years, even though the stubby .40-caliber bullet didn't perform as well in a handgun. Colt still sold more than 32,000 single-action Frontiers and 12,000 Bisleys in the less-popular .38-40 caliber.

Chambering the new handguns for cartridges which already existed and which had proven themselves in long guns made sense. Revolvers were made to order for those stubby, rimmed rifle cartridges. In short time, however, big rifle rounds and high-pressure rifle rounds surpassed a revolver's capability for handling them. Since then, of course, revolvers have grown stronger and are able to handle higher pressures, and cartridges like the .357 Magnum, which could turn up 45,000-pound pressures, became a reality; the same was true of the .44 Magnum. The .357 Magnum was introduced in 1935, and the .44 Magnum was introduced in 1956, but neither was initially chambered in rifles or carbines.

More recently, a nostalgia fad has struck gun buffs, and having a rifle (lever-action carbine) in the same caliber as a revolver has again become fashionable. As a result, we've seen the Browning 92, a copy of the old Winchester Model 1892, introduced in .44 Magnum. The Marlin Model 1894 chambered for the .357 Magnum came along. Rossi, Navy Arms, Winchester, and others introduced similar carbines which imitated lever-action counterparts made prior to the turn of the last century.

The .357 and .44 Magnums are modern counterparts to the old .38-40 and .44-40 cartridges. Unlike the old rounds, which were designed as rifle cartridges, the new numbers were designed as revolver cartridges and later chambered in carbines.

Most of the older cartridges, rifle and handgun alike, were of a straight or straight-taper design. While the .38-40 cartridge has a very slight bottleneck, it's nothing like rifle cartridges that came into vogue around the turn of the century.

Bottleneck cartridges have been unsuccessful for the most part in firearms which *most* of us call handguns—the revolvers and semiautos. Bottleneck cartridges had their day in the form of the .22 Remington Jet chambered in the Smith & Wesson Model 53 revolver and the .256 Winchester Magnum chambered in the single-shot Ruger Hawkeye. While the Hawkeye was a single shot, it resembled a revolver in appearance, size, and somewhat in operation. Neither cartridge became popular.

Now there is a different movement taking place. Instead of rifle cartridges adapted for handguns, rifles chambered for rifle cartridges and rifle actions have formed the basis for what it has become fashionable to call "handguns." The bolt-action XP-100, originally chambered for the bottleneck .221 Fire Ball cartridge, is now being chambered for the .223 Remington, .35 Remington, 7mm-08, and other rifle cartridges. The XP-100 *is* a rifle action. The barrel length, stock design, and overall length qualify it as a "handgun" by legal definition. By layman's definition, it's neither handgun nor rifle, but a crossbreed that's designed around the features of both. The same goes for the Thompson/Center Contender—rifle action, handgun stock, in-between barrel. Offhand, it shoots like a handgun; from a rest, it shoots like a rifle. With interchangeable barrels, it fires both rifle and handgun cartridges. It could be considered a rifle without a buttstock.

Actually, there's nothing you can't chamber in the current crop of . . . what shall I call them? They're not rifles or handguns. I think this relatively new subspecies of firearms deserves a name with pizazz. "Minirifles," "megapistols," or "megahandguns" are all close, but still not right on. "Pseudorifles" is too awkward to spell and pronounce. "Handrifle" is the best one I've come up with. I like it because it makes the group of firearms we're talking about clear; the name is descriptive.

I've long felt some separate name was needed for this class of firearm. It helps do justice to those who hunt with "real" handguns. It's a lot greater challenge to take an antelope with an iron-sighted single-action Super Blackhawk in .44 Magnum or one of the new semiauto Colt 10mm Delta Elites than with a handrifle weighing the same as a fiberglass-stocked rifle topped with a 7X scope and chambered for a long-range rifle cartridge.

I used to be awed by the ability of shooters with handrifles, thinking it was as challenging as handgun shooting. Then I borrowed a heavy-barreled T/C Contender chambered for the .223 Remington cartridge during a prairie dog shoot. The gun had a high-magnification scope, and from a rest, it was not a lot more difficult to hit prairie dogs with the handrifle than with a rifle in the same chambering. I've since had the opportunity to check out other handrifles at a benchrest and found the accuracy to be on par with rifles. The only disadvantage comes when they are fired offhand. Only in this situation does the rifle have greater potential than a handrifle for the average hunter.

Since these actions are from rifles, they have the strength to handle virtually any rifle cartridge. There really aren't any cartridges you can't chamber in a handrifle. Since the actions are rifle actions, they'll handle any high-pressure rifle cartridge. The primary limiting factor is recoil. Let's just say that firing a handrifle chambered for the .460 Weatherby Magnum, for example, might sting an ungloved hand a bit. Most shooters consider cartridges on the order of the .35 Remington or .30-30 Winchester to be the more practical limit in a handrifle.

While the XP-100 survived for years in the .221 Fire Ball chambering, that caliber has been dropped in favor of the .223 Remington. This round has proven to be an excellent performer for varminting purposes, even with the 14-inch barrels. The .35 Remington is fast becoming a big-game favorite as long as the game isn't too big, and it is also chambered in XP-100s available from the Remington Custom Shop.

When it comes to the Contender, there are no less than 24 different rounds listed in the T/C catalog. The Contender is chambered for all manner of cartridges: centerfire, rimfire, rifle, revolver, semiauto pistol, and even shotgun. Some of the popular rifle cartridges that are available in T/C factory barrels are the .22 Long Rifle, .22 Winchester Magnum, .22 Hornet, .222 Remington, .223 Remington, 7-30 Waters, .30 M-1 Carbine, .30-30 Winchester, and .35 Remington. Besides these standard rifle and carbine chamberings, there are several wildcat cartridge chamberings which have all the earmarks of rifle cartridges: the 6mm T/CU, 6.5mm T/CU, and 7mm T/CU. The .30 Herrett and .357 Herrett would also fit into this class.

I haven't even mentioned the nonfactory barrel wildcat chamberings in the T/C. Quite a few of these cartridges have received a degree of popularity. Some of the better known rounds come from J.D. Jones, avid handgun hunter and highly knowledgeable gun buff. The JDJ line of cartridges is based primarily on the .225 Winchester and .444 Marlin cases. The .225 has been necked up and blown out to fire bullets in diameters from .22 through 7mm. The .444 Marlin case has been shortened by .1 inch, necked down and blown out for bullets ranging from .30 caliber through .44. One of the most popular cartridges in this latter group is the .375 JDJ, which is capable of firing a 220-grain bullet at 2150 fps from a 14-inch Contender barrel. A Hornady 300-grain soft-point or full metal jacket can be fired at 1930 fps.

These loads buck and kick. For example, the 300-grain loading produces more than 40 ft-lbs of recoil from a 4¼-pound Contender (SSK barrel, mounts, and Leupold 2X scope included).

The Contender is great for wildcatters because it's so easy and relatively inexpensive to come up with a new chambering. But the XP-100 and Contender aren't the only firearms that fit into the handrifle category. Wichita has a bolt-action handrifle. Ultra Light Arms, the company that makes those fine-shooting, lightweight, synthetic-stocked rifles, is now producing one with a shorter barrel and a handgun stock. Anschutz has its bolt-action rimfire model called the Exemplar.

The movement is sweeping the country. Handrifles have become popular on the silhouette circuit, but hunters are also taking them in hand because most of these firearms can legally be used to hunt during handgun seasons in most states.

The same cartridges which work well in rifles also work well in handrifles for the same species. The .22 rimfire works well on small game, whether the bullet comes from a rifle or a handrifle. The .22 Hornet, .222 Remington, and .223 Remington work well on varmints, whether the bullets come from a Contender or TCR rifle. The 7-30 Waters, .30-30 Winchester, and .35 Remington are first choices for big game, whether the gun is a Contender or XP-100.

The only difference between rifles and handrifles is velocity. A 10- or 14-inch barrel is going to suffer considerable velocity loss from a 22-inch barrel. The amount of loss depends on factors like the cartridge used and the bullet weight and powder weight, powder used, etc. However, there are other consequences to velocity loss. It means energy, penetration, and bullet-expansion performance are often diminished.

Bullet expansion performance depends on velocity and on the design of the bullet. This is one factor to be concerned about if you're shooting a modern bottleneck rifle cartridge in a handrifle. Avid hunters who use the handrifles generally select bullets which expand readily from rifles. Sometimes all it takes is to select a bullet of a different weight, because lighter bullets are generally designed for lighter game and expand more readily. If you're shooting a .30-caliber handrifle, select bullets designed for the .30-30 Winchester rifle cartridge, not a .300 Magnum. If you're using a 7mm handrifle, pick bullets designed for the 7-30 Waters, not the 7mm Magnum. Some shooters lean toward varmint-weight bullets for handrifles. Someone shooting a .30 Herrett, for example, might use a 110- or 130-grain bullet rather than a 180-grainer, even for deer-size game. This helps ensure some degree of expansion at the low velocities received from the 10- or 14-inch barrels.

As you can see, rifle cartridges chambered in "handguns" have an entirely different meaning today than they did during the 1880s. Today's short-barreled handrifles are stronger, more powerful, and more accurate than even the rifles of that bygone era.

Selecting The Perfect Bullet

T HE SELECTION of a bullet for hunting deserves special consider-ation because it is *the* most important part of a handloader's assembly of components. Of all the components, the bullet is the most important because it is the primary contributor in producing a high degree of accuracy. Secondly, the tiny chunk of lead encased in a jacket has the awesome task of downing game efficiently and doing this under an infinite number of circumstances, angles, and distances.

The technology regarding bullet construction and production-line tooling has advanced to a point where there really isn't a "bad" bullet available—at least not from the well-known manufacturers—as long as it's properly matched to your hunting needs.

There's no question that bullets are different, and some of the impor-tant differences have nothing to do with brand names. For example, the external shape of a bullet is a difference we can see. There is an obvious difference between a blunt roundnose or flatpoint design and a spirepoint or spitzer. Regarding the expansion characteristics of spitzer versus roundnose bullets, many once believed a roundnose design, one with a lot of lead exposed at the tip, was necessary to produce the best expan-sion properties. Perhaps this was true years ago due to the bulletmaking technology available, along with the low-pressure, low-velocity cartridges the bullets topped. (Remember, the .30-30 was once consid-ered a high-velocity round.) In bullet expansion tests I've conducted, var-ious bullets in a given caliber, weight, and brand, intended for identical purposes, don't have perceptible differences in expansion characteris-tics. The spitzer or spirepoint expands just as reliably as the roundnose.

Roundnose bullets have also been reported to be more efficient at getting through heavy brush because they aren't deflected as easily as spitzers. There have been all types of tests conducted regarding what it takes to get a bullet through brush. The tests I've seen vary in their findings, but one point is consistent among them: you can't depend on *any* bullet to get through brush without being deflected, slowed down, or distorted to some degree. I don't think it matters whether the bullet is a roundnose or a spitzer.

The primary difference between roundnose and spitzer bullets? The spitzer bullet has a more efficient shape for overcoming the resistance of air during flight. The pointed bullet retains its downrange velocity and striking energy to a greater degree than does a bluntnosed bullet. Since the spitzer retains more of its velocity, it drops less and drifts less in the wind.

The more efficient the bullet's shape, the higher its ballistic coefficient. Ballistic coefficient numerically describes a projectile's ability to overcome the resistance of air. For example, the blunt Hornady 6mm 100-grain roundnose bullet has a ballistic coefficient of .216, while the pointed 100-grain spirepoint has a ballistic coefficient of .357. If both bullets are fired at 3000 fps (muzzle velocity), the roundnose bullet will be traveling 1811 fps at 300 yards, will be carrying 729 ft-lbs of energy, will have dropped 9.6 inches (with a 200-yard zero), and will have drifted 15.8 inches in a 10-mph crosswind; at the same distance, the spirepoint will have traveled 2232 fps with 1107 ft-lbs of energy, will have dropped 7.3 inches, and will have drifted 8.4 inches.

If you were to use the 1000 ft-lbs of striking energy "requirement" for deer hunting, the 6mm with the roundnose bullet at 3000 fps muzzle velocity is not a 300-yard deer cartridge. It lacks the necessary energy by a considerable amount. In fact, according to the Hornady tables, the roundnose is *barely* a 200-yard deer bullet with 1039 ft-lbs of energy. With the spirepoint bullet – same weight and muzzle velocity – the bullet exceeds the minimum energy requirement at 300 yards by a comfortable amount. Therefore, the energy difference between bullet shapes is significant. Though the difference in drop (2.3 inches at 300 yards) is a difference that will not be noticed in the field, the difference in drift is significant – nearly twice as much with the roundnose bullet. This is based only on the shape of the bullet's point.

One advantage to the roundnose bullet, however, is a bullet of a given weight is shorter than a spitzer design. On the surface, this might not seem to be much of an advantage, but it can be if the bullet is to be fired from a rifle with a limited magazine length. A roundnose bullet can be seated with its base farther out of the case to increase powder capacity (and a heavier roundnose bullet can be used in place of a spitzer). Besides, in hunting areas where even a 100-yard shot is a long one, the advantage of a spitzer bullet would be of no consequence. As a result, the hunter might select a roundnose.

Another obvious difference among bullets is the shape of the base. The flatbase bullet has been the standby for years, but boattail designs are becoming increasingly popular. The tapered tail is intended to make a pointed bullet even more efficient at retaining its downrange velocity and energy. As mentioned earlier, the 6mm Hornady 100-grain spirepoint has a ballistic coefficient of .400.

Let's take a look at the advantages in a boattail. The 300-yard figures for the boattail which started at 3000 fps (muzzle velocity) are: 2308 fps velocity, 1183 ft-lbs of energy, 7.1 inches of drop (200-yard zero), and 7.4 inches of drift (10-mph crosswind). Compared with the flatbase, the boattail has .2 inch less drop at 300 yards, 76 fps less velocity and energy, and one inch less drift. I haven't met a shooter yet who would notice the difference in any of these "advantages."

The cannelure is another difference among bullets. Some bullets have them; some don't. A cannelure is used basically to crimp the case mouth on a bullet that has no cannelure because it can distort the jacket. However, just because a bullet has a cannelure doesn't mean the case mouth has to be crimped into it, and it doesn't mean the bullet must be seated to the cannelure. The bullet-to-rifling-land distance is far more important regarding pressure and accuracy than the case-mouth-to-cannelure relationship.

If the bullet has a tendency to be pounded deeper into the case from being smashed against the front of the magazine box during recoil, or if the bullet has a tendency to be pulled from the case during recoil while the case rim is held fast, or if the magazine has a tendency to push bullets deeper into the case, then the crimp becomes important, and crimping the case mouth into the bullet can keep the bullets from moving.

A cannelure is rolled into the bullet jacket after the core has been seated; consequently, the bullet jacket is pressed slightly into the core, forming a type of inner ring around the core. Some shooters have reported that this has a tendency to lock the core and jacket together so the core is less likely to separate from the jacket when impacting game. As a practical matter, the bullet jacket generally mushrooms farther than the cannelure, so the latter has no core-locking effect whatsoever.

Generally, the cannelure is positioned on the bullet so that proper overall cartridge length is attained when the case mouth is crimped into it. This length is established for factory rounds so the ammunition will work through any action. A round won't be too long to feed through lever-action mechanisms or too long for box magazines in bolt actions; further-more, it will not be so long that the bullet is jammed into the lands when the round is chambered.

The wise handloader adjusts bulletseating depth to obtain optimum cartridge length relative to his particular rifle. Some rifles have longer magazines than others, allowing bullets to be seated farther out of the case to increase case capacity and performance. Similarly, some rifles have longer throats in the chamber, allowing bullets to be seated farther out and make better utilization of powder space.

Accuracy can also be affected considerably by bulletseating depth. Accuracy can frequently be improved by seating the bullet farther out of the case to be positioned in close proximity to the rifling lands when the round is chambered. For this reason, the handloader generally ignores the cannelure on a bullet unless it's absolutely necessary (for the reasons mentioned earlier).

Another basic difference among bullets is the shape of the ogive or curvature of the bullet nose. There are spirepoints, and there are spitzers; it is difficult to compare these bullets since both of them are pointed. Even among the spitzer bullets, there are differences in ogive shape. Spitzers of a given weight and diameter can produce different performance due to point and ogive shape. It's much the same with spirepoint bullets. As a practical matter, the popular bullets in any given weight and diameter are so similar – be they spirepoint or spitzer – that I doubt if any shooter would be able to discern the difference in the field. But there are other points to examine besides the bullet's performance in flight.

In most instances, I find the full bearing surface (the part touching the inside of the barrel when the bullet travels down the bore) of a spirepoint bullet is positioned farther from the bullet's base and closer to the bullet's point than it is with spitzer bullets. This might not seem like a difference of any consequence, but I have found it to be important in some instances. For example, on a rifle with a long throat or in a rifle with a worn leade, a spirepoint bullet doesn't have to be seated as far out of the case in order for it to come close to touching the lands. This way, the case neck has a better friction grip on the bullet's shank than might otherwise be possible with a spitzer bullet. I have encountered this situation in rifles with both long magazines and long throats. Spirepoint bullets shot better because they were seated closer to the lands.

On the other hand, the spirepoint design can be a disadvantage because the bullet's base must generally be seated deeper into the case for the same overall cartridge length when compared with a spitzer bullet.

Since there are so many excellent hunting bullets available to the handloader, selection of the perfect one can become confusing. However, the points I've made should provide some basis from which you can decide on the very best bullet for the task at hand.

1960-1985
25 Years Of Cartridges & Reloading

IN 1960, MAGNUM primers, ball powder, and the Ruger Model 77 didn't exist. Nor did calibers like the 7mm Remington Magnum, .300 Winchester Magnum, or .22-250 Remington.

Between 1960 and 1985, a great many developments in both the rifle and handloading components fields were brought about. Generally, when you think of new developments in the field of firearms, you turn your attention to new cartridge designs. Action types, for the most part, have remained pretty much conventional over the last century. Other than a move away from centerfire lever-action and single-shot rifles to a predominance of bolt actions, most of the "new" rifles or action designs are actually modifications of existing basic systems.

Since 1960, there has been a host of new cartridge introductions. Three were announced in 1962: the 7mm Remington Magnum, .340 Weatherby Magnum, and the .44 Remington Magnum. The .44 Magnum wasn't a new chambering altogether – it was just new to long guns when Sturm,

Ruger offered it in its semiauto carbine in 1962. Of these three cartridges, the 7mm Remington Magnum is perhaps the most notable and continues to be one of our most popular big-game cartridges.

In 1963, Roy Weatherby announced another new caliber to his lineup, the .224 Weatherby Magnum, and Winchester came up with two: the .284 and the .300 Winchester Magnum.

The .224 Weatherby remains the smallest belted magnum cartridge distributed in this country. Even though it has a belt and carries "magnum" in its name, its performance isn't quite on par with either of its nonbelted .22-caliber cousins, the .22-250 and .220 Swift.

The .284 Winchester is one of those cartridges that, from all appearances, seems to be barely hanging on. Still, I don't believe the .284 Winchester, with its fat body and rebated rim design, is ready to be buried. In my opinion, the basic case design is too good. It has never been appreciated for what it has to offer: high performance in short-action rifles on a par with longer cartridges (long action).

The .300 Winchester Magnum remains very popular today. As a long-range elk round that can be utilized in a standard action, the .300 Winchester Magnum is tops. It delivers flat trajectory and high energies to extreme ranges. It's versatile enough for all big game in North America and has gained a respectable reputation on the target range.

The standardization of the .223 by Remington, the introduction of the .225 by Winchester, and the announcement of Marlin's proprietary round, the .444, highlighted 1964.

The .223 has become popular not only in bolt-action rifles, but in semiauto rifles like an assortment of H&Ks, Ruger's Mini-14, and Colt's AR-15.

The .225 Winchester is another one of those cartridges that appears to be all but breathing its last. Unlike the .284, the .225, though an excellent cartridge in its own right, has competition that it hasn't been able to match—namely the popular .22-250 Remington and the .225's predecessor, the .220 Swift. In addition, the .225 was plagued with a semi-rimmed design which necessitated a special magazine box for cartridges to function smoothly. It's doubtful the .225 will be revived, as have some of the older cartridges during recent years.

The .444 Marlin, introduced in June 1964, has gained a reputation as being very final on deer and black bear at the shorter woods ranges when fired from Marlin's lever-action rifle. I was glad to see a rifle manufacturer besides Winchester, Remington, or Weatherby come out with its own cartridge design and have it succeed.

The year 1965 brought in the commercialization of the .22-250 Remington and the introduction of the .350 Remington Magnum.

The .22-250 was a popular cartridge in wildcat form before Remington commercialized it. As such, it was destined for success, and since its commercialization, many more varmint shooters have acquired rifles chambered for this fast, flat-shooting round.

The .350 Remington Magnum, though offering a lot of punch from a short action, apparently didn't have enough followers to make it go. It appears to be on the way out. Cartridges of this class really have to have something going for them in order to succeed because there aren't as many shooters going after the big bears or who prefer an extra-large cartridge for elk-sized game as there are hunters going after deer or elk with a .30-06-class cartridge.

Though there was a flurry of new cartridge introductions during the early '60s, only four additional cartridges arrived from 1966 through 1974: the 6.5mm Remington Magnum (1966), the .240 Weatherby Magnum (1968), the .25-06 Remington (1969), and the .17 Remington (1971).

The 6.5mm Remington Magnum, like its larger cousin the .350, seems destined to the same fate. There are no rifles currently being chambered for the cartridge, and it doesn't appear either cartridge will have a revival of any consequence, except perhaps as a special-run offering from Remington or possibly Ruger, two firms that have periodically done limited runs.

The .240 Weatherby Magnum, like most of the cartridges in the Weatherby line, offers ultimate performance for its bullet diameter. The .240 Weatherby is a belted case with a rim diameter the same as a standard .30-06 cartridge. This makes it relatively easy to come up with an action suitable for barreling and chambering for the .240 Weatherby Magnum. I have used several .240 Weatherby Magnum rifles and find the cartridge ideally suited for long-range coyote shooting. The round packs a punch that's enough to put a coyote down decisively at long ranges.

The .25-06 Remington, like its wildcat cousin the .22-250, was mildly successful in wildcat form even before it was commercialized by Remington. As a commercial cartridge, it is also mildly successful and is considered to be ideal for hunting deer and antelope-size game.

The .17 Remington was the first commercial .17-caliber cartridge. It quickly dominated the .17-caliber field and replaced wildcats like the .17-222 and .17-223. A 25-grain hollowpoint factory load is still available from Remington.

The years 1970 through 1974 produced virtually no new rifle cartridges. In 1975, Ferris Pindell and Dr. Louis Palmisano opened everyone's eyes when world records in the benchrest shooting game began falling to .22 and 6mm PPC cartridges. Based on the .220 Russian case and featuring a Small Rifle primer with a short, fat powder column, the PPC cartridge changed everyone's thinking regarding what it takes to make a benchrest cartridge. The .222 Remington had reigned as king on the benchrest circuit for many years before the PPC rounds came along. The PPC rounds continue to dominate the benchrest winnings today.

The 8mm Remington Magnum cartridge was introduced during 1977. This cartridge, of .375 H&H Magnum length, appeared to be a real hotshot to top all elk hunting-class cartridges with its 185- and 220-grain bullet weights. But Remington quit chambering the round last year, and it appears to be headed for the same fate as the .350 and 6.5 Remington Magnums.

The .375 Big-Bore Winchester came along in 1978. A rimmed cartridge for use in a lever gun, it is similar to the old .38-55 Winchester. A big difference, however, is that the new .375 Winchester is loaded to much higher operating pressures. In addition to being chambered by Winchester in the Model 94, the .375 round was also chambered by

Savage (Model 99) and Marlin (Model 336CS), but it has not been highly successful.

During 1979, Marlin offered the .357 Magnum handgun round in its lever rifle (Model 1894CS), which was a first in a rifle, much like the .44 Magnum was in 1972. The practice of converting older .32-20 lever-action rifles to the newer .357 Magnum handgun round had kept gunsmiths busy for many years previous to the introduction. The idea wasn't a new one, but it was legitimized by Marlin.

In 1983, Winchester announced two new numbers, the .307 Winchester and the .356 Winchester cartridges. Designed with rimmed cases and blunt bullets, these rounds were developed for the new Angle Eject Model 94 rifles. Like the .375 Winchester, they are loaded to higher operating pressures than most rimmed lever-action-type cartridges. The .307 Winchester is basically a .308 Winchester with a rim, at least in exterior dimensions. Similarly, the .356 Winchester is a rimmed counterpart of the .358 Winchester.

This list includes most of the new rifle cartridge designs, but there was a revolutionary introduction about the same time the 8mm Remington Magnum was announced. It was Remington's "Accelerator" cartridge—initially a .30-06 round loaded with a sabot that housed a 55-grain, .22-caliber projectile at a previouslsy unheard-of 4000 fps muzzle velocity. Remington later introduced the saboted cartridge in the .308 Winchester and the .30-30 Winchester.

The .22 Winchester Magnum Rimfire (WMR) came on the market about 1960 and was followed by the 5mm Remington Magnum. This was during the era when it was deemed necessary to attach the word "Magnum" to a cartridge name in order to give it some chance of success. The 5mm Magnum rifles and ammunition are collector items now. Remington no longer makes ammunition for this slightly bottlenecked rimfire cartridge. Winchester's .22 Magnum continues to sell, but it's not close to being as popular as the .22 LR.

From all these rounds, the commercialization of wildcat cartridges and military numbers encompasses many of the most notable introductions. These include the .223 Remington, .22-250 Remington, and .25-06 Remington. With those aside, the 7mm Remington Magnum and .300 Winchester Magnum take honors as two of the most significant new rifle cartridges introduced during the last 25 years. They're significant because they have become popular and respected.

I think it's of importance to note that there has been something of a nostalgic wave sweeping American shooters during the last 25 years. Not only with the reintroduction and repopularization of older cartridges like the 7x57, .257 Roberts, .45-70, etc., but also the move toward more conservative, classic-styled stocks like the Winchester Model 70 Featherweight, the Remington Model 700 Classic, and the Ruger Model 77 RL Ultra Light.

There has also been a vast improvement in handloading components during the last 25 years, specifically in propellants, bullets, and primers. The early '60s marked the introduction and popularization of ball and spherical propellants. These introductions were imn.ediately followed with the introduction of a Magnum primer from CCI in 1961. Omark says the new primer was offered in response to the harder-to-ignite

Winchester W295 ball powder.

Bullets have seen a vast improvement in selection, expansion performance, and availabililty. Prior to 1960, there were hardly any jacketed handgun bullets available to handloaders. Handloader offerings from Winchester and Remington were limited – and were not always obtainable. During the 1950s, Speer began distributing ½- and ¾-jacketed bullets, but it wasn't until the '60s that a magnum-type bullet with a long ogive jacket was introduced. Today, shooters have a vast array of jacketed handgun bullets for all calibers which produce reliable expansion performance, even at subsonic handgun velocities frequently encountered. In fact, today's handgun hunter may find it surprising that prior to 1960, jacketed handgun bullets of a reliable expanding type were practically nonexistent.

Not only have handloading components improved considerably, but so have the tools used to assemble them. Priming tools have improved to a large degree in the auto-priming attachments for bench-mounted presses and in hand-priming tools. The Lee Precision tool is a good example of the latter. There is a primer magazine holding a large number of primers that can be inserted into a case with the press of thumblever. To top it off, the tool is inexpensive.

Lee introduced several other items for the handloader which are fascinating. The combination of the Lee turret press with interchangeable turrets and the Auto-Disc powder measure makes an inexpensive turret press available for rapid reloading of metallic cartridges. The inexpensive Lee shotshell press is another revolutionary idea from that firm.

Powder measures have become more precise than ever, and there are measures that are matched for dispensing a given charge of a specific propellant. For example, there are a good number of measures designed specifically for dispensing pistol-type propellant in small quantities and doing it very precisely. Micrometer adjustments on powder measures are also better than ever.

Dave Corbin would be right at the top of the list of notables during the last quarter-century of handloading because he has made bullet presses and bullet-making dies available to the average handloader who wishes to make his own bullets, even bullets of a specialized design or diameter. Brass Extrusion Laboratories Limited (B.E.L.L.) also deserves mention for making obsolete cases available so old cartridges can be handloaded.

The introduction of reliable, compact, inexpensive chronographs for the average handloader is one of the most important developments for the handloader or serious shooter since 1960. Ken Oehler is the person responsible for this handy outfit. Today's shooter has the capability of checking the velocity of his own loads so he knows exactly what his particular rifle and barrel length are producing without depending on once-inflated factory figures or load manual data which was developed in perhaps another type of rifle or barrel length.

Another useful development in recent years was the Ainsworth electronic scale, which allows a handloader to weigh a bullet or powder charge more rapidly than ever. The Ainsworth scale provides the shooter with an easy-to-read LED display, making it possible to determine an unknown weight, like a recovered bullet, quicker and easier than ever.

Last, but certainly not least, are the improvements in loading manuals over the last 25 years. This aspect alone has probably done more for the average handloader than any other. Today's manuals offer a large accumulation of excellent, sometimes pressure-tested, load data. Different data is available from many sources. Today's load manuals offer reliable loads and a wealth of information.

There were a lot of developments between 1960 and 1985 that shooters can be thankful for. Even the introductions that are fading away were interesting and have added to our experiences and knowledge. Due in part to new developments, rifle shooting and handloading have attained new levels of sophistication.

2010
The Next 20 Years In Rifles/Reloading

TECHNOLOGY IS advancing at an astonishing rate all around us. Computers have made it possible to accomplish work with a higher level of efficiency and at a greater rate than was previously thought possible. In the shooting industry, we now have the technology available to push projectiles faster and flatter when fired from shoulder-held firearms than most shooters think is possible. The use of sabots, smoothbores, and flechettes makes extremely high velocity and high accuracy attainable. We have the technology available with electronics, microprocessors, and microcomputers to adjust sights based on velocity and ballistic coefficient to compensate for distance, wind velocity, barometric pressure, and other factors to make long-range hits practically a certainty.

Such a high degree of technology might very well be applied to military weaponry, but I don't believe it will be applied to sporting firearms, at least not to an extent that's limited only by the technology available. There are areas, however, where technology will affect changes in sporting firearms, changes I think can make our sport even more enjoyable. First, I'll look at the very near future—and the more conventional.

The increasing acceptance of fiberglass stocks will continue, and these stocks will most likely be supplied by most of the major firearms manufacturers in this country in the not-too-distant future.

I believe we're going to see the introduction of a family of rebated-rim .284-type cartridges. The .284 Winchester cartridge is more efficient and practical than the sales figures during its short existence would seem to indicate. This cartridge actually has a better reason for existence today than when it was introduced. With the popularity of short-action, lightweight rifles like the Winchester short-action Featherweight, the Remington Model Seven, the Ruger Ultra Light, etc., such a cartridge can increase the performance without having to increase action length. This is the primary reason for the existence of a cartridge like the

.284 Winchester.

The consistent powder ignition and consequent high accuracy potential of the short, fat powder column have only recently been documented and appreciated in the PPC cartridges—and since the .284's demise. As most shooters know, the .284 Winchester has a *large-diameter* body which increases case capacity rather than accomplishing the same end with a *longer* case, as has frequently been the solution to the problem of how to increase performance. The case rim diameter of the .284 is a convenient and standard .30-06 size. Due to its fatter body and shorter neck (for increased capacity), however, the case can produce ballistics on a par with the much longer .270 Winchester/.30-06 class of cartridges.

I believe there is also room for a commercialization of cartridges like the 6mm-284 and .30-284, two wildcats that produce high levels of performance and are well liked by shooters.

There was a time when the highest velocity obtainable with any given projectile was the goal of wildcatters and cartridge experimenters. Such thinking gave rise to the .30-30 Winchester many years ago when it was the high-velocity king and has continued through the .270 Winchester, .220 Swift, and the Remington .30-06 Accelerator. It was this thinking that produced the entire family of excellent Weatherby cartridges— cartridges which remain the top performers in most of their respective calibers. I don't believe we've seen an end to this line of thinking about high velocity, regardless of the fact that there appears to be an increasing popularity of older, milder cartridges like the 7x57 Mauser, .257 Roberts, and .45-70.

In the past, velocity was generally gained by increasing the size of the case or the powder capacity so higher velocity was attained without increasing pressure levels. I think this trend is reaching the end of an era, with one or two possible exceptions. First, I think we've yet to see an ultrahigh-velocity .22 centerfire with a case capacity appreciably greater than the .220 Swift. I'm thinking in terms of a cartridge that will be commercially available and of a conventional nature, but one that will fire a 55-grain bullet in excess of 4000 fps and have the potential to become popular with predator and varmint hunters alike.

For the most part, the high-velocity cartridge being all-important (at least insofar as it is being obtainable only with an increase in case capacity and at a sacrifice in muzzle blast, barrel wear, recoil, etc.) is a view that's seen its better days. I think shooters and inventors are going to be looking at cartridges which are more "efficient." These cartridges will produce a very high level of accuracy and velocity with no increase in case capacity.

I think one way we're going to realize vastly increased cartridge efficiency is in terms of propellants that will become available. During recent years, we have seen the introduction of propellants which have a greater density wherein a higher energy level can be packed into a given volume. What is really needed is a propellant that produces a flatter time/pressure curve to lower the pressure peak and maintains the pressure level over a longer period of time.

As most shooters know, peak pressure is what generally limits the amount of propellant that can be burned inside a case. Peak pressure is usually reached about the time a bullet starts into the rifling; it escalates rapidly until the slug becomes engraved and is accelerated to high velocity. Once the bullet's mass is accelerated, the peak drops off rapidly. The ideal propellant would build pressure gradually as the bullet moves down the barrel. It would not peak as high and would retain the pressure level almost to the point that the bullet exits the muzzle. In effect, this would produce a gradual acceleration without causing pressures to be excessively high.

The late Dan Pawlak, inventor of Pyrodex, the blackpowder substitute, worked primarily with his own resources during a major portion of the Pyrodex development. He was able to accomplish something large companies with unlimited resources were unable to do. He developed a propellant that had most of the characteristics of blackpowder but was as safe to store and use as smokeless powder.

Dan indicated to me that it was entirely possible to receive 4000 fps from a 150-grain bullet in a .30-06 with pressures no greater than 50,000 psi. All this hinges on the development of a super propellant with the characteristics I mentioned earlier. This was a project Dan wanted to pursue, and if not for his untimely death, I think shooters would be realizing those benefits today.

I believe we're also on the brink of seeing pressure-testing equipment made available to the handloader, just as chronographs have been made available during the last 25 years. It wasn't very many years ago that accurately measuring the speed of bullets wasn't possible. Thanks to Ken Oehler, we're able to with today's small, inexpensive chronographs. I think pressure equipment incorporating a strain gauge, oscilloscope, etc., will be in widespread use by the handloading hobbyist in the not-too-distant future. Pawlak was able to do this, and others have since. The system Pawlak was using had to be calibrated for each individual rifle or handgun barrel. Perhaps someone will develop a pressure-measuring system that operates in conjunction with the rifle's boltface or cartridge.

I also think we're going to see a definite improvement in bullet design, with radical changes in the offing. For example, a combination lead and fluid core bullet would produce more consistent expansion and a higher level of accuracy.

In rifles, I think the trend toward shorter, lighter, more compact long guns will continue. Maybe someone will introduce a rifle with a lightweight aluminum receiver and a steel insert to engage and retain the bolt lugs. Perhaps this idea sounds improbable, but custom riflemakers are already experimenting with the concept.

I also think we haven't realized the possible advantages in muzzle brakes and various forms of recoil-reduction devices. Most shooters scoff at the use of a muzzle brake, considering it too large, unsightly, muzzle heavy, and detrimental to fine accuracy. I believe most of these aspects will be overcome; some already have been. The muzzle brake will very likely become more accepted and will be used for more applications.

For example, muzzle brakes reduce felt recoil and muzzle jump. One of the best places to utilize this attribute is a varmint rifle with a high-magnification scope. If you fit your favorite heavy-barreled .22-250 or .220 Swift with a 36X Leupold (or even a 20X glass), you'll have excellent target definition when ambient conditions are right for it. The sad part is that you won't be able to see the bullet's impact due to recoil of the rifle and the high scope magnification. A good muzzle brake, possibly with a mercury stabilizer built into the rifle (similar to what archers use), could allow you to see the bullet's impact.

Actually, I don't think technological advancements in the shooting sports are going to keep pace with the level of our technology. We have the potential, in both shooting and sighting equipment, to fire projectiles at unheard-of-speeds and to hit targets at distances previously thought impractical. Here is the question that's going to come up: Do we really want this technology to be applied to sporting firearms? Such introductions will have applications in the military or possibly in competition shooting sports, where the unlimited-class firearms form the proving ground for equipment, but the real essence of the shooting sports is a lot more involved than just equipment efficiency. There's the challenge for the shooter in the competition shooting sports and the challenge of the hunt for the sportsman. To eliminate these elements would be to lose a large part of the skill and excitement–the reasons for participating.

The essence of the hunt has a lot of nostalgia wrapped up in it, and for some people, we've already come too far. This relates back to the old scope versus iron sight argument. Scope fans like the idea of being able to shoot effectively at a greater distance. It's argued that scopes offer a more humane alternative for dispatching game because shots can be placed more precisely at a greater distance.

In reality, there is probably no decreased incidence of wounding game when scopes are used. While a scope makes a sure-killing range perhaps 300 yards, some shooters try to push this distance to 400 or even 500 yards–usually beyond their own shooting ability–due in part to excellent target definition from the scope making the game appear to be closer. The users of iron sights cannot make clean kills consistently at great distances, nor do they feel confident of it due to poor target definition. For this reason, a hunter using iron sights limits his range to those sure-killing distances–under 150 yards.

No doubt, it would be more humane to shoot at a deer at 2000 yards with a laser-sighted, heat-seeking, explosive projectile, but does anyone really *want* it for hunting? Some hunters even balk at conventional range-finding scopes as going too far in terms of technology being applied to the hunt.

With the interest in older classic-style firearms like the Winchester Model 70 Featherweight, the Remington Classic, and Ruger Ultra Light, along with the reintroduction of the single-action sixgun, the Browning 1885 Winchester, and the continuing popularity of muzzleloading hunting, I think it's evident hunters want to retain our shooting heritage–a pride from those days when great-grandfather fed the family from his hunting skill, Kentucky windage, and a well-aimed shot. That's where the essence of the hunt lies and where it should be if hunting is to remain a sport that we'll be passing on to our great-grandchildren. For this reason, it is my feeling we've come close to reaching a pinnacle in the technology that is acceptable to American hunters.

But there will probably be an increase in the efficiency of propellants and in materials and methods used in the manufacture of firearms. Barrel metals will probably improve, meaning longer barrel life and lighter weight. Improved stock materials and bedding techniques will also make the guns shoot more accurately and consistently. For practical purposes, however, I think (and hope) there will always be rifles that closely resemble those used by our forefathers.

In any event, the next 20 years ought to be interesting.